A lark for the sake of their country

A lark for the sake of their country

The 1926 General Strike volunteers in folklore and memory

Rachelle Hope Saltzman

Manchester University Press

Copyright © Rachelle Hope Saltzman 2012

The right of Rachelle Hope Saltzman to be identified as the author of this work has been asserted by her in accordance with the Copyright, Designs and Patents Act 1988.

Published by Manchester University Press
Altrincham Street, Manchester M1 7JA, UK
www.manchesteruniversitypress.co.uk

British Library Cataloguing-in-Publication Data is available

Library of Congress Cataloging-in-Publication Data is available

ISBN 978 0 7190 9676 1 paperback

First published by Manchester University Press in hardback 2012

This paperback edition first published 2014

The publisher has no responsibility for the persistence or accuracy of URLs for any external or third-party internet websites referred to in this book, and does not guarantee that any content on such websites is, or will remain, accurate or appropriate.

Printed by Lightning Source

For Pearl Saltzman, who has waited patiently,
and for
Stanley Saltzman, Rose Kerrigan, Roy and Sue Band
- *olev ha shalom* -

Contents

		page
	Permissions	viii
	List of figures and tables	ix
	Acknowledgements	xv
	Preface	xxiii
1	Introduction: folklore, memory, and the volunteers of 1926	1
2	Building Jerusalem: The General Strike as social drama	27
3	Social distinctions, social actions among the upper and middle classes	43
4	Fides est servanda: keeping the faith	62
5	Images of the volunteers: media versus memory	82
6	Humours of the Great Strike	136
7	The volunteers' farewell: closing rituals, genteel ironies	156
8	From ethos to mythos: the General Strike and Britishness	170
9	1926 and all that …: Britishness and the volunteers	201
	Bibliography	214
	Index	253

Permissions:

Benedictus, David, 1985, *What a Way to Run a Revolution*. Portions used by the kind permission of David Benedictus.
Murray, Commander J. R. N., 'The Secret People', Imperial War Museum, Department of Documents (London). Portions used with permission of the Trustees of the Imperial War Museum. Every effort has been made to trace the copyright holder in Commander Murray's narrative. Both the author and the Imperial War Museum would be grateful for any information that might enable them to get in touch with his family.
Saltzman, Rachelle H., 1987, 'Folklore, Feminism, and the Folk – Whose Lore Is It?', *Journal of American Folklore: Folklore and Feminism (Special Issue)*, 100:398, 548–62. Portions used with the permission of the American Folklore Society (www.afsnet.org).
Saltzman, Rachelle H., 1993. 'A Feminist Folklorist Encounters the Folk: Can Praxis Make Perfect?' in Susan Hollis, Linda Pershing, M. Jane Young (eds), *Feminist Theory and the Study of Folklore* (Chicago: University of Illinois Press). Used with permission of the University of Illinois Press.
Saltzman, Rachelle H., 1994, 'Folklore as Politics in Great Britain: Working-Class Critiques of Upper-Class Strike Breakers in the 1926 General Strike', *Anthropological Quarterly: Symbols of Contention, Part II (Special Issue)*, 67:3, 105–21. Portions used with permission of *Anthropological Quarterly*.
Saltzman, Rachelle H., 1995, 'Public Displays, Play, and Power: the 1926 General Strike', *Southern Folklore: Façade Performances (Special Issue)*, 52:2, 161–86. Portions used with permission of the University Press of Kentucky.
Sassoon, Siegfried, 1926, 'The New "Black & Tans" (from White's)', Copyright Siegfried Sassoon by kind permission of the Estate of George Sassoon.

The author has made every effort to secure permissions to quote from letters sent to her and from recorded interviews she conducted.

List of figures and tables

Figures

1.1	Strikes! Restaurant exterior, near Trafalgar Square (R. Saltzman, ©1986)	*page* 2
1.2	Strikes! Restaurant interior showing photo murals (photo of murals, R. Saltzman, 1986)	2
1.3	'Army v. Navy! Student Coal Heavers', 1926, *Daily Graphic* (11 May), p. 1 (by permission of Solo Syndication)	3
1.3(a) left:	'Soldiers and sailors on duty at Lots Road Power Station hold a services' match'	3
1.3(b) right:	'Students and professional men acting as coal heavers at the Chelsea Power Station.'	3
1.4	Roy Band (R. Saltzman, ©1985)	22
2.1	'Curious effects of the strike: unusual scenes in London', 1926, *Illustrated London News* (15 May), p. 866 (by permission of the Mary Evans Picture Library)	35
2.1(a) upper left:	'A motor-bus recruiting office: volunteers enrolling at the LGOC Emergency Camp in Regent's Park.'	35
2.1(b) upper right:	At the Trades Union Congress headquarters after the stoppage of the strike was announced.	35
2.1(c) middle left:	'A "Test Match" in Rotten Row: volunteer workers in Hyde Park play improvised cricket with sticks for bats and boxes as wickets.'	35
2.1(d) middle right:	'"A flock of sheep that leisurely pass by": an unusual sight in New Bridge Street, connected with the maintenance of London's food supply.'	35

2.1(e) lower left:	'Keeping up the domestic coal supply in the East End of London: purchasers at the G.E.R. coaldepot at Custom house.'	35
2.1(f) lower right:	'Attended by women volunteers as waitresses: volunteer workers on the Underground Railway at a meal in their mess-room at Earl's Court.'	35
2.2	Marjorie Shipley Ellis (R. Saltzman, ©1985)	36
2.3	David Fremantle (R. Saltzman, ©1986)	39
3.1	Sid Rosenberg (R. Saltzman, ©1985)	49
3.2	Harry Crivan (R. Saltzman, ©1985)	55
4.1	'The Spirit of England at work: railway and dock volunteers', *Illustrated London News* 1926: 858 (by permission of the Mary Evans Picture Library)	73
4.1(a) upper left:	Right away!: A volunteer guard on the Metropolitan Railway in charge of a train during the strike'	73
4.1(b) upper middle:	'Important duty at a London terminus: a volunteer adjusting the points outside King's Cross station'	73
4.1(c) upper right:	'Ensuring the safe passage of Main Line trains into King's Cross: another volunteer adjusting points.'	73
4.1(d) middle left:	'Signalmen in Fair Isle Jerseys and "Plus Fours": Two Volunteer Undergraduates in Charge of the Chief Signal Box at Bletchley Station.'	73
4.1(e) middle right:	'Strenuous work at a London Terminus: a squad of volunteers turning a locomotive on a turn-table at King's Cross station.'	73
4.1(f) lower left:	'The arrival of the "Mauretania" at Southampton: Some of the volunteers who acted as shore-gangs loading a passenger's luggage into a car for the journey to London.'	73
4.1(g) lower right:	'As to the manner born: a volunteer engine-driver and his fireman on their locomotive during the strike.'	73
4.2	Allene and Arthur Toms (R. Saltzman, ©1986)	74
4.3	Phineas May in special constable uniform *c.*1926 (courtesy of Phineas May)	75
5.1	'Well Done – The light(hearted) blues!' 1926, *Tatler* (26 May), p. 267 (by permission of the Mary Evans Picture Library)	87

5.1(a) top:	'Plus-Fours And Flannel Bags – A cheerful group of volunteers on the quay at Dover	87
5.1(b) lower left:	'Two "Blues"' [Mr P. S. Douty and Mr A. D. Allen]	87
5.1(c) lower right:	'"Oh, Mr. Porter, Whatever did you do?"'	87
5.2	W. K. Haselden, 1926. 'Some Humours of the Strike Days', *Daily Mirror* (18 May) (by permission of The British Cartoon Archive, University of Kent and Mirrorpix)	89
5.3	E. T. Reed, 1926. 'Some "General" Favourites', *Bystander* (26 May), p. 445 (by permission of the Mary Evans Picture Library)	90
5.4	Frank Reynolds, 1926b. "Your son is looking very bored", *Punch* (2 June), p. 578 (reproduced with permission of Punch Ltd, www.punch.co.uk)	92
5.5	Leslie Jackson (R. Saltzman, ©1985)	93
5.6	Leslie Dover's Southern Railway work pass (courtesy of Leslie Dover)	95
5.7	Lord Denning with armband and truncheon from 1926 (R. Saltzman, ©1986)	96
5.8	'Where London Volunteer Bus-drivers and Conductors Slept during the Strike: The Chiswick Garage of the L.G.O.C. arranged as a dormitory' in 'Strike and Post-Strike Incidents, Including Trainwrecking', 1926, *Illustrated London News* (15 May), p. 865 (by permission of the Mary Evans Picture Library)	98
5.9	George Richardson (R. Saltzman, ©1985)	99
5.10	R. H. Dobbs' TUC certification for volunteer work, 18 May 1926 (courtesy of Phyllis Dobbs)	100
5.11	Edward Dunham (R. Saltzman, ©1986)	102
5.12	Frederick Coombes (R. Saltzman, ©1985)	106
5.13	Lots Road Power Station Volunteers, 1926 (Captain A.G.W. Herber-Percey, courtesy of Charles W. Cassell, Ret, RN)	113
5.14	Peggy Paten (R. Saltzman, ©1985)	114
5.15	'How they Helped in Hyde Park and Whitehall', 1926, *Sphere* (22 May), p. 158 (by permission of the Mary Evans Picture Library)	117
5.15(a) upper left:	'Miss J. Leveson-Gower helps in Hyde Park'	117

5.15(b) upper middle:	'Mrs. Grey Alderson and the Hon. Ivy Somerset seated in front of the mattresses in Whitehall car park'	117
5.15(c) upper right:	'Hanging out the washing in Hyde Park during the Great Strike – An interesting group of workers pictured during last week'	117
5.15(d) middle:	'A good-bye group of volunteer workers in the M. O. T. Park in the Horse Guards Parade. Forty per cent of the drivers were women'	117
5.15(e) lower left:	'Lady Betty Butler and Miss Collet help to fry bacon and sausages in Hyde Park'	117
5.15(f) lower middle:	'Lord Airlie and Mrs. Brinling commanding the fast-car service'	117
5.15(g) lower right:	'Miss Bridget Sherwood and Miss M. E. Gaunt at work in Hyde Park'	117
5.16	Frank Reynolds, 1926a. 'Repercussions of The Strike', *Punch* (19 May), p. 525 (reproduced with permission of Punch Ltd, www.punch.co.uk)	119
5.17	Arthur Wallis Mills, 1926. 'Riding Pillion', *Punch* (26 May), p. 541 (reproduced with permission of Punch Ltd, www.punch.co.uk)	120
7.1	Dinner menu and programme, Peterborough & District Electricity Users' Association (courtesy of George Richardson)	157
7.2	Note to Phineas May, 'May 14, 1926. The Street Patrols have been cancelled after tonight Friday so you will not have to report for that duty on Saturday morning. Please look up other duties in place of this' (courtesy of Phineas May)	158
7.3	Phineas May's Government thank you certificate (courtesy of Phineas May)	159
7.4	Charles Cassell's Metropolitan District Railway thank you certificate (courtesy of Charles Cassell)	160
7.5	Jack Santall's City of Birmingham Tramways Committee thank you certificate (courtesy of Jack and Brenda Santall)	161
7.6	Peter Kingsford's Great Western Railway thank you certificate (courtesy of Peter Kingsford)	162
8.1	National Portrait Gallery railing with General Strike and Queen Elizabeth II exhibit posters (R. Saltzman, ©1986)	191

8.2	Interior of National Portrait Gallery's General Strike exhibition (R. Saltzman, ©1986)	191
8.3	Lady Lindsay's Great Western Railway silver tray (courtesy of Lady Lindsay, R. Saltzman, ©1985)	193
9.1	'Police v. Strikers at a Football Match at Plymouth,' in 'Home News in Pictures', 1926, *Sphere* (15 May), p. 180 (by permission of the Mary Evans Picture Library)	202
9.2	Rose Kerrigan (R. Saltzman, ©1986)	204

Table

3.1	Traits of upper and middle-class General Strike volunteers	44

Acknowledgements

This book owes its existence to a great many people and institutions. During 1985–87, I corresponded with and interviewed members of the British upper and middle classes who had come out as volunteers to do the jobs of the workers during the 1926 General Strike. I interviewed many from the strikers' side as well as those who had family or friends on either or both sides. In all, I was in contact with over 300 individuals from England, Ireland, Scotland, the United States, Wales, and India. My correspondents and interviewees were forthcoming about their beliefs and prejudices. I exchanged more than one letter with at least a quarter of those I contacted, or who contacted me as a result of various advertisements and requests for information. One man sent me poems he had written, while another conducted an argumentative correspondence. Many invited me into their homes and told me their stories.

I was fortunate enough to reside in northeast London with journalists Alan Rusbridger and Lindsay Mackie. They offered me their services as cultural translators as well as the use of their electric typewriters and televisions, taught me how to lay a coal fire, and teased me about 'my' President Reagan and American international policy. Besides providing me with a place to stay, children to play with, and all the full-cream milk I could ever want, Alan and Lindsay were eager to hear about my research adventures and were uncommonly generous in listening, offering interpretations, and sharing their friends and family with me. Frequent visits to friends Gretchen and Robin Precey and their children, then in Salhouse, a small town outside Norwich, were a welcome respite from the intensity of London. The Precey house became my home away from home, and I was invited to share their holidays, family life, and local community.

British folklorist Steve Roud, then reference librarian at the Croydon Library, and fount of bibliographical knowledge, deserves more gratitude than I can put into words. He, his wife, Pam, and their daughter shared their home with me in 1987 and 1992 as well as for countless visits during 1985–86. Steve, especially, listened to and read my writing on the strike, challenged my interpretations, and tactfully educated me about British culture and mores.

I was well aware, and became increasingly so, that my identity as a postgraduate American student enabled me to cross class lines. Certainly, I knew enough of how the social hierarchy was constructed to know that I was entering a rarefied atmosphere, but I also had nothing to lose by writing letters and making phone calls to members of the upper classes.[1] I obtained interviews with Lord Denning, then the Master of the Rolls, and Lady (Loelia) Lindsay, the former Duchess of Westminster (thanks to Artemis Cooper for the introduction), and received detailed correspondence from other members of the peerage, whose time, thoughtfulness, and assistance I very much appreciate.

My disparate – from an English perspective – social and educational background provided me with access across the class spectrum. Yet while those with working-class, lower-middle-class, and middle-class backgrounds, interviewees and correspondents as well as folklorist friends, grilled me about my labour credentials (e.g. whether I knew the difference between a strike and a lockout) and my background (daughter of a millwright and a teacher, both union members who had been involved in several collective actions), very few of my upper-middle or upper-class interviewees asked about anything other than my university education – a pretty clear class marker in 1980s' Britain, where even today such a minority have advanced degrees. Most of those I interviewed and with whom I corresponded, regardless of class, seemed to assume that my beliefs were similar to theirs or that they were of no consequence – or perhaps it was just not polite to ask. Rather than being insulted by my questions, they seemed more intrigued than put off by my enquiries.

One of my first tasks after I arrived in England was to write to several local and national newspapers (see below) requesting that they print my letter seeking information about those who served as government volunteers in the strike. These media contacts resulted in over one hundred letters and included multiple exchanges with several individuals. During the winter, I contacted men's and women's clubs as well as various charitable organisations, and, in the spring and summer, I wrote to alumni from several Oxbridge colleges.[2] In the spring of 1986, I also put personal ads in the *Daily Telegraph* and *The Times*. In April and May of 1986, I followed up with several of the other newspapers and sent them a compilation of responses that I had received, concluded by welcoming further responses, and received another forty-one letters. To the editors of the *Brighton & Hove Gazette & Herald*, *Brighton and Hove Leader*, *Cambridge Evening News*, *Cambridge Weekly News*, *Daily Telegraph*, *Eastern Daily Press*, *Hampstead & Highgate Express*, *Inner London Education Authority Newsletter*, *Isle of Wight Mercury*, *Jewish Chronicle*, *Kelvin Times*, *Kensington News and Post*, *London & Westminster Newspapers*, *London Newspaper Group*, *Marx Memorial Library Bulletin*, *Morning Star*, *Navy News*,

Peterborough Evening Telegraph, Pensioners' Voice, Sheffield Weekly Gazette, Surrey Advertiser, The Times, and the *Willesden and Brent Chronicle,* and to Sue Wallace of Radio Solent I owe a great debt, for they provided my first fieldwork contacts. To those who responded in writing and by telephone to my letters, I offer my profound thanks for their reflections and memories.

The many kind and generous members of all classes whom I interviewed about their youthful experiences in the 1926 General Strike went out of their way to answer my questions, serve me a 'proper' tea, fête me with Christmas cakes and mince pies, and offer me a window into their personal history, social concerns, political views, and their sense of humour. Of particular importance were Sue and Roy Band (Roy was a retired Conservative Party manager) of Peterborough, who read my letter to their local paper, rang me, and invited me to stay with them. Roy and Sue fed me, brought morning tea to my bedside, explained why I had to watch the television series *Yes, Minister* and its sequel, *Yes, Prime Minister,* and took me round to visit and interview their many Conservative Party friends and acquaintances of all classes.

Rose Kerrigan, a still-active Communist Party member then in her 80s, also took me under her wing. Rose, widow of Communist Party leader Peter Kerrigan, responded to my letter in the *Morning Star*. She not only shared stories but jokes, songs, poetry, and art as well as her political views and personal philosophy (Saltzman, 1993). Rose also drew me into her circle and introduced me to family and friends whom I interviewed.

Peter Gathercole, then Dean of Darwin College, Cambridge University, and another *Morning Star* subscriber, became a gentle mentor. He listened to my theories and suggested readings. And when I became frustrated with the lumbering speed of British social change, he carefully and kindly pointed out that this was not my culture and that my role was, appropriately, restricted to that of a scholar.

Local libraries, historical societies, and archives also provided crucial information. I want to thank Chris Coates, Fran Mundin, Steve Mills, Jen Cox, and Kathy Granville, librarians at the Trade Union Congress Library for their patience, talk, and hours of research time from 1985 to 1987. Without them, I could never have gained access to the contemporary newspapers from 1926. The reference librarians at the British Library in the British Museum, the Imperial War Museum, the Marx Memorial Library, *The Times* Newspaper Library, the Greater London Record Office and History Library, the Oxford Public Library, the Croydon Public Library, Islington Public Library, the National Portrait Gallery, as well as those at the Newspaper Library at Colindale and at the Public Record Office in Kew Gardens, were similarly helpful. It was a pleasure to work with archivists so eager to help a researcher use their materials.

As part of my research, I also contacted the masters, deans, registrars, and mistresses of Clare, Girton, and Newnham colleges at Cambridge University and Somerville, St. Hugh's, and Corpus Christi colleges at Oxford University, as well as the librarians or archivists at Leeds and Liverpool universities. They sent me their alumni directories so that I could send out survey letters, printed my letters' requesting information in their annual newsletters, and invited me to explore their collections. To Suzy Johnston, College Archivist of Clare College, Cambridge, I owe a special debt for providing not only the Clare directory but also a photocopy of the invaluable undergraduate publication, *The Upside Down*. I am also grateful to the secretaries of the Athenaeum, United Oxford and Cambridge University Club, University Women's Club, Navy News, Distressed Gentlefolk's Aid Association, Honourable Society of Lincoln's Inn, and Society of Archivists as well as Boodle's, who printed or posted my letters as well as contacted people on my behalf. Thanks to them, I was able to correspond with people from all over the UK who served as volunteers, or who knew those who did. Particular thanks are due to as well to A. Phillips, Frank Sutton, and the Rev. Ria A. G. Plate, who also assisted with research and even interviews, in the case of Rev. Plate. To those who responded to my letters with theirs, and those who allowed me to interview them, I offer my deepest gratitude. This study could not have been researched or written without their time, experiences, and magnanimity.

Several historians, writers, and folklorists in Great Britain also played their part in this work. To Chris Wrigley (University of Nottingham), I owe great thanks for his many insightful and specific comments and corrections, references, and advice, then and now. David Benedictus (author, producer, and all-round Renaissance man), whom I interviewed in 1986 and again in 2009, has been uncommonly generous with his time and knowledge. To historian Peter Kingsford, literary critic and historian Lady (Rosalie) Mander, Artemis Cooper (author and granddaughter of Duff and Diana Cooper), Brian Durrans (Museum of Mankind), Chris Saunders, and Brian Harrison (Corpus Christi College, Oxford), I extend my gratitude for their encouragement, scholarship, and assistance with my research. To folklorists and scholars Gillian Bennet, Marian Bowman, Craig Fees, and Doc Rowe in England, and to Gregor Wienans of Cologne, as well as friends Leslie Currie and Pam Roud, I remain in debt for their cultural translation, patience with this impatient American, intellectual discussion, political arguments, and endless cups of tea and boxes of Jaffa cakes. Further appreciation is due to my friends' children whose everyday concerns, laughter, tears, crises, and jokes helped to keep the research in perspective – to remind me that I was dealing with real people and not just abstract constructs.

I've also received much assistance in locating current sources for illustrations and getting permissions of various sorts. Mack McCormick (University Press of Kentucky) spent more time and effort than anyone should

Acknowledgements

to clear a copyright. Tess Hines (Mary Evans Picture Library) was wonderfully patient with my endless questions and deserves a special thank you. Mel Knight and Nancy Curran (Mirrorpix), Andre Gailani (*Punch* cartoons), Nick Hiley (British Cartoon Archive), and Danny Howell (Solo Syndication) have also been generous with their time and assistance, enabling me to reproduce various images that I hope make 1926 a bit more real for readers. Roderick Suddaby (Imperial War Museum) facilitated permission for me to publish lines from Commander Murray's account of his strike-time activities. I am most grateful to John Wells, Alan Samson, Jean Moorcroft Wilson, and Barbara Levy for extremely timely transatlantic aid in securing permission to reprint one of Siegfried Sassoon's poems.

Further gratitude is due to dear friends and colleagues Patricia Sawin, Laurie Graham, Kip Lornell, and Carol Trosset. They kept me sane and provided support in the field and at different phases of the writing and editing process. Regina Bendix sent me enormously helpful comments for an earlier version of this book, and Joanne Mulcahy offered much appreciated encouragement. Erika Brady and Moira Smith deserve special mention for having waded through the entire manuscript in its near-final state. Erika has been wonderfully supportive, providing elegant editing and bibliographic suggestions for various articles and this book as well as comforting comments when the labour pains got bad. Moira provided detailed, thought-provoking, and critical comments and questions. Moira, Patricia, and Nancy Michael have all served as sounding boards with regard to theory and interpretation as we have travelled our various paths. Patricia has also provided talk, solace, feedback, comfort, and laughter as well as online articles at the eleventh hour. You all have my continued gratitude for listening as well as sharing your thoughts and friendship.

Thanks are also due to Deb and Steve Ohrn, Julia and Jeff Moats, Jill Downing, Gail and Joe Kotval, Lisa and Ira Lacher, Gail Klearman and Jake Jacobs, and Steve and Gabrielle Callistein in Des Moines, Iowa. They took care of my daughter at various times while I was writing, encouraged me, and have provided friendship, laughter, wine, and comfort.

Of those teachers who have offered me their insights over the years, I would first like to acknowledge folklorist Roger de V. Renwick, whose editorial comments, honesty, and advice over the past thirty years have served me well and kept me on track. My first folklore professors, dear friends and mentors, Bob Bethke and Tom Green, have read and edited versions of this work, encouraged me always, and made it clear that being a folklorist was about the most fun career anyone could ever hope to have. Historians Brian Levack, Standish Meacham, Gerry Straka, Bill Fletcher, and Jim Curtis provided me with a solid training in methods and research. Social anthropologist James Brow added his native understanding of British culture and his vast theoretical perspective, while folklorist Dick Bauman offered his insights, teachings, bibliographic suggestions, and advice at both earlier and later stages, as did Jane Young. I have also been inspired by the work of my colleague Amy Shuman, who has always expressed an interest in my analyses of the General Strike volunteers – little did I know early on how important her work on storytelling was to be to the intellectual framework of this book. I am grateful to all these scholars for their patience, friendship, and intellectual generosity. Any errors or failings in this book are mine alone.

This book might never have existed without the understanding of my supervisor, Mary Sundet Jones, and others with whom I work in Iowa. Mary's flexibility made it possible for me to take time off for this book. My friend and colleague Linda Lee Lovelace also encouraged me to get it done. Sincere thanks are due to Mary, Linda, Staci, Bruce, Sarah, Dawn, and Lara for taking up the slack. History curator Jack Lufkin read chapters and offered useful suggestions and encouragement. Staci Nevinski performed heroically and came to the rescue when my laptop crashed. Veronica O'Hern scanned and Photoshopped many images, making my photography look much better. And Wendy Stegall created an elegant index. Novelist Larry Baker also offered encouragement and inspiration.

My deepest debt goes to members of my family. To my aunt and uncle, Marcia and Marvin Shepard, my appreciation for their ready ears, emotional support, and total confidence. I cannot imagine that I would have started, much less completed, this project without the patience, financial help, and emotional support of my parents, Pearl and Stan Saltzman. Even when they have had their doubts about this pursuit and others I have undertaken, they always provided me with their love and understanding. Their ability to talk and listen to strangers, which totally embarrassed me and my brother when we were children, taught me the importance of listening and trying to understand the words and worlds of others. My mother, especially, has had an unwavering faith in me and my work.

Special appreciation is due to the Manchester University Press staff members, who have requested that they not be named individually. You all are amazing, and I cannot thank you enough for making this book possible.

Finally, I'd like to thank my husband, Nick Rieser, and my daughter, Eva Saltzman. They took care of domestic matters while I agonised over miniscule details and fretted over copyright issues. Eva, whose early years rightly put this work on hold for a while, entertained herself, drew me pictures, and wrote me notes, recently asked if I would be writing this book until I die. To that, I am now able to say a resounding 'No'! Nick, who came into this project near its denouement, has shown uncommon interest in my obsession, provided ongoing and repeated technical support when I was at my most hysterical, and gave much needed neck rubs. Both deserve credit for this book finally seeing the light of day.

⇜ *Acknowledgements* ⇝

Funding for my research during 1986 was provided by a dissertation Grant-in-Aid from the Wenner-Gren Foundation for Anthropological Research. An American Folklore Society Public Sector Residency at Indiana University provided time for research and rewriting in 1995.

Note: All General Strike related letters, interviews, manuscripts, newspapers, and so on, which are in the author's possession, will eventually be placed at the University of Texas Humanities Resource Center in Austin.

Rachelle H. Saltzman, Des Moines, Iowa, USA

Notes

1 I wrote to 41 individuals from the peerage noted in Merlin Waterson's *The Country House Remembered: Recollections of Life between the Wars,* in April 1986. I received 13 replies plus references for 5 others; 11 of the first were substantive, while 2 wrote that they were ill.

2 I wrote to a random sample of 39 Clare College, Cambridge University alumni during April 1986. Eighteen responded with information, 3 to say they were ill, and 6 relatives to inform me the person had died. Response rate: 46 per cent with actual information, 59 per cent overall.

I sent letters to a random sample of 71 alumnae from Girton College, Cambridge in December 1986. I received 36 substantive responses, plus notes that 5 had died and 4 too ill or too old. I exchanged multiple letters with 3 and interviewed 2. Response rate was 51 per cent.

I also placed requests for information in these Oxbridge women's colleges' newsletters and received 10 responses: Newnham College, Cambridge *Letter* (Winter 1987); St Hugh's College, Oxford *Chronicle* (spring 1987); and the Somerville College, Oxford *Report* (spring 1987).

In my letters, I noted 'I will give full acknowledgement of any information that I use (unless otherwise desired).'

Preface

This study of the 1926 General Strike volunteers started accidentally as a course requirement. Knowing of my interest in ritual and revolution, University of Texas folklore professor Roger deV. Renwick handed me an undergraduate's paper (Schenker, 1978) and recommended that I investigate its claims that coal miners and other strikers had been involved in rough musicking, a form of traditional dramatic protest and censure that typically involves anonymous threats, noisemaking and name calling, masking or face blacking, and mock funerals. There was, however, surprisingly little evidence of such behaviour from striking workers but quite a lot from strike-breakers – also known as volunteers. My subsequent research involved investigating the volunteers' role in the General Strike, an overtly political topic that concerned the traditional expressive culture, the folklore, of the peerage and gentry, and the volunteers' image in the national imagination as upper-class buffoons, the clownish side of the gentleman amateur stereotype.

Shortly before I came to England in 1985 to start my fieldwork, one upper-middle-class British folklorist informed me that what I was studying was not folklore. I respectfully disagreed and, somewhat indignantly, proceeded with my research in various archives and libraries and conducting interviews with former volunteers, strikers, and others. Unwittingly, I had stumbled into one of those British/American cultural divides.

Most American folklorists would agree that folklore (variously known as folk art, folklife, cultural traditions, or traditional arts), while rooted in at least one explicit and shared identifying feature (e.g. language, geography, ethnicity, occupation, gender, age, or religion), encompasses a range of expressive forms (e.g. storytelling, music, dance, craft, or others), which are 'learned as part of the cultural life of a community ... These traditions are shaped by the aesthetics and values of a shared culture and are passed from generation to generation, most often within family and community through observation, conversation, and practice' (National Endowment for the Arts, 2009). Writing about the confluence of memory, history, and expression, Finnish folklorist

Seppo Knuutila noted that 'folklore ... reflects and recreates worldviews and mentalities' (Knuuttila, 2008: 265). Although social class, a priori, does not determine whether or not a group possesses folklore, the very name of the field has pointed researchers in a particular direction and narrowed its focus, despite a history of debates about devolved forms, survivals, and aristocratic beginnings.[1]

In the UK, restrictions on place and class seem to be part of the accepted understanding of folklore, which is quite explicitly *not* found among middle and upper-class *English* men and women. Neither is it urban, unless one is cockney, non-white, or politically based. Rather, British and/or English folklore is quaint, rural, innocent of political intent, entertaining, and distinctly a preserve of the lower classes and those of a particular ethnic (Irish, Scottish, Welsh, or Cornish), occupational, or distinct regional background, for example Celts of various sorts, coal miners and sailors, cockneys or Yorkshiremen – preferably, hearty *yeomen* and, more rarely, women, who sing Child or broadside ballads, perform mummers' plays, Morris dances, or tell tales (Paxman, 1999: 148–9; 167; Sutton, 2008). It provides a basis for romantic nostalgia about England, for folklore is found as surviving among the elderly, children, and the rural working classes – the very groups from whom most nineteenth-century and twentieth-century folklorists 'collected' Child and broadside ballads, folk tales, folk drama, and folk dance.[2]

Folklore in British-speak fits precisely into that cultural definition of Englishness that has become such a bone of contention in recent years, one that was just beginning to surface in the mid-1980s. In fact, Robert Colls' and Philip Dodd's edited collection *Englishness: Politics and Culture 1880–1920* (1986) came out as I was writing my doctoral thesis. While I had endlessly documented that the strike seemed to evoke all sorts of stereotypical commentary about what British behaviour was and was not, Colls' and Dodd's work neatly summed up much of the recent cultural history that led to that particular constellation of characteristics labelled Englishness. In the intervening twenty-five years, there have been increasingly intense debates about definitions for Englishness versus Britishness. Historians, political scientists, sociologists, pundits, journalists, and national surveys (e.g. Colls and Dodd, 1986; Paxman, 1999; Kumar, 2003 and 2006; Ward, 2004; Aughey, 2007; Hutchinson *et al.*, 2007; Ministry of Justice Opinion Poll on Identity, Belonging, and Values, 2008; Wills, 2008) have entered into the fray for a variety of motives and perspectives and with regard to ethnic identity, devolution, nationalism, political consequences in Parliament, the relationship between the UK and the EU, immigration, and so on. The blurring of lines between cultural and political definitions has increasingly confused the debate to the point where no one is too sure any longer how to articulate either identity or its constituent features, but all are quite clear that they know it when they see it.

Nonetheless, how Englishness and Britishness are regarded today has little bearing on contemporary understandings of that identity in 1926. Those writing on the topic make the point that the terms 'British' and 'English' were found interchangeably in contemporary usage (Powell, 2002: 152–5; Aughey, 2007: 76). Both were generally taken to encompass the English living in England proper as well as certain Celtic peoples but not the non-whites and non-Christians who were part of the larger British Empire; they did not become British until much later. England clearly referred to the geographical land mass that was England specifically, including Wales but not Scotland; Britain included Scotland and Ireland, but not for the majority of Irish living in what became the Republic of Ireland. The British Empire included the above as well as all colonial nations. English and British – but not Englishness or Britishness – as nouns and adjectives were used during and in the years just after 1926 to describe very specifically who was and who was not part of the national polity, neither a political nor a cultural construct (Kumar, 2006; Hutchinson *et al.*, 2007) but a mix of both.

During this same period, the late twentieth century through the early years of the twenty-first, various other scholars have been puzzling over the relationship among history, collective and individual memory, key symbols and cultural paradigms and how identities are formed, passed on, and reformulated (e.g. Sahlins, 1981; Johnson *et al.*, 1982; Ladurie, 1982; Hobsbawm and Ranger, 1985; Samuel and Thompson, 1987; Portelli, 1991; Halbwachs, 1992; Thompson, 1994 and 2000; Shuman, 2005; Anderson, 2006; Rohdewald, 2008). Such scholars and others, whose work is discussed in Chapter 1, have relied on oral history, folklore, literature, memoirs, diaries, and popular culture to gain understanding of what has been variously labelled mentalities, world views, and cultural aesthetics. As they have realized that there is not one truth or one history but a multitude that form an overarching whole with aspects at odds with one another, scholars in this mode have come to understand that people tend to act in societies according to their particular perspective; there are particular cultural icons, key symbols, cultural constructs, and legends that provide enough metonymical resonance as well as enough vagueness to allow them to persist, acquire new meanings while simultaneously retaining the older ones, and thus be available to 'think with' when new situations arise. Paradigm shifts certainly occur when different mentalities collide and questions are reformulated or even cast aside for brand new ones. For the most part, however, societies and cultures are elastic enough to absorb such moments and even reframe their definitions to fit new outlooks and still make some kind of claim to cultural continuity, to preserve some thread of cultural authenticity, a connection with a past, imagined or otherwise.

For folklorists, 'the most important question is not whether the stories are fiction or not. Much more interesting is how the articulations of imagination and memory work' (Rohdewald, 2008: 267). We are concerned with how and why certain mentalities and aesthetic traditions interact to form and reiterate identities. This is not so different a perspective from that of late twentieth and early twenty-first-century British social historians such as Paul Johnson *et al.* (1982), Paul Thompson (2000), Edward Thompson (1991), and Sue Bruley (2010), except that folklorists shine a brighter light on particular forms of folklore (e.g. legends, jokes, songs) as well as how their performance reflects identity formation, maintenance, and reproduction.

Debates over Englishness versus Britishness clearly do have some bearing on a British understanding of folklore. Yet folklore as a discipline and as a construct have not been explicitly a part of the discussion, though all the ingredients are there (see Symons, 1957; Benedictus, 1986; Thompson, 1991; Perkins, 2006; Bruley, 2010: 60–85, 109–11), partly because of the field's and the term's highly restrictive definitions in Great Britain as well as a potentially suspect relationship with extremist nationalistic movements. Thus, framing my research topic as folklore made little sense to anyone but my working-class interviewees, who very much understood.

The strike polarised people from all classes in Great Britain. Yet regardless of which side they were on, volunteers, strikers, government, military, business people, or those simply caught in the middle, had remarkably similar notions about what constituted British identity. And they used that definition to claim that identity for themselves and their idea of the nation. Respect for good and right order as well as the law, patriotism, fair play, moderation, doing one's duty, service, good humour, keeping one's head in a crisis, and not taking oneself too seriously were all part and parcel of national identity for all concerned.

Notes

1 Early folklorists such as the Grimm brothers (Germany), Percy (England), and later Francis James Child and Cecil Sharp (England), and the Lomaxes (United States), working as they did during a time of romantic nationalism, looked to the folk, peasants, and working classes of their respective countries for evidence of some deep-rooted essence of cultural peoplehood (Buchan, 1972; Zipes, 1979; Harker, 1985; Bendix, 1997).
2 For more, see David Buchan's *The Ballad and the Folk*, Dave Harker's *Fakesong*, and also the works of Francis James Child, Cecil Sharp, Maud Karpeles, A. L. Lloyd, and Roger deV. Renwick.

1

Introduction: folklore, memory, and the volunteers of 1926

> I overheard a scrap of conversation at an At Home in Oxford yesterday. One lady said to another: 'When we landed at Dover during the strike, we were welcomed by Cambridge men, who slung our baggage over their shoulders as to the manner born, and then, having done all they possibly could, stood by the engine and cheered as our train steamed out. Then in London we fell into the equally kindly hands of Oxford men, among them an old pupil of my husband's ...' The other lady remarked: 'Charming manners – good temper! I hope historians will not fail to record those special characteristics of the voluntary workers in the great strike.' ('A Scrap of Conversation', 1926: 460)

> Parallels were vaguely drawn between the emergencies of the war and the general strike; and all but a few of them were imaginary. On the first day of the strike I met the most famous and only monocled special correspondent in England. He predicted, 'Within three weeks we shall hear tales about the miners having crucified a mine-owner in Yorkshire – you know, like the yarns about the Germans in Belgium.' (Bott, 1926: 171)

> The humiliation of 1926 was deeply embedded in the collective memory of the mining communities during the disputes of 1972 and 1974 [as is] ... another long memory – the folk memory of 'treachery at the centre'. (Wrigley, 1984b: 6)

In mid-1980s London, the restaurant Strikes! opened establishments in Trafalgar Square, a few streets from the National Portrait Gallery, and across from the National Design Centre (see figure 1.1). Strikes! served American-style barbequed ribs and ice cream sundaes. Its walls were adorned with huge photo reproductions of 1926 General Strike volunteers (as the middle and upper-class strike-breakers were known) driving buses, serving tea in canteens, and so on. In 1926, a plethora of such photographs accompanied newspaper and magazine accounts of the strike (see figure 1.2). The image that stands out for me is one with a group of smiling, laughing, happy young men, crowded together for a photo op and kicking a football, as soldiers did across no-man's land in the First World War (see figure 1.3).

1.1 Strikes! Restaurant exterior, near Trafalgar Square

1.2 Strikes! Restaurant interior showing photo murals

1.3(a) *left:* 'Soldiers and sailors on duty at Lots Road Power Station hold a services' match'

1.3(b) *right:* 'Students and professional men acting as coal heavers at the Chelsea Power Station'

The restaurants, which inexplicably seemed to be celebrating the strike, the strikers, and the volunteers with a bizarrely and iconically American menu, presented an interpretive challenge, especially for a folklorist who had solicited, listened to, and documented the memories of former volunteers and strikers. This seemingly anachronistic operation, which apparently opened around the time of the 1984–85 miners' strike, the biggest labour uprising since the 1926 General Strike, did not seem to fit – neither in theme nor menu choice. Its placement, within sight of Trafalgar Square and its dizzying obelisk commemorating Nelson and marking the beginning of the British Empire, had perhaps some more profound symbolic logic.[1]

The 1926 General Strike lasted officially from midnight on 3 May until 12 May. Over the course of nine days, four million workers came out in sympathy with coal miners, who were protesting against attempts by mine owners and managers to reduce wages and lengthen hours. A government subsidy had propped up the coal industry on and off since the end of the war in 1918; in the midst of an uncertain international economy, however, the government claimed that it could no longer afford to subsidize one industry at the expense of others. Mine owners were equally insistent that their profits not be reduced – hence the solution to cut miners' wages. Union representatives were understandably unwilling to accept these proposals, however, and on 30 April 1926, the Trades Union Congress (TUC), the representative body of and for British labour unions, voted in favour of a 'co-ordinated action' (TUC General Council, 1926: 32A).

Organized labour believed that a general stoppage would convince the public to put pressure on Parliament, whose members were involved in debates and negotiations concerning the coal industry, to preserve coal miners' then current wages and hours. The theory behind the notion of this broad-based action, first articulated in the 1830s (Benbow, 1936; Symons, 1957: 50–1; Morris, 1976: Jenkins, 1980; Wrigley, 1984a), held that even the dullest and most apolitical among the general public could not fail to notice the connection between labour and the maintenance of society if that labour were withdrawn all at once. Consequently, early in May 1926, workers in over 200 unions put their livelihoods on the line for the sake of one million locked-out coal miners. Yet, as with most strikes, the general public's hostility to being inconvenienced outweighed much of the sympathy they might have felt for the miners' plight. Most people tended to fear rather than applaud the sympathetic relationship among the labour unions, for a general strike (by the end of the stoppage, labour leaders were also using this term), carried to its logical extreme was, and is, a workers' revolution.[2]

In addition, the working-class tactic of evoking such potent symbols of the left as the Peterloo massacre, the Chartist movement, and the Tolpuddle martyrs, served only to frighten the upper and middle classes into thinking that, regardless of protests to the contrary, the TUC did intend the General Strike as an attack on their rights and property. The arguments of both labour and intellectuals were based on a moral sense that those who had sacrificed for the good of the community (the entire British nation during the First World War) were by all logic also a part of that community. And the 'innocent public', which had benefited and continued to benefit from the products of manual labour, owed the workers, specifically the miners, some reciprocal responsibility. Yet while this argument made good rhetorical sense, it had little resonance for anyone other than the working classes and the intellectual left.

To the surprise of contemporaries at home and abroad, however, the strike was conducted with relatively little violence – especially as compared to other workers' actions (cf. Perkins, 2006),[3] and strikers did not engage in traditional protest to any great degree. In fact, TUC leaders specifically ordered their constituents to behave in an orderly fashion – not to indulge in older, more subversive and traditional methods of coercion. Unlike their eighteenth and nineteenth-century predecessors, strikers did not blacken their faces, parade about at night, demand money and free food from propertied people, or threaten to indulge in arson and riot if their demands were not met. In fact, with the exception of several mock funerals for blackleg miners (Leeson, 1973: 102–3, 109; Gerard, 1976: 97, 221; Tucket, 1976), Gerald Crompton's note about a retired engine driver's being treated to some rough musicking with tin cans and kettles by striking railway workers in Peterborough (Crompton, 1988: 134), and a few other charivari-like examples of in-group censureship in South Wales and Swindon (Francis, 1976: 251; Tucket, 1976; 294–5, 298; Bruley, 2004 and 2010: 106–11), there is surprising little evidence of this sort of behaviour.[4] A fair amount seems to have come from miners' and railway workers' wives (Francis, 1976: 251; Tucket, 1976: 298; Bruley: 2010: 106–11), however. The TUC, on the other hand, was intent on showing that organized labour was a sophisticated and orderly force, comprising neither a rioting mob nor a bunch of street hooligans (Wilkinson, 1989: 66–7, 133; Laybourn, 1993, 1999).

At the same time, another group began to exhibit some very public displays of their own folk culture. All of a sudden, over half a million registered volunteers and countless others, most of whom the newspapers traditionally categorized as useless, disorderly, youthful, feminine, and, most importantly, non-workers, came out into the streets and parks of the nation, particularly in London and other major cities, such as (but not limited to) Manchester, Liverpool, and Glasgow as well as in small towns and rural areas. Despite the fact that people from all walks of life served as volunteers[5] and worked hard at doing so with no reward but a thank you,[6] undergraduates and society women volunteers dominated the contemporary media and later the memoirs, diaries, and a continuous stream of novels, plays, and anniversary exhibits as well as the walls of the restaurant Strikes! Upper and upper-middle-class university students, society women, titled people, and young businessmen drove trains and buses, ran canteens, printed and delivered emergency newspapers, worked in the docks, and had a great time 'carrying on'.

For the volunteers and those who sided with them, a general spirit of renewal, fun, and licence – the carnivalesque (Abrahams, 1987: 173–82; Falassi, 1987: 1–12) – came to characterize and frame much of the event – for contemporaries and in the collective memories of the event (Gerard, 1976: 95; Bruley, 2004: 237; Perkins, 2006). Sue Bruley also noted the existence of some of this same atmosphere, despite the hardships miners and their families faced, in South Wales, for example, jazz bands, 'cattie and dog' tournaments, carnivals, 'comedy' (often with men and women's teams) football matches with outlandish costumes, and concerts of all sorts (Bruley, 2010: 60–85; see also Norman, Letter, 1985: Buckley, Interview, 1985).

While behind-the-scenes negotiations proceeded among trade union leaders and the government, the public drama of the General Strike continued to unfold. And it did so in more informal and expressive, albeit no less instrumental, ways than those of the bureaucratic institutions involved. For the public enactment that became the General Strike had its roots in the unspoken rules that dictated certain customary forms of behaviour for interaction among the different sectors of British society (Davidoff, 1973; Thompson, 1974 and 1991).

Although the General Strike ostensibly began when printers at the *Daily Mail* refused to print an inflammatory editorial condemning the strike, this was more an excuse for negotiations to end rather than a reason. The causes of the 1926 lockout and General Strike were far more complex, as John McIlroy, Alan Campbell, Keith Gildart and their colleagues (2004) as well as other historians have detailed. As far as the public was concerned, the event was played out in the public byways. R. J. Cruikshank, who recorded 'A Diary of the General Strike' for London's *Daily News*, noted that the crowd's reaction to a military convoy that moved flour from the docks to an improvised depot in Hyde Park 'was typical of the public attitude during the strike ... The crowds that lined the roads from the east to west of London appeared to regard it primarily as an attractive spectacle, a Lord Mayor's show out of season ... Histrionics were never before at such a discount in a great national emergency' (Cruikshank, 1926: 15).

Chancellor of the Exchequer Winston Churchill noted this phenomenon as well, but he also pointed out that the strike was an attack by one sector of society upon the Establishment. Churchill warned: 'there were masses of people who "feel quite detached from the conflict; they are waiting, as if they were spectators at a football match, to see whether the Government or the trades union is the stronger"' (TNA, Churchill, 1926; Hutt, 1937: 139–40).[7]

At the same time that such a holiday atmosphere prevailed, however, there was also an uneasy fear that the General Strike might not be so easily resolved as a football match, for the threat of real violence underlay all the stories of comic bravado. In fact, the entire conduct of the strike cannot be understood at all, unless one can realize the impact of the First World War on all involved. For the volunteers in particular, the war was an ever-present spectre. If they were too young to have been involved in it personally, as most were, they had brothers, uncles, or fathers who had been, and mothers, sisters, or aunts who had served as nurses and ambulance drivers or run canteens. Boy Mulcaster, one of the upper-class characters and a General Strike volunteer in Evelyn Waugh's *Brideshead Revisited*, declared before he joined up: "'You and I . . . were too young to fight in the war. Other chaps fought, millions of them dead. Not us. We'll show them. We'll show the dead chaps we can fight, too'" (Waugh, 1979: 205).

The decade after the war was not only a time of rapid change in transportation and communication technologies, intellectual theories, and social expectations for young people, especially middle-class women and those men who had served in the military. It also constituted a time of hope for some that the war had been worth the sacrifices; for others, it was an era of increasing awareness that economic depression and labour unrest were clear signs that they had not come close to achieving David Lloyd George's 1918 general election promise of 'a fit land for heroes to live in'. Revolution in Russia, continued trouble in Ireland, rumblings in India – all filled in the troubled background of an age best known for its dance craze, wild music, and liberation from the rigid rules and ornamental but static conventions that were seen to have characterized English society before the Great War (Cohen, 2002: 85, 153).

The most deeply felt emotion just after the war was relief; mass disillusionment with its promises did not set in until the end of the 1920s. For Felicia Stallman, who came from a professional middle-class background and who was a student at St Hugh's College, Oxford at the time, once the war ended, 'Oh, it was wonderful! Of course everybody went mad!! Of course there was no social life [during the war, but afterwards] the parties came back at once. There was a wonderful upsurge after the war. [During the war] everything was so dull and so horrible. It wasn't funny not getting enough to eat. Then suddenly everybody came back and we thought everything was going to be just as it used to be' (Stallman, Interview, 1986).

On 11 November 1918, most of the country poured into the streets for joyous celebrations, dancing, fireworks, singing, and just walking about in disbelief and wonderment at their good fortune in having survived. Life soon returned to a kind of normal state for many: middle and upper-class women gradually left the workforce, working-class soldiers demobilised and tried to find jobs, many a middle-class ex-soldier went off to university, and society attempted to resume its pre-war round of parties, albeit with a somewhat desperate and frenetic air. The sedate majesty of the Edwardian summer had vanished, and in its place was a new, fast-moving age of motor-cars, country-house weekends, short-skirted, independent women, and parties – each more wild than the last.

Post-war social historians berated the upper classes for their thoughtless lives of luxury whose very existence mocked the harsh and cruel conditions experienced by the majority of British society during the 1920s. Scholars, journalists, and novelists have construed such behaviour as an escape from the horrible memories of war-time sacrifices or, somewhat less justifiably, as ignorant and youthful hedonism. Both personal journals and published memoirs by the era's elite also proffered these same explanations in token apology for socio-economic divisions. Yet such responses and explanations mirrored contemporary notions about what being British meant in terms of appropriate behaviours for all classes, for men and women, young and old. At the same time, only certain roles were permissible, only certain alternatives existed, and, much as heroes and villains in folk tales and traditional ballads are bound by strict rules and consequences for their violation (Propp, 1968; Zipes, 1979; Renwick, 1980), so there were absolute penalties in 1926 for violating the social relationships encoded in British national identity (Davidoff, 1973: 79–82, 96–9).[8]

The Great War itself represented the epitome of what it meant to be British, especially for the upper and middle classes. This symbolic identity emanated from the Victorian and Edwardian eras, which ensured that the public school rituals of debate, the hierarchy of forms and prefects, and the virtues of duty, honour, and good sportsmanship were extended from the classrooms and playing fields into the halls of Parliament, to the old-boy network in politics, business, and the armed forces. Public school traditions among the young, as well as the more serious theatricality of adults who performed as paternalistic lords, magistrates, and self-righteous social planners in Whitehall and Toynbee Hall, were the basis for the English upper and middle-class male world view (Lane, 1981; Mangan, 1986). A sense of hereditary rightness, combined with the disinterested public service required of these young men, left no honourable alternative beyond the ultimate sacrifice of their own naive selves in the quest for a perfect society – a society that they had no choice but to believe was possible.

To be authentically British, and more particularly, English, in the twentieth century, one was obligated to serve, to do one's duty obediently, without question, and most importantly, cheerfully, politely, willingly, and even enthusiastically – but never for personal gain (Colls and Dodd, 1986; Paxman, 1999: 197–9). Those virtues were crucial for a successful outcome to the war.

Such an ethos pervaded all classes – in public, state, and church schools and universities; in rural villages and on country estates; in Parliament; and in urban slums via middle-class sponsored clubs, the scouting movement, and popular literature. But the war's unfulfilled utopian rhetoric was its greatest felt effect. And the final betrayal of the so-called Great War was the realization that government could do little to ease the economic burdens of most of its people.

Whereas war experiences intensified certain aspects of the British character, the 1920s signified others – adaptability to change, eccentric out-of-context behaviour, and an extreme fondness for practical jokes, especially among young members of the upper classes (Nicolson, 1946; Davidoff, 1973: 79–81). It was not that the former qualities had disappeared; the quick response of middle and upper-class volunteers to defend the nation from the threat of 'revolutionary' strikes in 1919, 1921, and 1926 left no doubt about that. But the Great War had so emphasized the necessity of fulfilling one's duty to king and country that the more light-hearted, pleasure-seeking aspects of being British had been too long repressed and had to seek a release somewhere – or so popular psychological explanations of the frenetic search for new and risky diversions would have it (Balfour, 1933: 70–1, 154–60; Clephane, 1933: 191; Mannin, 1971: 55–6; Zangwill, 1972; Branson, 1976: 96–9). The larks, pranks, fast cars, fancy dress parties, and treasure hunts of the elite, as well as the motorbikes, dance craze, sports, and amateur theatrics – the play genres – of the middle and working classes, in addition to everyone's obsession with cinema and radio, were all designated as the means by which people could forget the war's horrors and its disillusioning aftermath. But in forgetting the bad, other transformations occurred: brave middle and upper-middle-class soldiers turned into 'feminine' aesthetes or dull hearties; competent women ambulance drivers and munitions workers of all classes became emasculated harpies; and working-class soldiers suddenly looked like Bolshevik revolutionaries (Clephane, 1933: 155, 170–2; Graves and Hodge, 1941: 112–13, 34; Mannin, 1971: 55–7; Branson, 1976: 210–11).

For the upper classes – the upper ten thousand, the aristocracy, or society – the 1920s were in many ways a golden age, despite or because of the various changes wrought by war (Thompson, 1984). These people had money, social position, political power, and the licence to enjoy all three, unlike a third of the population at the other end of the socio-economic spectrum (Lane, 1981; MacKenzie, 1984). As Barbara Cartland put it, 'We were young, we were alive, we could laugh and love, and our feet could dance. That was ecstasy, that was youth and it can never come again' (Cartland, 1970: 300). Explained Lady (Loelia) Lindsay,[9] 'As I said, we weren't at all seriously interested in the problems of the day. I really didn't know whether the miners had enough pay or not ... It sounds bad ... but I mean that is the *truth* of it. [We were] so *young*! I don't remember anybody sort of discussing the rights and wrongs' (Lindsay, Interview, 1985).

The main preoccupation of these youthful members of society was to forget war-time losses and have a good time. Some of the old traditions such as walking in Hyde Park after church on Sunday, when 'all society paraded at Stanhope Gate, where they sat on green chairs and watched their friends walk or drive by' had faded with the increased use of motor cars, which made country weekends far more accessible (Cartland, 1970: 25). Yet others continued. Lady Lindsay, for instance, recalled the revival of the Season with its debutante parties:

> Yes [there were] two or three sometimes [a night]. You didn't know which one to go to ... It was after the war, and there was this tremendous feeling – Oh! Some youth, and some joy. And then everybody would be – the war to end all wars. And then, well, people didn't expect so much of parties – elaborate decor. They had a garden if you had a country house, and some flowers ... A very good supper, and depending on which ball you went with which young man you wanted to see, and this one you went to one ball, and you crossed over, meeting and that sort of thing. (Lindsay, Interview, 1985)

As the then Duchess of Westminster wrote: 'People sneer with great hindsight at the idea that a "war to end war" had been fought and won, but when I came out that was what most of us sincerely believed. The sacrifices had been terrible but one assumes that the result was worth it' (Grosvenor, 1961: 83). 'The prevailing mood was one of relief mixed with hopes that the world would really be a place "fit for heroes to live in" – but I'm not sure that everyone truly felt that we could simply go back to the kind of society in which we had grown up' (Grieg, 1979: 76). Lady Phyllis MacRae recalled that 'people tried to revive [the Season] at once. 1919 was a wonderful Season – gay and bright, with all the men in uniform, throwing their money about any old how, they were so glad to be alive' (Waterson, 1985: 33). As Lady Lindsay told me, conditions then were '*so* different. You can't imagine it. Then there was no envy or hatred. We walked about in our dresses through the square, jewels. Nobody would have *thought*. And then people watched the ones arriving. There was never any nastiness; they were just thrilled to see pretty people. Gone forever' (Lindsay, Interview, 1985; Davidoff, 1973: 67–9, 88–93).

Yet the pleasures of post-war England were not open to everyone. The Countess of Haddington remembered 'the 'twenties and 'thirties as a golden age, an absolute golden age. But I don't regret the present age, not at all. I think I approve of it much more than the old days. It was rather a selfish life, really, except in between one did good works and that sort of thing, with one's various charities. But on the whole it was a selfish life' (Waterson, 1975: 250; Cohen, 2002: 51).

Truth be told, society men and women and university undergraduates were not expected to show much social responsibility (Davidoff, 1973: 68–9). They were, however, supposed to respond to calls for national service. But a context for national crisis had to be established in order to transform these 'effeminate degenerates' into gallant lads. And the economic troubles of the 1920s were not slow to provide the setting. As Irene Clephane explained: 'After the war, the heroic status of the fighters was of bitterly short duration. Within two years of the cessation of fighting the men who had fought, for whom nothing was to be too good – underwent transformation in the popular middle-class imagination into lazy good-for-nothings of revolutionary tendencies whose sole idea was to avoid work and live on the "dole"' (Clephane, 1933: 155; Wrigley, 1993b: 268–70, 286).

Such feelings did not come out of thin air. The general economic situation in the early 1920s belied the outwardly carefree attitude of the upper classes. Felicia Stallman, one of the first female recipients of an Oxford degree, recollected that 'there was a great deal of dissatisfaction and disillusionment – one remembers growing depression. If you were inclined to be pessimistic, as I was, seeing that it was becoming very difficult for everybody ... The whole situation had really got appalling: industrial unrest and trade union power, miners and railways and transport – the General Strike' (Stallman, Interview, 1986).

Fresh in people's minds in the immediate post-war years and into the 1920s was the Russian Revolution.[10] Endlessly repeated accusations and warnings about Bolshevism and incipient revolution among workers can be found in the *Parliamentary Debates* (House of Commons, 1926; Wrigley, 1993a: 17 and 1993b: 269–80).[11] Still, the propertied classes did have serious grounds for concern as to whether the post-war reduced armed forces could and would maintain essential services should a social crisis occur (Bagwell, 1971: 117). In early 1919, the government created the Supply and Transportation Organisation for citizen volunteers; in March that same year, the Middle Class Union was formed to break strikes and maintain services. When a police strike occurred in August, a call to defend the nation went out. Those accepted as volunteer special constables were 'untrained young men, most of them clerks and other white-collar workers from the suburbs'. These men joined with the CID to stop the police union marchers, who wore their cast-off soldiers' uniforms, displaying their medals and ribbons, a symbolic protest also employed during the General Strike as well as during the 1924 and 1930s' hunger marches (Sellwood, 1978: 171–2).

While strikers used their medals to signify the sacrifices they had already made and as symbols of unkept promises, many of the volunteers, too young to have fought in the Great War, did not know how to read such blatant signs, for they had yet to earn their own symbolic capital. They had not experienced the war as a rite of passage into a disillusioned adulthood, as had their older brothers and sisters. And they still persisted in believing that only through war – no matter where or with whom – could they achieve the ennobling, purifying transformation still promised to public school boys (Fussell, 1975).

Should any able-bodied young man have missed his chance to volunteer to defend his country from its working-class ex-soldiers in 1919, yet another opportunity presented itself in 1921. At the end of March, war-time government control of coal mines ceased; the owners declared drastic pay cuts and an end to nationally determined wages.[12] The Miners Federation of Great Britain (MFGB) voted to reject these terms, and a lockout began on the last day of the month. The government declared a state of emergency, sending troops into the coalfields and placing machine guns at the pitheads. The miners appealed to the National Union of Railwaymen (NUR) and the Transport and General Workers Union (TGWU), the other two branches of the Triple Alliance, which called for a sympathetic strike to commence on 15 April (Symons, 1957: 5; Morris, 1976: 122; Farman, 1974: 23).

On 9 April 1921, Evelyn Waugh, then a public school boy, noted his frustration at not being able to join in:

> A war fever has taken hold upon us just as it did in August 1914. All the week has been fiercely exciting with strike news. On wednesday [sic] Mother and I went to the wedding of one of our cousins, and the bridegroom, a regular officer, was called up that night. Yesterday the Triple Alliance came out. I am anxious to get some work, but the only people at present being called up are those over eighteen who can join for ninety days and to my disgust Mother and Father refuse to let me do this. I have written to the local Labour Bureau but I doubt if they will give me anything to do. It is quite exasperating. It looks as if we were going to have a civil war and I shall be out of it. I mean to try and get in somehow. It seems to me that it has now ceased to be a matter of right or wrong and is merely war. *One does not blame the miners particularly. If I was a miner I know that I should be only too anxious to strike; since I am not, I try to break them* [emphasis added]. (Waugh, 1976: 124)[13]

The miners' perspective was not the issue for Waugh. The accident of birth precluded any such notion, which had nothing to do with rightness, but with duty to one's own side. Had the miners not kept on fighting, had the hunger marchers not worn their medals of valour, neither would have been a respectable opponent. Playing the game was by no means an attribute of the upper classes but expected behaviour for all true British men (Newsome, 1961; Cunningham, 1986: 301).

Despite all the efforts, both private and governmental, that went into creating a volunteer force to counteract the General Strike, few scholars have taken seriously the political and symbolic import of the volunteers' activities. Since 1926, there have been no books and only five articles written specifically about the volunteers (three by Chris Wrigley, one by Gerald Crompton, and one by David Archard, Brian Harrison, and Tony Heath), not counting my own. In all of these, the focus was largely on unearthing demographic data about those who volunteered – not on proving or disproving either their effectiveness or their image as buffoons. In 1972, David Archard, Brian Harrison, and Tony Heath documented the undergraduate volunteers from Corpus Christi College, Oxford. They solicited and received responses from Corpus alumni, largely the sons of middle-class professionals. Corpus volunteers were responding to the atmosphere of the day; there was not much more on their minds than enjoying a patriotic lark and doing their duty. Much of the article is devoted to describing the activities of Corpus men in 1926, the details of which are reflected in Chapter 6 of this book.

Gerald Crompton (1988), who wrote about railway volunteers in the *Journal of Transport History*, posited that the major impact of the volunteers' activities was psychological: they mobilized anti-strike support and weakened the confidence of strikers. Using a variety of historical sources, Crompton focused on the employment and class background of railway volunteers in Great Britain. His findings confirm that while a substantial number of those volunteering were university students, the majority were never used; those who were, tended to be relegated to jobs requiring minimal skills. Those jobs requiring the most minimal skills such as portering or serving as footplatemen were often the most visible of the railway volunteer positions and tended to go to the students. The majority of volunteers generally were men employed in related industries whose employers offered their services, ex-railway workers angling to regain their jobs, and railway employees from different non-union grades.

Crompton, following his labour history sources, wrote of the very real accidents, injuries, and deaths that the volunteers' inexperience caused. He also pointed out that, despite the improvement in rail services during the course of the strike, such progress could not have been sustained for long, given the inability of the volunteer forces to stick to published timetables or to provide necessary maintenance services. His article is notable for its cataloguing and detailing of the General Strike's carnivalesque features: the volunteers' dress versus that of regular workers; their long hours and isolation from others; the spirit of democracy of 'men from all classes', especially in the GWR's Paddington canteen; the humour and word play; and, most importantly, the media's fascination with the amusing value of amateurism especially as displayed by titled folks, military officers, and the wealthy. But Crompton stopped short of framing the strike as carnival and concluded by citing the very real and long-lasting animosity felt by railway strikers toward volunteers.

Taking a somewhat different stance, Chris Wrigley, whose interest was in local history, investigated the Home Office records of the Organisation for the Maintenance of Supplies (OMS) volunteers (1982, 1984a, 1984b). While others have examined these records to discover how many volunteered and what damages they might have caused, Wrigley looked at them to discern social and geographical distribution. Not surprisingly, he, like Crompton and Archard *et al.*, found that most listed were from middle-class backgrounds and/or were unemployed; while not of aristocratic background, a good many were members of the Fascists or Loyalists (1982). My examination of these figures revealed further that a disproportionate number did come from the wealthier boroughs of London and the southeast counties (Wrigley, 1984a), which provides a partial explanation as to why such volunteers dominated media accounts – their social standing made them simply more newsworthy than regular citizen volunteers.[14] Wrigley also interviewed a few of those former volunteers and found, as Crompton, Archard *et al.*, and I did, that most who came out against the strike did so because they believed it was their patriotic duty. They may have sympathized with the miners, but they would not be bullied by a general strike.

Despite such evidence that most volunteers were *not* from upper-class or society backgrounds, neither these scholars nor anyone else has attempted to discover why that particular image of the volunteers as 'comically foolish Young Gentlemen' (Symons: 1957: 79) was so predominant at the time, and has continued to prevail ever since (Wilkinson 1989 [1929]: 41; Stansky, 2003: 121; Perkins, 2006: 121, 205–6, 253).[15] Even Julian Symons (1957), whose history of the strike contains the earliest analytical and insightful discussions of the volunteers (most of whom Symons claims were students), did not do so. Symons was, however, one of the few, and certainly the earliest historian, to note and comment in more than a disparaging way on the holiday-like atmosphere his informants recalled from the strike.

This feeling that the whole affair was really a holiday was expressed by a girl student at RADA, writing home to her mother in the country:

> It is really fine to see how nice and good-tempered everybody is about the strike. When I arrived at Paddington there were no ordinary porters, but I had a very good-looking man, medical student he looked like, who seized my suitcases ... Eventually he went out and stood in the middle of the road and shouted 'Baker Street' to the first car that came along. And it stopped, and I got in and luggage [*sic*], and went to Baker Street. There everybody carries your luggage for you, and is awfully nice. It is perfectly mad to hear, instead of "Arrer 'n' Uxbridge', a beautiful Oxford voice crying 'Harrow and Uxbridge train'. Ticket collectors say thank you very much; one guard of a train due to depart, an immaculate youth in plus fours, waved a green flag. Nothing happened. He waved again and blew a whistle, then said to the driver in injured tones, 'I say, you might *go*.' It's all very jolly, and such an improvement on the ordinary humdrum state of things. (Symons, 1957: 78–9)

Writing about the account of one volunteer who remembered being served by 'glamorous debutantes' in a canteen, Symons remarked, noting without classifying them as such,[16] the features of festival licence (play, humour, role reversal, parody, alcohol, and hints of some degree of sexual licence) that characterized the volunteer experience:

> Several things about this account are typical: the hard work willingly undertaken and carried out with at least reasonable efficiency, the compensatory bottles of beer at every station (and the lack of discipline implied by them), the dormitory sleeping conditions and the debutantes running canteens. The absence of discipline was important; it gave many of the volunteers a delightful feeling of slight irresponsibility. It was important that you should do your job, but there were no real penalties for making mistakes; and, providing you did the job, nobody minded if you drank quite a lot of beer or played a few practical jokes ...
>
> These good-humoured, charming and efficient young men were, it must be remembered, volunteers of exactly the same sort as the comically foolish Young Gentlemen seen attempting to take the buses out of the garage: so different does the same activity look when seen from the other side. (Symons, 1957: 78–9)

While most scholars did observe the existence and persistence of this image, their essentialising of it allowed them to diminish, trivialise, and dismiss the meanings inherent in such 'class' symbols (Hughes, 1968; Perkins, 2006: 206, 240, 253, 263). In his book of General Strike photographs, Patrick Renshaw noted the conflation of the upper and middle classes in popular memory, further underscoring the belief that all volunteers were of a privileged status:

> The folk memory of the General Strike is full of quaint period charm, redolent of the Gay Twenties. In the popular picture, undergraduates in Oxford bags drive buses and trains, medical students shift goods and luggage, and pretty typists thumb lifts to work in steam lorries and sports cars ... Those self-confident middle-class strikebreakers [sic], with their pipes and plus-fours, those debutantes peeling potatoes perhaps for the first time in their lives, knew nothing of the lives of ordinary people. For though the strike brought industrial life to a standstill, it was not allowed to interfere with the social life of the privileged classes. (1975a: n.p.)

Thirty years later, on the 80th anniversary of the General Strike, journalist Anne Perkins in *A Very British Strike* wrote: 'the amateur [tram] conductors, wearing the uniform of the golf course – plus-fours, gloves and ornamental stockings with tasselled garters – and liberally dispensing their "Thanks awf'ly", caused delighted amusement'. She further observed, not having devoted much space to the volunteers, that 'they were not workers but actors in a drama being directed by the government and its supporters in the press', and credited the media with stirring up interest in society, fashion, and royalty

(Perkins, 2006: 206, 24). Finally, though, citing A. J. P. Taylor's summation of the volunteers' effort as 'Tom Brown's last stand', Perkins concluded that 'the undergraduate bus drivers and the temporary dockhands looked a little misguided, and at worst more like the bully Flashman than the eponymous hero of the schoolboy tale' (Perkins: 2006: 263).

Thus have the General Strike volunteers passed from ethos to mythos, from public school boys out for a lark to the now legendary image of the foolish, well-meaning gentleman amateur, in the canon of symbolic events cited to illustrate the unique British character. Certainly the volunteers acted in accordance with their perceived role in society – as did strikers, TUC leaders, and government officials (Symons, 1957; Farman, 1974; Morris, 1976; Skelley, 1976; McIlroy, 2006; Perkins, 2006). But they were all also responsible for what contemporaries and later people understood to be the meaning/s of the volunteers' and their actions, and how their story was repackaged. Examining the historical development of this process as well as at its contemporary meanings is critical to understanding how folklore and history can and did intertwine – in the media, in scholarly works, and in the minds of those who witnessed or heard about the General Strike long after it was over (Shuman, 2005: 24, 26).

Remembrance is a delicate business, and there are many theories about how it works, especially with regard to national memory and history making. Nostalgia, forgetting, appropriate or inappropriate audiences – all are at play, and one must be cognisant of them. Sociologist Iwona Irwin-Zarecka has noted that 'the initiative and ultimately control over the framing (or reframing) of remembrance belongs on the outside of a community of memory' (1994: 96). Certainly, people were intrigued that I, an American, was interested in their lives and particularly in their role as volunteers. Many also commented on some encounter or relationship to other Americans, either during the Second World War or as the result of travel, work, or familial relationship. They were eager and willing to talk or write to me, possibly because no one else had asked – or would have thought to ask – about class and behaviour. Some found my approach intriguing, while others found it sufficiently irritating that they were compelled to respond (and said so!).

Another factor in the high response rate (over 40 per cent to direct survey letters sent to individual alumni from several Oxford and Cambridge colleges) was the high degree of literacy among this cohort. Furthermore, because I conducted this research from 1985 to 1987, people were still in the habit of writing letters, by hand or with typewriters. Home computers were just at their beginning and then mostly in university and business settings; email had not yet taken hold and laptops had not yet been imagined, much less smart phones, blogs, or tweets. In reviewing the many letters I sent and received during that time, I was struck also by their length (many 3–4 handwritten pages), even from colleagues who were my contemporaries, but more so from those who had experienced the 1926 strike. People still took the time, had the time, and assumed it was important to take the time to write, even if just to tell me that they had nothing to tell me.

Nostalgia for a long-gone youth was undoubtedly also a factor in their narratives as well as in the memoirs and novels written years later (Coser, 1992: 28–9; Halbwachs, 1992: 48–9; Thompson, 2000), for the intervening years along with media and historical interpretations have filtered and structured participants' memories to a degree. The 1984–85 miners' strike was clearly fresh in people's minds when I interviewed them about the 1926 strike, and did influence their perspective; in particular, neither the strike nor the strikers in 1926 came across as militant or as bitter as those in 1984–85, at least to those with whom I was in contact (e.g. Bemrose, Letter, 1986b; Benedictus, Interview, 1986; Benson, Letter, 1986b; Brockway, Interview, 1986; Bullard, Letter, 1987; and see also Bruley, 2010: 137–42).

Despite the passage of so many years and the inevitable comparisons with major events from the intervening years, accounts reported sixty-odd years after 1926 hold up to scrutiny amazingly well. Contemporary media accounts as well as published and unpublished diaries from the period, confirm the accuracy of those memories, which differ in perspective depending on social class, but are remarkably consistent in terms of the type of information and detail they provide.[17] They represent a form that scholars often refer to as contested narratives: those stories that subvert and run counter to the dominant discourse (Portelli, 1991; Bodnar, 1992; Radner *et al.*, 1993; Bennett, 1994; Saltzman, 1994a and 1994b; Noyes *et al.*, 1995; Tuleja, 1997; Sawin, 2004; Shuman, 2005). Such recollections interrupt to provide a corrective to volunteer stereotypes, to put the personal back into the collective (Thompson, 1994), but they also are complicit in the construction of the national story, the allegory, of the General Strike (Samuel and Thompson, 1987; Halbwachs, 1992: 182; Shuman, 2005: 71–88; Bruley, 2010).

For example, Sue Bruley's *The Women and Men of 1926* specifically took on the challenge of providing a gendered history of the strike and subsequent miners' lockout and made pointed use of her own (2004) and previously collected oral histories (1970s and 1980s) to refute assumptions of working-class women's activities and motivations in 1926. Finding that nearly all previous studies ignored the role of women in the 1926 General Strike/lockout, she uncovered the untold story of what women did in the South Wales coalfields before, during, and after 1926. Bruley ably defends her use of oral histories (interviews recorded years later as well as autobiographical accounts) against those who warned of its pitfalls (errors, forgetfulness, nostalgia) by showing how oral histories provided a much needed corrective to the gaps in the written record. Further, she makes the case, noting the work of Dai Smith, Hywel Francis, Sheila Rowbotham, and others, for creating a history of an entire community (an ethnography) that is simply not available from written sources alone, which provides a much more comprehensive and complex sense of how people in different interest groups were active agents in creating and understanding their history.

Not only are ethnographies the only sources for certain topics, they can also, when one is forthcoming with one's interviewees, provide a dialectical approach to research, which is impossible with archival and other static records. Leslie Bloom has argued that many feminist researchers, in particular, 'believe that reciprocity and interpersonal relationships help "to create conditions in which [the respondent] enters into the process as an active agent" of the research ... (Acker, Barry, and Esseveld 1991: 136) ... Feminist methodologies strive for more reciprocal and less mystical relationships between researchers and those respondents whose lives are the focus of the research (see, for example, Ascher, Desalvo, and Ruddick 1984; Fonow and Cook 1991; Geiger 1991; Harding 1987; Heilbrun 1988; Lather 1988; Personal Narratives Group 1989; Reinharz 1983; Roberts 1981; Stanley 1990)' (Bloom, 1997: 111; and see Saltzman, 1993).

Thus, for my own fieldwork, which occurred when reflexive and feminist ethnographic methodology was coming into its own, part of the accepted practice was to engage interviewees with the research topic. Not that researchers of this type try to load the questions – just that when particular issues come up, we do not make assumptions about what may seem obvious but query our subjects instead. During the first phase of my fieldwork in 1985–86,[18] an overwhelming number of those I interviewed and with whom I corresponded used terms usually reserved to reference the upper and middle-class scripted play behaviour (lark, rag, joke)[19] to describe their experiences in 1926. After repeated instances of this usage, I realized that it was not a coincidence that they were referring specifically to such play genres, and I started asking interviewees and correspondents to define the terms and to explain the implicit comparisons they seemed to be making (Saltzman, 1997).[20] No doubt, memories sixty years after the event, the contrasting experience of the very recent 1984–85 miners strike, and, at a certain point, the kinds of questions I asked, focused their accounts in certain ways (Coser, 1992: 22–3, 28–30; Halbwachs, 1992: 48–9). Yet there was sufficient commentary about the mundane and even boring nature of the volunteer experience as well as reports of threats and even violence on both sides, that the story painted by the range of working, middle, and upper-class accounts, when combined with the written record and primary documents, provided a much more detailed and accurate picture of the volunteers' activities in 1926 than has previously been documented.

In my own work and in Bruley's, the authenticity of the narratives we elicited emerged from what individuals experienced, combined with their perceptions about what occurred. Such perceptions of collective memory, of folk history,[21] are not mere 'myths' – to discount and correct with historical veracity (McIlroy, 2006). They are valuable contemporary resources that enable us to examine and understand the perspective of those we study (Saltzman, 1993: 449; Bruley, 2010: 6–8). It was the world view of both volunteers and strikers that dictated their contemporary actions and reactions as well as later interpretations about the General Strike (Saltzman, 1997a: 448–52; 1997b: 452–5), whether in 1972, 1984–85, or in 2010.

Over the past half century, folklorists, labour and social historians, social anthropologists, and sociologists have written about the interaction among the processes of collective memory, contested narratives, and history making.[22] They have provided imaginative and important analyses that present the voices and stories of marginalized peoples as counter-narratives to the dominant historical discourse. Those scholars, all of whom draw from social history, anthropology, and folklore theory, have demonstrated how people and societies use available and particular categories to think with, and frame, experiences when they construct their histories.

A variety of other works came out just prior to, and in the wake of, the 1992 publication of Lewis A. Coser's editing and translation of Maurice Halbwachs's *On Collective Memory*.[23] Halbwachs's work focuses on how collective memory functions as a 'socially constructed notion' that individuals, '*as group members*' (emphasis added), use to reconstruct the past locally, within families, among religious groups, and within social classes (Coser, 1992: 22). 'Commemorations, festival enactment, and the like', that is, public displays, keep memory alive (Coser, 1992: 23), and that collective memory in turn fills the gaps between public events, those Durkheimian periods of collective effervescence (such as community festivals or socio-political events like the Civil War, the Great War, the Blitz, or the 1926 General Strike) and the everyday. Collective memory serves to reinforce and strengthen key events through their commemoration and re-enactments (Coser, 1992: 25).

Further refining this point, Howard Schuman and Jacqueline Scott hypothesized that events with the maximum impact on collective memory occur during adolescence and young adulthood (Coser, 1992: 28–30; Halbwachs, 1992: 48–9), a notion that has particular resonance for my work on General Strike volunteers and for scholarship about the impact of adolescent rites of passage. In particular, Halbwachs wrote of the historical power of key events in a nation's history. These 'collective traditions ... leave their traces in the memories of people ... [O]nly those recollections subsist that in every period society, working within its present-day frameworks, can reconstruct' (Halbwachs, 1992: 182–8). Although Halbwachs's focus remained on the ways 'the present situation affects the selective perception of past history' (Coser, 1992: 33), he stopped just short of concluding that it was the coincidence of young adulthood and a key national event combined with the resonance of *other* key events in a nation's history that enabled an event to acquire a historical significance that could span centuries of national history and identity.

In the last quarter of the twentieth century and into the early twenty-first century, a number of scholars, many of them folklorists, concentrated specifically on collective memory and the ways memories (re)construct history/ies, identity/ies, genres, nations, ethnic groups, gender, and social class (e.g. Schwartz *et al.*, 1986; Samuel and Thompson, 1987; Portelli, 1991; Bodnar, 1992; Greenhill, 1994; Graham, 1995; Eber and Neal, 2001; Shuman, 2005; McIlroy, 2006; Bruley, 2010). Studies involving displaced or dominated populations especially employ this model for uncovering and/or reviving contested narratives and anti-hegemonic histories (e.g. Thompson, 1984; Schwartz *et al.*, 1986; Saltzman, 1988; Friedman, 1992; Landsman and Ciborski, 1992; Guss, 1993; Saltzman, 1994a and 1994b; Workman, 1995; Ben Amos and Weissberg, 1999). Their focus helped to set the stage for the subsequent influence that Halbwachs's studies would have on the study of collective memory, history, and identity formation. What distinguishes the scholars noted in this paragraph from earlier ones is their emphasis on the *shifting* and selective roles of memory, narrative authority, and context in the process of (re)constructing pasts, how pasts become histories, and which histories become hegemonies and/or part of the dominant discourse about identity.

Much folklore scholarship during this time has explored the interplay among narrative, structure, individual creativity, performance and their power to formulate, preserve, and transmit group identity. Of particular use to this analysis have been folklorists' insights about history making, especially those of Roger deV. Renwick and Amy Shuman, whose works pick up where Halbwachs's leaves off; this is a subtle, but critical, point. Renwick's analysis of traditional ballads as well as individually authored folk songs and poetry about local events demonstrated the meaningful symbolic and generative role of commonplaces[24] in particular historical contexts and in the construction, remembering, and significance of those texts (Renwick, 1980). Shuman's work on the relationship between allegory (the larger cultural paradigm) and personal experience narratives urges scholars who tell other people's stories to consider issues of ownership, function, intent, and impact (Shuman, 2005: 162).

When personal experience narratives draw on collective societal metaphors – the commonplace expressions that we use to think with and categorize our lives – they make the particular more general, comprehensible, and eventually transformative. Such narratives also particularize the general, making history and, consequently, identity the products of actions, events, memory, and performance. When this phenomenon occurs, as it did with the General Strike, the paradigmatic meaning of the event and all the other key symbolic events and their attendant meanings invoked by contemporaries (1066, the Civil War, the Revolution, Peterloo, Boat Race Night, etc.), move into time – into the present and the future – transforming that event into a dynamic and generative symbol for national identity. Such youthful and seminal experiences, especially when they coincide with national crises, become generational markers, a phenomenon that further imprints memories for those who live through such times.

Political scientist Arthur Aughey (2007) posited a similar theory about the formation of English identity and recommended examining a society's legends or underpinnings. Using a rather lovely and accidental phrase from Joan Scott, Aughey noted that Scott's way of thinking about history and identity formation allowed for imagination, dynamism, and the interaction between individuals and society. Aughey (quoting Scott) stated, "'fantasy is the means by which real relations of identity between past and present are discovered and/or forged". It is that act of historical imagination, which imposes order on events and thereby "contributes to the articulation of political identity'" (Aughey, 2007: 11). 'Historical identification ... operates as a fantasy echo, "replaying in time and over generations the process that forms individuals as social and political actors"' (Aughey, 2007: 12).

Most Britons alive at the time, even those who were young children in 1926, had some memory of the General Strike; they knew where they were and what they were doing. Roy Band of Peterborough, for instance, who was aged 4 in 1926, remembered that the strike prevented his mother and him from moving house (see figure 1.4). Pamela Cavendish,[25] who was just 8, noted that 'it made very little impact on us in the nursery. I do remember Nanny being very excited about it! Also my parents' friends, the young men, were all driving trains and buses, and thinking it great fun' (Cavendish, Letter, 1986). The strike appears in various media as the event that quintessentially defines what it was to be English[26] – for the Establishment and the upper classes as well as for the working classes. Working-class and leftist studies have continued to be reproduced on each significant anniversary of the event to reiterate the 'never again' message that the strike's failure came to embody for the Labour Party. Novelists, historians, educators, museum curators, playwrights, songwriters,[27] my informants, and even I have selected and 'reproduced' certain aspects of the event.

Former volunteers made it clear to me that the General Strike still had enormous resonance in the 1980s – as the existence of the Strikes! restaurant

1.4 Roy Band

as well as a number of 60th anniversary publications, an exhibit at the National Portrait Gallery, and Channel 4's airing of David Benedictus's musical, *What a Way to Run a Revolution*, would indicate. And the more recent publications (Laybourn, 1993 and 1999; McIlroy *et al.*, 2004; McIlroy, 2006; Perkins, 2006; Bruley, 2010), especially Anne Perkins' *A Very British Strike*, point explicitly to the ongoing relationship between national identity and the 1926 General Strike.

Yet the contentious debates at the end of the twentieth century and at start of the twenty-first regarding the meanings underlying Britishness and Englishness (civic versus ethnic)[28] were not the issue in 1926. Rather, it was the ability to define what being English or British meant, as opposed to being French, German, Russian, or American. The gaze was far more outward at that time, and the inward, more domestically inclined definitions following the Second World War, were not at all the issue, at least not for the English (Paxman, 1999; Powell, 2002). In the 1920s, to be British was indeed merely an extension of the essential English identity.[29]

The General Strike was not merely evidence of class divisions and a post-war society in transition; the event and its participants have become national folk symbols for Britishness – a more broadly construed identity than Englishness in 1926, and one that extended beyond the Home Counties, both literally and symbolically. Although different aspects of it are manifested depending upon one's socio-economic class or political affiliation, those who claim it cite well-behaved, cheerful, and mannerly strikers, volunteers, or average workers 'carrying on' as typical of the English in a crisis,[30] and contrast those positive traits with the rude, disorderly, unpatriotic, and violent behaviour of others – that is, whoever one is not (from the groups above) and especially those in similar situations in other countries.

Together, people remember, write about, and 'co-memorate' the past in ways based on implicit categories that they use to structure their identities and their world view (i.e. their ethos). But they also do so as individuals with fragmentary, particular experiences that are meaningful *because of* a larger than life event (Shuman, 2005). Memories of participants and witnesses contest historical stereotypes and reify them. Exploring such processes can demonstrate why events like the General Strike unfold as they do, as well as how they become powerful cultural symbols, that is, our mythos, the taken-for-granted seemingly root-metaphors that encode the stories that tell us who we are and through which we understand our identities. This study explores the folk image of the volunteers, how it provides a key to the iconic British gentleman amateur (Berberich, 2007), and what that image conveys about British social structures as they existed in the early twentieth century and as they persist in the popular imagination at the start of the third millennium.[31]

Notes

1 Trafalgar Square, a public symbol of the Empire, has long been the site of irony, thus a perfect place for protests by suffragettes, miners, CND supporters, and more (Mace, 2005).
2 W. H. Crook (Crook, 1931) discussed the function and intent of various types of strikes. At the beginning of the action, the TUC and labour leaders avoided the use of the term 'general strike' because of its political connotations; by the end, the term was in common parlance, for example, in the NUR bulletin, entitled *General Strike News Bulletin*, editorials in the *British Worker*, TUC General Council statements, and writings by Aneurin Bevan, Arthur Pugh, and Walter Citrine (Farman, 1974: 280, 282, 291, 293, 296, 301, 334; Laybourn, 1999: 119).
3 Leslie Dover, employed in 1926 as a clerk by the British Iron and Steel Federation, volunteered as a ganger with others from his firm; he reported stone throwing and threats. When the group left him alone one night, 'something like 30 strikers invaded the Railway platform (no. 5) which was our group HQ and where those of us who could not get home at nights slept. I was loudly reviled and threatened, but was more scared than hurt!' (Dover, Letter, 1986b).
4 A. M. Clark, whose father was a corporation bus driver in the West Midlands, reported that in Birmingham, one strategy that strikers used against blackleg drivers was to add sugar or urine to their gas tanks (Clark, Letter, 1986a).
5 University men and society women certainly dominated the popular image of the volunteers, but whether or not they actually constituted the majority is unknown. Certain statistical records, which classified special constables and those in the civilian constabulary reserve by residence, indicate that the highest proportion

came from the wealthier urban areas and county seats (Wrigley, 1984a; PRO HO 45/12336/2130/1926/OMS/484910; PRO HO 45/13364/1923–29/SC/447130).

6 Marjorie Lathbury wrote: 'During the strike I drove city workers to their offices in my Morris Minor car. Public transportation was nil. I got up fairly early & walked to the garage & picked up passengers, who became regulars. Marble Arch London was the starting point. No charge of course …' (Lathbury, Letter, 1987a). Lathbury, whose father was a Liberal MP, attended St Felix. School in Southwold, Suffolk and then Newnham College, Cambridge. She noted, 'I received no recognition other than a bouquet of flowers, nor did I expect any' (Lathbury, Letter, 1987b).

7 For more about this letter, see *Strike Nights at Printing House Square* (1926: 34) and Hutt (1937: 139–40). *Strike Nights in Printing House Square*, which *The Times* printed privately and with no author listed, appears to be an edited version of Harry Pirie Gordon's 'The Story of "The Times" During the General Strike'.

8 See Ellen Wilkinson's *Clash*, her 1929 novel about the 1926 General Strike/lockout (Wilkinson, 1989), in which it is impossible for the protagonist, Joan Craig, to succeed with her upper-class love interest, Tony Dacre. He wants a woman to devote herself totally to him (and their potential children), not to her career (Wilkinson, 1989: 176–88). Class boundaries combined with social expectations prevent her from marrying 'up'; in turn, the upper-class women in the book may have their careers, but they cannot succeed in love. The mores of 1926 did not allow for anyone to have it all.

9 Lady Lindsay, born Loelia Ponsonby, was the only daughter of Sir Frederick Ponsonby, later Lord Sysonby, who served under Queen Victoria, Edward VII, and George V as Keeper of the Privy Purse in 1914 and Treasurer in 1920 (Lindsay, 1983: 11). Lady Lindsay was first married to the second Duke of Westminster, whose family name was Grosvenor. After they divorced, she married Sir Martin Lindsay of Dowhill. I reference her books as Grosvenor, 1961 and Lindsay, 1983, respectively.

10 On 9 December 1915, the Triple Alliance (miners, railwaymen, and transport workers) approved their constitution, which provided for the possibility of united action, though not the likelihood, given the different aims and situations of the three partners. While a general strike was possible, an actual revolution was highly unlikely, despite the expressed syndicalist views of two railway leaders, Charley Cramp and Robert Williams in 1920 (Bagwell, 1971: 101–3).

11 This despite equally repeated denials by the Clydesiders as well as Communist MP, Saklatvala, who was elected more for his housing policies in the London borough of Battersea than for his party affiliation (Graves and Hodge, 1941: 146; Benedictus, Interview, 1986).

12 During the previous three months, coal prices had fallen by 50 per cent and unemployment had doubled. 'The average price of British coal for export in the last quarter of 1920 was 83*s* 2*d* a ton. By January revived competition from the European mines had brought the price down to 65*s*. 4*d*. and by March of the same year to 43*s* 6*d*' (Bagwell, 1971: 117). During this same period, the Ministry of Labour reported that unemployment was at 1,615,000, 'more than double that of December 1920' (Bagwell, 1971: 121).

13 On 17 April 1921, Waugh wrote in his diary, 'The Daily Herald admitted that it was

the "biggest defeat of the labour cause in the memory of man". The miners are still holding out, but there is no fear of the Triple Alliance strike. I suppose that all along they expected the country to give way and then got frightened of the volunteer movement. I signed on for fatigue duty' (Waugh, 1976: 124).
14 See PRO, HO 5/12336/2130/1926/OMS/484910; PRO, HO 45/13364, Part 1, 1923–29/SC/447.130; PRO, HO 45/13364, Part 2, 1923–29/SC/447.130/108.
15 In Wilkinson's novel, *Clash*, Joan Craig comments, "'It will be the War atmosphere back again. Young men in plus-fours looking important, and silly Society girls patting their heads and sitting up all night to give them cocoa'" (Wilkinson, 1989: 41). Three-quarters of a century later, Peter Stansky, in his biography of Philip (Siegfried Sassoon's cousin) and Sybil Sassoon, wrote, 'Most Oxford and Cambridge undergraduates . . . were notorious for their mindless opposition to the strike and for regarding it as a great lark' (Stansky, 2003: 121).
16 See Crompton, 1988, as per above.
17 Gerontologist Robert N. Butler has noted with regard to older people's reminiscences about their early lives that this process was not a 'pathological condition'; instead, it was engagement in 'the important psychological task of coming to terms with the life they had lived' (Butler, 2007: xv; see also Rohdewald, 2008: 287).
18 See Acknowledgements for a detailed account.
19 See Chapter 3 for an in-depth discussion.
20 Bloom further notes that 'placing oneself on the same critical plane must go beyond "a gesture that is enforced by politically correct convention" (Marcus 1994: 572), and be truly and openly self-critical' (Bloom, 1997: 117).
21 Folk history represents a group's collective perception regarding what is significant about its past and that history's effect on the group's present. Oral history, which is generally officially recorded by a designated interviewer, is more about an individual's or group's take on events the interviewer designates as important. For folklorists, folk history is significant because it involves a group's take on what has been culturally meaningful over time (Saltzman, 1993: 448–52).
22 Most notable are those by Roger Abrahams, Richard Bauman, Barbara Babcock, Maurice Bloch, Peter Burke, Bob Bushaway, Robert Colls, Natalie Zemon Davis, Robert Darnton, Phillip Dodd, Paul Fussell, Clifford Geertz, Eric Hobsbawm, Paul Johnson, Emanuel LeRoy Ladurie, Eleanor Leacock, Jerome Mintz, George Rudé, Marshall Sahlins, E. P. Thompson, and Victor Turner.
23 Halbwachs's landmark studies, *La Topographie Légendaire des Évangiles en Terre Sainte: Etude de Mémoire Collective* (1941) and *Les Cadres Sociaux de la Mémoire* (1952) were virtually unknown by most English-speaking scholars until years after they were translated and published.
24 In ballad and folk song theory, commonplaces refer to phrases once thought of as throw-aways or clichés such as 'milk-white steed', 'the glorious month of May', or 'lily white hand'. Such phrases are critical mnemonic devices; more importantly, however, they provide and recreate the deep cultural meaning of ballads and folk poetry in relation to their specific time, space, and world view as well as to other texts in the same corpus (Renwick, 1980: 11–15, 185–230, 231–2).
25 Cavendish was cousin to the Duchess of Buccleuch. Her sisters-in-law were the

Viscountess Gage and the Dowager Countess of Crawford and Balcarres (Cavendish, Letter, 1986).

26 There was a particular magnification of English identity at the time, personified in the writings of Prime Minister Stanley Baldwin (1971), himself of Scottish and Welsh as well as English ancestry, which emphasized the pastoral English countryside of both the gentleman and yeoman farmer (Paxman, 1999: 142–3; Powell, 2002: 155–6, 183, 270; Aughey, 2007: 146). This place-identification had little to do with the personal characteristics required of citizenry; place-based allegiance was available as a justification for attributions of foreign, alien (not British), and just plain un-English (inappropriate) behaviour when non-native-born British residents (Asian Indians, eastern-European Jews from London's East End) or women, workers, Irish, Scottish, Welsh, fascists, communists, socialists, Tories, or Labour joined with their fellows to oppose attempts to control their destinies.

27 In 1974, the musical group, The Kinks, brought out an album entitled *Preservation Act 2*, which included the song 'Nobody Gives'. That song includes commentary about the 1926 General Strike, linking it to the Holocaust in its comparison of victims (miners and Jews) (The Kinks, 1974).

28 Krishan Kumar (2003, 2006) and others (e.g. Colls and Dodd, 1986; Paxman, 1999; Powell, 2002; Ward, 2004; Winder, 2004; Anderson, 2006; Hutchinson *et al.*, 2007; Aughey, 2007) have written extensively on this topic, which largely comes down to various ways of drawing the distinctions between a larger British (read civic) identity, which encompasses the many ethnic groups that populate the British Isles as well as national beliefs in regarding civic virtues, and a more narrowly constructed English (read ethnic) identity that refers more to cultural heritage; the latter also emphasises a romantic and nostalgic notion of the rural upper and middle classes.

29 Those Celtic peoples included in this extended identity were sometimes categorised as belonging to the fringes if the behaviour they displayed was too violent, leftist, or somehow disruptive to the workings of the government.

30 Stanley Baldwin wrote in 1924 for a lecture 'On England': 'The Englishman is made for a time of crisis, and for a time of emergency. He is serene in difficulties, but may seem to be indifferent when times are easy. He may not look ahead, he may not heed warnings, he may not prepare, but once he starts he is persistent to the death, and he is ruthless in action. It is these gifts that have made the Englishman what he is, and that have enabled the Englishman to make England and the Empire what it is' (Baldwin, 1971: 3–4).

31 See Powell on the memory of empire and the persistence of British identity (2002: 232).

2

Building Jerusalem: the General Strike as social drama

> The striking workers were not out to break the law or anything like that. They were just withholding their labour in order to stimulate their employers to make a change in their attitude ... At that time there was considerable poverty. In that district, in the working-class areas in and around London, it was not infrequent to see children without shoes and stockings running about in the street ... A bus driver would be earning about £3 a week, which is quite inadequate ... The pound was worth ... at least twenty times [what it is worth today]. (Edward Dunham, retired stockbroker, Interview, 1986) (see figure 5.11)

During the 1920s, the British coal industry was faced with both a sagging international economy and a reduced market for its product. In late 1925, the Samuel Commission, the second Royal Commission on coal mines within six years, was appointed to investigate and make recommendations to reform the coal industry. Previous government-appointed investigative bodies (the Sankey Commission in 1919 and a Court of Inquiry in 1924) had recommended nationalization of the mines, recommendations that the government and owners had ignored. The Samuel Report (March 1926) advised somewhat less drastic solutions: 'State ownership of the royalties accruing from them, amalgamation of many small, unprofitable mines', research into more efficient mining techniques, improved work conditions, profit-sharing, and family allowances. Most of those recommendations favourable to the miners were to be carried out in the indefinite future, however. In contrast: 'the suggestions unfavourable to them [i.e. wage reductions and lengthened hours] were to be put into effect immediately' (Symons, 1957: 33–4). With this support from the Samuel Commission, mine owners were able to persist in their efforts to lengthen hours and cut wages. As noted in Chapter 1, these proposals were unacceptable to both the miners and the TUC, which voted in favour of a 'coordinated action' at the end of April 1926.

Contemporary testimonies indicate that, although most residents of Great Britain did not really fear a revolution per se, events of the previous decade had so threatened and attacked traditional notions about what constituted a stable society that people were both wary and defensive about any indication of further assault (Weinberger, 1987: 34; Powell, 2002: 124–5). As retired solicitor Bruno Marmorstein – a middle-class, Jewish public school boy of 15 in 1926 – commented, 'I think the Russian revolution made a lot of difference to the way people looked at things … In those days, in 1926 if you were sympathetic to Labour, you were branded as a communist!' (Marmorstein, Interview, 1985; see Graves and Hodge, 1941: 141). Unstable social conditions, economic disruptions, and Britain's increasing loss of colonial and industrial power contributed to the polarization of attitudes that crystallized in the 1926 General Strike. No other event in British history has evoked such a defensive, class-based response from all sectors of society. Lord Brockway, author, life peer, and editor of the *British Worker* in 1926, remarked, 'I think it was the most evident example of class division, the General Strike, that there's been' (Brockway, Interview, 1986).

During the First World War, the government's desperate need for the services and goods that only labour could provide had given the latter a certain amount of leverage. While pre-war Liberal reforms resulted in better wages and improved conditions for the very poor, the general economic upturn during the teens had more to do with the war's stimulus effect, which resulted in improved wages overall. The granting of universal manhood suffrage in 1918 also seemed to confirm the Labour Party's accession to economic power as a political reality. And, as David Powell has noted, the very national character of the capital versus labour struggle reinforced this sensibility (Powell, 2002: 140–1, 166–8). Partial labour union victories (for coal miners, the 1919 Seven Hours Act and the 1925 nine-month subsidy; for railway men and dockers, the 1919 Arbitration Act) as well as the first Labour government under James Ramsay MacDonald in 1923, further encouraged the working man's sense that he deserved, and was capable of attaining for himself, certain rights as a British citizen. These successes also led him to believe that such rights were attainable via legitimate, overt displays and public negotiation, and not by way of the more 'old-fashioned' and covert 'folk' methods of the previous century.[1]

Despite some economic gains during the late teens, however, the post-war years were far from being an era of progress for labouring men and women. Like workers, businessmen had also grown accustomed to better industrial conditions created by the First World War. High profits, controlled wages, and war-time monopolies misleadingly created an atmosphere of rising expectations. The 1919–20 boom, followed by a severe recession during 1921–

22, as well as a lifting of trade restrictions – especially in the older industries like coalmining – resulted in falling prices and profits from 1920 to 1924. This situation was not improved by Great Britain's return to the gold standard in 1925 (see especially Laybourn, 1993; Foster, 2004). Although real wages took a slight turn upward in 1925, so did unemployment. Strikes in all the older industries marked the post-war years, for workers, like owners, refused to believe that the economy and their own place in it would not continue to improve. Their confidence was misplaced. Stanley Baldwin's Conservative government could not afford (economically or politically) to subsidise coal at the expense of other industries.

In the pre- and post-war years leading up to 1926, protests at home (labour and suffragettes) and in the Empire (Ireland and India) combined with the war and a Red Scare to challenge old notions of pre-war Liberal England (Dangerfield, 1935). While the various social, economic, and political uprisings certainly contributed to the sense of a disintegrating world, it was the First World War that afterwards had the greatest effect on the world view of the Establishment: the upper-middle-class and upper-class elite in British society. As Paul Fussell has so eloquently demonstrated, 'playing the game' was not always successful – especially when it became uncertain what winning the game was going to mean in terms of lives and the decline of an accepted way of life for the privileged (Fussell, 1975; Girouard, 1981: 241–8, 275–93; MacKenzie, 1984; Mangan, 1986). Finding one's military comrades waiting at tables or begging in the streets added to a collective sense of imminent doom (Cartland, 1970: 20; Powell, 2002: 136; 147; 150–2).

The success of the Russian revolutions further made it clear, as had the French revolution in the eighteenth century, that those from the base and fringes of society could indeed join forces and challenge the dominant ideology (Williams, 1978; Rudé, 1979). Middle and upper-class apprehensions only increased when Scottish workers on the Clyde threatened to strike in support of the Russian government in 1919. And members of David Lloyd George's coalition government lent more fuel to the Red fire by declaring a policemen's strike in August 1919 and a railway strike a few months later to be the first stirrings of revolution in England (Jones, 1969: 97–101; Middlemas, 1979: 149–53; Geary, 1985: 61–2). During that 1919 rail stoppage of nine days, newspapers used war-time terms to describe the industrial situation. Comments like 'doing one's bit', 'seeing it through', 'fighting to a finish', and 'saving the women and children' signified that, for upper and middle-class volunteers, the strike indeed represented a war (Clephane, 1933: 161). Given this atmosphere, it was not surprising that the general populace could be roused so easily to fight bolshies. Even the Labour party itself publicly refused to permit the Communist Party of Great Britain (CPGB),[2] an amalgamation of three socialist groups, to be a part of their association in 1920, for 'to be in any way associated in the popular mind with a massacre of the nobility and gentry was most damaging to its cause' (Graves and Hodge, 1941: 141).

The spring of 1921 brought further economic woes. A plunging economy, coal prices reduced to half their rate of the previous year, and employment numbers that had doubled since December of the previous year resulted in a hastier than planned end to government control in the coal-mining industry. When mine owners responded with announcements of a return to district rather than national wages levels as well as wage reductions of as much as 40–50 per cent in many areas, the miners refused those terms. The owners shut down the mines, and a lockout began on 1 April. The Triple Alliance threatened a sympathetic strike on 12 April unless further negotiations occurred. Fearing revolution, the government reacted quickly, mobilising the Supply and Transport Organisation under the Emergency Powers Act. Infantry units were brought back from abroad and a camp with infantry and cavalry established in Kensington Gardens; 'tanks and armoured cars were concentrated at London, Glasgow, York, and Worcester' (Jeffery and Hennessy, 1983: 60–1). Negotiations were tried but broke down: although the government was willing to offer a temporary subsidy to avert substantial wage cuts, the miners also held out for a national pool (effectively nationalisation), which the government believed would result in state regulation and refused to countenance (Jeffery and Hennessy, 1983: 62). Thus the Triple Alliance called a strike for 15 April. At the eleventh hour, Lloyd George offered to take up the issue of wages alone, but the Miners Federation of Great Britain (MFGB) refused, although the railway and transport workers urged them to reconsider. The precipitous change in the labour market, which more directly threatened railway and transport workers than miners,[3] caused a breakdown in the sympathetic outage by the Triple Alliance, a breach of trust from which it could not recover (Bagwell, 1971: 117–26; Jeffery and Hennessy, 1983: 62–4).

A deepening depression after mid-1921, which did not facilitate labour uprisings, followed by an improved economy in 1923, somewhat lower unemployment rates, and the first Labour government in 1924 defused any collective labour unrest for a time. Involvement by the TUC, the Labour government's switch in approach from avoiding revolution to maintaining the movement of essential supplies, and that government's involvement of trade unions themselves in the latter effort prevented a series of strikes in early 1924 from gaining much ground. A real reluctance on the part of MacDonald's Cabinet to avoid overt strike breaking and instead engage in and encourage negotiations between employers and workers also helped. Not until early 1925 did organized labour begin collectively to re-group, partly as a result of the TUC General Council's increasing involvement in trade union leadership. In June of that year a more comprehensive industrial alliance included 'foundry workers, engineers, and shipbuilders as well as the three railway unions, the miners and' the transport union (Bagwell, 1971: 126). In contrast to the fiasco of 1921, all agreed to act together, enabling the miners to wrest the offer of a nine-month subsidy from Baldwin's Cabinet at the end of July. This averted the increasing possibility of a general strike and gave the government time to ready its then skeletal emergency forces (Clynes, 1937: 74; Jeffery and Hennessy, 1983: 66, 71, 77, 80–6, 91–3).

By April 1926, events had come to a showdown once again. Mine owners insisted on lowering wages and lengthening hours, resulting in greater production for lower cost; they mistakenly believed this would return profits to inflated war-time levels. Coal miners, however, refused to acquiesce to such a proposal, responding with secretary A. J. Cook's catchy slogan, 'not a minute on the day, not a penny off the pay'; they also pointed out, as did the *Oxford Magazine* ('How Will the Strike End', 1926: 525), that the production of yet more coal – the result of increased working hours – was not a logical solution given the already coal-saturated world market.

The government subsidy of 1925 was due to run out at midnight on 30 April 1926. Months of negotiations could not break the stalemate. The MFGB gave the TUC General Council the authority to negotiate for them with the owners and government. Yet both the government and TUC were busy preparing for a large-scale collective action, rather than proposing any realistic compromises for what was probably an uncompromisable situation; the intractability of miners and mine owners appeared insurmountable.

Although the MFGB's unwillingness to yield on wages and hours and the mine owners' equally intransigent refusal to settle for smaller profits clearly set the stage for the strike, there were two incidents that combined to trigger it. When the subsidy ran out at midnight on 30 April, some owners posted notices advising workers of new hours and wages; the notices promised a lockout if these provisions were not accepted (McIlroy *et al.*, 2004). Thus, one million miners were not technically or legally on strike as of 1 May, although the TUC's General Council was already making plans for one as well as for a sympathetic strike. Then on 2 May 1926, the *Daily Mail* printers refused to set type for what they considered to be an inflammatory editorial in favour of a volunteer work force – should a general strike occur. Following is the editorial that *Daily Mail* printers refused to set; single quotation marks appear in Symons (1957):

> 'The miners after weeks of negotiation have declined the proposals made to them and the coal mines of Britain are idle.
>
> 'The Council of Trades Union Congress, which represents all the other trade unions, has determined to support the miners by going to the extreme of ordering a general strike.
>
> 'This determination alters the whole position. The coal industry, which might have been reorganized with good will on both sides, seeing that some

'give and take' is plainly needed to restore it to prosperity, has now become the subject of a great political struggle, which the nation has no choice but to face with the utmost coolness and the utmost firmness.

'We do not wish to say anything hard about the miners themselves. As to their leaders, all we need say at this moment is that some of them are (and have openly declared themselves) under the influence of people who mean no good to this country.

'A general strike is not an industrial dispute. It is a revolutionary movement intended to inflict suffering upon the great mass of innocent in the community and thereby to put forcible constraint upon the Government.

'It is a movement which can only succeed by destroying the Government and subverting the rights and liberties of the people.

'This being the case, it cannot be tolerated by any civilized Government and it must be dealt with by every resource at the disposal of the community.

'A state of emergency and national danger has been proclaimed to resist the attack.

'We call upon all law-abiding men and women to hold themselves at the service of King and country.' (Symons, 1957: 48–9)

The Cabinet, led by Minister of Health Neville Chamberlain, supported by Chancellor of the Exchequer Winston Churchill and Home Secretary William Joynson-Hicks, forced Prime Minister Stanley Baldwin to end negotiations (cf. McIlroy, 2006: 99). They regarded the refusal to print the *Daily Mail* article as a premeditated and organized working-class attack that marked the commencement of a general strike. Although the TUC General Council insisted that the refusal was an unauthorized and unofficial action, Baldwin refused to meet with the General Council after this incident. Left no alternative, the TUC declared a sympathetic strike in support of the locked-out miners at midnight on 3 May 1926.

Archibald Fenner Brockway, 'the oldest member of the NUJ [National Union of Journalists]', became the editor of the *British Worker*, the TUC's strike-time newspaper (Brockway, 1942: 185–95). Brockway recalled:

> The General Strike was received with enthusiasm by the young people in the Labour movement. The whole staff of the ILP, which had premises near the House of Commons, agreed they would bring their sleeping bags and sleep during the strike [there] and devote themselves during the day to activities. They proposed specially to Photostat the edition of the British Worker and distribute that throughout London ... [T]ransport workers distributed the paper all over North Wales, as far as Carlyle in the north, as far as Hull in the east, and I don't remember ... what our circulation was. Oh, it must have been over 80,000. (Brockway, Interview, 1986)

Churchill, who was placed in charge of editing the *British Gazette*, which was intended to promulgate the government's position during the strike, regarded the printers' action as a proclamation of class war calculated to overthrow the constitution and Parliament, a view that many Liberal politicians supported as well. But according to those on the Labour side, since the General Strike was intended to be an economic and not a political strike, it could not be proved illegal. Sir Henry Slessor, MP, who had been Solicitor-General in Ramsay MacDonald's Labour government, wrote that, according to the 1906 Trade Disputes Act, 'there was nothing illegal about a sympathetic strike unless it was accompanied by provable treason, felony or seditious or criminal conspiracy' (Morris, 1976: 225). That this position was not without its merits is evidenced by the Trade Disputes Act of 1927, whose passage made sympathetic strikes designed to coerce the government illegal. If they were already illegal, why the need for a new law (Goodhart, 1927)?[4]

Uninterested in continuing this debate, Baldwin refused to resume further official negotiations until the strike was called off and demanded unconditional surrender. But the Executive (the officers) of the Miners' Federation adamantly refused to enter negotiations with an *a priori* agreement to lower wages, which was the government's condition. Thus with both sides backed into their respective corners, the resulting performances were not only unprecedented, but completely unpredictable – though an astrologer had reportedly forecast the event ('Right or Wrong?' 1926: 4).

The volunteer machinery dominated the London scene especially; its effect diminished in cities increasingly further away from London. Urban areas certainly depended more on volunteer services, particularly for public transportation, than rural areas, which were hardly affected by the General Strike. Ports, especially in the south and northeast of England, depended more on dock and ship workers. In areas between cities, especially between London and nearby towns, drivers for food and supply lorries and private transportation for commuting workers were necessary, though they tended more to be non-union working-class men and middle-class women – not at all the sort who volunteered in ports and major urban areas. For example, Ralph Steel, who worked for a wholesale tobacconist in the 1920s, remembered,

> It wasn't much that I did in the General Strike really – just a couple of journeys. But the organization, well, it was quickly got together and it really did work ... At that time of day I was working for a ... Mr. Hunting ... and he also owned the Westco Motor Company ... in Peterborough. And they had a motor coach, very rough and ready it was ... They wanted a vehicle to get a man to collect some potatoes and cabbages and take them to ... market ... Mr. Hunting asked me if I'd drive it, so I said, yes I'd take it. And he said, 'You know what you're in for, don't you?' I said, 'In what way?' 'Oh', he said, 'you might find it a bit rough.' I said, 'I don't mind, I'll put up with that.' It didn't worry me in those days; I didn't know the word fear. I'd just come out of the first war and you learn not to be afraid of anything. (Steel, Interview, 1986)

Those who came out for anti-strike duty in 1926 were drawn from a wide range of social statuses – from the Earl of Meath (a retired military officer of 85), to middle-class women with cars who picked up walkers, to non-union working-class men who simply needed the money to support their families. Overall, however, volunteers tended to fall into four main types. Many of those I interviewed and with whom I corresponded told me that the majority of volunteers were working-class and middle-class men of no particular social distinction who felt duty bound and/or in need of money from temporary jobs.[5] They recalled middle-class women who contributed to the volunteer effort spontaneously and usually anonymously by just doing whatever they could to help people get to work and children to school. Far more noticeable, and noticed, were the society and upper middle-class women, some of whom had had war-time experience in organising canteens and ambulance corps, and most of whom had done some kind of charity work. But the group whose image was most responsible for defining the stereotypical volunteers was comprised of upper middle-class and upper-class males between the ages of 18 and 25, either at university or employed as young professionals.

The initial call for volunteers emphasized the patriotic duty of all men and women to keep order, maintain transportation, and ensure the movement of essential foods and utilities. Yet more than one editorial noted:

> There was a sort of picnic feeling in the air. No one minded inconveniences; walking to work, sleeping in the office, special emergency activities – all were taken as 'jolly good fun' ... Lightheartedness [*sic*] was especially in evidence on the railways. Countless young men realised their boyhood ambition to drive a train [see figure 4.1(g) and 5.2(c–d)]. Clad in their oldest suits, they sallied out and, scorning the meaner delights of ticket-collecting, demanded to be given an engine of their own. The real trouble was that there weren't enough engines to go around. (*Answers*, 1926: 10)

People went to their local Guild Halls or public parks (see figure 2.1(a)), queued up, and received assignments; some received special insignia to indicate their new status. Volunteers often enrolled as a group, like those from Clare College, Cambridge or Boodles', a London men's club. According to *Time and Tide*:

> many of those who spend a good part of their time in playing games have set a splendid example to others in volunteering for duties for which their fitness and physique makes them particularly suitable. Large numbers of polo players are acting as mounted police and ... special companies and sections of Special Constables being formed from footballers. Hospital students are cheerfully shovelling coal supplies for the hospitals at some of the great stations, and everywhere one hears the same story. ('The World of Sport', 1926: 22).

Freed from the strictures of everyday life, they worked together, slept in

2.1 'Unusual scenes include a motor-bus used as a recruiting office, a flock of sheep walking down a road in London, and volunteer workers improvising a cricket match in Rotten Row.'

(a) *upper left:* 'A motor-bus recruiting office: volunteers enrolling at the LGOC Emergency Camp in Regent's Park.'
(b) *upper right:* At the Trades Union Congress headquarters after the stoppage of the strike was announced.'
(c) *middle left:* 'A "Test Match" in Rotten Row: volunteer workers in Hyde Park play improvised cricket with sticks for bats and boxes as wickets.'
(d) *middle right:* '"A flock of sheep that leisurely pass by"': an unusual sight in New Bridge Street, connected with the maintenance of London's food supply.'
(e) *lower left:* 'Keeping up the domestic coal supply in the East End of London: purchasers at the G.E.R. coal depot at Custom house.'
(f) *lower right:* 'Attended by women volunteers as waitresses: volunteer workers on the Underground Railway at a meal in their mess-room at Earl's Court.'

communal quarters, ate special rations, and usually had their fill of free beer (Symons, 1957: 78; Greene, 1971: 177–8).

Male volunteers drove buses, underground trains, trams, railway trains, and lorries; served as special constables; or worked in docks or electrical plants. Women served in canteens (see figure 2.1(f)), as telephone operators, and as drivers; they also delivered mail, newspapers, and messages. Most of the volunteers regarded their temporary jobs not as a dangerous duty but rather as an exciting adventure; few thought, or admitted to thinking, that it was the revolutionary crisis so touted by the press and certain members of government.[6] For volunteers, the strike was a welcome break in the ordinary routine of school, banking, clerical work, or even leisure – a chance, as in wartime, for everyone to contribute to the defence of the realm. As Marjorie Shipley Ellis of Peterborough (see figure 2.2) told me:

> My cousin, who was a railway enthusiast [and I] ... were listening to the radio in a friend's house ... and Joynson-Hicks, the Home Secretary, was appealing for volunteers for the railway. At the flash, Norman was out of the room, down to the station, offering to fire an engine up to King's Cross. And so he did. *Never was a boy so happy!* ... It was a jolly thing ... [I saw him] coming from the train one day: he was coal black! ... And you realized what a magnificent set of teeth he'd got! Oh! He was never so happy! You see, that boy knew every signal box,

2.2 Marjorie Shipley Ellis

every crossing, between here and King's Cross – of course he was invaluable. Had a lovely time! (Ellis, Interview, 1985).

Social capital could be earned even by walking, as the streets became the site of a communal exhibition of national unity and goodwill. In communities of strikers, and nationally among those sympathetic to them, people gave money for soup kitchens, pooled their resources, gave rides to each other, and organized a series of singing and jazz band concerts, and even a traditional Sword Play in one community (Lester, 1979: 10; Buckley, Interview, 1985; Norman, Letter, 1985; Bruley, 2010: 60–85), to raise money for those without food. Even non-union working-class and lower-middle-class volunteers were invited to enter the periphery of this holiday world by having their ordinary work declared a social service. Sir Richard Terry noted in the *Queen*, another Society journal,

> Everyone now has a list of adventures during the late strike. Every newspaper has commented on the amazing amount of things we all found we could do without.
> For the first time in most of our lives we have enjoyed the sensation of 'having it both ways'. If we did without something we were congratulated on our self sacrifice; if we were determined not to do without it, we were complimented on our pluck – 'carrying on' as we called it. (Terry, 1926: 7)

The General Strike polarized Parliament with the Labour opposition on one side, the Conservative government on the other, and remnants of the Liberal Party (most notably David Lloyd George, Sir Herbert Samuel, and Sir John Simon – an array that spanned their party's political spectrum from left to right respectively) – all attempting to mediate various compromises. Two major arguments came to the fore. According to those in government, most of whom tended to take the part of colliery owners, the strike represented an act of war by the TUC General Council. The government claimed that the elected leaders of organized labour went beyond their 'legitimate' powers and used the economically coercive forces of a General Strike to put political pressure on an innocent, uninvolved public. According to Baldwin, his Cabinet, and much of the media, the strikers were staging a treasonous attack on government, Parliament, King, community, people, nation, public, law and order, and most importantly, the constitution. To their minds, the strike was an attempt to impose the will of a minority upon an innocent majority.

From the perspective of the Labour Party and the TUC, the General Strike used the rational, organized pressure of a general work stoppage to persuade the community at large of parliament's moral responsibility to the miners. It was an economic measure, a morally justifiable method of demonstrating the vital contribution that workers and especially coal miners made to the entire society, a demonstration of the interconnectedness of human responsibilities and industrial reform. Most importantly, it was a last-ditch attempt to force the government and mine owners to recognize organized labour's stake in the polity. Unfortunately for the striking workers, the government refused to acknowledge that any authority but itself had the right to appropriate labour for what the government designated as political ends.

When the TUC General Council agreed to resume negotiations with the government on 12 May 1926, the General Strike officially ended. The General Council did this on the basis of the Samuel Memorandum, which would have ensured that miners would not be subjected to temporary wage cuts without guarantees that the industry would be reorganized for more efficient production of coal. The miners refused, however, thus releasing the government and mine owners from any responsibility to adhere to the agreement. This enabled both to blame the miners for being 'obdurate' ('End of the Strike. An Unconditional Withdrawal', 1926: 3), for all three parties had to agree to the Samuel recommendations for them to be obligatory. Furthermore, the government disassociated itself from the Memorandum, claiming that it was only the report of a private but interested bystander, which was in no way legally binding. Samuel himself acquiesced to this view and wrote in reply to a 8 May letter from Sir Arthur Steel-Maitland (which stated, 'it is imperative to make it plain that any discussion which you think proper to initiate is not clothed in even a vestige of official character'), 'I have made it perfectly clear that I have been acting entirely on my own initiative and without any kind of authorization from the Government' ('Sir H. Samuel's Basis. No Authorization From Government', 1926: 3). On 14 May 1926, Baldwin sent proposals to the miners and owners more severe than those that Sir Herbert Samuel had proposed. The MFGB refused to accept these, and the government declined to accept MFGB counter-proposals made later that summer.

While it might be interesting to speculate about what might have happened if the miners had agreed to the proposals (the majority of opinion claims that the owners would have backed out) and the owners were publicly shown to be intractable, neither occurred. With the miners' remaining adamant, other unions refused to return to work. In fact, in the first few days after the strike, more came out in sympathetic outrage for the plight of the miners. Further adding to the chaos, many volunteers – having been told that the strike was off – did not come to work either. Thus the aftermath of the General Strike was perhaps more discomfiting than the official event itself.

Within a few weeks, though, life had more or less returned to normal for the majority of Great Britain's population. As Sir Robert Speed (at Trinity College in 1926) recalled: 'Everything went on as usual when we got back to Cambridge. We had to do our exams for the Tripos in June' (Letter, 1986). David Fremantle, whose father was Commander in Chief at the country's largest naval base in Portsmouth, was a Clare College, Cambridge student at the time. Fremantle, who came down to work unloading passenger ships at Southampton, recalled, 'for a few days I think it was a three-days' wonder. And ... people told their most interesting experiences that we'd had. You see, things collapsed so quickly and completely, suddenly, that life got back to normal almost immediately, although the miners' strike went on another six months I believe. They had a terrible time. But otherwise, everybody else went back to work and life became absolutely normal' (Fremantle, Interview, 1986) (see figure 2.3).

Stressing the importance of retaining that supremely British quality of order, the King urged his subjects to 'forget whatever elements of bitterness the events of the past few days may have created, only remembering how

2.3 David Fremantle

steady and how orderly the country has remained' ('The King to the Nation', 1926: 2). According to George V, a lasting peace could be created only by 'forgetting the past', which would enable the nation to 'look only to the future with the hopefulness of a united people' ('Pictures of the Strike – The Police Cope with Disturbances' 1926: 857; 'The King's Message', 1926: 3).

Unlike the King, Stanley Baldwin preferred to recall the past, to credit Britain's historic tradition with ending the strike. Welcoming back the prodigal strikers into the national fold, though not without first scolding them for 'engaging the constant attention of the Government', the Prime Minister stressed:

> Our business is not to triumph over those who have failed in a mistaken attempt. It is rather to rally them together with the population as a whole in an attempt to restore the well-being of the nation ... It would not, however, be right that I should let to-night pass ... without expressing the heartfelt thanks of the Government to all those of our countrymen who have supported us ... We conceived it to be a matter of absolute duty to call upon the whole country to resist the menace of the general strike. The people of these islands responded ... as in our long history they have answered every claim made upon their love of freedom and sense of fair play. ('Mr. Baldwin's Thanks ...', 1926: 3)

Despite those pleas for brotherhood and forgiveness, thousands of workers were victimised, especially those working for the yet-to-be nationalised railways. The railway unions were forced to admit publicly that their sympathetic strike was a wrongful act – though no law existed to that effect. In many industries, workers lost their jobs or were forced to take reduced wages. A notice appearing in *The Times* the very day after the strike ended and on the same page as the Prime Minister's statement urging 'a spirit of co-operation, putting behind us all malice and all vindictiveness', declared:

> NON-UNION LABOUR ONLY
>
> OMNIBUS COMPANY'S DECISION
>
> In a notice issued yesterday the directors of the Southdown Motor Services state that, having regard to the withdrawal of the company's drivers and conductors without notice ... in spite of an agreement entered into as recently as April 27, they regard the agreement as automatically terminated, and have decided that in future they will not recognize any trade union. They further state it is their intention not to engage union labour in future. ('Mr. Baldwin's Statement', 1926: 3)

Right next to this notice was the 'Government's Statement', noting that 'His Majesty's Government have no power to compel employers to take back every man who has been on strike, nor have they entered into any obligations of any kind on this matter. Some displacements are inevitable ...' ('Re-Engagement of Strikers. Government Statement', 1926: 3). The effect was to disassociate the government or employers from responsibility for enforcing Baldwin's 'hope ... that we should resume our work in a spirit of co-operation, putting behind us all malice and all vindictiveness'.

Outraged by what they saw as the General Council's betrayal of their cause in agreeing to the Samuel Memorandum's recommendation of reduced wages and securing no guarantees for a renewed subsidy, ending the lockout, and further negotiations, the miners stayed out for seven more months. Although attempts at charitable fundraising for 'miners' wives and children' helped in a small way, thousands went hungry. Baldwin made his loyalties clear when he tried to block international aid with 'official' reports to the United States that miners and their families were not under any real hardship.[7] In November 1926, the MFGB surrendered and negotiated district settlements with local mine owners – at wages below March, May, and July proposal levels for those who were re-employed. And in January 1927, the House of Commons passed the Trade Disputes and Trade Union Act.

Its very passage, however, seemed to support the TUC's contention that a general strike had indeed been legitimate, for the new act now made sympathetic strikes, mass picketing, the 'political levy' in trade unions,[8] and the affiliation of civil service unions to the TUC all illegal. Furthermore, local authority workers were threatened with imprisonment for breaking their employment contracts. In November 1927, in a desperate move to remind the rest of the country that little had changed, 250 unemployed miners staged a march from the Rhondda Valley to London.

The Mond-Turner talks began in January 1928 with Sir Alfred Mond, head of the Federation of British Industry (FBI), an industrialists' group, and Ben Turner, representative of the TUC, alternately chairing the first Joint Conference of the two groups. This resulted in a July 1928 report, which 'welcomed measures for rationalization of industry and proposed the setting up of a National Industrial Council of the TUC and the FBI, with compulsory arbitration through a Joint Standing Committee' (Skelley, 1976: 412).

Notes

1 This brand of protest, which relies on models derived from the ritual folk dramas that mark calendar customs, can include night-time raids, masking, parades, anonymous threats, arson, smuggling, and poaching. Such activities have been documented as early as the seventeenth century and as recently as today (Alford, 1959; Smith, 1966; Williams, 1971; Thompson, 1971, 1974; Burke, 1983; Simms, 1978; Hay et al., 1975; Hebdige, 1979; Bushaway, 1982; Pearson, 1983; Pettit, 1984; Underdown, 1985; Thompson, 1991).

2 The CPGB held its first conference on 31 July 1920 ... but 'complete unification was only achieved at a later meeting, in Leeds, on January 29, 1921. The new party

at once sought affiliation with the Labour party, and received the first of many refusals in a letter from Arthur Henderson on September 11, 1920' (Mowat, 1971: 20; see also Cole, 1948: 96, 102–3, 112–13). In 1924, The Labour Party Conference decisively rejected affiliation with the CPGB (Klugman, 1980: 51).

3 Bagwell, Jeffery, and Hennessy have argued that railway and transport strikes were more easily averted because so many volunteers were eager to drive trains, buses, and lorries; such volunteers also could be easily mobilized. Bagwell further asserted that the Cabinet's circumspection in not provoking the NUR by threatening the railwaymen's gains, kept the railwaymen from going out in sympathy with the miners. The railwaymen had no interest in risking their guaranteed week, much less in courting unemployment. As well, miners' strikes were far less likely to be troubled by blackleg labour – no one who was not already a miner really wanted to go down into the pits, a point that made it far more likely for miners to use strikes as a bargaining tool (Bagwell, 1971: 116–25; and see Jeffery and Hennessy, 1983: 63).

4 This is a facetious question. The goal of the Trade Disputes Act 1927 was to forestall any chance of another general strike by eliminating all possible loopholes as well as to damage the financial relationship between the Labour Party and the unions.

5 Ralph Steel explained, 'strikebreaking never entered our heads; we were just doing a job of work ... No, never dreamt of it. You see, it was a question, the whole country was at a standstill and if you weren't, didn't do something about it, people would be starving, wouldn't they?' (Steel, Interview, 1986).

6 Steel recalled, 'No, I don't think we gave any thought to [revolution] at all. We were doing a job and that was it. And we certainly hadn't any political views or anything like that ...' (Steel, Interview, 1986; and see Bullard, Letter, 1987).

7 Baldwin's action lends support to McIlroy's conclusion that Baldwin was not a man of peace or interested in really helping the miners (McIlroy, 2006: 99) as opposed to Perkins' contention that Baldwin's goal was to strike a middle ground (Perkins, 2006: 233–5, 265).

8 Before, union members had to 'contract out' of contributing to the Labour Party, as per the 1913 Trade Union Act; this law reversed that, resulting in reduced funds for the Labour Party (Renshaw, 1975a: 242; Richardson, 2003: 207).

3
Social distinctions and social actions among the upper and middle classes

> It was an era of practical jokes and being young and carefree it all seemed as it was, natural, innocent and harmless. No one got hurt, but the kind of life we led didn't include much thinking about a larger world. Soon afterwards that was unavoidable. (Grenfell, 1976: 85)

> A lot of nonsense is talked about the strike and the 1920s. It was not really like that. The 1920s, for example were not gay if you had no money. (Hodgkiss, Letter, 1986)[1]

In Great Britain between the wars there was little ambiguity as to who was at the top of the social hierarchy, though the distinctions do blur for those of lower rank. But as social historian Raphael Samuel has noted,

> the upper class, however its membership is defined, [was] seen as qualitatively different. At the top of society there was a conspicuously privileged ruling class, made up of public persons and social leaders – what had been known in mid-Victorian times as the 'upper-ten thousand' and what was variously referred to in the inner war years as 'the aristocracy' 'the upper classes' or 'society'. In one aspect it was the Establishment. In another, a leisure class of prestige who took part in the London Season, and followed the country house round. More rarely it might be extended to take in the leaders of industry and finance, but only when they were taken up in high politics, or caught up in the social round.
>
> 'Society' was a descriptive term for titled and influential people who monopolized prestige roles. (1983b: 29–30)

Social identity is a matter of negotiating among the differing group identities each person maintains (Royce, 1982). In each instance, identity is determined by contrast and contact with others: 'we' can be defined as 'us' only if there are others who can be designated as 'them'. Social enactments serve to express and legitimate these distinctions and the status roles, behaviours, and social functions that are constituting and constitutive of social identity (Davidoff, 1973; Turner, 1973; Colls and Dodd, 1986; Halbwachs, 1992: 140, 166, 172–3; Greenhill, 1994). Manner of dress, accent, social activities, choice of reading matter and cultural activities, political views, and so on are all factors in keying identity (Davidoff, 1973; Goffman, 1975; Smith, 1995; Eber and Neal, 2001: 176–7) and in creating and maintaining group solidarity (McKibbin, 2000: 2–23, 36).

Specific behaviours were deemed appropriate for, and were expected of, certain social categories of men and women, which limited not only what they could or could not do but what they were remembered for doing (Halbwachs, 1992: 148, 172–3; Shuman, 2005: 154). Particular criteria marked social place and thus served to define the conditions for work and play, as well as that intermediary practice known as 'good works' – a peculiarly privileged genre that combined features of both work and play. There was some flexibility, but in most cases social status, age, sex, geographical location (e.g. north *v.* south, London *v.* the rest of Great Britain), and occupation limited the degree to which people could 'fiddle' with these social categories and the relationships that they implied. For the most part, categories matched up as follows: young upper-class men (play) are opposed to older middle-class men (work) and mediated by married, upper-middle-class women (social service). Spatial categories also map on to these social and behavioural classifications: that is, country houses and universities oppose urban work environments such as the City, Parliament, and the Inns of Court (law offices). Public spaces – streets, highways, railways, and parks – provide the passage-ways between spaces for play and work; they also provide public sites for various demonstrations of social service and duty. Those categories, in my structural analysis (see also McKibbin, 2000), work out as a series of paired oppositions, as per the table and discussion below:

Table 3.1 Traits of upper and middle-class General Strike volunteers (Saltzman, 1988: 14)

Dramatis Personae	Play	Charity	Work
Adolescent	x		
Mature		x	x
Male			x
Female	x	x	
Unmarried	x		
Married		x	x
Unmarried women	x	x	
Unmarried men	x		x
Married women		x	
Married men	x		x
Unmarried women	x		x
Married women		x	
Unmarried men	x	x	
Married men			x

Male university students were the members of British society with the most licence to play and to be publicly and socially irresponsible. In 1925 the *Daily Express* denounced 'the modern girl's brother[s]' at the universities as 'weary, anaemic, feminine, bloodless ... Exquisite without masculinity ... they would never fight – their fathers had died for a degenerate offspring' (Graves and Hodge, 1941: 117; Cartland, 1970: 183) – not quite the image of British manhood typified by the 'golden-haired young Apollos' of pre-war days. Personal amusement rather than duty to anyone or anything else was the major preoccupation of most well-off young men.

Although there were certainly a good number of undergraduates from grammar schools at Oxford and Cambridge, and somewhat more at the other universities, public school boys tended to dominate political and social life, as their fathers and brothers did in Parliament and the city, and as their mothers and sisters did in society and charity work. In the opinion of noted historian A. J. P. Taylor, Oriel College at Oxford was dominated by Charterhouse, one of the nine 'Great' English public schools:

> Its products were agreeable young men, obsessed with Association football and with not a thought in their heads, at least none in theirs that were in mine. They had never heard of Marx ... [They weren't at Oxford for the learning but to receive] the necessary social stamp for well-paid jobs in the civil service. Work was a tiresome interference with more interesting things such as Association football and the drinking of beer ... [At Union debates] they were play-acting, pretending to be the House of Commons. (Taylor, 1983: 68–72)

But these young men could afford to play-act, were even encouraged to do so; they occupied a temporal space between childhood and adulthood and a physical space removed from both the leisurely pace of country house life and London's urbane society. Like adolescents in more 'primitive' cultures, they were expected and permitted to indulge in certain types of licentious behaviour that emphasized ingenuity, especially when it could be employed in inventing new pranks and elaborate practical jokes. Also in keeping with the English 'passion for dressing up' in the 1920s, elaborate disguises usually accompanied their dramatic enactments (Davidoff, 1973: 68; Hawarth, 1978: 64), which were well publicized in the popular press (McKibbin, 2000: 28–34).

Such activities were known collectively as 'rags' to people of the day, who were quite careful to differentiate between those activities and behaviour that could be described as hooliganism – a contemporary gloss for lower-class pranks. Irene Bullock of Norwich, a Girton alumna, noted that a rag, was 'a more organised, bigger affair than a "lark", something harmless but unusual, even outrageous, often organised in aid of a charitable object' (Bullock, Letter, 1987). According to the *Cambridge Gownsman and Undergraduette* of 1926, with regard to the annual bacchanalia on 5 November, 'a rag is a matter of careful organization, and not mere hooliganism. This university is a university for gentlemen' (Hawarth, 1978: 64).

Unlike undergraduates, professional men, mostly of the upper-middle class and at work in the City, finance, law, or business, were required to display a greater degree of social responsibility before and after the war. Such young men, the younger sons of the aristocracy or members of the wealthy upper-middle class, were frequently involved as Boy Scout leaders; sponsors of boys' clubs such as the Church Lads' Brigade, the (Nonconformist) Boys' Brigade, and the Jewish Lads' Brigade in the East End; or as officers in the Territorial Army reserve. They did not have the freedom to indulge in the deliberately meaningless pranks of their school days, but neither were they as removed from the world of outdoor amusement as their older colleagues who spent their leisure time playing bridge at London men's clubs. And not accidentally, they were able to set an example to young working-class boys as to the proper attitudes concerning obedience, service, and hierarchy (Ward, 2004: 119–20). While taking young lads on country outings and going off to army camps for rifle practice were clearly enjoyable, these activities signified service, not play.

Although many of those men tended to be from the professional middle classes, the perception of those on the receiving end of this social work – boys and girls who benefited from the various scouting organizations and camps – was that the *upper* classes were helping them. Public focus tended to be on the fashionable. Their efforts were what stuck in people's memories, possibly because of the very juxtaposition of their privileged status with that of the poor they tried to assist.

Yet the perception of upper-class largesse was not completely wrong, especially with regard to the many war-related charitable activities led by titled women (de Vries, 2005). And sometimes relatively small financial donations, made a large symbolic impact (e.g. the Prince of Wales' donation of £10 to the miners' relief fund after the 1926 strike collapsed). But while there were fewer examples of aristocratic largesse in the countryside after the Great War (Dawes, 1974; Waterson, 1975), the press, whose proprietors were part and parcel of society, went all out to publicize such instances when they occurred.

Changing demographics after the war also had their own impact. The land transfer between 1918 and 1921 of some eight million acres (affecting the landed gentry far more than the peerage); death duties of 50 per cent at a time when two or three generations passed on within four years; and the increased costs of running country estates for those who were land rich and cash poor, led many men who would have remained members of the leisure class before 1914 to seek careers. Not only did they work alongside their upper-middle-class counterparts in the City, law, and business; they were also associated with corresponding charitable activities (Graves and Hodge, 1941; Branson, 1976; Newby, 1980; McKibbin, 2000).

But these finer points of status distinction were of little importance for the working classes. Many believed that the sons of the aristocracy were out there to serve, in the same way that they had sacrificed themselves during the war. Ironically, middle-class 'social-climbing' charity efforts, which inadvertently benefited working-class children, along with a tendency to identify 'up', may have, in fact, done a good bit to justify the existence of an increasingly dysfunctional aristocracy. Bruno Marmorstein recalled that those involved as leaders in the Jewish Lads' Brigade, for instance, were all from public schools or universities (Interview, 1985). Phineas May, himself a leader in that organization, explained that he and his peers were 'definitely aware' of the poor conditions – had they not been, there would not have been a Lads' Brigade.[2]

> People who were in better positions ... did ... try to help those in not such a fortunate position as they were. And anybody who came from my type of home [and who went to a public school] would have volunteered for something like that, the same way as we volunteered for the special constables [during the General Strike] ... you felt it was the proper thing to do, in the same way, when there's a war you, you join up, or join some service that will help your country. (May, Interview, 1986)

Unlike their younger or single counterparts, older middle and upper-class men, whose role was defined by their work rather than by their charitable or leisure activities, were too busy managing their businesses or performing in the more serious dramas of local and national politics and government to need much in the way of home-grown theatrics for mental stimulation. Certain men from the very top levels of society, or men aiming toward those heights, did indulge in more creative forms of entertainment, however. Thus, one finds such eminent figures as Winston Churchill and Duff Cooper, as well as Lord Birkenhead, joining younger society folks at fancy dress balls – perhaps in an effort to recapture their own youth or to acquire a certain amount of social cachet by association with the younger members of society. The Duchess of Westminster recalled the Duchess of Sutherland's party at Hampden House in 1926, at which 'Lord Birkenhead [F. E. Smith] came as Captain Hook' (Grosvenor, 1961: 110–11). Significantly, both Cooper and Smith were originally members of the well-to-do middle class; their theatrical displays were likely more representative of a continued striving for social status by those not quite securely within the inner circle of elite power. As historian Ross McKibbin has noted, there was a significant blurring of the lines among various sectors of the upper classes during the interwar years. The 'tendency to associate upper classness with social display' further conflated the upper class with society (McKibbin, 2000: 2; see also Taylor, 2007).

For older or married women, 'good works' (not play) were their primary activity outside the home. Women were supposed to support others, their public acts an extension of their domestic role of nurturers and maintainers of order (Houghton, 1979; Mackay and Thane, 1986; Saltzman, 1994a: 112–13; Cohen, 2002: 51, 85–6, 152). Many a young person in the 1910s and 1920s could tell of titled and wealthy landowning grandmothers and mothers who showed a high degree of responsibility for their tenants, villagers, workers, and servants. Mrs Richard Cavendish, whose grandfather was a multi-millionaire tea planter in India, recalled when the words 'Lady Bountiful' signified a distinctive category for upper-class women rather than a sarcastic reference.

> In those days [the words] were taken literally. My grandmother was amazing: it didn't matter who wanted her – anybody in the village, anybody on the place who needed help – she was always available...
>
> [A]t Welbeck ... the Lady Bountiful there was the Duchess of Portland. On the night of an enormous party, an old man in the village, who was dying, asked to see the Duchess. The moment all the other guests disappeared, off she went down to the village. She sat with him all night, talking to him, looking after him, until he died. Next morning, there she was at breakfast, beautifully dressed and not a word said. (Waterson, 1975: 37)

Besides helping out those in trouble who depended upon them, the upper classes also provided special treats, usually at Christmas time, twenty-first birthday parties, or weddings. Brenda S—— of Suffolk, who grew up in a Warwickshire village, recalled that the

> Lord of the manor ... was a dear called Boughton Leigh, whose people had come over with the Conqueror. And they were a very old established family, and they ruled the village ... [On New Year's Eve] we all took plates and knife and fork and went to the church rooms. The Lord of the manor and his family came. Everyone sat down at the very long table, and we had a super meal with food provided by local farmers and my mother used to make a trifle.... [The Lord of the manor] used to give a party for tenants in his grounds, but you didn't go into his house. (S——, Interview, 1987)

The Duchess of Portland also used to hire waiters to wait on her servants at the annual Boxing Day ball. After she had danced with the steward, she and the Duke left, and the ball became more relaxed (Dawes, 1974: 133–6; see Cannadine, 1980: 37, 339–41, 424).

Rather than indulge in such grand and impersonal gestures, however, most mistresses of large estates, unlike masters, were much more likely to demonstrate goodwill towards the lower classes in more personal and traditionally maternal ways. Brenda S—— noted that the Boughton Leigh family 'did a great deal of charity. Old Lady Boughton Leigh used to take soup to the parishioners, if they were ill, and food' (S——, Interview, 1987). Esther

Social distinctions, social actions

(Cohen) Segal, who grew up in London's East End, recalled annual invitations to Lady Rothschild's home. Neighbourhood children would have tea in the pavilion, where they were waited upon and served watercress sandwiches. Afterwards, the children received carnations from the estate's greenhouse. Once, Mrs Segal remembered, she got to walk around the gardens with Lady Rothschild herself (Esther Segal, Interview, 1985).

Although some members of the working classes who benefited from such efforts appreciated such glimpses into another world, others took it for granted. As Sid Rosenberg told me, 'Yeah, the [society ladies] used to run canteens] in the stations. Yeah, sure ... They were all very rich women ... titled women. They used to run like they do now for the down-and-outs, but they ... well they paid out of their own pocket. All right – what'd it cost in those days: tea, sugar, milk? A penny, a bottle of milk?' (Rosenberg, Interview, 1985) (see figure 3.1)

Given the very real limitations imposed on women during the Victorian age and for some time afterwards, it is not surprising that upper-middle-class women performed so much charity work (Davidoff, 1973: 92–5). As generic maternal figures to the poor, whose poverty gave evidence of childlike incompetence, these women were actively able to do something measurable to demonstrate their own power without violating the domestic boundaries of their cultural role (Cohen, 2002: 85–6). They posed little if any threat to their male peers and none to those above, who were probably just as relieved to

3.1 Sid Rosenberg

have others diffuse their own diminishing social responsibilities. The gap between very rich and very poor could be made to seem less apparent, especially when some token titled women could be invoked (sometimes repeatedly) as proof of the social and economic function of the aristocracy.

As the middle classes took on more and more charity and welfare work, the upper classes, particularly the women among them, seemed more involved in purely symbolic media displays. Contemporary photographs show society ladies enjoying themselves at balls to raise money for charity, replacing much of the formerly local and active social work undertaken by the upper classes, many of whom now lived primarily in cities where such small, hierarchical communities of personal obligation did not exist.[3] Still, much of the same affective function may have been served, since these magazine and newspaper photographs reached a larger audience than attending to one's tenants could ever do.[4] But rather than being used to signify mutual obligations, such presentation of elite charitable activities encouraged a lack of personal responsibility for the conditions of others. The (charitable) exception was invoked to prove the rule, which both made it more memorable and allowed it to assume greater symbolic significance as a result.[5] For example, during the General Strike, every major newspaper mentioned Lady Mountbatten – better known for her shopping capabilities than for her charitable endeavours – for her volunteer efforts. It is no wonder that society became the more restricted 'society', as public representations of group identity came to exclude rather than include the middle and lower classes from membership.

Women's work during the Great War provided an even more blatant violation of those rules for acceptable female activities, however, and many of their early contributions did not meet with a very cordial reception. This situation did not begin to change until 1915, when the War Office finally recognized their temporary and replacement roles as doctors, nurses, ambulance drivers, canteen organizers, railway signal operators, tram drivers, taxi drivers, munitions workers, conductors, and special constables – ironically, many of the same jobs male volunteers took over in 1926.[6] With their work reframed as 'service', women workers of all stripes were recast as supporters of the war effort (Woollacott, 1994; Thom, 1998 and 2005; de Vries, 2005; Noakes, 2005; Andrews and Hobbs, 2010). They came to be praised by such enemies of the women's movement as Lord Northcliffe, who declared even suffragettes wonderful because they were 'devoting themselves whole-heartedly to the prosecution of man's game of war' (Clephane, 1933: 114). Once the war was over, however, women, both working- and middle-class, 'ceased to be splendid patriots serving their country, and became instead selfish vampires depriving men of jobs' (Clephane, 1933: 170; see also Leacock and Safa, 1986; Thom, 1998 and 2005; Cohen, 2002: 152; Andrews and Hobbs, 2010: 107).[7]

After the war, although a few upper-class women rebelled against their restricted status by working to earn money[8] or taking part in the supposedly serious and public arena of politics,[9] they, like young upper-class men, were allowed to do so only in a playful context. Yet even this realm was restricted for older and married women, for whom play was relegated to mealtime jokes and planning parties (i.e. matchmaking) for single men and women. Their innovative themes and overturning of conventions constituted a 'safe' form of rebellion – seemingly limited to the spheres of domesticity and play at country house weekends and fancy dress parties.[10] The Duchess of Westminster recalled lunches at the home of Mrs Richard Guinness: 'I loved going to her house in Great Cumberland Place ... Often the curtains were drawn and the lights lit and the food was unconventional too ... One felt that one had got into a topsy-turvy country, where all that mattered was to be amusing' (Grosvenor, 1961: 117). Particularly striking about much of this rebellious dramatic activity was the predominance of women, mostly young, but some older, in creating and carving out new identity markers. Much of the intent seemed to be to confuse and invert normal social relationships.

While older women tended to engage in inversion mostly within the domestic sphere, younger women constructed the rebellious side of their social identity more publicly. The 1920s may well have been the era of the 'It' girl,[11] sex appeal, and the flapper, which evolved from meaning a teenage girl to 'a daring young rebel who openly defied convention' (Grenfell, 1976: 79), but only within limits. As the Duchess of Westminster stated, 'flappers were definitely middle class' (1961: 79). New forms of amusement did allow the Mayfair set, most of whose members lived in that well-appointed London neighbourhood, to explore new possibilities and roles. But such entertainments also provided these young people with an opportunity to rebel against their parents' rules and customs without completely rejecting the old world.

For young unmarried women between the ages of 18 and 25, prescribed activities included 'becoming' adult, that is, getting married. Yet for most women of this class, there were simply not many options open beyond the social life and charity work that defined their domestic sphere. According to Lady Phyllis MacRae, for upper and upper-middle-class women, 'it was considered unpatriotic to have a paid job during the period after the 1914–18 war, with as much unemployment' as there was (MacRae, Letter, 1986b; Davidoff, 1973: 63; Cohen, 2002: 152). As MacRae explained:

> It would have been considered very caddish to get a job when there was so much unemployment. You had a home, you had money, you had everything you needed: it would have been very wrong to take anyone's job. You were expected to do a lot of voluntary work. You might be a secretary or chairman of the Women's Institute or the Red Cross; you might run the Girl Guides and Boy Scouts. You did not get paid for it. Of course if it was really necessary, people like war widows, poor things, did work. (Waterson, 1985: 34)

Thus, while their male counterparts' minimal 'work' responsibility had to do with getting through university, most young women of the upper and upper-middle classes had the responsibility of a court debut and the subsequent social life, both of which were aimed at finding a husband. Doing so involved leading their peers in a series of new and original entertainments.

For the upper classes of Great Britain, then, certain types of social behaviour tended to reinforce and legitimate their unique status and its social value within and across class boundaries and in specific historically constraining contexts (Shils and Young, 1953; Hay *et al.*, 1975; Moore and Myerhoff, 1977; MacAloon, 1984; Cannadine, 1985). Certain groups in particular perceived themselves, as did those outside, as possessing especially ambiguous status: that is, young male adults and women from their 20s to their 40s. Like those of 'betwixt and between' or liminal status in other cultures, these folks turn out to be the very people with limited social responsibilities and functions; surrounded by the most rules and behavioural boundaries, they also had the greatest licence to violate those limits and incur the least severe of penalties – at least in the eyes of the larger society (e.g. Van Gennep, 1960; Geertz, 1973; Babcock, 1976; Humphries, 1980; Turner, 1982; Pearson, 1983; Davis, 1986; Brandes, 1988; Graham, 1995).

In ordinary times, those who fit the stereotype of the General Strike volunteers were best known for the way they both flaunted social conventions prior to the First World War and took advantage of their privileged status to stage treasure hunts, fancy dress parties, charity rags, activities on the night of the annual Oxford-Cambridge Boat Race, and elaborate, often public, spoofs in London and in the university towns of Oxford, Cambridge, Liverpool, Edinburgh, and Glasgow. As Marjorie Shipley Ellis noted, 'we were all young in those days you see and people hadn't got the regular jobs as they all have now' (Ellis, Interview, 1985). The Duchess of Westminster explained, 'The Press made out that we were an organized gang who called ourselves the Bright Young People and that we found modern times so dull that we were deliberately trying to brighten them up. Any wild party, Bohemian rag or large-scale practical joke which took place in the West End between 1924 and 1930 was supposed to have been perpetrated by these Bright Young People' (Grosvenor, 1961: 122). Yet it might also be argued that 'the parties, the sensations ... were quite consciously public activities which would not have occurred but for the press' (McKibbin, 2000: 28).

For upper-middle-class and upper-class men and women in the 1920s, play[12] rather than work came to represent their sphere of social action – regardless of a reality in which many continued to serve charitable functions, study at university, work in offices, and pursue relatively mundane pleasures like hiking, sports, cinema, theatre, concerts, reading, and music halls. Few took them seriously or assumed their larks to have any particular, if any, meaning – except possibly those few members of the lower classes who were the direct or indirect victims of their 'jokes'. In May 1926, a London taxi cab driver wrote in to *Titbits* to report that he'd lost his cab; members of the Bright Young People had hired it for a late-night treasure hunt. They left the driver and ran off with his vehicle, which police found in a ditch miles away with its radiator and head lamps smashed. When the driver found out who had engaged him, the young man had gone abroad (London taxi cab driver, 1926: 372). Barbara Cartland, by way of an apology for such situations, noted that the Bright Young People were original, gay, and enjoyed themselves; 'if a few people got mobbed up and made fools of in the process, well it really didn't hurt them. We made a lot of people laugh' (1970: 208).

The execution of carefully planned jokes was one of the most popular activities of this set, a tradition traceable to the eighteenth century (Balfour, 1933: 162–3). Sylvia Baron, an alumna of Girton College, Cambridge, told me that larks, rags, and jokes 'all mean approximately the same thing – a light-hearted happening of a jokey nature which also sometimes – but not always – served a useful and even a serious purpose' (Baron, Letter, 1986). Evelyn Waugh noted that the point of 'rags' was to 'score off' people generally designated as authorities, such as political speakers, policemen, or schoolmasters (1976: 117). Further refining Waugh's definition, Marion E. Massey, another Girton alumna, related that a rag 'was something a group of you might do, usually discomfiting someone else, or a group of others. It would be somewhat at their expense, but not vindictively so' (Massey, Letter, 1986).

As a criterion for rating performance, ingenuity ranked high, especially when it could be employed in inventing new pranks. In one example, Mr George Edinger, an Oxford undergraduate, lectured as a 'well-known German psychologist ... Many distinguished professors and heads of colleges turned up to hear what the great thinker had to say. The lecture was a *tour de force*. A brilliant parody of all the jargon that psychologists use, but without one word of meaning' (Balfour, 1933: 169). Both Oxford and Cambridge also had climbing clubs, and 'almost every year at Oxford someone performed the classic climb up the Martyr's Memorial to stick a chamber pot on top', wrote Robert Graves and Alan Hodge (1941: 112).

Back in London, Brian Howard came up with the 'Bruno Hat' hoax, for which he 'painted a number of absurd pictures in obvious parody of the more advanced French schools. They were framed in rope, and some of them were on cork bath-mats. He gave them pretentious titles, like "Leda and the Swan" [and] ... "The Adoration of the Magi"'. Not only did Howard send out invitations to a 'First Exhibition of Pictures by Bruno Hat', he also appeared at the exhibition in a wheelchair and 'wore smoked glasses, a drooping black moustache, and the sort of black clothes which a penniless German artist might easily wear if had had put on his "Sunday best" for the occasion'. The Mayfair intelligentsia came out and tried to make appropriate comments in German to Mr Hat. The exhibition itself was a success, and few discovered the hoax until the next day (Balfour, 1933: 167–8).

Students did not design rags to disturb those outside of their students' milieu – except for those who posed a challenge to its boundaries. Most rags involved juxtaposing inappropriate contexts, costumes, and actors to create situational puns. Lady Harrod related that at one country house, jokes went along with the marvellous food: mustard in miniature champagne bottles, for instance, 'was quite funny at the time, and quite original. Then [Gerald Berners] had those lovely fishes, made of overlapping scales, and there was also a large cock. Maggie Taylor, who was the very highbrow, pretentious wife of Alan Taylor, used to go and see Gerald and yap away in her highbrow way. One day ... he ran after her, holding this, and shouted "Maggie, Maggie, I want you to see my cock!"' (Waterson, 1985: 116).

Sometimes rags did get out of hand, especially during occasions like Boat Race Night or a charity rag, when university students invaded the outside world. According to one report, an Oxford crew sneaked into Drury Lane theatre and upset a performance by changing the spotlight colours on the singer ('Excerpt', 1926: 306). A more traditional activity for Boat Race Night was to snatch a policeman's helmet. Mary Talbot recalled:

> It wasn't only among the undergraduates, because all sorts of other people latched on. On Boat Race Night the young went a bit wild in the West End and a certain amount of larking about [took place]. And if you could sort of bag a policeman's helmet, it was a terrific trophy! Certain people were hailed up no doubt the following morning [...] just drunken undergraduates! Simple as that! It just happened to be that that was reckoned to be a trophy. (Talbot, Interview, 1986b)

While most people did seem to accept such pranks for what they were – unofficially sanctioned and relatively non-threatening (to the upper classes and government) ways to defy authority – charity rags were not always so well received, despite their overt function to collect money for a good cause. Harry Crivan (see figure 3.2), a college student in Glasgow in the 1920s (later teacher then principal at Edinburgh Technical College), recalled that University of Glasgow students, carrying cans to collect money, would meet at a certain point and march through the streets.

> Some of the students used to get themselves into trouble ... See the tram cars were trolleys, run by trolleys and if you pulled the trolleys out the guard's tram car was stalled ... Some of them did this and some of the tram drivers got annoyed with them and used to chase them you see. And then sometimes they used to go into the picture houses and upset people, as well. Then eventually

3.2 Harry Crivan

they came into a big place in George Square ... where they used to finish off dancing. And of course all the young girls came over to dance with the students. (Crivan, Interview, 1985)

After singing popular and local songs and dancing with those who watched their performances, students would collect for charity, transforming their apparent hooliganism into acts for a worthy cause.

Besides engaging in these planned rags and pranks and more spontaneous larks, the young indulged in fancy dress balls and amateur theatricals – homemade, albeit elaborate, entertainment. Fancy dress was 'by no means a new pastime for the upper classes. In the nineteenth century, amateur theatricals were often the most popular form of after-dinner entertainment for a house-party, and many houses ... had their own theatres ... Fancy dress balls became all the rage after the great Devonshire House ball, given by the Duke of Devonshire in 1898' (Sykes, 1980: 182; see also Davidoff, 1973: 67). England's fancy dress tradition – disguising oneself as someone else for amusement as opposed to more pragmatic purposes – dates back at least to Shakespeare's time. Count Heidegger, a Swiss, introduced 'masking' as a public entertainment in London circa 1710 (Jarvis and Raine, 1984: 4). Although the style and themes for costumes changed over the centuries, the practice has continued up until the present, for example, fancy dress Coronation parties in 1953, society 'costume balls' photographed for *Vogue* and the *Tatler*, and the Princess of Wales and Sarah Ferguson, masquerading as policewomen just before the latter's wedding.

In the 1920s, 'the wearing of fancy dress reached near epidemic proportions ... Costumes had to be amusing, bizarre, or shocking to be a success' (Jarvis and Raines, 1984: 23). 'After the war everyone wanted to get away from the gloom of wartime clothes and wartime austerity', recalled Barbara Cartland (1970: 190). 'Smart' people wanted to disguise themselves, 'as if they all wanted to escape from reality into a gay irresponsible world of pretence' (Cartland, 1970: 203). The primary context for fancy dress was parties: 'masked parties, savage parties, Victorian parties, Greek parties, Wild West parties, Russian parties, circus parties, parties where one had to dress as someone else and almost naked parties in St John's Wood, parties in flats and studios and houses and ships and hotels and night-clubs, in windmills and swimming baths' (Waugh, 1946: 27). As the Duchess of Westminster wrote:

> We ... spent a great deal of time and money devising dresses for fancy-dress balls. We went to great lengths to be amusing or mystifying, sometimes changing half way through into a totally different kind of costume, or arranging an elaborate team effect. [For example,] fourteen members of White's Club, headed by the present chairman of Watney, Combe and Reid, were monks escorting Lady Diana Bridgeman dressed as a saint ... My mother wore a gold mask, gold hair and said she was the Last Trump, which, for some reason, was considered a joke in bad taste. (Grosvenor, 1961: 110)

In her autobiography, Lady Diana Cooper painted a vivid picture of another fancy-dress ball at Lord and Lady Ribblesdale's home, describing members of the aristocracy and government at play. 'All the women looked fifty per cent worse than usual – S. as Little Lord Fauntleroy quite awful, P. as a street Arab just dirty ... Gerald Berners [Lord Berners] was good as a hunting man with a marvellously funny mask by Oliver Messel. He had announced his intention of going as Nurse Cavell but was dissuaded. Winston [Churchill] as Nero was good. F. E. [Smith, the Earl of Birkenhead] went as a Cardinal' (Cooper, 1959: 105). Particularly noteworthy was how those endowed with official rank and power chose roles that intensified certain aspects of their authority: Churchill as Nero and Birkenhead as a cardinal. Those society members of no particular political importance used their disguises to invert gender, class, and occupational roles. Even costume parties could not completely escape the social structures of everyday life.

Baby parties became the next rage. The *Daily Express* reported, 'The so-called young people arrived in perambulators ... The guests were dressed as babies in long clothes, Girl Guides, Boy Scouts, nurses. They had comforters in their mouths and carried toy boats, dolls, pails and spades... Cocktails were served in nursery mugs, and the "bar" was a babies' pen' (Cartland, 1970: 194). Unfazed by media censure, however, the BYP merely continued in their efforts to subvert the everyday order of the most basic things. At their next event, a 'Pyjama and Bottle' party, drinks ranged from champagne to beer to ink, petrol smelling salts, Thames water, and tadpole water (Cartland, 1970: 194).

What such seemingly senseless activities symbolized was not a disregard for distinctions and differences – just the reverse: a desperate effort to assert the right to control those distinctions. Again, it was competition of a different sort – a game in which the actors gambled at losing their identity in the hopes of winning an idealized representation of it. The stakes were raised to dangerous heights, however, when strangers started to cross social boundaries. Yet fear of what might come of this uncontrollable development only added to the excitement of gambling with social façades. The threat imminent in such events, especially those that encouraged guests to hide their identities totally, was 'the great problem of the twenties – the uninvited guest. There was really nothing to prevent complete strangers from hiring a fancy dress and slipping into any party' (Cartland, 1970: 191; see also Davidoff, 1973: 69). According to the Duke of Sutherland, uninvited guests appeared at a party in Hampden House. The object for this particular occasion was for guests to disguise their identities and when recognized, to change their costumes. With princes acting as drunken waiters, and the Prince of Wales switching disguises from Bonnie Prince Charlie to 'a Chinese Coolie' (Granville, 1957: 91–2), who could tell which guests were authentic and which were not?

At a time when the entire world was changing at an unheralded pace, constantly redefining upper-class membership markers was the only way to know who was and, more importantly, who was *not* a member. To be deemed authentic was never to appear to be oneself. 'It was necessary, also to be a rebel, to defy the older [members] of high society by doing something outrageous that had not been done before' (Margetson, 1974: 39). The semi-exclusive nature of seemingly senseless activities appealed not only to their appreciation for the melodramatic (Grenfell, 1976: 82), but gave youthful members of the upper classes a sense of identity quite different from the old society or the young adults of other social strata.

A craze for spoofs and leg-pulls represented a further extension of this obsession for trying out new roles, for making life into a game they could control – merely by switching their outfits and thus their personae. Not surprisingly, members of the same families and social groups tended to dominate in this realm. In keeping with the predilection for fancy dress, elaborate disguises usually accompanied these little dramas. Loelia Ponsonby, the former Duchess of Westminster, recalled that two of her friends 'had the nerve to pretend to be reporters and go and interview film-stars in the Savoy or, more daring still, dress up as important foreigners and pay calls on strangers' (Grosvenor, 1961: 119). Lady Eleanor Smith, the Earl of Birkenhead's daughter, masqueraded as a Russian princess and deceived a young man with stories of her adventures (Mitford, 1960: 14–15).

Members of the BYP indulged in games, such as playing hide-and-seek in Selfridges, in the London Underground, and later, in the streets for paper chases and treasure hunts. The Duchess of Westminster and some of her friends started a new paper-chase: 'Zita and Eleanor were the hares with five minutes' start and they zigzagged about London using buses and undergrounds and leaving clues behind them as they went.' It was such an exciting game, they asked others to join them and they 'used to amuse [themselves] on blank afternoons by chasing each other around London. And that is how the Treasure Hunts began' (Grosvenor, 1961: 119–20).

Once men joined in, however, the whole character of treasure hunts changed; they became more wild and dangerous – and more overtly invasive of the lives of non-society people. People used cars and 'were tremendously noisy. There were no traffic lights and we used to race madly through the empty streets, rushing out to suburbs and the East End, regardless of the feelings of the inhabitants who were trying to get to sleep' (Grosvenor, 1961: 120).

Although the various hunts were much the same in structure, particular incidents made certain of them noteworthy. At one, participants caught a prominent MP removing a clue in little courtyard off St James's Street; there was a scuffle, but the clue was recovered and replaced on the sundial face. This particular hunt also sent the players to Buckingham Palace, where, according to the Duchess of Westminster,

> we bore down on the sleeping Palace with screeching tyres, jumped out of our cars and rushed up and down the railings, looking for the clue in the sentry boxes and shouting and screaming while every moment more cars kept arriving. Next day my father came home with the story of the extraordinary things that had happened at Buckingham Palace...; swarms of lunatics had tried to break in, the Captain of the Guard had turned out every available man, had telephoned for reinforcements, and, suddenly, the whole crowd had disappeared as mysteriously as they had arrived... I was able to fill in the gaps... the reason for our sudden departure was that we had found, at the foot of the memorial to Queen Victoria, the next clue; a bunch of white roses with a card, 'All good Cavaliers will know where this should be laid,' which had sent us helter-skelter down the Mall to Trafalgar Square. (Grosvenor, 1961: 121)

Not only did the BYP seem to regard the imperial icons of power as theirs to play with, but the good Cavaliers also showed no hesitation in transforming the public by-ways into their personal playgrounds – and as Cavaliers they were certainly not denied the right to do so.

The goal of the fashionable, youthful elite was to be as different from others as possible – not to be 'the best' but to alleviate boredom. Their continual need to indulge in new pastimes and to remove themselves from competition in appearance, intellectual accomplishments, or political sensibilities with the upwardly mobile middle classes, were what enabled upper-class youths to maintain their own differentiated status. They seemed to be trying their hardest to recreate the innocent and meaningless games of their childhoods – whether as an attempt to escape into an idealized past that never existed, as many popular psychologists of the day would have it, or as acts of rebellion against the Establishment's outmoded power structure (Middlemas, 1979). Their forte, according to Patrick Balfour, was 'the act of doing nothing gracefully' (1933: 61).

A more detailed examination of university students, society women, debutantes, and the young professionals of the City does reveal that their lives did not consist only of mad escapades and wild parties. Like their middle and working-class counterparts, most were intrigued by the cinema and the new craze for dancing. According to many of those with whom I was in touch, as well as texts on the subject, playing sports such as tennis, cricket, rugger, hockey, and billiards; watching football; hiking and walking in the countryside; playing the piano, listening to the wireless or records, and reading; going to dance halls and attending the theatre; playing cards; and participating in singing groups and amateur dramatic societies tended to occupy the leisure time of most young people of all classes in the 1920s (Clephane, 1933; Walvin, 1978; Walton and Walvin, 1983; Bruley, 2010: 60–72).

Although more mundane entertainments did not attract the media publicity to anywhere near the degree that the enactment of dramatic childhood games by the social, political, and artistic leaders of tomorrow did, the very organization and orderliness of such amusements provided the context from which the more celebrated activities gained their meaning. Baby and bath parties could thus be viewed merely as the entertainments of a society eager for playful abandonment after the intensity of war, industrial upheaval, political threats, and economic depression.

Designated no real responsibility and often denigrated for developing any keen interest beyond their wild social life, neither the BYP nor their less publicized age and status cohorts at university, in the City, at charity institutions, and in provincial areas had much purpose in society other than to entertain themselves.[13] Its women were ridiculed for working, its young men portrayed as effeminate for not working – and suspected of being communists if they took any more than a casual interest in the poor and working classes. Many a member of that group as well as those on the fringes of it seemed to take it upon themselves to represent their privileged status in a fashion so blatantly public that it could not be ignored. Yet because both in-group members and outsiders framed and designated what they did as 'play' (Bateson, 1972; Goffman, 1975, MacAloon, 1984), their protests against a society that offered them no practical function could not be seriously entertained.

Notes

1 Winifred Haward Hodgkiss of Dewsbury, Yorkshire was a lecturer in history at Bedford College, University of London in 1926. She was the author of *Two Lives* (*A People's History of Yorkshire*) (Barnsley: Yorkshire Art Circus, 1983).
2 Robert Winder has noted that Jewish immigrants tried to be more British than the British, founding Lyons tea shops, Marks and Spencer, and Sadler's Wells Theatre (Winder, 2004: 244–9), and a 'Jewish Lads' Brigade ... to promote Anglophilia' (Winder, 2004: 246).
3 David Cannadine also argued for the urban nature of society (Cannadine, 1980: 30).
4 Note the vast number of articles and photo-spreads' detailing Diana, Princess of Wales's charity work, before and especially after her divorce.
5 Ross McKibbin pointed out that 'the political role of Society was essentially one of public display ... An endlessly publicized glamour, an emphasis on smartness and modernity ... were powerful weapons in legitimizing privilege and making it acceptable to a mass electorate' (McKibbin, 2000: 33; see also Davidoff, 1973: 68–9).
6 The largest increase was in commercial work (factories, dockyards, arsenals), followed by local government, hotels, agriculture, and civil service. Working-class women were most often employed in factories (textile and munitions), while middle-class women were more often employed in office work as well as in medicine and engineering at significantly higher numbers than before 1914 (Thom, 2005).
7 Angela Woollacott made a similar point about working-class women. Like their male cohorts who became soldier heroes during wartime, when women workers sought to control their own destiny, 'they were harshly and publicly condemned ... and were widely criticized for exhibiting autonomy in their social behavior [sic] ... Because women's experience of war was constituted by the opening up of a temporary liminal gender space between normal expectations of feminine and masculine behavior [sic], in which women appropriated masculine roles and characteristics, it posed a threat to the hegemonic gender order of peacetime' (Woollacott, 1994: 10).
8 Despite the bad press, some titled women did work, as they had before the war. It became quite the thing for titled ladies to run high-class shops, though not everyone was pleased their attempts to make a living. One magazine editor received a letter from one indignant reader, upset because society girls' going on stage was making it difficult for professional actresses to do so ('The Editor to His Readers' Letters', 1926: 319).

9 See comments in Parliamentary debates directed to Lady Astor (House of Commons, 1926: 322).
10 Lenore Davidoff has noted that while much of what went on at country house parties looked like play, a great deal of serious, albeit informal, political and social business got done; hostesses were able to invite certain people to interact at private residences and not at formal political events (Davidoff, 1973: 17, 59–66).
11 An 'It' girl was a charming, sexy young woman of the day; novelist Elinor Glyn likely originated the term and published *It*, a novel on the subject, in 1927.
12 I am defining play as consisting of actions designated and bounded by a frame of 'not real' in time and intention (Huizinga, 1955; Caillois 1961; Bateson, 1972; Goffman, 1975).
13 See Davidoff regarding the 'jack of all trade' fate of the aristocracy (Davidoff, 1973: 98–9).

4

Fides est servanda: keeping the faith

> My parents [were] middle class Liberals ... They were third generation Jewish immigrants and excessively patriotic. I was brought up on stories of the First World War and the General Strike. My parents volunteered for service during the strike and obviously enjoyed the experience. My father was a conductor on the buses ... and my mother worked in the canteen in Baker Street station in London ... serving meals to the volunteers.
>
> They always spoke of this time as being a return to the spirit of war-time service i.e. a patriotic duty and were proud to have served. It never struck them that they were 'strike-breakers' as the General Strike appeared to be so abnormal that it could not last – it was 'not British'. (Zeitlyn, Letter, 1985a)

> [My mother] was a V.A.D. during the 1914–18 war ... My parents always spoke of themselves [during the strike] as 'we volunteers' and I think this was literally so – no payment made or offered (like blood-donors in Britain today). (Zeitlyn, Letter, 1985b)

> As far as I myself and my immediate circle were concerned I think that we were amazingly selfish ... we really only thought of ourselves. I can remember enjoying the General Strike very much with never a thought for the miners. We were quite sorry when it came to an end ... My contemporaries and I had no particular feelings about the rights or wrongs of the strike. (Lady Smith, MD, Letter, 1986)

Before, during, and after the General Strike, the government and media used metaphors of war, revolution, and sin to validate their response and persuade the populace of the wrongness of the strike and the necessity of national service. In so doing, they evoked key historic events that defined and reaffirmed the British character. As many scholars have noted, this period of British history was characterized by a 'moment of Englishness', a time between 1880 and 1920 when certain key characteristics crystallised into a popular sense of what it meant to be English *and* British, which as J. G. A. Pocock has noted, were more or less the same thing (Colls and Dodd, 1986; Paxman, 1999; Powell, 2002: 152–5; Kumar, 2003 and 2006; Ward, 2004: 45 *et passim*; Aughey, 2007: 76; Hutchinson *et al.*, 2007). Certain behaviour was expected, no matter the crisis. In wars, during revolutions, and in the face of religious apostasy the average Briton came through and carried on. He served his King and country, defended the Constitution, and kept his head. Anyone who deviated from this ethos in 1926, the Establishment dismissed, castigated, or condemned as a Communist. Ironically, and as if to assert the very strength of British character, much of the dramatic rhetoric in Parliament and in the newspapers stands in sharp relief to the commonsensical reaction of most citizens.[1] What follows takes on that rhetoric, the give and take among the media and parliamentary reactions, and intersperses it with citizen commentary.

As the stoppage wore on, metaphorical statements proliferated in the Conservative (the *British Gazette, Daily Telegraph, Daily News, Daily Mirror, Evening News,* and *Daily Sketch*) as well as the middle-of-the road press (*The Times*). As early as 3 May 1926, the *Daily Sketch* warned: 'Not since the war has the country been faced with a graver crisis than that which has been brought about by the decision of the General council of the Trades Union Congress to call a general strike' (Man In The Street, 1926: 7). The strike had yet to be called.

Other newspapers soon followed suit, proclaiming 'No surrender! Troops on Move' (*Daily Mirror*, 1926: 2; 'Food By Convoy', 1926: 2). The bellicose nature of the Government's anti-strike forces was left in no doubt as newspapers published photographs of convoys, armoured cars, our 'reserve army', Welsh Guardsmen in full kit marching to the London docks, tanks leaving Wellington Barracks in London, and barricades at Smithfield market. Photo captions reinforced this tone: 'The canteens were reminiscent of war days', 'Called Up', and 'Steel Helmets in Fleet Street: A Column of Troops in Full Marching Order' ('Pictures Of The Great Strike', 1926: 4; Sabretache, 1926a: 268; 'Equipped with Steel Helmets...', 1926: 423–4; 'And Eve Said Unto Adam', 1926: 347; 'Military Force Displayed But Not Used', 1926: 856–7; 'The Volunteers Play Their Part', 1926: 170, 176). The *Evening News* of 13 May 1926 – the day *after* Prime Minister Baldwin had urged the nation 'to forget all recrimination' – proclaimed 'The Bus Victory', in which 'London's best battle was fought and won, in the L.G.O.C. Depot at Chiswick. There, with Grenadiers standing with fixed bayonets at the gates, and with 4 armoured cars drawn up just outside, 2960 volunteers were trained ...' ('Bus Victory', 1926: 2).

In contrast, the Liberal press (the *Manchester Guardian, New Statesman,* and *Daily Chronicle*) tried to persuade its readers that military tactics were inappropriate. 'The action of the Government in abruptly breaking off negotiations ... drew a barbed-wire entanglement across the sole line of approach to national safety. In a conflict of this character let no one even think of 'fighting to a finish' ... Remember that the combatants are fellow citizens' ('The Liberal Point of View' 1926: 1). The *New Statesman* drew parallels to major uprisings in Ireland to point out the misguided logic of those who urged

> the Government to refuse to resume negotiations till the General Strike has been 'called off.' ... This, it may be admitted, was a logical enough attitude, if you care more for the vindication of the British Constitution than for the happiness of the British people ... [But] of what use it would be to vindicate the British Constitution if the peace and prosperity of the British nation were destroyed in the process ... The Ulster of Sir Edward Carson was not told that its demands could not be considered till it had laid down its arms. The Ireland of Michael Collins was told so for a time, but in the end negotiations took place ... Why then, should the constitutional issue be the supreme issue in an industrial dispute to-day if it was not the supreme issue in a really revolutionary dispute then? (Y. Y., 1926: 118–19)

Such attempts at reason were rare, however, and even the Liberal media began to depict the government's approach as defensive manœuvres against yet another in a series of historical attacks on the Constitution and all that true Englishmen held dear.

In Parliament, Tory and Liberal members (with the exception of Lloyd George)[2] differed only by degree in their condemnation of what they deemed a labour uprising. The right-wing Liberal MP Sir John Simon, first in Parliament to declare the strike unlawful on purely legal grounds, announced that the strike 'threatens the life of the nation and the liberty of all' (Editorial, 1926a: 2; 'Without Permission of the T.U.C', 1926: 2). But the basis of that threat was not the strike itself, as pronouncements in Parliament and by unauthorized judges made clear. It had to do with an attempt to carve out a position in the national polity by an entire class who had fought for their country's existence just a few years earlier.

This challenge called forth a series of responses that referenced cultural symbols deeply rooted in the national psyche. In particular, the basic 'English' concept of the 'sacred contract' (as one commentator called it), became an issue – as if a labour contract were the equivalent of the Puritans' covenant with their God. According to *The Times*'s editorial on 'The Astbury Judgement', an unauthorized opinion deeming the General Strike illegal because it caused men bound by employment contracts to violate them without due warning (see also Goodhart, 1927):

> Long ago, in the troublesome times of the seventeenth century, John Selden, the English apostle of ordered freedom, insisted upon the principle that all human society is based upon good faith between man and man. 'If two of us make a bargain, why should either of us stand to it? What need you care what you say, or what need I care what I say? Certainly because there is something about me that tells me, *Fides est servanda*.' ... Men have not a right to cease work who have made a bargain, a collective bargain, not to cease work except on certain

conditions which under the illegal orders of the Trades Union Council could not arise ... [A]ll progress depended upon ... the sacred character of contracts. ('Astbury Judgement', 1926: 3)

Noting similarities between the General Strike and other constitutional challenges, Hugh Cecil, Tory MP and younger son of the eleventh Lord Salisbury, claimed in a letter to *The Times* that the General Strike 'arose out of an industrial dispute, but it is directed to coercing the Government and Parliament, and it operates by punishing the community. The purpose is revolutionary, and the method is revolutionary ... The wars of the sixteenth and seventeenth century arose out of religious disagreements, but they were not theological controversies – they were wars' (Cecil, 1926: 3).

The ease and frequency with which contemporaries invoked and combined key historic symbols like the Reformation and Civil War, as well as more modern threats such as the Russian Revolution, Irish uprisings, and the Great War, made evident just how threatening the General Strike was to the British Establishment in the 1920s. The strike was designed to disrupt 'business as usual' among the men who had declared themselves defenders of the faith. It was not just an attack on the mine owners and other businessmen; this was, declared the *Daily Telegraph*, a 'War On Work-Girls' (1926: 2). Yet for the government, much of the media, and the Establishment, the General Strike was much more than a war for industrial rights; it was a secular devil whose spectre already overshadowed another great empire, and it was to be condemned as such. Thus, Cardinal Bourne, the Archbishop of Westminster, proclaimed the strike 'a sin against the obedience which we owe to God' ('The Strike a Sin', 1926: 3).[3] The Lord Advocate and Chief Commissioner in Edinburgh declared: 'We are fighting for freedom, for democratic government, and for the breaking of that type of tyranny which has reached its culmination in Russia' ('An Improvement in Scotland', 1926: 3). By drawing such comparisons, editorialists were able to differentiate between loyal British workers and alien infiltrators out to destroy the nation. As the *Tatler*'s A. A. B. explained,

> Philosophically considered, the General Strike is as important an event in our history as the Great War. Just as the Great War rid us of the sabre-rattling of Berlin, the General Strike has freed us from the strike-rattling of the Trades Union Congress. The triple alliance of miners, railwaymen, and transport workers has been dissolved as effectually as the Dreikaiser Bund that dominated Europe for so many years. Never again will the mouthing of Mssrs. Cook, Purcell, Bevin, and agitators mysteriously connected with the Third International of Moscow, make our flesh creep with threats of revolution ... The curious thing is that all the men named above as responsible for the call to strike seem to have acted half-heartedly, doubtfully, even unwillingly. What, then, was the unknown force, the person or persons,

pushing them from behind? ... [C]ould it have been any of the emissaries of the Soviet or the Third International, who ... are always lurking about the country? (A. A. B. 1926a: 240)

There was a careful line to be walked in such indictments. Since it was not politic to call four million striking workers hooligans or revolutionaries, the blame for leading them astray was put on 'leaders' specifically classified as 'not English' – the facts not withstanding. Labour leaders so tarred included Secretary of the MFGB, A. J. Cook – not the Welshman he was often identified as being but a Devonshire man; Harry Pollit, head of the Communist Party and in jail for seven months at the time; Asian Indian MP Shapurgi Saklatvala; and others publicly associated with the Communist Party. The mainstream and right-wing media depicted such men as being under Moscow's sway and all too eager to lead gullible union members down the red path to perdition. As the strike progressed, Cook himself apotheosized in the popular mind into a satanic archetype, folded in with others of his ilk. Mrs Nancy H. Burton, an alumna of St Hugh's College, Oxford, explained that 'the solid middle class regarded Arthur Cook, the miners' leader, as a devil incarnate – talked of him in terms like the ones we later used of Hitler. He seemed such an enormous threat to the peace and security of our lives' (Burton, Letter, 1987). Such fears, triggered by the Russian Revolution and Labour's solid support of the 'Hands off Russia' campaign, as well as the Clydeside political strikes of 1921, were all too real to be ignored. Anything that deviated from mainstream notions of Britishness had to be defined as alien ('Volunteers – And The Others', 1926: 3; see Ward, 2004: 103).

Reports in the *British Gazette*, the strike-time quarter-folio newspaper edited by Winston Churchill, and other papers fanned ordinary people's fears by headlining such stories as: 'Foul Play on Railways', 'Innuendos about a Soviet contribution to the TUC', and 'False News'. Bruno Marmorstein, a retired barrister, remembered, 'We took it seriously ... [and] felt it was a threat to the government, a threat to order ... We felt there was something sinister and menacing about this ... [According to the newspapers] it was sort of a war fomented by Russian gold, Soviet gold ...' (Marmorstein, Interview, 1985). Mrs Mary Chitty, a Girton alumna, admitted, 'I suppose there was a fear lurking at the back of one's mind. After all, the Russian Revolution was still young' (Chitty, Letter, 1986a).

This notion that Russian communists were responsible for the General Strike came from the populist as well as the elite press, which variously invoked versions of this international legend. The *Daily Mail* insisted that the strike was part of a full-blown 'red plot that was hatched in 1918 [with] revolution the aim' of already (falsely) implicated conspirators such as Zinoviev, a 'Soviet official' supposedly directing the Labour Party ('Zinoviev on the Strike', 1926: 1).[4] On the same page, the headlines of another article, unrelated to the supposed 'red plot', trumpeted 'Surrender of the Revolutionaries' and 'Triumph for the People', lent credence to the neighbouring article. Using a different tactic, the more upper-class *Tatler* magazine printed seven 'cartoons from foreign and American papers dealing with the General Strike ... the general world opinion seems to be that the original inspiration of the movement for a general strike is Russian in origin' ('Through Foreign Glasses', 1926: 238).

In a war well-defined sides are crucial: us and them, heroes and enemies. And the papers were adept at dehumanizing 'enemies'. Besides laying the blame on Cook and the TUC, the London press portrayed those at the greatest geographical and cultural distance from the Empire's capital as the source of disorder (e.g. 'Riotous Scenes in Glasgow', 1926: 2; 'Glasgow Rioting', 1926: 3). To preserve a cohesive notion of British identity, most mainstream newspapers did not fault striking workers for any violence that occurred. Instead, *The Times* as well as the *Daily Telegraph* and other papers noted that 'gangs of ruffians' or 'youthful hooligans', not strikers, were responsible for damages done to transport vehicles ('Attack on Omnibuses', 1926: 2; *Daily Telegraph*, 1926a: 1; 'A Few Reflections', 1926: 2; *Children's Newspaper*, 1926: 1–2).

Compared to hooligans, communist leaders, and aliens, the press portrayed the strikers as well-behaved if politically unsophisticated blokes. Fortunately, Herbert Smith, president of the Miners Union, was a typical Yorkshireman, noted the *Daily Graphic*. While the ethnocentric racism of what follows grates on twenty-first-century ears, the perspective reinforces the writer's intent to differentiate the English from all others.[5] 'Suppose', the editorialist asked,

> that [Herbert Smith] had been a lean man in a sombrero instead of a stout man in a cloth cap, might not the temptation to theatricalise the whole affair have had dangerous encouragement? All the familiar phrases about sinister forces working underground seem rather absurd when set beside this portrait of Yorkshire in the flesh ... The Yorkshireman is as tenacious as his terrier, and such obduracy may work fatally at such a time as this. But the notion of Mr. Smith as Moscow's pawn could not survive the spectacle of his cap and carriage. (Onlooker, 1926: 6)

Most commentary specifically set the peaceful strikers in opposition to foreigners and hooligans. The *Morning Post* reported an absence of incident between strikers and police or soldiers, even in those areas of London where it was considered likely – except from those from whom such behaviour was to be expected.

> Indeed, the general attitude of the strike pickets and their comrades towards troops ... has been one of good-humoured chaff. There have been several

> instances where strikers and their wives have expressed open satisfaction at the presence of the soldiers with its guarantee against 'deeds of frightfulness' by the hooligan element.
> Particularly has this been the case in 'Dockland', where many of the men had protested that the disturbances during the first two days of the strike were engineered and carried into effect by roughs – including a considerable sprinkling of foreigners – from the East End. ('How London Was Made Safe', 1926: 4)

That last was a gloss for Eastern European Jewish immigrants whom mainstream Londoners believed to be Communist agitators – definitely not British and certainly not English (Pugh, 2006).

At an even further remove were several accounts that described an almost picnic-like atmosphere in reports that indicted nearly everyone on the strikers' side but the strikers. At the pre-strike May Day gathering at Speakers' Corner in Hyde Park,

> The huge crowd that swarmed over ... the Park might have been a Pleasant Saturday Afternoon gathering. There were no mutterings of revolution in the air ... Some of the demonstrators with their families encamped on the grass in perfect oblivion of the speeches [by Cook, Mr Saklatvala, and others]. People strolled over from Mayfair before tea to listen to the orators, and a young man in top-hat and morning-coat was neither mobbed nor booed, or even chafed. The hundreds of policemen sat on the railings and smoked cigarettes, and the only people who seemed at all intent on the mission of the day were the groups of Indians and East-End aliens. Some of these who got excited were told to shut up with shouts of, 'You aren't British'. The alien demonstrators, too, seemed to be the only people with voices and spirit enough to chant the 'Red Flag'. (London, 1926a: 5)

A similar report in *The Times* describing the crowd behaviour of those watching a military convoy to the London docks noted, 'there was no sign of hostility ... The few remarks levelled at the soldiers were made either by women or by young men of obviously foreign extraction ...' ('Undemonstrative Crowds', 1926: 3). Even the *Children's Newspaper* (overtly apolitical but a strong supporter of the Establishment's Conservative values), which marvelled at 'the friendliness and humour that were seen everywhere' and the 'patience of a much-tried people', took a conciliatory attitude toward the strikers:

> We hope that none of our readers will feel that the millions of our working people who have been idle for nine days are disloyal to their country; or want to see it brought to the miserable pass that Russia has come to. If there is one thing that has been made clear in these wonderful nine days it has been the solid loyalty of that great mass of people who are the backbone of our nation. There cannot be a Class War in England; the marvellous way in

which all classes rallied to the Government is everlasting proof of that. (Mee, 1926: 1)

Much of the media contended that English workers were too complacent and short-sighted to be successful revolutionaries. According to the *Daily Graphic*, 'the English trade unionist is little affected by [the] pedantic phraseology of the class-war manual, nor does he follow their romantic glances at the red horizon. His error is not in looking too far, like a scatter-brained romantic, but in staring too closely at his own job without relating it to industry as a whole' (Onlooker, 1926: 6). *Tatler* reporter A. A. B. noted that the 'revolutions of the seventeenth century were the affairs of the aristocracy. The British masses will never be good revolutionists. Their sense of humour and their love of settled government are too strong; besides, they are too well off' (1926b: 288).

In sum, the General Strike was fundamentally different from uprisings elsewhere because it was so characteristically British. Many articles presented a picture of a society that was well organized by the volunteers and barely affected by the strikers. From all sources came descriptions of cheerful, patriotic, orderly, well-mannered, unflustered British folks (strikers and volunteers) 'carrying on' 'business as usual'. Such expressions specifically evoked wartime usage – carrying on in a crisis, the country's purpose closely allied with that of business. Not carrying on meant disrupting business.

Such a scenario made for a paradoxical situation if one happened to compare it to reports of all those Communist-inspired attacks staged by hooligans and mobs in northern cities and London's East End. Yet there seemed to be a concerted media campaign to have it both ways, and reports of order throughout the land worked to transcend such contradictions. From across the political spectrum and in stark contrast to reports of revolutionary plots, came headlines such as 'Order and Quiet Throughout the Land', 'Work as Usual', 'Uneventful Days in Yorkshire', 'Patriotic Women – All Classes Helping the State', 'No Scenes of Disorder – Government Plans Works Well – Volunteers in Great Number', 'Philosophic Business Men Thousands Walk to Work', and 'No Disorders of any Kind' (*British Gazette*, 1926: 1–4; *Emergency Press*, 1926: 1).

Even the theatre went on as usual, according to *The Times*, which stated: 'No change has been made in the Shakespeare programme at Stratford-on-Avon' ('Shakespeare at Stratford', 1926: 4). The *Evening News*, however, indicated that London theatres were not doing quite so well: '20 London theatres are now closed; ... 2 big variety theatres may close at the week-end, and other managers are today conferring about suspension of programmes. At one West End theatre only £5 was received at an evening performance' ('Strike Brevities', 1926a: 2). Despite problems with theatre attendance, many other businesses claimed to be doing even better than usual. A typical article in the

Evening News reported that 'volunteers at Hull docks are unloading ships quicker than the regular men do' ('Beaten at their Own Game', 1926: 2).

According to Sir John Foster Fraser in the *Tatler*, Prime Minister Baldwin's 'call to the nation to "Stand Fast!" was admirably timed and met with an immediate and magnificent response from a nation which prefers law and order to being dragooned by Trade Unionism'. 'No wonder foreigners cannot understand the English. Sometimes I wonder whether the English understand themselves', wrote Fraser. The nation had experienced the ultimate tragedy: 'a rebellion to overthrow constitutional government', but 'we have kept on smiling'. In any other country – the United States, France, or Germany – troops and gunmen would have been slaughtering one another. In England (not Great Britain) 'the nation remained good humoured' (Fraser, 1926: 236; see also Clynes, 1937: 80, 82).

Yet such an unhappy event was not the fault of the 'hundreds of thousands of workers who joined the general strike'. They were merely acting

> with an inbred British regard for authority – they recognised their duty to obey their leaders and chiefly, because they felt they should give a helping hand to their mates in the mines.
> ... By all historical precedents there should have been bloodshed, our streets should have been barricaded, valuable property destroyed by general arson. These tragedies have been avoided, not because the struggled lacked reality but because the fight was tremendously sincere.
> ... Never in the story of the industrial world was there such a dramatic stoppage. Other countries were aghast. They thought a revolution had taken place. But they did not know England. (Fraser, 1926: 237)

Despite such efforts to reassert the essential national character of the striking workers, the mainstream media did not go so far as to try to persuade the general public that the strikers were in the right.

The Labour press (the *British Worker*, *Daily Herald*, *Scottish Worker*, and locally produced union newssheets) were quite intent on making readers understand that workers, even coal miners – the militant red centre of the British labour movement – comported themselves as proper Englishmen. Instead of mounting the barricades, striking workers busied themselves with concerts, church-going, sing-songs, soup kitchens, and organized sports ('Nation Behind the TUC', 1926: 2; *British Worker*, 1926a: 4 and 1926b: 1–2; 'Comments', 1926: 14; 'Strikers' Parade', 1926: 5; see also Norman, Letter, 1975; Bruley, 2010: 60–85). The *British Worker* and other sympathetic papers tried to establish the strikers' role in maintaining both order and solidarity among their ranks – especially in comparison to the government's militaristic (i.e. non-British from the strikers' perspective) tactics involving tanks, barricading ports, and parades of soldiers' carrying bayonets ('Barricades in the London

Streets', 1926: 174). Besides reiterating that the General Strike was not an attack on the Constitution, strike bulletins maintained the 'Britishness' of their own conduct – as opposed to the incompetent and dangerous behaviour of the volunteers.

But such efforts were largely fruitless, since few non-labour sympathizers actually read the working-class papers. Most middle and upper-class people, as well as non-striking workers, reacted indignantly against what they regarded as an organized force aimed at coercing them, hurting their livelihoods, impinging on their pastimes and ways of getting to work, hearing the news, or feeding their children. Even so, the majority did not think matters were quite so far gone as some in government and inflammatory media reports implied.[6] As Ruth Connolly pointed out, we 'didn't even think nationally in those days' (Letter, 1986). Mrs A. M. S. Maddox, a Girton alumna, explained, 'though we were all sorry for the miners, we thought the Strike must be defeated, as it was based on the rule of force rather than law, and we all heartily encouraged the volunteers. No, it never entered our heads that it would lead to revolution ... I just feel instinctively that revolution didn't happen in Britain' (Maddox, Letter, 1987). Still others felt that revolution was unlikely because 'the majority of the "working" people were not really in favour of it' (Oatley, Letter, 1987b).

Lord Brockway noted that while the General Strike 'wasn't planned as such ... I remember James Maxton, the leader of the ILP, saying that it was a revolutionary action and out of it a revolution might occur. But to be honest, my meeting with the Manchester and Salford Trades Council and others, didn't suggest that they were thinking in terms of revolution at all' (Brockway, Interview, 1986). According to Lady Wilhelmine Harrod, a general's daughter, 'I certainly do not remember any talk of a possible revolution – and I do not think for a moment that ordinary people were as panicky as that ...' (Harrod, Letter, 1986). Even Sid Rosenberg, an East End furniture-maker who went out on strike in 1926, agreed: 'In our own mind we never thought there'd be a revolution ... Now you got these riots and burning and looting, but in those days you didn't have no burning and looting ... You see in the twenties it was entirely different, a different world! A different outlook!' (Rosenberg, Interviews, 1985 and 1986).

While most people did not view the General Strike as a revolution, many of those who volunteered did regard it as an unreasonable attack upon the whole country. Leslie Dover, employed as a clerk by the British Iron and Steel Federation, volunteered 'because I felt it to be intolerable that any minority should bring the whole country to a standstill by sheer force' (Dover, Letter, 1986b). Dorothy Whittle told me that for most 'ordinary people, the General Strike was a nuisance in getting to and fro to our work and like most strikes, did no one any good, least of all the people on Strike' (Whittle, Letter, 1986).

T. G. Benson,[7] a Clare alumnus, on the staff at Harrow public school during the strike, recalled:

> The atmosphere was very calm, and no sense of class war. It was a challenge to the public, and our reactions were towards carrying on as best we could, as for example patrolling urban areas in the role of volunteer police (a very peaceful job, nothing at all of note, and naturally rather tedious) ... Accounts of how supplies were coming to London were stimulating, for example how milk churns came to Hyde Park for distribution. We carried on school without a stop. (Benson, Letter, 1986a)

> We didn't smell revolution in [it], no, nor was it a lark, but it gave an opportunity to look outside and we certainly needed to be jerked out of our complacency ((then) and now!). (Benson, Letter, 1986b)

Those who joined up as volunteers did so because it was what one did in a crisis. Volunteers' motives ranged from feelings of duty and patriotism to a desire not to miss the fun, from a fondness for larks to a desire to earn some money. People volunteered because 'everyone else' was doing it. Ken Harman, whose father worked in the railway offices for fifty years and drove a train in the strike, noted: 'I think the decision to drive a train must have been partly philanthropic, partly political, partly class. Most of the office staff would have regarded themselves as middle-class and were probably mainly Conservative supporters' (Harman, Letter, 1985b).

Despite this overwhelming political party loyalty, most volunteers insisted that they were not acting politically: they were not against Labour and for the Conservatives or Liberals; they were *for* their country. Elizabeth Stamp wrote:

> My father, who was killed in the [second] war, and his brother – now Lord——, manned the signal box at Bletchley Junction (after only a few hours training) during the General Strike. There was a rather splendid photo of them in the *Illustrated London News* of the time [see figure 4.1 (d)]. They were currently students at Cambridge ... Don't call it strike-breaking. They didn't see it that way. Hundreds of students offered to help 'to keep the country going'. (Stamp, Letter, 1985)

Most people felt that, regardless of the rightness of the miners' position, a General Strike was not a 'British' solution. Even Allene Toms, then a 14-year-old working-class schoolgirl whose father was a tailor and whose mother had been in service before marriage, recalled:

> Although ... we knew it was all very tragic because it was awful about that time ... we used to get the Welsh miners ... They'd walk from Wales and they would be singing in the streets and they were starving! They'd got no soles to their shoes. Of course work was very difficult to get, and it was all, very tragic, but when it came to the General Strike – well, I think most people thought, 'Oh well, we can't have this, you know ... No, can't let anybody get away with that.' (Toms, Interview, 1985; and see Massingham, Letter, 1986) (see figure 4.2)

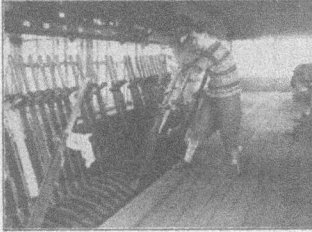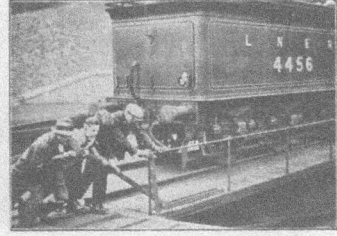

4.1 'Volunteers on the railways during the General Strike. "Nothing was more remarkable during the General Strike than the skill and efficiency with which the railways were carried on, largely by amateur workers. During the latter part of the crisis, thousands of trains were running."'

(a) *upper left*: 'Right away!: A volunteer guard on the Metropolitan Railway in charge of a train during the strike'
(b) *upper middle*: 'Important duty at a London terminus: a volunteer adjusting the points outside King's Cross station'
(c) *upper right*: 'Ensuring the safe passage of Main Line trains into King's Cross: another volunteer adjusting points.'
(d) *middle left*: 'Signalmen in Fair Isle Jerseys and "Plus Fours": Two Volunteer Undergraduates in Charge of the Chief Signal Box at Bletchley Station'
(e) *middle right*: 'Strenuous work at a London Terminus: a squad of volunteers turning a locomotive on a turn-table at King's Cross station.'
(f) *lower left*: 'The arrival of the "Mauretania" at Southampton: Some of the volunteers who acted as shore-gangs loading a passenger's luggage into a car for the journey to London.'
(g) *Lower right*: 'As to the manner born: a volunteer engine-driver and his fireman on their locomotive during the strike.'

4.2 Allene and Arthur Toms

Sir Robert Speed, a (Trinity College) Cambridge undergraduate who volunteered at the Dover docks, echoed those sentiments: 'I thought the miners had solid grounds for complaint – bad working conditions – low pay; but I was against a *General* strike' (Speed, Letter, 1986).

Further evidence of this very natural disjunction between cause and effect was the overwhelming reason most people gave for volunteering: the Great War. The paradigmatic power of that time cannot be underestimated. Margaret Diggle, an alumna of Girton College, Cambridge, wrote that her 'concern was mainly with the prevention of war. The memories of the first war were a haunting cloud' (Diggle, Letter, 1986). Andrew Man, who had just left his public school in 1926 and whose father was a vicar in Kent, wrote:

> At that time, [we] ... all realised that the miners may well have had a case for better conditions against the Coalowners. But their action and that of the other unions involved in the General Strike ... was irresponsible and unpatriotic. The Country had rallied as a team to defeat Germany and her allies in the 1914–18 war which had ended less than eight years before, and there could never be a sound reason for any citizen, by himself or collectively, to endeavour to bring the day to day life of their Country to a halt. (Man, Letter, 1985)

For the most part, and despite the strong gut reactions for and against the strike, the public had little explicit information about the strike once it started. With the press nearly halted, all people knew was that transportation and newspapers had been severely restricted. Lady Smith, MD, then a junior doctor in London, told me, 'this sympathy for the miners ... was rather for us masked by the transport [problem]' (Smith, Interview, 1987).

The apparently united stance of government, mine owners, volunteers, and media dominated the national consciousness; it rallied people by evoking their common notions of Britishness. The war medals the strikers were urged to wear by the TUC leaders ('Wear Your Medals', 1926: 4) made little impression on those convinced that they were defending Great Britain and not taking part in a political contest at all. Miners were not a part of everyday life for most urban dwellers, even less so in the 1920s than in the 1980s, when there was virtually no mass media other than newspapers. As Lady Smith recalled, 'I expect it was very different if one lived in a mining area. But in London miners are strange creatures that you don't really know very much about. It didn't hit anybody personally in London ... It was just too distant' (Smith, Interview, 1987).

Phineas May,[8] a former special constable and newspaper cartoonist from an upper-middle-class family, told me, 'You knew what a hell of a life a miner had ... But you can't let a whole city close down and therefore you do what you can to keep things going.' Patriotism was an overriding motivation. 'I think you volunteered for service because you felt that it was a proper thing to do', May continued. 'In the same way, when there's a war you join up, or join some service that will help your country' (May, Interview, 1986; see figure 4.3) 'The young men of my generation were very

4.3 Phineas May in special constable uniform, 1926

conscious of the terrible threat to our freedom of 1914–18', Cyril Spencer[9] wrote. 'The general strike was regarded as another threat and all of us, as our forbears did, wanted to do our bit' (Spencer, Letter, 1986a). David Fremantle (see figure 2.3) echoed that ethos: 'My family had always been a service family; for generations we served the country in one service or another, mostly in the railway ... To have not done what one could – it wouldn't seem to be the patriotic thing to do, anymore than not to join up in a case of war' (Interview, 1986). Yet, Fremantle noted, to compare the General Strike to the beginning of a war 'seems rather shaming in a way ... because it was erected against our own people in a way. I mean we were taking sides against our own compatriots ... It was to compare it with the war against foreign nationals' (Fremantle, Interview, 1986).

In fact, the majority of volunteers were not aware of the political issues – radio broadcasts were few and far between, and most newspapers were neither printed nor delivered, a situation dramatically different from our present-day lives, as many took pains to note. Ellen Havelock, a Girton alumna, recalled,

> The call went out 'our country needs you'!! And, of course, the best and the brightest responded including my fiancé who joined up at once and dashed off to London with a truck full of volunteers as special constables. When my fiancé returned a few days later he reported that they had been given hard hats and kaki [sic] arm bands and did a lot of waiting around to be told what to do. My impression is that the most they really did was to direct traffic.
>
> A year later we visited my fiancé's spunky little grandmother in London – She, out of a tiny budget, had sent money to the miners – out of sympathy for their terrible working conditions and minimal pay.
>
> I have wondered whether my husband ever questioned his hasty response because his sympathies were with Labour. (Havelock, Letter, 1987)

Again and for most of the middle class, participation rather than political affiliation was the key – to keep things moving, almost regardless of where that motion led. Sylvia Makower, the daughter of 'landed gentry' and at Newnham College, Cambridge in 1926, wrote:

> I have two clear recollections from the 1926 General Strike, and both throw light on the delight with which the Academic young of that day seized the chance it gave them to do something more practical than Academic studies, and at the same time to win social approval, not usually available as a result of neglect of their studies.
>
> My first recollection is of carloads of undergraduates ... setting off in high glee, in the streets of Cambridge, to do volunteer work of various kinds. I noticed with interest that those who were going to help the strikers and those who were on the side of the Establishment travelled cheerfully in the same car without apparent ill will. The strikers' struggle was not the point, the escape to 'real' work was the big thrill. (Makower, Letter, 1987a)

As Makower and others have noted, for undergraduate volunteers especially, the strike was a working holiday, a welcome break in the ordinary routine, and differing political views were taken as a matter of course, a difference of opinion among gentlemen, not altogether dissimilar to the difference between German and English officers during the Great War. Sylvia Makower's recollections elucidate this point.

> I wrote to my mother that the safety of the Realm demanded that she should lend me her car to make it possible for me to sign on as Volunteer Motor Transport in an office somewhere near the Guildhall in Cambridge ... I knew she would approve of my working for the Establishment, though like the young men I didn't worry which side I was on, myself. I just wanted the car.
> ... [T]he first (and only) job I was given during the strike was to drive two stout and elderly women to the funeral of their sister somewhere near Nottingham. They ... were enraptured by the delight of the drive, striving to express sorrow at intervals but unable to suppress their surprise and joy. Cars were not yet in very general use in 1926, and this was their first experience of such a drive through the lovely English countryside. (Makower, Letter, 1987b)[10]

Although many expressed some sympathy toward the miners, most were unable to see the strikers' point of view. Instead, the volunteers accepted the government's opinion, which enabled them to escape the paradox their very actions created. They could say and believe that volunteering was not strike-breaking, since it was directed against those 'others' or, more to the point, *for* the country, and not against the miners or the strikers themselves. Many volunteers regarded the strikers as essentially harmless good chaps, variously misled by Communists, betrayed by their leaders, or hoodwinked by the Russians into this unnecessary show of support for their mates. As Andrew Man wrote:

> The feeling between the Strikers and us volunteers was always friendly – bar an incident here and there of harmless stonethrowing [*sic*] – troublemakers were few and far between – in fact, hardly noticeable ... The 1926 General Strike was a 'disagreement' between the citizens of Great Britain to be settled, by and large in a Civilized way. Strikes since, and especially these days, have foreign connections, often undemocratically elected leaders, and too often are vicious in execution. (Man, Letter, 1985)

Underlying everything, however, was the deeply held belief that the British were essentially different (Ward, 2004: 103; Aughey, 2007: 32–8, 62–79). Joan Bedale, a graduate of Girton College, Cambridge, in France at the time of the strike, was amazed at the fears of her Parisian hosts.

> Being at heart essentially British in my attitude, I was unable to take the Strike as seriously as did all my French friends and acquaintances ... 'L'Angleterre, elle est finie' was their opinion. They were amazed to find that I did not sit and weep

for the downfall of my country. To them it was just the Russian Revolution of 1917 all over again. Every day they expected to hear that our King and Queen and all their children had been put to death. (Bedale, Letter, 1987)

Mainstream media accounts expressed this sentiment with much more dramatic hyperbole than did individuals. The *Children's Newspaper*, never one to understate matters, proclaimed,

> it is an hour of triumph for the most precious asset of our English-speaking race, the common sense that saves us from a host of troubles ...
> It has been a time without parallel in living memory – a time indeed without any parallel in British history, unless we think of the civil war in Cromwell's days ... If there is one thing that has been made clear in these wonderful nine days it has been the solid loyalty of that great mass of people who are the backbone of our nation.
> There cannot be a Class War in England; the marvellous way in which all classes rallied to the Government is everlasting proof of that ...
> Our people are not to be frightened by bogeys. They know quite well that Old England has been tried in the fires as no other nation in the world has been tried, and that she is pulling through ... The General Strike began at midnight; it ended at high noonday, with the Sun shining bright in the heavens, the Sun that shall never, never set, please God, on British liberty. (Mee, 1926: 1)

Particularly noticeable about all these attempts to describe British character put to the test was the way the papers claimed it for 'everyone' of 'all classes' – thus obliterating the dissenting definition put forward by the TUC and the striking workers. A column entitled 'The Fortnight of Folly – Brave Volunteers – Miners Beware! – Back to Work Again' in the *Daily Express*, 'the organ of imperial democratic opinion' (which added the sobriquet, 'for King and Country' to its banner on 5 May 1926), especially illustrates this point – the inherent heroism of the common Briton – *because* of his or her Britishness.

> It is easy, and in some quarters popular, to make fun of patriotism, but the love of one's country is still the first of the virtues. Patriotism is not only shown on the battlefields of war. It inspires the village girl's free gift of service or the tired clerk's unobtrusive performance of some humdrum necessity for the sake of the State, as much as the valour that earns the Victoria Cross or the statesmanship that is crowned with the thanks of the nation. ('Fortnight ...', 1926: 2)

At a time when the Empire was already in decline, the strike provided an opportunity to define Britishness in opposition to others – to those others outside the Empire as well as to those aliens within (Barth, 1969). One sign of this phenomenon, an article in the *Daily Graphic* was at pains to point out, was the English obsession with order and the law. 'The strike is now over, but, so far, the most surprising thing about the General Strike, and one which has excited the mingled astonishment and admiration of foreigners, is that not a single shot has been fired. No other country in the world could have kept its record so clean ... Truly, we are an amazing people' (Candidus, 1926: 2).

Part of the mythos of the General Strike was the belief that the British, as a unique people, got through it without violence, disorder, chaos, serious injury, death, or destruction. The United States and France, not surprisingly given their own experiences with violent revolutions, figured prominently in these comparisons; the Russian Revolution was apparently a little too close to cite for reassurance, however. The *Daily News* editorial of 14 May 1926 noted, 'It has been the best humoured civil war in history. Heavens, what blood would have flowed in France, in Italy, in America with a tithe of some commotion and challenge! I repeat, we are a great people' (Editorial, 1926: 2). The Liberal *Manchester Guardian* published similar comments from its French correspondent on the same day, coming 'consequently [to] the general conclusion that the British are a people apart, not subject to ordinary rules' ('French Perplexities – Commentators Nonplussed by British Calm', 1926: 2; see 'The Strike and After', 1926: 6).

By reifying Britishness, the strike enabled Britons to criticize and poke fun at foreigners – particularly at their eternal rivals, the French. According to the satirical *Punch*, for example, 'as many as 228 demonstrators and 118 police were injured in the course of the Jeanne D'Arc fête in Paris. It is rumoured that the French intend to borrow our next general strike and use it as a Bank Holiday' ('Charivaria', 1926a: 537). Claiming the style in which the General Strike was conducted as peculiarly British, the press was able to point fingers at 'foreigners', both at home and abroad, who supposedly instigated it, or at those countries that – according to the British press – could never have carried it off with the same good humour and sense of order endemic to the British character. Rather than admit to a failure of government or industrial organization, blows were directed – in fun and in all seriousness – at those outsiders who threatened the status quo *because* they were not English. As one 'British Observer' wrote to *The Times*,

> The true lesson of the General Strike, in the eyes of those 'foreign observers' ... is not that England is unlucky to have had to withstand the assault of reactionary Germanism and revolutionary extremism but that the English people are singularly fortunate in possessing a balance of mind and a dispassionate determination ... Not a few foreign observers feel, England may have helped to save Europe from the tyranny of minorities on the Right and on the Left. ('British Observer', 1926: 3)

In sum, the government and papers sympathetic to it attempted to create the impression that not only were volunteers, military, police, special constables, and patriotic citizens promoting and engaging in orderly behaviour, but that they were able also to control the disorderly elements – strikers, communists, socialists, foreigners, hooligans, and unruly women – by their actions and example. The strikers, and papers in accord with their point of view, also tried to put forth this desirable quality as their own (e.g. 'Nation Behind the TUC', 1926: 2). So far as they were concerned, inept and reckless volunteers, the government, and especially Churchill constituted disorder. But organized labour's tactics persuaded very few.

Those allied with the Establishment attempted to convince people that the national community should resist threats to their Constitution, King and Parliament, and most of all order, by way of patriotic action as the government defined it. Community, nation, and public – for those opposed to the strike – came to include only those who agreed with the government's policy of refusing to acknowledge the legitimacy of the TUC General Council's actions and authority. Parliament represented order only of a certain sort (i.e. hierarchy and non-violence to property and volunteers). The government as well as the right wing and centrist media framed the General Strike as threatening that order; by claiming it was instigated by so-called foreigners, it was designated 'not British'.[11] In response, the community marshalled all of its cheerfully dutiful forces to put those outsiders back into their social and economic place, exclude them from the national body through unemployment or imprisonment, and make sure that all who remained behaved in uniquely British ways, ways that the volunteers were eager to demonstrate.

Notes

1 Of those who have focused on the volunteers, neither Archard *et al.* (1972) nor Wrigley (1982; 1984a; 1984b) found that either the print media (local or otherwise) or the BBC had much, if any, influence on their informants' perceptions about the strike – in contrast to Anne Perkins' take (2006). Crompton (1988) credited the media with rather more clout than did Wrigley, however. Most of Archard's correspondents looked on the *British Gazette* as the propaganda sheet that it was, and few ever saw the *British Worker*. Even fewer owned or had access to a wireless or a crystal set, contrary to the claims of BBC historian, Stephen Usherwood (1972).

2 A notable exception among the Liberal leadership was Lloyd George, who sympathized with the strike, much to the dismay of Lord Asquith (Jones, 1951 and 1969; Campbell, 1977: 136–40; Wrigley, 1990). Lloyd George's stance, which put him at odds with the leadership of the Liberal Party, precipitated the Liberal Party crisis in which Asquith was the loser (Campbell, 1977: 144–56).

3 In contrast, the *Daily Mail* did not publish the Archbishop of Canterbury's plea for peace and resumed negotiations; neither the BBC nor the *British Gazette* recognized its existence until the document became so well publicized as to cause a debate in Parliament.
4 In 1924, Labour lost the national election, in part due to a fraudulent but successful attempt to implicate the Labour Party and Ramsay MacDonald in a communist conspiracy. Though the infamous Zinoviev Letter, which 'revealed' this plot, had been proved false, its spirit was revived. The *Daily Mail* printed purported comments from Zinoviev in Moscow to 'prove' that the strike had been planned in 1918 'when the first Council of Action [local strike committee] was organized. At that time an attempt was made to rule the country by committees of workers. Many years have passed of very hard work by the Communist International, and those committees ... have now grown into giants ... displaying their force against the bourgeoisie to-day' ('Zinoviev ...', 1926: 1).
5 See Arthur Aughey's discussion of the 'English exemplary' (2007: 32–41).
6 Lloyd George, though he 'opposed the General Strike', did not view it as 'a revolutionary threat' (Campbell, 1977: 138).
7 Benson was later a lecturer at London University in Bantu languages.
8 Phineas May's mother was Sir Herbert Samuel's cousin.
9 Spencer worked at a small Manchester business in 1926.
10 Makower told me that 'my family regarded me as a "Red" but when I reached Newnham I found I appeared to be a stuffy, establishment figure to my fellows there. I was prepared to play it either way. It made arguing more amusing' (Makower, Letter, 1987b).
11 See comments about the fear of aliens in Great Britain during this time (Powell, 2002: 124–5: Ward, 2004: 103–5; Winder, 2005: 250–73, 278–84), which was particularly heightened by the 1917 Russian revolution and unsubstantiated rumours about connections between the Russian Communist Party and the British labour movement (Ward, 2004: 103–5), for example, the Zinoviev Letter of 1924.

5

Images of the volunteers: media versus memory

'Seeing It Through'

Tommy is stoking an engine,
Grandpa waves flags red and green,
   Innocent Florrie
   Is driving a lorry,
While Millicent runs a canteen.

Daddy, of course, is a Special,
Mother is ready to nurse,
   And we all think alike
   That this jolly old strike
Is bad – but it might have been worse!

(Tristram, 1926a: 327)

The men rolled milk churns, unloaded fish, meat and vegetables at the expense of shins and hands, muscles and sleep, to say nothing of the wear and tear on '22' flannels and Jermyn Street pull-overs. Driving and stoking trains, driving buses and lorries ... they risked quite a lot at the hands of pickets and roughs.

And the women fed them at the many impromptu canteens – at the Y.M.C.A., in Hyde Park, at Paddington under Lady Churston, where Lord Portarlington marshalled the volunteers and handed out cigars and witticisms to the Specials; at Scotland House where a collection of girls and women who names would gladden the heart of any social paragraphist worked in shifts in the basement Canteen. ('Taking It Standing Up, Hats Off to the People who took their Coats off', 1926: 323)

The General Strike provided a special opportunity for the Bright Young People to reinvent Britishness in their own image, particularly that of the quintessential English gentleman amateur and, to a lesser degree, the charitable, gracious English lady. The paradox, of course, was that the gentleman amateur could be both a bumbler and a hero; what he could not do was take himself too seriously or overtly display a purposeful expert knowledge. He could be a Rupert Brooke, the fallen golden-haired Apollo of the First World War, or the Antarctic explorer Robert Falcon Scott – both possessed of an unseemly degree of hubris that clearly defined them as gentlemen. The antidote to these flawed heroes' identity was the foolish yet charming Bertie Wooster or that accidental detective, Lord Peter Wimsey. Being an amateur was the point, for to be overly professional was to be ungentlemanly (Berberich, 2007; cf. Davidoff, 1973: 98–9). As author, producer, and playwright David Benedictus observed, 'Bertie Wooster would have been one of the first on the transom' (Benedictus, Interview, 2009).

The implicit British attitude that made such an overwhelming volunteer response possible in 1926 was that a gentleman could be a better stevedore, engineer, or lorry driver than the real thing – if only he were not so busy being a gentleman.[1] As volunteers, Varsity men aimed to prove that they were not the effeminate, Bolshevist, pseudo-intellectual aesthetes that everyone assumed but, instead, innovative and service-oriented young men with a sense of duty and loyalty to their King, country, Parliament, and community. They demonstrated that they could protect, defend, and save their nation from the 'enemy' within. And unlike their brothers and fathers in the Great War, they proved that a sense of humour *could* save the day. As the *Bystander* declared: 'Our young men showed up magnificently. A week before the strike there were Jeremiahs who spoke gloomily of the modern tendency in our Universities. Hotbeds of sedition they were! ... But the way those youngsters ran our trains and manœuvred ten-ton lorries without killing us was a joy to all beholders' ('Bystander Comments', 1926: 419). Echoing the sentiments of more plebeian magazines and newspapers, the *Tatler* declared:

> We have often heard it said ... that the post-war crop of our nation was hardly a vintage one. We have been told that Jazz and Oxford bags and pork-pie hats had sucked all the sap out of the rising generation and that we could not hope to find a new breed of fighters ... That which they discovered was a quiet, confident, and highly-competent young man who, under good officers, stepped into his place in a flash, and learnt his job in an incredibly short space of time. High efficiency, unquestioning submission to discipline, a wonderful spirit and good manners, these were, and are, the high lights in the picture of our fine young reserve. (Sabretache, 1926a: 268–9)

Fashion historian Doris Langley Moore, a newly married writer in 1926, wrote, 'Everybody I knew volunteered whatever side they were on ... There were no particular persons volunteering – students and undergraduates of course but they always get into the action' (Moore, Letter, 1986; see Moore, 1929). Implicit in this presumptuous 'everybody', however, were the people whom 'one' noticed. And what the newspapers and magazines of the day, memoirs, novels, and plays, and many individuals noted were the Oxbridge undergraduates, well-known sports figures, and members of the upper classes, particularly those with titles.

Male volunteers

Distinguishing markers

> [The volunteers] came into their own as special constables. So training as school prefects was of some use after all. (A. J. P. Taylor, 1983: 79)

Media accounts emphasized the strike's levelling effect, the emergence of a cheerful, classless, spirit of fraternity among volunteers and those they helped. The *Daily Express* reported that 'thousands of special constables were in constant attendance. Many of the officers were N.C.O.s in the war, while in the ranks were peers, baronets, knights, admirals, peers' sons, medical students, professional men, clerks and mechanics' ('Wonderful Police', 1926: 3). Photographs of volunteers intensified a feeling of social inversion. The *Daily Mail* pictured 'a Savoy Hotel chef who volunteered to cook for the Daily Mail staff in Carmelite House' and 'Lord Monkswell as Signalman' (*Daily Mail*, 1926b: 1). Another issue of that newspaper displayed a photograph with the caption about the usually spotlessly dressed 'city clerks, grimy but happy, leaving King's Cross terminus after a day's work in the engine yards' (1926a: 1). 'The convoy [of newspapers] to Cardiff on the last night of publication consisted of one Rolls and ten Bentleys', reported the *Daily Express* ('Fine Service', 1926: 3). And the *Daily Graphic* noted the unusual sight of 'a bus in Piccadilly, yesterday, manned by four youthful stalwarts. The driver was a medical student; the 'special', resting indolently on the bonnet, a Marlborough half-back; his colleague, in the rear, a stock broker, and the conductor, his head bandaged, a Balliol man ...' ('Wonderful London Yesterday', 1926: 2). See also figures 4.1 (a–g), especially 4.1(g) and 5.1 below.

Certain jobs attracted specific media attention, especially when members of high society volunteered for them. The *Daily Graphic*, the *Daily Mirror*, and other papers announced with relish that there was at least one 'peer [who acted as a] ... Signalman. Lord Raglan,[2] who succeeded to the title upon the death of his father, the late Governor of the Isle of Man, was working as a railway guard yesterday. The Earl of Caledon is working at an L.N.E.R. engine shed, and Lord Monkswell in a signal box on the same system' ('Peer as Signalman', 1926: 3; 'Strike Brevities', 1926b: 3). Writers for the *Sketch* stressed the participation of upper-class men's clubs:

> White's supplied a full quota of members who volunteered as bus and train drivers and special constables ... I saw five well-known young hunting men come down the club steps into St. James's Street wearing smart blue uniform or

armlets. Most of the other clubs did the same. Lord Chesham was one of the first to drive a train. He got his training in the railway strike five years ago ... Major the Hon. Lionel Tennyson, the cricketer, was also a special constable. So was Sir John Milbanke, the boxing baronet. (Beveren, 1926: 270)

According to the *Daily Chronicle* of 13 May, even the royal family – or at least their retainers – were involved 'to free men for public duties. Admiral Sir Lionel Halsey, Controller of the Prince's Household, and Sir Godfrey Thomas, Principal Private Secretary, spent much of their time at the Horse Guards, and all the footmen were special constables, despatch riders or acted in some other useful capacity'('Prince Visits the Food Depots', 1926: 2). The *London Opinion*'s gossip column, 'Round the Town', also made mention of the social status of volunteers, particularly 'the Ministry of Transport's pool of motor cars on the Horse Guards' Parade, where a considerable slice of Society was busy throughout the strike under the direction of Viscount Curzon. In the small hours of a Sunday morning I saw the Prince of Wales there' ('Round the Town', 1926: 262).

Of course, not everyone who volunteered was from the higher echelons of society. As the *Daily Telegraph* noted, 'London in ordinary times is well supplied with specials ... [T]he Metropolitan Special Constabulary Reserve and the Metropolitan Special Emergency Constabulary' were made up of 'patriotic citizens ... willing to give their spare time to helping the police in keeping order and protecting the public'. The government deemed those 25,000 specials 'insufficient to meet the difficulties occasioned by the General Strike, and ... determined to establish the Civil Constabulary Reserve'. This new force was to be 'paid, whole-time, sworn-in special constables, organised in units, wearing plain clothes, and supplied with armlets, steel helmets, and truncheons. Territorials, O.T.C. men, and ex-military men up to the age of 50 years, were eligible' ('Specials' Fine Work', 1926: 4).

The social status of those volunteers who worked for the transportation industry – on buses or trains – or who acted as special constables meant that these were the positions for which the (male) volunteers were known and celebrated. That the majority of volunteers served in the docks, drove lorries, or spent most of their time installed in temporary barracks, waiting for action, was not highly trumpeted. What caught the media's imagination were the more visible and romantic activities, which ostensibly kept the nation moving. Industrial issues at the heart of the strike were relegated to the back pages, and the iconic symbols for upper-class British identity became the focus of public discourse.

Juxtaposition of upper-class status with working-class activities made news and called attention to a particular sort of volunteer, best known for his accent, manners, and style of dress. Clothing was the most outward and thus noticeable indicator of social class for everyone concerned. According to the

Westminster Worker, 'the clothes of the volunteers show their CLASS INTEREST IN BEATING THE STRIKERS' ('The clothes ...', 1926: 2). Either military and police or leisure clothing predominated. 'At White's, Duff Cooper found half a dozen of the members in full police uniform, including the Hon. Lionel Tennyson, who had the rank of inspector. Sir John "Buffles" Milbank looked very "smart as a sergeant"' (Farman, 1974: 241). Dorothy Whittle, a middle-class woman working in an office in 1926, wrote that 'the only volunteers I noticed were driving the buses, mostly undergraduates wearing their normal Plus-fours or Oxford bags' (Whittle, Letter, 1986). Such aberrations as 'busmen with Oxford accents', 'whose "bags" were of the Oxford type', became the norm during the General Strike ('Some Strike Snapshots' 1926: 2). See figure 4.1 (d), the middle left photo, as well as the three photos in figure 5.1 (a–c) and the explanatory captions ('Well Done ...', 1926: 267).[3]

Two retired, working-class men told me that the volunteers were also known as the 'plus force', so prevalent were university students and their typical manner of dress (Segal, Burt, Interview, 1985; Elsden, Interview, 1986). Contemporary cartoons also used this pun, pointing to the extra-ordinary nature of the 'force' (Blam, 1926: 428).

The *Sphere*, a glossy magazine, made note of the heightened meaning the strike had given to another item of upper-class leisure wear:

> One thing the strike has done – it has given the pull-over a place in history. If there had been no strike, the 'fair-isle' would have dwindled into a mere incident of fashion ... As things are, it will remain for ever a symbol of the gallant outburst of the spirit of youth, which brought a glory of high and joyous endeavour in among all the dismalnesses [sic] and meannesses [sic] of the strike-fortnight, as it did into the years of war, and will ever do.
>
> In signal-boxes and train-cabs, dockyard and mean-street, engineroom and workshed, the 'fair-isle' throughout those wonderful days stood for courtesy, keenness, courage, *for all that it means to be young in England* [emphasis added]. (S. R. L., 1926: 155)

That passage in the *Sphere* emphasized particularly the normally 'betwixt-and-between' status of male volunteers. Their Fair Isle pullovers became a symbol for upstanding young manhood in the midst of battle especially when such garments were conspicuously misplaced at 'work'. Edward, Prince of Wales made the garment a highly fashionable accessory in the early 1920s when he wore a Fair Isle pullover at the Royal and Ancient Golf Club of St Andrews in Scotland. This resulted in a successful revival and reinvigoration of the cottage hand-knit industry in the Shetland Islands. As patterned pullovers and waistcoats became the rage, the hand-knit items assumed a new status thanks to the Prince's endorsement and rapidly became identified with the upper and upper middle-class sports of tennis, golf, and badminton (Pearson, 1984).[4]

5.1 'These snapshots were taken at Dover, where the Cambridge volunteer flag flew bravely during the strike. The Cambridge volunteers, the light blue brigade, attired in berets, pull-overs, flannel bags and voluminous plus-fours, worked efficiently as porters and dockers.'

5.1 (a) *top:* 'Plus-Fours And Flannel Bags - A cheerful group of volunteers on the quay at Dover.'
5.1 (b) *lower left:* 'Two "Blues"' [Mr. P. S. Douty and Mr. A. D. Allen]
5.1 (c) *lower right:* '"Oh, Mr. Porter, Whatever did you do?"'

The inverted and recontextualized meaning of upper-class leisure wear also became a common theme of post-strike anecdotes, for example:

The Uniform

On the day after the strike was settled a gentleman, dressed in the most aggressive of plus fours, arrived in his London club, declaring that he had come up from the country to take a hand, and was bitterly disappointed that he had arrived too late.

At last another member, irritated by this belated zeal, turned on him and said: 'Well, we managed without you. And, anyway, what do you mean by coming in here dressed like a bus conductor?' ('The Strike and After', 1926: 6)

A multitude of contemporary cartoons also dealt quite pointedly with the issue of clothing. For the two reproduced here, notice the captions and the identity markers: for figure 5.2 (a) and (d), upper left and middle right, respectively, the striped armband signifying a special constable, the striped scarf and lack of cap typical of undergraduates; and figure 5.3, the plus fours and Fair Isle sweaters of the undergraduate volunteers versus the working man's cap. A third cartoon, unavailable for reproduction and in same issue of the *Bystander* as figure 5.3, shows two specials with armbands, apparently undergraduates from their mode of dress – plus fours, and Argyle socks. The caption reads: 'Our Plus-Force! None but the brave deserved the fare!' (Blam, 1926: 428). The pointed reference to courage, service, and manners, as well as the tolerance displayed for those involved in an accident clearly connects chivalrous service with its traditional reward; there is little question that fare referred to 'fair' or female customers – not to the 3*d*. 'fare'.

Accent was probably the primary indicator of social status for the class-obsessed society of the 1910s and 1920s. Shaw's *Pygmalion* did not accidentally premiere in London in 1914. The endlessly remarked upon upper-class or 'U' accent – a very distinctive, clipped style of speech with post-vocalic Rs eliminated and broad vowels emphasized (Buckle, 1978) – came to indicate not only status but also character. These features, combined with that all too recognizable outfit, were inextricably associated. The following typifies the multitude of volunteer descriptions and includes all three class markers – clothing, manners, and accent:

Smart young men who by their Oxford trousers and multi-coloured pull-overs marked them as of the caste of Vere de Vere, acted as porters. Their politeness was almost overpowering; and so clear was their enunciation that case-hardened travellers for the first time in their lives perhaps recognised the names of the stations at which the trains would call. 'Eringyornsyoodgn' became divided up into its three proper parts of Harringay, Hornsey and Wood Green; while on the tubes, for instance, 'Mblarch' blossomed into 'Marble Arch', 'Totcoro' into 'Tottenham Court Road'. ('London in Strike Time', 1926: 2)

5.2 'Some Humours of the Strike Days'

5.3 'Believed to have come from Oxford, Cambridge, and other "health resorts", London will not soon forget these cheery knights of the road. Their efficiency and endurance, their courteous and courageous service were equalled only by that of their comrades on the tubes and trains'

Members of the working classes also noticed. Kay Ekevall recalled the way in which after the strike, regular workers would employ exaggerated upper-class accents and manners:

> The aftermath of it was the funniest ... Students in those days were very sort of reactionary. They were all wealthy people who could afford to go to college and ... apart from ... the scholarship boy, with the occasional sort of wealthy person who was socialist minded ... most of the students ... came from the wealthier classes. And they manned the tubes.
> And after the strike was over the real tube men had great fun because they used to stand on the platform and say [very U-accent] 'Mind the doors please, pahss along the cah please'. They had us in stitches for weeks afterwards. 'Pahss along the cahs please'. And they had great fun taking them off, you know, the students, imitating their highfaluting voices, you know.
> ... We did hear it on the tubes because they were all on the platform and you could hear everything that was said ... It was really funny on the tubes... [It lasted] about three months, yeah ... They couldn't do anything about it because everybody was laughing you know. They would show themselves up ... [There was no question about what they were doing?] No. (Ekevall, Interview, 1986)

Thus, the regular labourers transformed the volunteers' efforts and the volunteers themselves into something trite and superficial by mocking the manners and accents of their upper-class replacements (Saltzman, 1994: 114; S. R. L.; 'Whipped Topics', 1926: 259).

These plays on class markers were appropriate only when they revealed working-class inadequacies, however. Working-class attempts to 'pass' and thus muddy the boundaries between classes were frowned upon. For example, a *London Opinion* report about the secretary of the National Union of Railwaymen, Mr J. H. Thomas (known in the workers' papers as 'Gentleman Jim'), noted that Thomas 'has been still further defying the opinion of his fellow trade unionists by playing the aristocratic game of golf on one of the aristocratic courses near Windsor. His driving, as one might expect from his experience of the footplate, is strong, but his putting is on the weak side. And as a rule he does not tempt Providence by launching out into plus fours' ('Round the Town', 1926: 262).

All of these ambiguous images, verbal and visual, rely on the ever-present double-entendres, the puns that teasingly referred to the undergraduates' liminal status in society – as clowns or tricksters likely to reveal the profane side of the most sacred moments – and at the same time, recategorised them as the faithful 'knights of the road'. No one regarded them as the workers of British society, yet the General Strike led them into that temporary position. Anne, Countess of Rosse, who volunteered in the food service at Hyde Park, while her husband, the 6th Earl of Rosse, helped out with the milk churns at the main railway stations, went to some trouble to point out to me (via her secretary) that 'praise is due to the immediate organization of young people which now are termed the "Bright Young Things". Not rotters at all! Lady Rosse's recollection was … [T]hat splendid service was as much enjoyed by those who helped – even more than if they'd been wasting their time in Night Clubs!' (Rosse, Letter, 1986a).[5]

The cartoon of a bored young man in *Punch* (see figure 5.4) further makes this point by conveying the absurdity of normal life for the upper classes in the 1920s and goes some way to explain the eagerness of so many to pitch in during the strike. For Marjorie Shipley Ellis of Peterborough, that cartoon 'absolutely sums it up! Because the railways were flooded with volunteers and the tubes and the buses, and all the things these young people had longed to do and not been able to do' (Ellis, Interview, 1985) (see figure 4.1).

Such characterisations emphasised the functions expected of persons in particular positions in the social structure. But men and women volunteers had vastly different experiences. For men, the more public a job was and the more room for dramatic, active display it allowed, the more prestigious – despite the higher financial rewards that could be earned in other positions, such as lorry driving. But for members of the upper classes, financial reward

5.4 '*Visitor.* "Your son is looking very bored."
Fond Mother. "Yes. You see, he misses the strike so dreadfully."'

was not the point, while it was much more so for members of the working classes who took on emergency jobs.[6] Victor Paul, for instance, heard that vehicles were needed to deliver all the fish that had piled up at the docks; he was paid £24 for his efforts, just over one-half the cost of his lorry. Mr Paul's average weekly pay at that time was most likely £3–4 a week as a farm worker and lorry driver (Paul, Interview, 1986; Letter, 1985).

More glamorous jobs – generally taken by Oxbridge undergraduates and peers – included driving buses, underground trains, trams, and railway trains, preferably in and around London. Harry Goodby, then a young insurance agent, a veteran of the First World War, and himself a volunteer bus driver, recalled, 'people who were helping with driving these buses were people from the Varsities – the universities, students, all kinds of students – they helped ... [There was] a mixture of students and business people, mostly younger people, the 20 year olds ... The older men they've got more responsible positions you see in those days, in industry' (Goodby, Interview, 1985). The next best positions, in descending order, were special constable, docker, electrical plant worker, and lorry driver – the more public and involving a group of fellow students, the better.

Volunteer work and social status

> Many people who were free volunteered and drove railway engines, buses, etc. to keep things moving! (Alec Bawtree, Clare College, Cambridge alumnus, Letter, 1986).

Although media reports and certainly most of the published histories give the distinct impression that the majority of volunteers were from the upper classes, those with whom I spoke or corresponded had a very different opinion. A former resident of Raynes Park, a middle-class London suburb, 'on the borders of Surrey', wrote: 'My father was at the Air Ministry in London. He hired a bicycle & cycled to London & back each day ... Our neighbour's son, then about eighteen or nineteen years of age, became a special constable. He guarded the sorting office of the General Post Office, I believe. His mother, a nursing sister was a widow & and we were far from being "upper crust"' (Anonymous, Raynes Park, Letter, 1985).

Leslie Jackson, a retired musician in the mid-1980s, was particularly intent on shattering my class theories about the volunteers.[7]

> The reason why I rang you was because of this mention of upper class [in your letter]. I felt that I wanted to question it. I just wanted to show you. It was dire

5.5 Leslie Jackson

poverty, dire poverty in London at that time at the beginning of the century. And as I said, my father had this barbershop ... where I was born in South London ...

So you see, this is why I was stunned to see upper class, because I would never consider myself – I don't really consider myself now other than working [class] ...

Now we'd go out in our Ford, my dad driving or my brother driving ... and you'd go along and you'd see the queues, I can remember right about near ... near the House of Commons, opposite there's the Westminster tube station ... or Waterloo station. And people would be queuing up for transport ... You never solicited anybody, but they'd wave and point which way they're going ... One or two others would say they're going the same way, and there was no, as far as we were concerned, ... there was no financial arrangement ... But usually at the end journey, they'd give you six pence or three pence or whatever. That was during the strike ...

It wasn't a business, don't misunderstand me. It was done as a service, a service. It wasn't intended deliberately to break the strike. And it wasn't intended deliberately as a financial act. But we just did it as a service, as a service! (Jackson, Interview, 1985) (see figure 5.5)

According to Gordon Hobson, a retired merchant navy man, those who volunteered to be special constables, an auxiliary service of 'public-spirited men who gave up their leisure time to perform a public service, [were] from all walks of life – butchers, plumbers, clerks, bank-managers, etc., and I have no doubt there were University students also' (Hobson, Letter, 1986). Andrew Man explained further that it was not only young middle and upper-class men who volunteered, but also 'retired Trades Unionists – retired members of the Forces, and Business people – undergraduates – and individuals like me with the time to spare and a good cause to support' (Man, Letter, 1985; and see Jeffery and Hennessy, 1983: 128). In fact, many of the jobs of policing London's parks, the West End, and the warehouse and factory sections of the East End went to those who already had a record of service to their country. In the countryside, ordinary working people offered their services, sometimes in exchange for quite high wages.

The majority of those who joined up did tend to be of an age when they had more free time and fewer responsibilities than others who might have wanted to join up – a point that has bearing on the pleasant memories most reported. In contrast to media accounts, more were lower-middle-class than upper-middle-class, and in need of jobs and money (Archard *et al.*, 1972; Wrigley, 1984a; Crompton, 1988; GLC, ACC 1297 MET 10/564; GLC, ACC 1297 MET 10/564). George Richardson, a retired electrical engineer, pointed out that the volunteers he knew 'were all too young to have fought in the First World War' (Interview, 1985). Mary Talbot, whose husband volunteered as a special before they were married, recollected, '[The specials were] just middle class people basically ... twenty or twenty-one; it was that sort of age group' (Interview, 1986b). Leslie Dover, born in 2008 in Upper Norwood, near the Crystal Palace, 'about seven miles from the center [sic] of London' was a clerk at the British Iron and Steel Federation. His volunteer experience in 1926 was clearly a memorable one, as he still had his work pass (figure 5.6) and thank you certificate from the Southern Railway (Dover, Letter, 1986a). Explaining his involvement, Dover wrote, 'The London Director of my Company was an acquaintance of the Regional Engineer of Southern Railway, and as a consequence about 20 of the London office personnel volunteered to work as gangers[8] maintaining sections of the railway track between Clapham Junction and Battersea, and between Clapham Junction and Wimbledon' (Dover, Letter, 1986b).

People most frequently mentioned that volunteers they knew served as special constables or lorry drivers, positions held by working men as well as those with titles. A man could be a special constable and still hold down a regular job, as well as carrying out family responsibilities. Lord Denning,[9] retired Master of the Rolls and still in possession of his armband and truncheon (see figure 5.7), told me that many young barristers, himself included, served as special constables in the mornings when they were free and then returned to their law offices in the afternoons (Denning, Interview,

5.6 Southern Railway work pass for Leslie Dover

5.7 Lord Denning with armband and truncheon from 1926

1986). Such assignments usually did not require the time and travel demands of the highly visible 'glamour jobs' (Verdin, Interview, 1986) of bus and train drivers, or even dock workers, which seemed to be reserved for socially connected undergraduates.

The following extended narrative from David Fremantle (see figure 2.3), a Clare College man in 1926, provides a detailed description of a typical volunteer experience working as a docker.[10]

> Well I was in a fortunate position, because my father at the time was Commander in Chief at Portsmouth ... our biggest naval port, ... So I was able to go to my tutor and tell him that I'd heard from him that volunteers were urgently wanted in the dockyards of Southampton ... It wasn't true at all ... a good friend of mine and I decided Southampton would be quite a nice place to go to work in the docks ... So [my tutor] said all right and ... off I went with my friend who'd also got permission under the same terms.
>
> We went out to the docks when we arrived and found the office of the main shipping lines and signed on so to speak. And they said, 'Delighted to see you, please report at seven in the morning', or whatever time it was. So we went off and drank a lot of beer in the pub ... [We] started work that morning.

From that time onwards for the next twelve days, I think, we practically never stopped working. But we were very well paid and we enjoyed our work, which was very largely, as luck would have it, dealing with the big passenger liners ... We were paid trade union rates, [which] ... weren't so very much if you were just doing an absolutely normal day ... We were paid extra for working the tea hour in the afternoon ...

They said we did the job in about half the time as the normal stevedores ... would do it in. I know it got up to £7 a week, and ... that was a tremendous wage in those days ... It was ten years I should think before I got to that on the annual basis ...

And as well we got some tips. We had a pact ... all the volunteers who were doing this job, that you wouldn't accept tips [under] 10s. Ten shillings meant a piece of paper, a note ... and if it was just a piece of silver, we said, 'No, we don't accept tips; we're volunteers'. But if it was a note, then it was worth having, so we swallowed our pride – and accepted it. I did a record: I got a pound from one man ...

When you got the passengers' luggages out of the ship, you used to go into the hold first of all and thrust all the baggage into the nets ... We would take the baggage on trolleys ... and put them all on long row tables inside a great long low shed ... in alphabetical order of the owners ... And we used to ... select baggage which we thought looked nice and rich and comfortable and stick by that ... This particular one, which I selected on the stare, ... (on the labels was an international bankers corporation or something of that kind), I thought, 'This'll do me fine, very rich looking luggage'. And I sat by this and waited 'til he came, and sure enough he came with his wife ... They had a Daimler hired, which was the posh car company ... and [I] ... put his luggage in, and tucked his rug round him, around his wife's feet, and he slipped something into my hand, which I had the strength of mind not to look at 'til he was out of sight. And when I looked at it, it was a pound. That was the record tip that any of us got – quite a lot of 10s notes – a pound made my day. It was a lot of money in those days, equivalent to about £25 now.

... There were a few pickets at the gates sometimes ... and there were a few police there always, but we never had any trouble at all ... We never had any contact with them at all. They didn't [try to stop us;] they used to catcall a bit and you know, make a bit of a noise, try to scare us and that sort of thing, but only very mildly ...

Of course I saw nothing of the fun that went on the buses and the underground in London, which I believe was well-worth seeing. (Fremantle, Interview, 1986)

For most volunteers, the physical milieu of their strike-time activities also presented a new experience, a point that newspapers and magazines frequently mentioned. In London, little villages sprang up to nurture volunteers (Croft, Letter, 1987b), and Hyde Park 'became for the time a self-contained community' ('Hyde Park as London's Food "Citadel"', 1926: 862).

'Every railway company [also] had its own offices [in Hyde Park], equipped with gas, electric light, heating, and telephones. In the middle of the Park were placed Y.M.C.A. canteens, rest houses, libraries, and recreation rooms' ('The Spirit of England – "Carry On"', 1926: 854). Whether volunteers were put up in Mayfair mansions or in military barracks at the Tower of London, in hotels or railway cars, sleeping conditions were crowded and often uncomfortable. According to one account,

> One of the discoveries of the strike has been the new style of 'camping out' – in the office. Owing to transport difficulties a number of business men have been sleeping in the office, on made-up 'beds', and cooking their morning bacon and eggs on the office fire.
>
> 'Just like a camping-out holiday', is the general verdict. All the same, it is rather doubtful whether any of the office 'campers' will spend their this year's vacation in quite this style. ('The Humours of the Great Strike', 1925: 10)

The *Illustrated London News* displayed photos of sleeping quarters in the LGOC's Chiswick garage, which was arranged as a dormitory (see figure 5.8), and at Earl's Court at meal time (see figure 2.1 (f)). Washing facilities, if they existed, were crowded, and hot water was a luxury. Volunteers were often given the food of common labourers – food that was also referred to as 'nursery food' by those who had experienced the same: tea, bread and butter or jam, bacon and eggs, buns, cocoa – nourishing and quickly-made bland dishes.

5.8 'Where London Volunteer Bus-drivers and Conductors Slept during the Strike: The Chiswick Garage of the L.G.O.C. arranged as a dormitory'

5.9 George Richardson

The strike-time emergency lent a festive and egalitarian spirit even to dirty and tedious volunteer efforts. George Richardson, an apprentice electrical engineer in Peterborough in 1926, volunteered because his father[11] expected him to do so, though strikers at his local power plant at first tried to stop him.

> All sorts of people came in and did the rough jobs around the power station. They cleaned out the boilers, they did everything! I can see these poor chappies now, sweating as they came out of these hot boilers, scarves around their neck, you know to keep the ash from going down ... There must have been at least ... two dozen volunteers ... We just had one student from Cambridge ... There were all sorts of people helping. Everybody mucked into the job and got going ... It was a great spirit, it was a wonderful spirit, we all had, there's no doubt about it. (Richardson, Interview, 1985) (see figure 5.9)

While their employers encouraged most young men to volunteer, not everyone with business interests regarded this as an effective solution. Clive Bemrose, at Clare College, Cambridge during 1920–23, was working with his family's printing company, Bemrose and Sons, in Derby in 1926, when all of their work people (about 1,500 men) came out, 'but the office staff remained at work ... I had gone off to see if I could help in any way by driving a lorry or some car, & got ticked off by the Chairman for sort of deserting the ship!' (Bemrose, Letter, 1986a).

Robert Errington had the reverse experience:

> I was asked by my boss when I was going to volunteer to drive a bus, and I told him I sympathised too much with the miners for that. He told me he didn't want any b. reds in his place and I could take the sack. I was out of work for about a month with millions of others and I remember only too well my 12/6 [*sic*] unemployment pay. After about a month I found another job where a young man had gone off to drive a bus without asking permission from his boss. Poetic justice. (Errington, Letter, 1986)

```
TELEGRAPHIC ADDRESS:                          Telephone: VICTORIA 9820 9821 6410
TRADUNIC, CHURTON, LONDON.

            The Trades Union Congress General Council,
  Acting Secretary:
  WALTER M. CITRINE,
  To whom all communications
  should be addressed.                        32, ECCLESTON SQUARE,
  Your Ref.:    Our Ref.:                                 LONDON, S.W. 1.
       Department:
                        The Heart of the World.

                                              18th. May, 1926.

        (Tuesday 11th – Sat 15th May 1926)

        Mr. R.H. Dobbs.

        Dear Mr. Dobbs,

                 TRADES UNION CONGRESS. GENERAL STRIKE.

             I have much pleasure in certifying that
        during the last three days you have been engaged
        upon beneficent work in connection with the
        General Strike.  I much appreciate the work you
        have been able to do.

                              Yours faithfully,

                              Herbert N. Elvin

                         For the General Purposes Committee
                             General Council of the T.U.C.
```

5.10 TUC certification for the volunteer work of Mr R. H. Dobbs, 1926, 18 May

Still others, whom one would expect to have volunteered for the government side, worked instead for the TUC or actually went out on strike. Dr Phyllis Dobbs, alumna of Newnham College, Cambridge, wrote that her late husband, Richard Dobbs, who volunteered at the TUC, had to request proof of his service because 'Cambridge University students who left during the General Strike had to bring a certificate to say they had been to "help their King & Country" (i.e. it was assumed they would work as blacklegs)'. Apparently, the certification was accepted (Dobbs, Letter, 1987).[12] (See figure 5.10.)

Vernon Booth, who became an undergraduate in 1930 at Trinity College, Cambridge, was in a different position at the age of 23:

> I was not interested in politics. I did not know what the strike was about, and still do not know (Booth, Letter, 1986b).
>
> I worked in a tin printing office, the St. Christopher Press, Letchwood Garden City. There were three of us. I was the 'manager' and also the skilled craftsman. I was a member of the printers' trade union, the Typographical Association.
>
> When the instruction to strike came, I consulted the managing directress of the Trust that employed me. I said 'do you think I should strike?' She considered ..., then said 'Yes, I think so'. I did that.
> This odd situation was probably unique. (Booth, Letter, 1986a)
>
> The managing directress wanted its 'image' to be good. That is why she recommended me to strike. (Booth, Letter, 1986b).[13]

Many volunteers maintained a neutral stance and worked for peaceful compromise. Ivor Bulmer-Thomas 'took round the Archbishop of Canterbury's petition for mediation ... I thought the strike was an alarming mistake ... I thought the strikers were misled by bad leaders. I thought the miners were being badly treated ... The miners' leaders and the mine-owners were equally bad – both bloody minded' (Bulmer-Thomas, Letter, 1986).

Some men refused to volunteer at all. Edward Dunham, a retired stockbroker, who answered my letter in the *Morning Star*, was a member of the Territorial Army, a part-time volunteer force, 'an auxiliary army' (see figure 5.11). According to Dunham, 'membership ... would be mainly young fellows ... the officers ... by virtue of their standing in society would get ... the King's commission ... Those who hadn't got such privilege would have to join as ordinary rankers ...; I was a ranker' (Dunham, Interview, 1986). He belonged to the London Rifle Brigade, the Fifth City of London regiment, whose colonel was a member of Lloyds Bank.

> [The Territorial Army] ... weren't exactly called out by the government ... [but] the government would approve of their action without necessarily sanctioning it or ordering it.
>
> ... I was just over sixteen ... I joined because my companions at home in the village I lived in [joined] ... As a young man, I thought it was a jolly good organization to belong to ... I hadn't really formulated any views ... Although I was socialistic in my outlook, ... my ideas hadn't gone fully into that stage. Now, don't forget I was young. And I enjoyed the going away to camp, I enjoyed the exercise, the rifle practice ... and I won quite a few silver medals ... It's a sport you see. Today my attitude'd be quite different ...
>
> I was working [as a clerk] in the office at that time, and we were expected to get to the office ... So I'd have to walk into my office, quite a walk ... There were some buses running by the blacklegs and we'd use those buses if you could get on one ...

5.11 Edward Dunham

> ... [When I didn't volunteer] I came under a certain amount of criticism ... I got a bit of stick from the company commander, and with whom I was in very good relations in the ordinary way ... And he felt it was the duty of every citizen to indulge in this activity ... It seemed to be a patriotic thing to do. That's how a lot of other people would look upon it, wouldn't they? Because these strikers are a nuisance, aren't they? ... The automatic opposition to the strike, the lack of understanding, the lack of understanding in the public is tremendous.(Dunham, Interview, 1986)

Unlike Mr Dunham, most of those who volunteered did so willingly and were envied by their peers in other professions. Dr Alan McGlashan, a Clare College alumnus, recalled, 'by 1926 I was a doctor working as a GP in the country ... and had to carry on with my mundane local medical work. I remember how fiercely envious I was of my brother who as an ex-Naval Officer was free to act as a volunteer driver of a London bus' (McGlashan, Letter, 1986).

Regardless of geography, class, or age, the predominant pattern for male volunteers was to join up in groups with friends, fellow club members, and colleagues and to take on the stereotypical jobs attributed to the undergraduates and young businessmen[14] as well as a wide variety of other services, such as tending boilers and driving lorries. Professor Sir Norman Jeffcoate[15] told me, 'I was a 2nd year medical student at the time and ... spent most of the Saturday and Sunday before the strike collapsed, transporting by small lorry meat from one of the docks to a distant warehouse ... My fellow student drove the lorry and I acted as 'driver's mate'. ... the general attitude of the students was pro-establishment if not anti-strikers' (Jeffcoate, Letter, 1987). Viscount Eccles drove an Underground train (Eccles, Letter, 1986), while Harold Churchill, a medical student in 1926, worked as a bus conductor (Churchill, Letter, 1986)

R. A. J. Williams, a veteran of the Somme, and Peter Kingsford were diverted from their ordinary jobs to help out with transportation. Williams, on the management staff of the Great Western Railway, 'drove GWR buses and parcel trains with my father and had some amazing experiences' during the strike (Williams, Letter, 1985). Kingsford, in later years a distinguished railway historian,[16] was a grammar school boy who had won a scholarship to a public school.

> I left Christ's Hospital, a public school, in December 1925 and through the influence of the Deputy chairman of the Great Western Railway, who employed my father as a butler, I was appointed as a junior clerk in the Office of the Superintendent of the Line, Paddington Station, from the beginning of May 1926 ...
>
> I knew nothing about politics or trade unionism and so when the clerks were told to help the company I went along with it. Another, older, clerk and I were sent to the Acton marshalling yard to help with the shunting! ...
>
> For one whole day we did that and I learnt the difficult and dangerous art of using a shunting pole, connecting and disconnecting railway wagons.[17] But after that we returned to the office, probably because there was no traffic to deal with, or because we were useless. (Kingsford, Letter, 1986a)

Working-class men such as Burt Segal recalled that many of the volunteers whom he knew of were officers of the Jewish Lads' Brigade. 'The officers [were from] ... well-connected wealthy families in this town ... And when the strike broke out a lot of them became strike-breakers. As a matter of fact they joined the special constables' (Interview, 1985).

Members of London's upper-middle-class and upper-class men's clubs also volunteered together. The Carlton Club even tried to organize a joint meeting of other clubs and sent out a letter 'offering to assist [club members] who desire to volunteer to help the Authorities during the present crisis, by including their names, together with a statement of the manner in which they are to help' (Boodles', 1926: 408). Some, like the Oxford and Cambridge Club, were not interested, though its members did contribute fifty guineas (£52 10s) to the National Police Fund (Chandler, Letter, 1986a; Oxford and Cambridge Club Minutes, 1926). The Athenaeum sent a representative to an emergency meeting held at the Carlton club (Webb, Letter, 1986), and Boodles' appointed one Lt Col. Cradock to act on the Headquarters Committee (Boodles', 2735: 408).

Amateur sports teams, most of whose members were upper-middle-class, also volunteered en masse. The Harlequin Rugby Football Club, a particularly popular subject of newspaper copy and photographic spreads, 'were kept together and used as a "flying squad". They organised a canteen at the Yard with a team of Harlequin ladies to run it and act as waitresses' (London, 1926b: 2). Cyril Spencer, who emphasized the connection between the strike and the Great War, explained that 'the Harlequin Rugby Football Club ... was of the highest class in membership (by invitation only – for playing ability) administration and management [in the 1920s]. Probably all its members had lost a relation or dear friends in the war, and with the wonderful team spirit and espirit de corps it would be perfectly natural for them to "do their bit"' (Spencer, Letter, 1986b). *Time and Tide* also pointed out that 'many of those who spend a good part of their time in playing games have set a splendid example to others in volunteering for duties for which their fitness and physique makes them particularly suitable. Large numbers of polo players are acting as mounted police and ... special companies and sections of Special Constables [are] being formed from footballers' ('World of Sport', 1926: 22).

Territorial Army members were among the quickest to sign up for antistrike duty. One member, the Hon. John Jones (pseudonym), of the Suffolk country gentry, was working in a London shipping office at the time of the General Strike. Jones's lengthy narrative gives a detailed sense of what was a typical experience and attitude for his class.

> I belonged to the Honourable Artillery Company – which were the Territorials. And we all went up to headquarters and ... they turned us all into special constables to start. We were given a truncheon and an armband and told to stand by; if there were any trouble we'd go out and try to settle it. We stayed at headquarters and we slept up there, just on the floor, anywhere ... We had paillasses on the floor and – well, we just laid down where we were. We had plenty of beer and we were all right! ... And we had a very good time ...
>
> And then they came along after a couple of days and they called for anyone who could drive a motor vehicle of any sort. 'Who'd like a volunteer to drive buses?' Well, I'd driven a certain amount, and I went down to Chiswick, which was the headquarters of the LGOC [London General Omnibus Company]. They'd got their skid track there, a big flat concrete track; they covered it with oil and everything else to teach you how to correct skids and everything else ...
>
> The whole thing was a joke. You got up on the bus and you had a 'special' sitting beside you with a truncheon, so if anyone tried to get up on the bus [he'd] knock him off.
>
> And [when] people got on the bus ... you'd say, 'Oh where do you want to go love?' and –
>
> 'We want to go round to Tack Street.'
>
> 'Oh, well – where's that?'
>
> 'We'll show you!' And they pointed and we'd go down and we didn't mind

about the proper route. As long as we got to the end eventually it didn't matter. And everyone was roaring with laughter. And we'd go round and we'd drop some of the dear old ladies that wanted a lift. They got on and we'd take them to their front door, and we'd see them off there, and go on to the next one! And we had a lot of fun with this...

But that was what broke the strike, because everyone then who was my age in those days – we simply treated the whole thing as a joke – which it was! And eventually it broke the strike!

... The coal miners? It was all supposed to be in sympathy with the coal miners. I had nothing to do with that at all, no ... I had nothing to do with the politics of the thing at all ... What happened in other areas, I don't know ... With London it was the transport workers there who came out in sympathy with the miners and tried to cripple London ... they failed entirely because we took on the jobs.

... [There was] no question of pay, oh no. [When it was over] we just went back to our jobs again ... Oh, we had a jolly good time! One of the best holidays I ever had, eh! (Jones, Interview, 1987)

Volunteers from different social classes in the regular armed forces also took part as volunteers in the strike. Commander J. Murray, RN, was a London bus conductor during the strike. He was convalescing from an illness when the strike began but obtained permission from the Admiralty to volunteer. Like many individual accounts of the strike, his was detailed as well as philosophical and articulate about broader social issues. With its interjections of the strikers' point of view, this dramatic and colourful tale offers a contrast to the previous one.

In order to volunteer, Murray journeyed to London to report to the Admiralty and then to the Medical Director General, who gave him a note saying he was employable in an emergency. He met up with Glen Kidson, a well-known racing driver, at the United Service Club, where he discovered that rank, or at least social connections, certainly had its privileges.

The room was clamorous...
'And what will they do?' said Kidson, as one who mistrusts oratory.
'What are you going to do?' I asked.
He explained that Lord Ashfield was a friend of his and had promised him a bus...
'Take me with you. I'll conduct your bus.'
'Right!' he said. 'Just what I was looking for...'
And so it was that I found myself ... sitting alongside him in a stream-lined Bentley, with a suitcase on my knees. (Murray, n.d.: 7–8)

Upon arriving, the two found the bus depot surrounded by pickets, but they decided to drive right on through. Once mustered in, they were issued with blankets and then staked out their sleeping billets on the floor. The drivers were put through a course of 'gradients, curves, turns', and so on, while the rest were taught how to punch tickets. Drivers and conductors were issued with brassards but not sworn in as special constables.

The two men did not experience much trouble on the road, though they did see many brickbats being thrown and only one bus with its windows intact. Nonetheless, Murray said that he 'felt as secure as an oriental potentate ... I do not know that every Briton can still be said to love a lord, but he likes to think twice before he assaults a crowned head, and there was not time for that' (Murray, n.d.: 11). At one point he observed 'a bus that was loaded ... with fascists wearing black shirts and flourishing revolvers, passed us on its way out'[18] (Murray, n.d.: 18). He and Kidson learned to tell hooligans from the 'righteous indignation' of crowds lining the roads but considered the government's directions 'to all authorities to repress and overcome' the strikers – a threat that was neither necessary nor helpful (Murray, n.d.: 29).

The observations of Frederick Coombes, a Royal Navy chief petty officer in 1926, provide a non-commissioned perspective on Commander Murray's narrative as well as a working-class counterpoint to that of the Hon. John Jones. Coombes, who was stationed on a submarine during the strike, had some poignant reflections about class differences (see figure 5.12).

> The news came that there was going to be a General Strike so off we went from Chatham to London docks ... Our people were asked to volunteer – if they would drive railway engines and things like that, because we were engineers.

5.12 Frederick Coombes

And a fair number of people, of the submarines, volunteered on account of the fact that they thought it was a damn good lark ... I don't think they did it from any sense of patriotism; they did it as a change from their ordinary life.

We were actually sent up there, the submarines; the engines were going to be used to pump up the refrigerators for meat in the London docks ... Well, then some of our fellows would get on the railway engines and run them against the buffers; they thought that was great fun ... They thought it was lovely, they weren't experienced ... I didn't do anything like that ... I wasn't going to volunteer anyway.

In the evenings they went over to the Port of London authority Canteen, a big canteen inside the dock yard. And you found all the students, Oxford, Cambridge, and people like that ... It was pretty obvious that they were ... the way they talked. They talked differently from us as well, and everybody knew that they were students. They didn't have to say that they were ... You could tell by the way that they carried on and that sort of thing – their attitude and everything ... Somebody told me one of them was Lord Burleigh ... a great hurdler he was; he won the Olympics.

... As I said, they were all there and they thought it was great fun even – [lifting] crates, because they were great big athletic fellows, even moved lumps of beef. They didn't mind doing it for that week. They would not like to do that forever – for a living – but they thought it was all fun. And then they used to go in and they'd sing songs, all lovely singing, all getting half-drunk and all that! ...

We talked like it was anybody else, we talked to them ... Sometimes you could tell because they ... are much more casually dressed than a lot of working [men]. You could tell the quality of the clothes they were wearing. We knew perfectly well who they were. Anyway, they were very happy, that sort of thing. No snobbery amongst them when they had a few pints of beer. And they're never snobs, those sorts of people ... They're always very nice; that's part of their charm, you know? They were just having a good time, perhaps a few felt patriotic ... Perhaps they started off with that – all for Britain and – of course their Britain was lovely, isn't it? Their Britain is all right. They keep what they've got. Don't blame them in some respects. (Coombes, Interview, 1985)

Of course, the majority of those in the military were neither like Coombes nor the university volunteers he observed; most had little real knowledge of the strike. L. T. Studley, in the Royal Air Force in 1926, noted that he 'was 21 ... and with little news media one rarely had any means of assessing the rights or otherwise of the situation' (Studley, Letter, 1985b). 'Some of our Squadron aircraft were used to ferry newspapers to the north of England. I believe that the crew carried spades so that in case of a forced landing, their cargo could be buried' (Studley, Letter, 1985a).

While many men joined up in groups, there were a number of upper-class individuals in their 20s who signed up on their own and then ran into compatriots on the job. The Duke of Richmond, who encountered several of his peers while volunteering, explained,

At the time of the 1926 General Strike I was 22 years old and working with Bentley Motors Ltd Kingsbury. In the service dept. We had just built a complete 3 litre Bentley chasis [sic] out of reject parts ... I got permission to use this car with which I joined a convoy fleet of about ten cars that went to Lypne (airfield) each morning to collect Daily Mails printed in Paris and flown across in ex-War 1 aeroplanes like the DH9 etc.

We then proceeded back to the secret distribution centre in Woburn Square. This meant leaving London in convoy about 6 a.m., and arriving back about noon. I then returned to my Bentley Service dept. work, and after about three days one was very short of sleep as you can imagine. In the convoy was the then Duke of York's (King George VI) Armstrong Sidley Shooting Brake, as well as the Rolls Royce of Sir Bertram Mills the famous circus promoter. We didn't encounter much opposition although our route traversed some pretty hostile areas such as the Old Kent Road. One Sunday I attended a Scotland Yard car parade on the Horse Guards Parade and I recall a lecture from Prince Serge Obelensky [Alice Astor's husband] relating from his fairly recent riot experiences in Russia, telling us always to approach a mob in reverse gear so that should you threaten to be overwhelmed you could instantly escape at speed in a forward gear. Good sense I guess! But my Daily Mail work precluded me from further Scotland Yard Operations. It was all over in about ten days ...

Oh yes! I also did a paper round in Clapham one Sunday morning, again in that wonderful Bentley! (Richmond, Letter, 1986a)

Many members of the middle and upper classes responded to my newspaper queries and letters to Oxbridge alumni to tell me that friends or relations of theirs had served as special constables or volunteer drivers (e.g. Coulson, Letter, 1986). Lady Patricia Hambleden, laid up with a tooth ache during the strike, reported: 'My youngest brother drove a train I remember and my other 2 did various things. I remember my husband telling me (I was not married then) that he and several others drove all night delivering the only paper published at the time – and they had quite an adventurous time getting through the picket lines' (Hambleden, Letter, 1986). Mary Talbot recalled,

My late husband, who was then living in Holland Park, ... joined the 'specials' and he and a friend used to walk the streets of North Kensington to relieve regular police for more important duties ... Hyde Park was used as a big food storage place, and general storage place ... which needed troops and police to guard it against looting. The specials had no special uniform, just an armband ... My father also joined the 'Specials', but that was down in Carshalton ... and I think they had nothing down there; it was a very quiet sort of area. (Talbot, Interview, 1986a)

Correspondents also reported on the variety of services that they and others had performed. According to David Smithers, MD, a Clare alumnus,

I was too young (just) to take part in the General Strike of 1926 being a schoolboy. My brother, who had often been illegally in the signal box (hand operated) at our local station, was allowed by the signalman to pull the long shining handle post over the signal ... a friend of mine drove busses [sic] in London and in the evening he piled into the bus to go the theatre, parking their bus outside. My brother-in-law helped print the special daily paper. (Smithers, Letter, 1986)

Those with automobiles offered rides to those without. L. Oldham, another Clare alumnus, wrote, 'What I, together with many more private motorists, did was to put a destination label on our windscreens and, as we drove past regular bus stops where passengers had continued to wait, pick up anyone wishing to go our way' (Oldham, Letter, 1986). Such private motorists had no 'official' status as volunteers and did not receive any official certificates or tokens of thanks, as did those who worked in mass transportation.

Besides driving people to work, volunteers also delivered mail (Croft, Letter, 1987a) and printed local news sheets. Lt Col. William Owen, Ret. RN,[19] the son of a local schoolmaster, was

in the sixth form at a local grammar school in North Wales, in a small town in a coalmining community ... Both I and my school chum ... were both due to leave the school in the summer of 1926 and to go up to Oxford in the autumn, John to Exeter College and I to Magdalen.

... our contribution to events took the form of providing the local community with 'News'. We spent some hours each day in the Head Master's study, listening to 'news' broadcasts by the B.B.C. John and I took it in turns to commit alternative news items to paper and prepared a 'News Bulletin' which we had typed and posted in the window of a local stationers. So far as we were aware, this was the only 'News Bulletin' to reach the town for several days. (Owen, Letter, 1986a)

Individual efforts were often more successful than those organized by official organizations. John Mellanby, an undergraduate at Emmanuel College, Cambridge and a member of the University Officers Training Corps Signals Company, told me that he and some other signallers were '"volunteered" in true Army style to take over the railway telegraphs. [We] were bundled into a car and taken to Peterborough, where a senior railway man gave us a very cool reception ... The railway man told us that he had had experience with Army Telegraphists before, and it took at least two weeks hard training before they could use the single needle instruments effectively. We were therefore returned to Cambridge' (Mellanby, Letter, 1986). Mellanby did succeed in a later attempt to provide transcripts of BBC bulletins for his College.

Schoolboys also managed to involve themselves in transport work. G. M. E. Paulson was soon to enter Cambridge when he volunteered his services. Paulson, born in 1908, was a senior boy at Westminster School in London. His father was a Colonel in the Royal Signal Corp serving in India while his mother remained at home in Brighton. Even at a distance, his father thought that it was a good idea that everyone, regardless of age or position, should do what they could to help. [The school authorities] were in touch with the underground authorities ... and selected a number of us senior boys to help ... What was left of the underground management told us what to do ... [I regarded volunteering] as a change from school – something new, original and rather exciting! ... I do remember it was great fun. (Paulson, Letter, 1986)

Experiences such as driving a bus or train, serving as a special constable, or even loading crates in the docks were exciting, in part, because such activities lasted a relatively short time and were, as many noted, so different from their regular lives. Removed from their everyday world, volunteers developed a camaraderie typical of those in potentially dangerous situations and isolated from outsiders (Geertz, 1968; Turner, 1974; Fussell, 1975). Many a media account emphasized how the nine days enabled men to rediscover the joys of masculine companionship with military comrades. 'Many of the men [who volunteered at the docks] ... had served in the War, and they could "swop" [sic] yarns of the old days at Ypres and elsewhere. "My first real holiday for years", one of these men said. "You see, though I have a fortnight at the seaside every summer, I've always got to take the wife with me"' ('The Humours of the Great Strike', 1926: 10).

Individuals also noted the 'time out of time' feeling of the strike, reminiscent of the 1914 Christmas ceasefire. B. W. Pendred, at Regent Street Polytechnic in 1926, served as a special constable on the Great Western Railway. He related that during his time as a ganger, 'one lunchtime [sic], there was a heavy shower. The gateway was picketed. While some of us were sheltering from the rain in the hut there was a knock at the door. "Could we come in?" asked the picketers? We welcomed them to join in the tea and sandwiches, hard boiled eggs, etc., all animosities forgotten' (Pendred, Letter, 1986a).

George Richardson (see figure 5.9), working at the Peterborough power station during the strike, emphasized the playful aspects of strike-breaking:

> Everybody thought it was a great game! We were keeping the power station going! ... We enjoyed ourselves ... we had some slide shows ... we played darts and skittles ... we played all sorts of public-house games ... as if you were in a club or pub, all men, no ladies ... I can remember some of the people used to sort of write poems and skits and things like that .... And of course there was a ... a bath system at ... the old power station. We used to all get in this tank and this bath together, like a rugby club! We used to bath together. That was the thing that I remember about it – I don't think there were any bad times, we were so proud of what we were doing! ... We were all too young to have fought in the First World War. (Richardson, Interview, 1985)

Besides reporting on the excitement, most also noted that much of the volunteer work (if there was any) was hard and sometimes tedious.

Particularly for those who joined the Civilian Constabulary Reserve and the Special Constables, monotony was relieved only by homemade entertainment or an occasional foray into the East End to demonstrate their potential force to the 'alien' element. But *not* to have been part of the volunteer effort would have been far worse than a bit of boredom. The relatively short duration of the strike in comparison to other instances of national deprivation made the experience bearable – especially since it did provide material for tale-telling sessions after the strike (e.g. 'The Great Exodus, or How It Was Arranged', 1926: 13; '"All Aboard." or How Bournemouth got their Potatoes', 1926: 6), a point that Varsity publications made all too clear.

Newspaper reports tended to focus on fraternity rather than tedium. For instance, *The Times* told of

> University men, medical students, clerks, costermongers, and a considerable sprinkling of strikers who have found their way back to work ... Little gangs who had finished their job early hurried across to help their slower mates at another chute. At Victoria Dock a medical student in 'plus fours' and a Rugby football jersey could be seen giving a hand to a fellow-labourer in drab blue overalls ... Soldiers and volunteers workers fraternised in a tin hut where coffee and sandwiches were served. ('Undemonstrative Crowds', 1926: 4)

Detailed reports of the more strenuous volunteer work experiences did occasionally appear in newspapers but more typically in magazines. For instance, Edward Benn, then at Clare College, Cambridge, submitted his memoirs to the *Nation*, an American magazine that described him as a '"class-conscious" young author' (Benn, 1926: 666). Mr Benn kindly sent me a copy of his article in the *Nation* and the letter from the managing editor. That letter further noted that the diary 'reveals what was probably the mood and attitude of a large number of young men of your general social position who looked upon the strike as a combination of a lark and a serious national emergency' (Managing Editor, 1926).

Although Benn tells his tale with the typical tongue-in-cheek deprecation of the upper classes, also apparent is his trepidation and excitement, as well as his disappointment at the mundane reality of volunteer duty. Throughout is also a very clear sense of what was expected in the way of British behaviour for all involved. The diary commences on Monday, 3 May 1926.

> Found a letter from dad on coming in from golf:
>
> '... situation looks bad, but somehow I refuse to believe that the General Strike will really take place. It is a Continental notion, and the British workingman is too sensible a being ...'
> Still ... I signed on with the O.M.S. at the Guildhall. Put myself down as a lorry-driver – pity the lorry that gets me.

Tuesday, May 4

> ... Talked with S. the historian. He drew an alarming parallel between the present situation and the start of the French Revolution. Went and played golf, feeling that it was very much 'fiddling while Rome burns.' Still what can one do? (Benn, 1926: 666)

Placing the strike and volunteer duty in the same category as events like the French Revolution had the contradictory effect of emphasizing the tedious nature of volunteer service. The *Cambridge Gownsman and Undergraduette* reiterated this point in a two-page 'diary', similar in tone to Benn's account but more self-consciously lampooning the experience (and, as always, referencing other national crises). Entitled 'The Gallant Six Hundred!' the account began: "'Brick-bats to the right of us,/ ...Volleyed and thundered./Into the midst of them, ... /Went our Gallant Six Hundred!" That was our dream. This was our reality' (H. A., 1926: 12).

H. A. reported that once the volunteers got to their stations, 'Whitechapel was quiet, annoyingly quiet. With six-hundred "idle well-to-does" confined in a couple of warehouses in their midst, in Leman Street, all chafing to quell a riot, the people of Whitechapel and the district grew strangely docile.' They grew even more so as the days wore on, and 'the Cambridge University Contingent of the Civil Constabulary Reserve ... had to content itself with visits to the Bloody Tower and throwing pennies to the leading comedians and musicians of the district.' Volunteers were 'considerably embarrassed by the remarks and jeers of the crowd which surround[ed] them, and soon pick[ed] out Cambridge bags, plus fours, and other articles of clothing and mannerisms peculiar to ourselves' (H. A., 1926: 12).

Six 'Roberts' (police) told the crowd to move on, and the next morning the volunteers were given a lecture about 'Jews, Chinamen, and agitators, which was most illuminating!' A brief scare later that day caused the troops to don full kit, complete with truncheons, but nothing happened. The next day, they had the opportunity to march to the Tower, get tickets for a play, have tea, and 'play at 'buses' (H. A., 1926: 12).

The following day included a game of cricket on the constabulary cricket grounds, followed by 'inspection and P.T. ... with press-ups, O'Grady, leap-frog, and the rest – football comes later, and one enterprising gang made a push ball out of a palliass!' (see figures 1.3 (a) and 2.1 (c)). Confined to quarters for the afternoon, waiting for an emergency that never happened, they amused themselves with 'bridge, swearing, letter-writing, reading and fitful sleep' (H. A., 1926: 12). The Cambridge volunteers' final day in London was devoted to sightseeing: museum-going and photographing the Tower Moat. General Sir T. Scott told the men 'how proud and happy he is to have served with us, but regrets we may not retain our tin hats' (H. A., 1926: 13).

5.13 Charles Cassell identified himself in this photo of the Lots Road Power Station Volunteers, 'This was taken after the strike was over before we all went our different ways. I am the little sailor in between two big guardsmen in the top right hand corner.'

In his article, Benn also noted: 'We were allowed to keep our truncheons, but not the tin hats, much to everybody's disgust. Lunch, and then paid off. Another five bob – this extravagance will break the Government! Got my pay, seized my suit-case, and jumped into a taxi ... back to Cambridge and ordinary dull work' (Benn, 1926: 667).

What stands out in these accounts is not only the variety of jobs done, but also the matter of fact way volunteers did them. Charles Cassell,[20] a 19-year-old stoker (boiler tender) in the Royal Navy in 1926, said that while he never met any of the student volunteers, he remembered, 'they worked hard, "trimming" the coal that supplied the boilers, so we never met for drinks or a farewell party' (Cassell, Letter, 1986). Mr Cassell sent me a photo of the Lots Road Power Station volunteers (see figure 5.13), as well as his certificate of thanks from the Metropolitan District Railway (see figure 7.4).

Women volunteers

Society women in the media

A Versatile Volunteer Worker.

'In this office Lady L. M. has been managing the telephone.' *Sunday Newspaper.*

'Lady L. M. sold more than 1,000 copies [of the newspaper] in twenty minutes.'
– *Another column, same paper, same day.*

'Other well-known people who rose nobly to the occasions were Lady L. M., whom I saw gaily wielding a frying-pan at Marble Arch ...' *Another paper, same day.* ('A Versatile Volunteer Worker', 1926: 540)

On the surface, the duties of women volunteers did not seem very different from those of their fathers and brothers. Women who were able volunteered in 1926 because not to do so was inconceivable. Yet they did not want merely to fulfil a one-dimensional feminine role prescribed by their society, their government, and the media.

Young women volunteers preferred to have jobs in transportation or official public service, positions that provided a certain amount of licence in their public comings and goings, driving speed, and social interactions. While they might have wished for more adventurous jobs such as bus-conducting, those were reserved for their male counterparts. Outside London, fewer male volunteers meant that jobs for women were not so restricted, and upper-class unmarried women more often got a crack at the more adventurous jobs involving driving or bus-conducting. Peggy Paten (see figure 5.14), from an upper-middle-class family near Peterborough, told me, 'I was a bus conductress with another woman ... I was given a wallet purse with a band on my shoulder and across my chest, took money and gave tickets ... Oh, I enjoyed it, yes!' (Paten, Interview, 1986).

5.14 Peggy Paten

Marjorie Shipley Ellis (see figure 2.2), from a prominent Quaker family in the same town, was thrilled to be given the opportunity to deliver newspapers.

> The last paper that came out, the last issue of *The Times*... told us the strike was coming.... And then we all charged down to the little Guild Hall. There were *streams* of people waiting to be given a job!... You went up and said, 'Please give me a job.'... And then they said would I like to take the newspaper run? And I said 'Yes, very much my cup of tea.' And so that was how I took the papers round. I'd forgotten all about it until you rang.
>
> [I drove myself when] I started out, and then when the papers got more, and I got a pal to drive me, and ... I leapt out with my increasing bundles of newspapers and dumped them down ... Of course the news-agents were thankful to have the papers to deliver! Because it was an absolute emergency, and Winston Churchill was in charge of course ... I was given two newspapers, two copies and told to make it go round two villages ... The great thing was to find the most public-spirited man in the area ... I went to the publican, at the Queen's Head ... and I explained that I was giving him this one precious copy, and he'd got to make as many people in Nassington see it and in the nearby village ... The next day I reported for duty at the Guild Hall and I was given four copies and that had to go round six villages ... By the end of the General Strike ... I had got a newspaper route through all the normal newspaper agents from Spaulding to Arundel, which is quite a big area ... They were all so keen to see this paper ... Very few people had radios ... so they were very eager for any centre of news ...
>
> And I was positively upset when the thing ended; I'd enjoyed my newspaper route *so much*! It was all such fun! (Ellis, Interview, 1985)

Most women volunteered as individuals and not as members of a formal group. Unlike male volunteers, who both lived and worked in the docks, at newspaper offices, or various plants, women were not quite so removed from their normal lives; even those among the upper classes who joined up with friends returned home each evening. While many did get the opportunity to deliver newspapers and messages, providing an outlet for their 'wild driving habits' (*Daily Graphic*, 1926b: 1), in only a few cases did women serve as conductors of buses or trams[21] and even fewer as special constables[22] – all of which they had done more than competently from 1914 to 1918.

The jobs remaining were in the domestic sphere – work for which most upper-middle and upper-class women had little practical experience. In an inversion of everyday social roles, women with the most social cachet performed a sort of public housework – precisely the jobs maids would do in the homes of these well-off families. Society women with war-time experience recruited their daughters and friends to organize food stalls in Hyde Park and in railway stations. Lady Lindsay told me:

> My mother ran the canteens during the war ... and that was why perhaps she was thought to be capable of running this thing, and she certainly was ... It was just my mother and some of her friends were given the job ... at Paddington

Station. So her friends all corralled all these debutante daughters ... And this was so absolutely filthy dirty, this canteen. It'd never had a proper cleaning in its life ... And so she decided that the burden had been put on us to clean it up ... It was not particularly a pretty job because it was absolutely knee deep in old grease, where things had been spilt down. We were literally scraping it off the floor. And we spent most of our time on our knees. Well of course we were young, and we were giggly and also in a way it was what my mother said we were to do ...

As I said, we ... shared our parents' political views ... we never questioned anything – or wondered if there was a right or a wrong. We merely slogged away at this job. (Lindsay, Interview, 1985)

While those in charge tended to be married women, those working in the canteens were more likely to be unmarried and to have the lesser positions of service, rather like the hierarchy of house maids, kitchen maids, and so on – all jobs aimed at supporting the male-dominated and much more public and publicized activities. Other women ran errands, served as telephone operators, and delivered newspapers and messages, secondary jobs that tended to go to those of lesser social status or situated at a distance from London. And they were generally not given as much publicity in the media.

Instead, the papers overwhelmed their readers with articles about well-known members of society who cooked, served food, hung out laundry, peeled potatoes, swept up, ate, and took cigarettes breaks in Hyde Park canteens. These articles further noted those who worked as drivers, for Queen Mary's Auxiliary Service, and for the G.W.R. horses ('How Women Helped During the Great Strike', 1926: 159; 'Were We Downhearted? The Answer is in the Negative', 1926: 235; 'Noblesse Oblige', 1926: 340; 'Over in Ireland, and the Strike from the Social Point of View', 1926: 246; 'How the British Empire Came on in Spite of The Strike', 1926: 240–1).

Garbed in overalls, pearls, and fancy hats, titled women were photographed and mentioned by name in those articles noted above and others ('How the Flag was kept Flying' 1926: 251). A particularly good photograph of this sort illustrated an article in *Eve* entitled 'Noblesse Oblige'. Capitalizing on the uniqueness of the situation, the caption reads: 'Strange happenings at Scotland Yard! The Hon. Mrs. Lionel Tennyson, the Hon. Mrs. Fitzallan Howard, the Hon. Diana Skeffington, Miss Cameron and Lady Sara Wilson busily engaged at the canteen in Scotland Yard' ('Noblesse Oblige', 1926: 340). As another photo caption in the *Sphere* declared, 'There was no job, no matter how lowly its character, for which volunteers were not forthcoming – volunteers drawn from the ranks of the highest aristocracy in the land and from those who are often described as Society butterflies' ('How they Helped in Hyde Park and Whitehall' 1926: 158; see figure 5.15(a–g)).

5.15 'Typical volunteer workers in Hyde Park and Horse Guards, helping in the canteens and hanging out the washing'.

(a) *upper left*: 'Miss J. Leveson-Gower helps in Hyde Park'
(b) *upper middle*: 'Mrs Grey Alderson and the Hon. Ivy Somerset seated in front of the mattresses in Whitehall car park'
(c) *upper right*: 'Hanging out the washing in Hyde Park during the Great Strike – An interesting group of workers pictured during last week'
(d) *middle*: 'A good-bye group of volunteer workers in the M. O. T. Park in the Horse Guards Parade. Forty per cent of the drivers were women'
(e) *lower left*: 'Lady Betty Butler and Miss Collet help to fry bacon and sausages in Hyde Park'
(f) *lower middle*: 'Lord Airlie and Mrs. Brinling commanding the fast-car service'
(g) *lower right*: 'Miss Bridget Sherwood and Miss M. E. Gaunt at work in Hyde Park'

The photo in the lower left of this spread in the Sphere appeared in three papers with three different captions:
Sphere: 'Lady Betty Butler and Miss Collet help to fry bacon and sausages in Hyde Park' (22 May), p. 158.
Sunday Worker: 'Lady members of the idle class "caught" doing something useful in Hyde Park', Caption, 1226, Sunday Worker (16 May), p. 8.
The Sketch: 'Armed with their frying pans: Lady Betty Butler (left) and Miss Collett Doughty' (12–19 May) p. 13.

While upper-class women were taking on such domestic responsibilities, the numbers of working-class women employed in service was in serious decline, a situation regarded as both a problem and a threat in the 1920s. During the General Strike, this decreasing number of female servants coupled with women's entrance into previously male-dominated fields came to be used as a metaphor for the changing position of women of all classes. Arthur Tristram's comments in *Eve* parodied what such social change could entail: 'The House of Commons charwomen have been travelling to their work in Rolls Royces. This sort of thing is going to make the servant problem more acute than ever' (Tristram, 1926b: 327). A satirical piece in *Punch* detailed just how the strike enabled female servants to gain the upper hand, for the coal shortage empowered them to give orders to their male employers (Evoe, 1926a: 526). Such commentary underscored the very real post-war fear that women, particularly lower-class women, might not remain in their proper place.

Unlike their male friends and relatives, women did not receive recognition for having 'saved' the nation – only with 'helping out'; they merely served as intermediaries between the (male) volunteers who did the 'real' work and the loyal public who 'carried on'. Headlines such as 'Women's Work in the Crisis' (1926: 1) and 'Women Helping' (1926: 1) did not accidentally entitle stories about society 'girls' (many married and most over eighteen) who joined up to cook food and wait on male volunteers. A caption beneath a photo of Mrs J. Leveson-Gower (see figure 5.15 (a))[23] who 'convoy[ed] "sausages and mashed" at one of the Hyde Park canteens', read: 'They also Serve—' ('Who, When, and Where', 1926: 424). The ending to the well-known phrase did not need to be printed. Yet it was only the temporary nature of this particular dramatic encounter and the volunteers' popularly acknowledged victory that enabled magazines such as *Punch* to discuss explicitly the advantages of a society in which the leisure class did the jobs of idle workers.

At the same time that the press was touting the 'good-tempered' attitude and hard work of society members, it defended their entertainments with a sanctimonious fervour unknown in the days before the General Strike. More middle-class publications such as the *Sphere*, the *Bystander*, and the *Illustrated London News* echoed those sentiments. After the strike, 'the most serious problem confronting Mayfair hostesses at the moment is the re-organisation of the dance programmes. It will scarcely be possible to make up all the balls postponed during the last fortnight' (Corisande, 1926: 11).

Frivolous pastimes were suddenly transformed into patriotic acts. The *Bystander* cavalierly but pointedly noted,

> the Season, like the rest of the country's activities, will carry on *après la grève*. It would have been a thousand pities if it had been found necessary to cancel any of the Courts, as apart from the bitter disappointment caused to some hundreds of *debutantes*, the set-back to business would have been very badly felt in certain

quarters. Your rabid revolutionary, in his fulminations against the existing order of things, usually takes good care to forget the amount of employment which depends upon such functions as these, a point which many folk would do well to remember. ('Who, When, And Where', 1926: 426)

Such comments further trivialized the role of women in the 1920s, and society magazines gave the distinct impression that feminine interest in the strike rested solely in the benefits that could be derived – particularly concerning fashions, men, and gossip. Thus, several articles praised both the loyalty of fur and dress shops for 'carrying on' and those patriotic women who did not cancel their orders for the May Courts or Ascot frocks. Despite the disconsolate emptiness of the West End shops, proprietors kept their stores open, demonstrating that they, unlike the strikers, were well aware of their responsibilities to the nation ('Wear and Tear. The London Shops and the Strike', 1926: 335; 'Keeping Smiling', 1926: 246; 'From Town and Country – A Striking Contrast', 1926: 666).

Advertisements and fashion columns in *Eve* and the *Cambridge Gownsman and Undergraduette* further reinforced this portrait of selfish frivolity with captions such as 'The Present Emergency is not National, but Personal. "What Gown shall I buy?" Come round to Arthur House, Regent St. And let them help in your choice' (1926: 4), and 'A striking model for non-strikers: a three piece suit …' ('Wear and Tear. The London Shops and the Strike', 1926: 335). A cartoon in *Punch* was more explicit in its attack, and scathingly summarizes the upper-class female image prevalent during the strike (see figure 5.16).

The tongue-in-cheek 'Diary of a Mondaine' in *Punch* (1926: 572) detailed how the strike affected romantic relationships. The number of cartoons and quips detailing the 'dangers' undergone by 'unsuspecting' men who gave rides to office 'girls' (see figure 5.17) demonstrates how, and how much, the British class structure was threatened ('Chances for Cupid', 1926: 10; 'Charivaria',

5.16
'Repercussions of The Strike'
'*Maid*. "What will madam wear?"
Mistress. "Well, I really don't know. What does one wear for a strike?"'

5.17

'*First Young Woman*: "Riding pillion all through the strike, I was; and such nice young chaps!"
Second, Ditto: "Really, dear! I suppose one does find one's level in a crisis. Personally I never sank lower than a limousine."'

1926b: 565; Evelyn, 1926: 234; Mills, 1926: 541; 'Strike Notes', 1926: 527; 'Strike Sparks', 1926: 327; 'Whipped Topics', 1926: 259).

Middle-class women and unofficial service

Besides their presumed interest in the various activities of upper-class volunteers, if the overwhelming amount of media coverage is any measure, middle-class women tended to be involved in the strike in unofficial ways. Newspaper articles emphasized how these anonymous women could and did fulfil their duties. 'The Ladies' Mirror' recommended in all seriousness, 'In these times when the workers are apt to return at all times and want to be fed it is a good idea to have a cold buffet laid out in the living room' (Phillida, 1926b: 4).

Another difference between middle and upper-class women was that the former did not have the ready-made service or charitable organizations that upper-class women and middle-class men did. Jean Rowntree,[24] an alumna of Somerville College, Cambridge, was in the rare situation of having a female don who organized her female students to drive local children to school. When I asked Felicia Stallman, a student at St Hugh's College, Oxford until 1920, if the women joined up like the men she told me, 'No, it wasn't necessary to join anything. You see the whole thing only lasted a little over a week … The suburbanites, [the women] were not a very organized – [the canteen volunteers were] more the upper-class women who always have more freedom and of course they met more people of a different type' (Stallman, Interview, 1986).

Despite a lack of official encouragement, many middle-class women performed a variety of tasks to help out. Mary Talbot who had a full-time job during the strike and could not volunteer, related: 'Until the *British Gazette* newspaper started the only way of getting news was by the radio, which rather came into its own at that time. An aunt of mine, who was a shorthand writer, used to take down the bulletins and have transcriptions available for husbands on return from their work and for people who had no radio. That was just sort of a way in which she helped ... In small ways, everyone tried to help' (Talbot, Interview, 1986a).

Dorothy Whittle, like Mary Talbot, did not volunteer because she also had a full time job. As with most people, the main impact the strike had on her life had to do with personal transportation.

> I was 19 ... years of age. Father bought a Bicycle [*sic*] so that I could get into the Office without excuse. I could not face 6 miles of cycling in the rush hour and refused to use it, but [my sister] Hilary who worked in Kennington for the Waifs & Strays, found that once she had crossed a few main roads, the traffic was not too bad. We belonged to the Conservative Party, who ran a Coach each day ... and sometimes I was able to use this means, though the times were difficult. Mostly I waited in the Main road till I got a lift, or got on a Pirate bus, driven and conducted by University Students in Plus Fours and by paying 3*d*. for any distance, managed to get to the Office without any absenteeism. Very often I walked most of the way, sometimes going past a long line of strikers, which felt a bit menacing but never troubled me. (Whittle, Letter, 1985)

Mary Talbot, who responded to my ad in the *Kensington News and Post*, concurred.

> I don't think it ever felt dangerous to me, but then I was young – at eighteen you don't, I think, feel that. I mean ... there was a great deal of talk in the family obviously and at offices and so forth, was this a communistic ... because of the Russian revolutions ... But at my age, you don't think really in terms of that, you just think it's all rather a lark.
>
> And of course it didn't go on too long. That was the thing. It didn't go on long enough to be a bore ... [I asked] another friend of mine ... 'What did you do in the great strike?'
>
> 'Oh well [reported with an exaggerated upper-class accent], actually it was rather fun', she said ... If you'd been fifty I should think it was less funny. (Talbot, Interview, 1986a)

The strike also contributed an unforeseen bit of adventure even for those unable to volunteer. Mrs Talbot continued, 'a friend of mine ... [who] was working for an architect at the time ... said, 'Oh! They made us stay in a hotel in Holborn ... so we knew nothing of the strike at all! We used to just walk round the corner to our office! And she said to me – as a girl who'd never done anything very much – this was all rather exciting! To stay with just a friend in a *London* hotel!' (Talbot, Interview, 1986a).

Middle-class women who did not work outside the home had the greatest opportunity to serve as unofficial volunteers. Those with access to a motor car offered lifts to office workers walking into the city or ferried children to school. Mary Talbot told me that a relation of hers, age 5 at the time of the Strike, remembered 'the Headmistress of his Kindergarten School driving round the villages in her small open sports car & picking up those of her young pupils who had no transport & cramming them into her little car' (Talbot, Letter, 1986).

Felicia Stallman had to leave her job as secretary to the managing editor of the (politically Liberal) *Daily Chronicle* in 1925 because of the growing economic depression. As a result, she was free to drive others to work. She explained,

> When I was in my newspaper job, I learned how to drive, just because I wanted to ... So I just – put my car up and volunteered as a ... relief car. I ferried people up and down. We lived in Dulwich, near here; my father worked in the City. Every day, to and fro I went up and down to the City: take him in, leave him there, go up again, fetch him back ... [I picked up anybody] no matter who it was. After the first day, somebody in the car held a cardboard out saying which centre I was driving to – whether I was going to London Bridge-Victoria, which meant West End, London Bridge. (Stallman, Interview, 1986)

Such acts impressed both the left and right-wing media, but no particular women were mentioned by name or photographed. The *Emergency Strike Bulletin* accorded the 'highest praise ... to private car owners, especially the ladies, who have responded so admirably to our Government's call by assisting the loyal workers, and placing their property and themselves at the disposal of the working public' (*Emergency*, 1926: 1). The *Daily Mail* reported that 'Women who own motor cars are using them for workers, secretaries are cutting up sandwiches, independent women are looking after other people's children' ('Women Helping', 1926: 1). Such praise was not unqualified, however; the media continued to snipe at middle-class women, portraying their efforts as excuses to drive 'smart little cars', enjoy crowd-free shopping, and obtain 'many bargains as a result of the strike' (Phillida, 1926a: 4).

The government did not do much to acknowledge the work of middle-class women volunteers either. As Marjorie Lathbury,[25] an alumna of Newnham College, Cambridge told me of her car driving, 'I received no recognition other than a bouquet of flowers [from one of the passengers], nor did I expect any' (Letter, 1987b). In fact, the role of middle-class women in charities had always been relatively anonymous (e.g. YMCA, Women's Institute); such women were not in leadership positions, so they were not considered newsworthy. Nor did they seek such attention, which would have been considered unseemly. Their contributions during the strike worked in much the same way.

Besides driving people to work, middle-class women helped to keep others informed. Marjorie Vincent, then a shorthand typist for Twinings, volunteered her services to the Guildhall in Cheapside. A friend of one of the directors even wrote a thank you note to Twinings for Vincent's services – even though, as she told me, 'they hadn't done a thing about it'. She had volunteered quite on her own (Vincent, Interview, 1986). Phyllis G. Croft, a veterinary surgeon and an alumna of Newnham College, was 8 years old during the strike. Her father, a stockbroker, had been killed in the First World War. Croft was educated at home by a governess but remembers going about with her mother during the strike.

> During the Strike there were no trains, and hence postal services were threatened. So, a rota was formed in the village and those who had cars, volunteered to carry mail bags from one sorting office to another. My mother and I carried mailbags from Roydon in Essex to Ware in Hertfordshire every Sunday afternoon for several months. The distance was about 6 or 7 miles and the whole process took us about an hour. No one checked my mother's credentials – she was well known to everyone in the village. I was <u>thrilled</u> – I felt we were doing something very important and from childhood onwards I was always looking for ways to serve the community. My mother did a lot of things normally restricted to men – and driving a car in 1926 was one of these. (Croft, Letter, 1987a)

When I asked her if the strike-time atmosphere was similar to that during wartime, Dr Croft told me that this was indeed the case.

> You're quite right about 'grass roots' organisations springing up among the people concerned. The same spirit <u>did</u> appear in the 1939–45 War. I was in London during the worst of the bombing – & just the same spirit was evident. In some ways one is sad that the same thing doesn't appear more often in this country. (Croft, Letter, 1987a)

> [I]f the community is sufficiently isolated you do get it. I live in a very scattered small village (no post-office, or village shop) and ... we do a lot of organising & general neighbourliness among ourselves. It's a pleasant life. (Croft, Letter, 1987b)

University Women

Outbursts of an Undergraduette of a Frivolous Nature during the Strike.
(by F. de L'A.)

> Will you lend
> Me one ear,
> Dearest friend,
> ...
>
> – – – this strike!
> I, for one,
> Would quite like,
> Just for fun,
> To have done
>
> Some odd job
> Up in town.
> I could sob!
> She-Dons frown.
> 'Can't go down'!
>
> No one's left
> But us hags
> Place bereft
> Of all 'bags';
> No more rags ...
>
> Dearest friend,
> Lend an ear
> And attend
> While I swear:
> X!! ***! There!
> Did you hear? (L'A., 1926: 6)

Unlike their stay-at-home female counterparts and their male classmates, most university women (all upper-middle and middle class) were not able to serve as volunteers, usually because they were not permitted to be absent from college during the term. Instead, many did what they could in areas near enough to Oxford or Cambridge to permit afternoon excursions. Mrs Rosamund Tosh, an alumna of Somerville College, Cambridge, explained, 'in the twenties the great majority of undergraduates came from middle class, professional, and therefore 'conservative' families, and their natural impulse was to support the establishment. Since we had all grown up while the 1914–18 War was in progress there was even an element of "doing one's bit for one's country" in the attitude of many people' (Tosh, Letter, 1987b).

Residence in certain Oxbridge colleges seemed to provide for a greater opportunity to act. Jean Rowntree, in her second year at Somerville College, Oxford in 1926, told me:

> We were reading Political Science that Summer Term, which made any decision to volunteer to keep services going a matter of political principle – or so it seemed to us then. The Principal addressed students about this decision, reminding us rather firmly that, for every student at present in College there were x number of well-qualified students for whom there was no room – i.e. that our membership at College was a precious thing, which should not be lightly interrupted. In spite of this, a fair number of my contemporaries did in fact volunteer to run various essential services, and I and a friend settled with our consciences by doing our service as well as our normal work, and in a form – driving country children to school – which we thought a special category, as it seemed important that education should not be interrupted. This service ... was run by Mrs. H. A. L. Fisher, wife of the warden of New College ... The main operation went well and we were allotted a car lent by Mrs. Everett, a temporary English Tutor who was in fact a Socialist, but shared our views about uninterrupted education ...
>
> Of course we were pretty well cut off from the possible centers [*sic*] of trouble and lived in rather an unreal world in which the issues involved were seen in terms of <u>theory</u>, and the condition of the miners was outside our experience. (Rowntree, Letter, 1987a)

In contrast, Phyllis Legh, a Girtonian, told me, 'I remember sitting outside the town council's offices ready to act as messenger. I don't remember being called upon to act!' (Legh, Letter, 1986). Elisabeth Kitson, also of Girton, had a similarly frustrating experience: 'a few friends at Girton and I had bought an old 2 seater car which we put, as well as ourselves as drivers, at the authorities' disposal. I think they only used us once or twice. From that and [my brother's] experience it seems that there were far more volunteers than needed' (as sent to Chitty, Letter, 1986). Kitson's cousin, Mrs Mary Chitty, explained to me, 'hers was a gayer and more get-up-and-go set of girls than mine. We certainly never heard of clubbing together to buy a car; in fact to most of us it would have been beyond our financial means' (Chitty, Letter, 1986).

Rosamund Tosh tried her best to volunteer for work in the Hyde Park (London) canteen,

> but was told, firmly but politely, to stay where I was! All that I could do was to join some of my friends at the Oxford Town Hall, where ... our task was to interview and record the particulars of men from the town (mostly self-employed, non-Union members) who came to volunteer; many of them seemed to be taxi-drivers, lorry drivers or lorry drivers' mates. My friend and fellow-Somervillian, Janet Adam Smith,[26] however, got herself a far more glamorous job. An undergraduate friend from St. John's College, on leaving to unload ships at Hay's Wharf, had offered her the loan of his motorcycle during his absence,

and on this she was allowed to drive round to neighbouring villages delivering copies of the British Gazette. (Tosh, Letter, 1987a)

The ability to perform such services required access to a vehicle – something that was not within the financial scope of most women students. According to Mrs Tosh, however, 'there was no objection to Janet's riding round the neighbouring villages during the afternoons, and there was absolutely no question of favouritism or class privilege!' (Tosh, Letter, 1987b). Nonetheless, it was evident that a minimal family position or political connection was necessary for any female who desired to serve in the area of transportation, if only because of the cost of a vehicle (Makower, Letters, 1987a and 1987b). In her second letter to me, Jean Rowntree noted that Janet Adam Smith was a member of the Conservative Club and speculated that this was why she had the glamorous job of delivering the Government's *British Gazette* (Rowntree, Letter, 1987b).

The prohibition against women's leaving university during term no doubt limited the numbers of women undergraduate volunteers relative to others in their social class, but it also marked another important distinction between male and female students. Similar restrictions were lifted for men undergraduates who wished to serve as volunteers outside Oxford and Cambridge. While there were perhaps a sufficient number of local women volunteers outside London, the real reason for the disparity in numbers was that male undergraduates were simply considered more appropriate volunteers than females. Class was another factor; there were simply more middle-class than upper-class women at university (McKibbin, 2000: 36), and the latter tended to dominate the volunteer scene, just as they did the social scene. There was also a pervasive attitude that most university women did not 'join up', which must be distinguished from 'helping out', because they did not believe it was right or necessary. Marion Massey, at Girton in 1926, explained:

> If some needed work had come my way I have no doubt I would have volunteered, partly for a change and out of interest, but it did not.
> The curious thing was, that the men almost all volunteered and did something active and exciting, but the women were not asked to and did not. But at that time, unless you were an ardent feminist, you took no exception to this state of affairs, and certainly I did not think there was anything particularly discriminating in it. We women did not question whether we were suitable for the fairly heavy jobs that the men did. This was still a time when women were tolerated at Cambridge but not particularly welcomed, certainly not by some of the older academics. (Massey, Letter, 1986)

Mrs Ruth Connolly, another Girtonian, noted: 'We were still practically all of one class and we discussed music and poetry and philosophy and Art rather than social questions. Our lot were all "nice" girls, and we didn't go to political meetings' (Connolly, Letter, 1986).

Even those sympathetic to the miners' cause felt they could do little to help, though the whole experience seems to have shifted and solidified their lifelong political views. According to the Countess of Longford, who was waiting to go up to Oxford:

> I think I can say honestly that I had practically no interest in politics, except in so far as the plays of G. B. Shaw fired my imagination. My sympathies, if I had any were with the under-dog because of this reason ... During my last year at Oxford (1929/30) I became interested in politics for personal reasons and when I went down became a lecturer for the Workers' Educational Association. Ever since then I have been on the left ... During my first year at Oxford I met Hugh Gaitskell who had been inspired by GDH Cole to help the strikers. He made me feel on their side, but this was long afterwards. (Longford, Letter, 1986a)[27]

Sophia F. Baron, whose 'student friends [and I] ... were all on the side of the miners ... wished them well. We all felt indignation, anger and sorrow when within sight of victory, the miners' union leaders sold their members down the river, did a deal with the coal-owners and the Government and called off the strike, forcing the miners to take a cut in their already wretchedly inadequate wages' (Baron, Letter, 1986). And Mrs L. Hodgkiss, a Girtonian and 'a poor solicitor's daughter from Suffolk ... well born but poor', wrote:

> The strike turned me into a Socialist, and I have remained one ever since ... I did not <u>like</u> using the volunteer buses for fear of helping to break the strike. I know a lot of girls picked up volunteer buses just as a joke, and would count up how many 'rides' they could get. You see, we were <u>for</u> the strikers, who had just had their wages cut, and what was a joke to the 'volunteers' was grim for us. I remember the brief newspapers – all, of course, against us. No one to plead for the miners, who were starving ... The strike converted me to the justice of nationalisation.
>
> ... My parents were poor, but proud! We are 'gentry' (aristocrats of the small type), but I hope working class in sympathy, too ... I suppose the better off had quite a good time [in the strike]. For us it was a sad world ... It is obvious, isn't it, that 'volunteer' is a 'bad word' to use. It means trying to break the strike. <u>We</u> had to fight on. ... I don't think the volunteer movement made much difference. It was economic forces that decided the struggle. (Hodgkiss, Letter, 1986)

University women opposed to the strike tended to take a more activist stand than those who sympathized with the workers. Lady (Rosalie) Mander,[28] remembered: 'The part I took was that with others of the same Liberal opinions in going round houses in North Oxford (not Colleges) to get people to sign a Petition for industrial peace ... organized by some Bishop' (Mander, Letter, 1986a).

Regardless of their political attitudes, however, most university women regarded any such participation as simply not appropriate. Only 'ladies' were wanted, and for narrowly defined tasks. As several of them put it, they were *not* society women – though many could have been debutantes if they'd wanted.

Society women redux

In contrast to their undergraduate sisters, society women volunteered en masse and delighted in the unusual and novel experience of cooking, sweeping, and waiting on their men folk. 'As a teenager', Lady (Rachel) Bowes Lyon,[29] like many of her class, 'volunteered with friends ... at Paddington Station and fry[ed] hundreds of eggs and bacon for other amateurs' (Bowes Lyon, Letters, 1986b and 1986a) – a scenario echoed by the reminiscences of Lady Lindsay, Lady Phyllis MacRae, and others. As a photo caption in the *Tatler* put it, 'Lady Betty Butler is the unmarried sister of the Duchess of Sutherland; and was one of the large company of society girls who worked at the Hyde Park, Scotland Yard, Whitehall or other canteens for the benefit of transport and workers, Special Constables and other Volunteers' ('Were we Downhearted? The Answer is in the Negative', 1926: 235). Such women may have dressed 'down' in overalls, yet they retained their jewellery and fancy hats – as if to emphasize the social cachet of the occasion, as well as the dramatic and playful role-reversal their dress and behaviour signified (see figure 5.15).

While they did have a great time, many also did some hard work, although the media did not emphasize this aspect of volunteering. Lady Lindsay reported that, 'we spent most of our time on our knees ... [The overalls we wore] were very dowdy, [but with] ... buckets on the floor, they were the very thing really. We hadn't many clothes in those days that we would have wanted to spoil them ... It was so filthy. And when we gave it back, when the strike was over, they were *overcome* with what it was like!' (Lindsay, Interview, 1985). Other debutantes took care of exercising horses at different depots, while still others worked as telephone operators, messengers, newspaper delivery women, and office workers.

In 1926, Lady Phyllis MacRae, the daughter of an upper-class English family, was 27 years old and living with her husband and his family on the west coast of Scotland. She not only remembered the General Strike, but she also saved the voluminous correspondence between herself and her mother, the Marchioness of Bristol, who travelled between London and the south of England during the crisis. Those letters give a detailed picture of the strike from women of different generations. Both observed its effect from quite distinct geographical perspectives. Lady Phyllis explained, 'my mother wrote very fully to me, as ... I had been so involved with voluntary work and politics up to my marriage – in the South. Life was so different 1) before 1914, 2) during the war, and 3) in the period 1919–1939 – when so many tried to get back to the days before the war, or tried to become "equal"' (MacRae, Letter, 1987b). A letter dated 9 May 1926 from the Marchioness of Bristol brought news about their London neighbour: 'Mary Byng is driving her car for a firm that requires it's [*sic*] employees transported.' Explained Lady Phyllis, 'Lady Mary Byng (at that time aged 27) would have considered it her <u>duty</u> in a National emergency' (MacRae, Letter, 1986b). MacRae's sister not only put up volunteers in her home but also sent her children to her mother's in order that she might volunteer during the strike (MacRae, Letter, 1986a).

Reporters wrote about such women as if they, like the titled men and socially prominent undergraduates who served as volunteers, were involved in yet another fancy dress ball, treasure hunt, or charity rag – or engaged in a war effort. They were portrayed as if they were playing dramatic roles in a theatrical production about a fashionable war. Five photographs of well-coiffed women 'doing their bit' appeared under the headline 'Noblesse Oblige' (1926: 340). The caption under one photograph of two women (one with a special's armband) serving tea to a well-dressed volunteer, informed the reader that 'the canteen at Scotland Yard was Mrs. Loeffler's own "show" and a very good show too ... Everyone did yeoman service from 10 a.m. till 10 p.m.' ('Noblesse Oblige', 1926: 340; and see 'Helpers at the YMCA canteen in Hyde Park busily serving out "rations"', 1926: 427).

Befitting their station, upper-class married women participated in less public, yet more markedly maternal, ways than their single friends. The Countess of Crawford and Balcarres, for instance, played hostess and then nurse to the 'two students billeted on us. As far as I remember they went out on different shifts working in the docks and railway yards till one of them developed pneumonia and had to be looked after till he recovered' (Crawford, Letter, 1986). These married but socially prominent ladies of the peerage held the most anonymous volunteer positions. Interestingly, the job of telephone operators, which required the least amount of physical contact with outsiders, was co-opted by those of the highest social standing, such as Lady Louis Mountbatten (see quotes at the start of this section). Besides that job, she worked in the Hyde Park YMCA canteen, and, like other 'distinguished women, sold copies of the Sunday Express in the streets as cheerfully as they sold Armistice Day poppies'. And 'two duchesses, a viscountess, and the daughter of a marchioness drove lorries for the *Times*' (Farman, 1974: 178). Apparently, if one were of high enough position, one was entitled to violate even the rigid structures of the emergency state; conversely, high social status might simply override everyday gendered social restrictions and entitle such persons to more, rather than less, licence and privilege. Or – like the Bright Young Things during less critical times – Lady Mountbatten may simply have decided that more exposure would enhance her position rather than diminish it; she took advantage of the possibilities that women's service in the First World War and the actions of the BYP indicated were available options.

In the 1920s, power did not come to any women by right. Although men of certain social classes were 'naturally' expected to become volunteers, women who held some kind of power – even if only temporary – had to be described as the exceptions. There were the occasional photographs that pointed to some overcoming of gender bias, such as one captioned, '"Specials" of both sexes at Ranelagh where Polo players enrolled in the mounted section' ('"Specials" of both sexes', 1926: 4). And the *Daily Telegraph* did print a short paragraph about the women who took care of the Southern Railway's horses. Without reading the article, entitled 'Volunteer Stablemen', however, one would never know that 'the presiding genius of this cheery group ... [of] nine ex-cavalry officers ... [was] Miss Smythe, normally secretary of the British Italian League' ('Volunteer Stablemen', 1926: 4), and apparently granted temporary masculine status by virtue of her abnormal position – and upper-middle-class status.[30]

Although 40 per cent of volunteer drivers in the Transportation Corps at the Horse Guards Parade were women (see figure 5.15 (d)), only those like the Duchess of Sutherland, Mrs Roberts, and Mrs Allen were given particular publicity ('How they Helped in Hyde Park and Whitehall', 1926: 158; 'Cheery London. Business as Usual Despite the Strike', 1926: 1; 'Who, When, and Where', 1926: 427). Both the society and popular media implied, whenever they wrote about women like Mrs George Norrie, CBE, of the YMCA, Commandant Mary S. Allen of the Women's Auxiliary Service Emergency Corps, Lady Londonderry of the Women's Legion, Mrs Stanley Baldwin of the Emergency Transport Section, Dame Florence Simpson of the AMAAC Old Comrades Association, or the few others with positions of authority, that these women held such positions by virtue of their wartime experiences, their husbands' positions, or their social titles – all the result of their relationships to certain men (e.g. 'Women's Organisations', 1926: 4; 'How Women Helped During the Great Strike', 1926: 159; 'Were we Downhearted? the Answer is in the Negative', 1926: 235; 'Who, When, and Where', 1926: 427). Their power could be justified only if framed in this way (Rogers, 1978; Sanday, 1981; Leacock and Safa, 1986). And only those women acting as 'women' – either as glamorous domestics or intermediaries for men – and those with government sanction to masquerade as men and thus qualify as official drivers, were explicitly acknowledged as volunteers. The uniforms, which officially acknowledged female members of the transportation corps wore, had the effect of temporarily transforming them into men or 'sexually ambiguous, a person-in-uniform' for the duration of their work (Cohen, 2002: 54–5, 133–4).

The 'Diary of a Mondaine' picked up on this particular phenomenon with its farcical account of Rosebud, who slipped into one of her husband's suits and went off to try to be sworn in as a special constable. She was recognized at the last minute, however 'by one of the Saxonburys ... [whom] she called a good many things and, still wearing Teddy's suit, went and got a job to drive a motor-bus. She's an absolute top-notcher' (1926: 572).

As in war time, a woman was permitted to do 'a man's job' only when that man was otherwise occupied and her reason for doing so was in the national interest (Thom, 1998: 169; Noakes, 2005). The media applauded 'strike insurance clerks, both men and women, [who] stuck to their jobs in most difficult circumstances with the utmost good humour ... the work was carried on efficiently and without complaint for the insurance clerk of both sexes is a good fellow' (King-Page, 1926: 2). The anomaly of women doing 'men's work' could be avoided; the solution was for them to become temporary men – 'good fellows' – so long as they were not acting like suffragettes and emasculating men in the process.

Despite the reality of so many women's experiences, however, it was all too clear that following the domestic ideal was the only legitimate pathway for English womanhood during the General Strike. As one gentleman, who had driven a bus in London, remarked, 'I never came across any ladies driving or that sort of thing. I don't think anyone would have dreamt of asking them to do it ... There were quite enough of us I think!' (Jones, Interview, 1987). The Victorian 'angels on the hearth' (Houghton, 1979) became, in 1926, pearl-draped canteen maids. They'd moved out of the houses in which their fathers and husbands had installed them but only physically: those tent kitchens and spruced up railway canteens became merely an extension of the home front (see figure 5.15 (a, c, e)).

The strike enabled upper- and middle-class women to fulfil an exaggerated maternal model – just as Wendy in J. M. Barrie's play *Peter Pan*,[31] a cultural icon deeply embedded in the public consciousness of this generation, was able to play at taking care of the Lost Boys. Once the play was over, the role was easily discarded in anticipation of the next fancy dress opportunity. Volunteer activities transformed the oppositional nature of actor and activity into complementary forms:[32] the menial labour of 'lady volunteers' of high character became their 'noblesse oblige' when those unaccustomed to such labours successfully performed them – and thus regenerated one image of British 'community'.

Volunteers who mattered

The university lads, society women, Bright Young People, and businessmen who served as volunteers did not regard their acts as motivated by class divisions but fuelled by a desire to keep their country moving. Clearly, volunteering was an adventure, a way of making oneself important to the community at large. But it was also an act limited to those of a certain age and socio-economic status, those who had both the leisure and few responsibilities to others. The very nature of the activities required of volunteers restricted who could or could not join up. Furthermore, the semi-official nature of the organization of the call-up dictated that the more desirable jobs would go to those of higher social status – those with access to unofficial channels of government communications.

Other considerations further structured the nature of the volunteer experience. Those who fit the stereotypical characteristics of the volunteers were also those in peculiarly liminal status groups, that is, university men and society women. They constituted a relatively small group of people from very similar backgrounds: they played the same games, held the same attitudes, went to the same schools and parties, and even dressed and spoke alike. But more importantly, they were considered by themselves and others to belong to a particular group and to act in a fashion readily identifiable as marking membership in that group (Isherwood, 1947: 176–80; Dundes, 1965: 2; McKibbin, 2000; Taylor, 2007).

A general strike at another time might not have designated the Bright Young People (BYP) as stereotypical volunteers. But the BYP, those associated with them, and those who aspired to such an association were especially devoted to play acting, treasure hunts, fancy dress, charades, jokes, larks, and rags, all forms of upper-middle and upper-class folk drama. They were used to creating their own alternative worlds and identities and hungered for an excuse for something even more dramatic to engage their imaginations. For young people who considered themselves deprived of the opportunity to prove themselves in the Great War, the General Strike provided an appropriately theatrical setting for another sort of dramatic enactment.

Notes

1 I am indebted to Erika Brady and Michael Bell for teasing out this line of reasoning and to Erika for suggesting I look at Robert Falcon Scott.
2 Lord Raglan (Major FitzRoy Richard Somerset, 4th Baron Raglan), was the author of *The Hero: A Study in Tradition, Myth and Dreams* (1936), which introduced a motif checklist for classifying mythical heroes; Raglan became widely known for his myth-ritual theory about the origin of religion. During the First World War, he served in the Grenadier Guards in the Middle East after stints elsewhere in the British Empire. From 1921 to 1926, he ran his late father's estate. As an aristocrat, soldier, and accomplished yet amateur scholar as well as General Strike volunteer, he totally fitted the stereotype of the gentleman amateur whose birth and experiences in other realms made him apparently capable of serving as a signalman (and see Davidoff, 1973: 98–9).

3 The rest of the text for 5.1 identifies the 'Rugger blues' and makes a bit of a jibe about their 'hard labour'.
4 Erika Brady pointing me towards this connection between a traditional, local handcraft and its fashion ascent – particularly significant, given its symbolic import during the General Strike.
5 Her secretary further noted, 'Lady Rosse wishes to add that real fear never came into it. So to many of them it was their first answer to "the country's need and service"' (Rosse, Letter, 1986a).
6 See Chapter 7, note 2, regarding the specifics of miners' pay.
7 While Mr Jackson insisted that his background was working class, his father owned both a barbershop and a Ford, which Chris Wrigley believed more likely placed him as lower-middle-class.
8 Dover explained: 'The gangers' job is quite a vital one, swinging a 14lb hammer to keep the keys (wedges) taut in the rail chains' (Dover, Letter, 1986b).
9 Lord Denning, a self-described middle-class grammar schoolboy from a village north of London, received a scholarship to Cambridge and came up through the Inns of Court. His title was earned, not inherited, and stemmed from his position in the judicial system and as a Law Lord.
10 M. R. Pratapsinhji, also of Clare, went 'to work with the volunteers of our College ... helping the loading and unloading at the Southampton harbour. One of the things that pleased us was that we were usually well tipped by the rich America passengers using the big trans-Atlantic liners! ... As far as my personal inconvenience was concerned I missed my daily hot water bath, which I was used to, owing to lack of coal supply and was glad when it was all over' (Pratapsinhji, Letter, 1986).
11 Richardson's father worked as stable boy and then horseman for the Dukes of Bedford and Buccleuch. Later, he became a hotelier (Richardson, Interview, 1986).
12 Richard Dobbs was a nephew of Beatrice Webb. Richard and Phyllis Dobbs were educated at Bedales, a very left-wing school (Dobbs, Letter, 1987).
13 The St Christopher's community where Booth attended school and became an apprentice printer at age 16 'was different from other factories and workshops in various ways ... As part of a socio-industrial experiment, various craft departments were set up. One was printing. At age 20 (Jan 1924) I left the Temple Press and I became the "manager". I had one apprentice. Then I took on another employer. Next came a compositor: he was the chairman of Letchworth Urban District Council' (Letter, 1986b).
14 According to Metropolitan Railway records, 801 outside persons volunteered. Of these, 750 were men and 51 were women; there were three titled male volunteers, 17 military officers, and 23 belonged to London clubs. Over 100 of these volunteers, who included those educated at public schools, ex-soldiers, and clerks, applied for permanent employment after the strike (GLC, ACC 1297 MET 10/564, 'Alphabetical ...', 1926; GLC, ACC 1297 MET 10/564, 'General ...', 1926). The 'Minutes of the Metropolitan Railway Officers' Monthly Conference' record that both passengers and profits were half of what they were for May 1925 (GLC, ACC 1297 MET 1/103, Numbers 1854–2100', 1926).
15 Jeffcoate was former Chair of Obstetrics and Gynaecology at the University of

Liverpool and former President of the Royal College of Obstetricians and Gynaecologists.

16 Kingsford, who passed away on 2 June 2010 at the age of 101, was the author of several books about North Mymms in Hertfordshire as well as books on the hunger marchers and Victorian railwaymen, electrical workers, and more.

17 'When a train was made up of goods vehicles for various destinations the wagons had to be put in the proper sequence for them to be dropped off later. This was done in the sidings by the shunter who coupled and uncoupled wagons with a long pole as a shunting loco pushed them to and fro. It was the most dangerous work on the railway and I certainly was not competent after one day' (Kingsford, Letter, 1986b).

18 The Fascists tried to organize their own volunteer corps but the government rejected them, presumably because giving official sanction to such a group would have been too provocative even for the most radically right-wing in the Cabinet.

19 After attending Magdalen College, Oxford, Owen became a research physicist in the Ballistics Directorate of the Armaments Research Department at Woolwich, then Bursar of a boys' preparatory school (Owen, Letter, 1986a).

20 Cassell noted, 'Us sailors were just sent where we were required, but I still feel very pleased that little bit of help that I, and my mates did, helped to keep the country moving and out of a complete shut down. I never believed in strikes. And I don't now, as it's only the public suffers' (Cassell, Letter, 1986).

21 The *Sphere* published a photograph of a stylishly clad woman on the upper platform of a bus captioned: 'A girl conductor collects fares on her brother's bus' (X. X., 1926: 179).

22 According to the *Bystander*, 'Mrs. Marshall Roberts, who is well known in the polo world, ... enrolled as a Special Constable in order to drive a police car' ('Who, When, and Where', 1926: 427).

23 This is the same photo as 5.15 (a) but with a different caption from that in the *Sphere* spread.

24 Rowntree worked at the BBC, first in the Talks department, later in Adult Education, and then as Head of the Further Education Department.

25 Lathbury's father was a Liberal MP. She attended St Felix School, Southwold, Suffolk before Newnham.

26 Janet Adam Smith, whose 'father had been Principal at Aberdeen University' and an associate of the father of J. C. W. Reith (BBC founder), was a scholar, editor, mountaineer, biographer, professor and more. She was an editor at the *Listener*, the *New Statesman*, and *Nation*; wrote a biography on Robert Louis Stevenson in 1937, and 'edited an edition of Stevenson's Collected Poems (1950)' (Miall, 1999).

27 Longford's future husband was a volunteer during the strike, but later changed parties. In her first letter to me, she related 'one little story from my husband ... Frank Pakenham, a Conservative but later converted to Labour (and now in the House of Lords of which he has been Leader) joined the Varsity Squad which was sent up in the middle of the summer term ... to deal with the strikers'. Instead, they were installed at what 'is now the Spanish Embassy at the corner of Belgrave Square ... for a week during absolutely nothing. At the end of the week their commandant assembled them to meet an elderly general. "Here is the Varsity

Squad, sir," he said to the general, "and a fine lot of men they are. They mean business, I can assure you." "It looks like it", replied the general with a quizzical glance. The commandant then looked behind him and saw that every one of his men was smoking like chimneys except for Frank who happened to be the only non-smoker among them' (Longford, Letter, 1986a).

28 Lady Mander noted that she was a biographer and lecturer at Queen's College, London. She researched and lectured in Austin, Texas on Rossetti's letters and published works on Mary Shelley (1936), Trelawney (1950), Rossetti (1965), and Mrs Browning (1980) (Mander, Letter, 1986a).

29 Lady Rachel (Pauline Spender Clay) married the Hon. Sir David Bowes-Lyon, the brother of Elizabeth Bowes-Lyon (who would later become Queen Consort to George VI).

30 Angela Woollacott (1994: 10–11) and Lucy Noakes (2005) drew conclusions about women taking on masculine roles (uniforms, tasks) during the First World War. See also Grayzel (2005).

31 J. M. Barrie's play *Peter Pan: Or the Boy Who Would Not Grow Up* was first performed in London in 1904, revived in 1915 and again in 1924. Barrie published *Peter and Wendy* as a novel in 1911, and the tale was first released as a film in 1924.

32 Roger Abrahams noted in his paper 'Can You Dig It? Aspects of the African Esthetic in Afro-America', presented at the African Folklore Institute, Indiana University in 1970, that a community celebrates: 'its sense of groupness by coordination of energies in the common creative enterprise, and [does] so by taking binary oppositions, embodying them in a complexly integrated traditional form which utilizes these oppositions in the form of complementarities. This group focus is guaranteed through the practice of interlock, in which the distinction between performer and audience is made meaningless, for all perform to some degree. The good performers ... gain status not because of their virtuosity but for their ability to bring the community together in performance' (cited by G. Davis, 1987: 156).

6
Humours[1] of the Great Strike

In reality the spirit in which the strike was faced was amazing. There was a sort of picnic feeling in the air. No one minded inconveniences ... all were taken as 'jolly good fun.' Perhaps this was partly because everyone was sure that the stoppage would not be of long duration ... there was certainly no doubt as to the sporting spirit in which every discomfort and difficulty was met and conquered ... Young men ... became ticket collectors or porters and filled the bill as to the manner born. ('The Humours of the Great Strike', 1926: 10)

I am frequently hearing from friends of witty things scrawled in chalk on buses and tubes during the strike. Here are some new ones:
'To stop bus, wring conductor's neck – once only.' ...
'None but the brave deserve the three penny fare.'
On Friday: 'Positively our last appearance.'
'Gentlemen are requested to throw their matches on the lines,
as I have been detailed to sweep the platform each night.'
('Humours of the Volunteers', 1926: 5, *Star*)

The defining features of the General Strike were its good humour and the ways in which all involved used a variety of comic forms of speech and behaviour to frame the event and express particular visions of the national community.[2] Contemporary accounts of activities during the General Strike very clearly delineate Britishness for different status groups, institutions, and individuals. Reference to generic stereotypes – frivolous, sometimes reckless, but sincere Varsity men and society women, misguided yet well-behaved strikers, and brave and loyal average citizens who simply carried on – appeared in headlines, quips, slogans, conversation, poems, photos, cartoons, published 'true tales', and parodies.

The latter two genres, true tales and parodies, provided more elaborated descriptions of undergraduates who drove trains and served as bus conductors, ladies who served tea in Hyde Park, middle-class men and women who gave rides to office girls and clerks, strikers who played football with village constables or volunteers. The shorter speech forms, quips and slogans, function as what I call 'collapsed narratives', a form of speech totally dependent upon understanding the contemporary context and significance of the reference – as well as the point if not the details of the longer stories (Kalčik, 1975; Bauman, 1986: 76). These collapsed narratives refer to two types of tales: 1) the fully elaborated and detailed personal experience story and, 2) the less detailed but far more widespread urban legends of the day (i.e. those topics that retained a common theme and thread but got attached to a variety of actors and places) (Brunvand, 1981).

These verbal art forms particularly relied on the transparent ambiguity of puns (Green and Pepicello, 1984 and 2000) to indicate who was not a part of the polity of good English*men*. The media were particularly partial to bus slogans. Though volunteer drivers were no doubt responsible for most of these one-liners, the slogans' appearance in newspaper columns and their word-of-mouth repetition increased their spread and popularity. Those I interviewed presented these joking comments, quite similar to one-liners that also appeared in university and society publications, as examples of typical English humour in the face of adversity (Nicolson, 1946; Freedman, 1999). Bus slogans used humour to point explicitly to class and political differences, and the triumph of one political system over another.

In particular, the national media gave attention to slogans that focused on how upper-class volunteers claimed the mantle of Englishness and transformed a Labour-controlled transportation system into a Tory stronghold, for example, 'The Red Bus with the Blue Blood' ('Strike Diary', 1926: 3). A *London Opinion* reporter noted, 'a volunteer bus conductor claims that at Highgate, Hendon, Holborn, Hampstead, Hackney and Harringay he dropped passengers but not aspirates' ('Whipped Topics', 1926: 259). A *Daily Chronicle* reporter further commented on those volunteers, who were

> quite likely up at Oxford in the same destination and year as the conductor who demands my fare in the accents of the university and wears plus fours and a pull over. They are both humorists of a sardonic vintage. They have 'christened' the vehicle 'Soviet Sue' and chalked up on the other flank is the announcement 'By permission of nobody' ...
>
> Wonderful this English humour that is exclusively English ... There is proof of this quality writ large on bus after bus. ('London's Day of Disillusion', 1926: 2)

The *Children's Newspaper* interpreted the slogans in a similar vein, though it raised the stakes by referring to the buses as 'a brave little army, each with some kind of peculiar badge'. Bus slogans thus became military insignia and invoked other battles. 'One ... which had been in the wars and lost its glass, had a card fixed where the window should have been, and on it was written: *I have no pane, dear mother, now*' ('The Good Side of it All', 1926: 2), an unintentionally ironic quotation from Edward Farmer's 'The Collier's Dying Child', a much parodied story (Roud, Letter, 1987), and a not-so-subtle reference that framed the volunteers' behaviour as a selfless (Christian) sacrifice. But it also was a very conscious parody of that characterisation, as evidenced by the reaction of the 'thousands of people [who] saw that card and went on their way laughing'. The Duke of Richmond reported, although 'it got very ugly at times especially with the bus-driver volunteers ... [that chalked comment] shows the type of wit this extraordinary country of ours can produce when things are in crisis!' (Richmond, Letter, 1986a).

Newspapers also noted the ability of sloganeers to turn injuries into joking puns. The *Children's Newspaper* reported that those people who had had a laugh at the one bus, 'presently ... had another laugh. A bus which had also been in the wars drew up to the kerb, and over a hole was written, *All stones this way*' ('The Good Side ...', 1926: 2). And the *Daily News* noted, 'A rolling 'bus gathers no stones' and 'A board put across the vacant space left by a shattered window bore the words: "Emergency Exit"'. The columnist commented: 'Fortunately, we have not lost our national gift of turning our discomforts into jokes' (London Calling!, 1926a: 2). Two days later, the same column explained that such bus slogans have 'the characteristic English quality of giving a comic twist to an incident which in other countries would lead to torrents of solemn rhetoric, or even to a riot' (London Calling!, 1926b: 2).

Yet these comments were not only the response of those able to turn injury to sarcastic insult; they also displayed a black humour that more than hinted at the threat some felt the strike posed. In both the *Daily Telegraph* and *Daily Mail* the following story appeared:

> A privately owned omnibus, which was plying between Liverpool-street and Victoria yesterday, was 'protected' with wire and boarding. The driver was encased in wire netting of fine mesh, which extended over the engine-bonnet, while the windows on each side of the vehicle were strongly covered with long thick boards. The driver, who was humorously hailed in the Strand as the 'Surrey Fowl,' declared that he was 'taking no chances'. ('The "Surrey Fowl"', 1926: 4; '"Surrey Fowl" Bus Driver', 1926: 1)

Although the *Daily Mail* printed no other examples of such humour, the *Daily Telegraph* was so taken with this image that it printed another story on the subject in which 'the London humorist rose to the occasion and promptly chalked "The Hen-Coop" on the sides of these particular vehicles' ('London in Strike Time', 1926: 2).

But such interpretations focused on the dangerous nature of the volunteers' job and missed the point. Both creators and consumers of those puns used them to collapse oppositions by remarking on the strike and the volunteers' performance, their social status as opposed to that of the usual workers (and their knowledge of sayings that could easily be parodied), practical matters and the placards that directed everyday life, and the relationship between playful anarchy and Armageddon. See, for example, those quips at the beginning of this chapter ('Humours of the Volunteers', 1926: 5).

Of course not all publications printed all comments. University magazines noted sarcastic quips about the volunteers (most often made by Varsity men themselves). Women's magazines, more expensive journals, and national newspapers cited this genre to comment on the problems caused by the strike itself, the politicians in charge, the strike leaders, and the strikers or regular workers. A number of these weak puns, perhaps not accidentally, indexed a sick society; the *Sunday Pictorial* noted 'A Strike Time Epidemic. Rumour-tism'.

Even leftist papers such as the *British Worker*, *Daily Herald*, and *Scottish Worker* joined in the joke-making, though theirs more explicitly disparaged volunteer efforts. Some of the nicknames given to the OMS were the 'Order of Mugs and Saps', the 'Order of Mugs and Scabs', and the 'O'Messers' (Everard, 1926a: 4 and 1926b: 4; Gadfly, 1926: 5). More common than those sobriquets were short, biting quips. One, entitled 'Cannibalism?' observed, 'One of the sights of London yesterday [11 May] was an exquisite limousine labelled "For food", and bearing a cargo of substantial men and women' (1926: 4). A similar cartoon in the *Bystander* pictured a lorry containing only women and labelled 'for food only' (Cottrell, 1926: 421). The *British Worker* and other Labour papers used this image to aim its venomous humour at well-to-do blacklegs, presumably from the upper classes, whereas papers that catered to a middle-class or higher status group used it to denigrate women. In fact, there was a great deal of hostility against working women's usurping the places traditionally reserved for men; numerous anecdotes and quips complained about women in silk stockings getting all the rides and women workers' trapping unwitting and generous car drivers as husbands (e.g. Tristram, 1926b: 327). Unsaid yet implied, however, was the point that while certain types of people used the strike as an excuse for missing work, meals, and so on, those unaccustomed to responsibilities were volunteering for them – the back-story behind those collapsed narratives.

Other topics of humour included class and political differences as well as contemporary political and economic issues. The mainstream press ridiculed both strikers' slogans and upper-class status customs (e.g., the *Sunday Pictorial* noted 'Our Milk Headquarters [was] Cow-Hyde Park' and 'Road Traffic: The Common Wheel'). Mr Mayfair reported, 'Pour Encourager Les Autres. An official says that the names of all who have created disturbances should be displayed publicly. A sort of 'Who's Hooligan,' in fact' (Mayfair, 1926b: 5). Churchill's militant empire building attempts were a particular topic of jibes, e.g. 'In Pekin [*sic*] Dr. Yen has formed a Cabinet of one. How Winston must envy him this accomplishment of his ideal' ('Asterisks', 1926: 8; cf. Tristram, 1926: 327). Government workers also came in for some attacks, for example, 'during the strike many public officials slept at their offices. "Business as Usual"' ('Asterisks', 1926: 8).

Besides those pointed comments, others simply picked up on the more obvious and easy puns that the strike situation made available. Mr Mayfair of the *Sunday Pictorial* seemed especially fond of this genre, typical British humour of the period, hence his reports of the 'Hopeful Walkers' song: "Any Lorry"', and 'The Times we Live in: Sole Stirring' (Mayfair, 1926a: 3).

Stories and jokes about the volunteers also proliferated among individuals and in the media, which not only recirculated anecdotes that might otherwise have been lost but also offered a prize for the best strike story ('Strike Diary', 1926: 3). In fact, so many stories about the undergraduates' role were circulating during and just after the strike, that editors of university magazines such as the *Cherwell* felt compelled to state, 'We feel that care should be taken not to overstress reminiscences of the strike, as these are bound to pall in time ... Let us begin to talk about something else and pick up again the threads of our life here' ('Strike Reminiscences', 1926: 122).

Near and actual accidents with trains and buses were a common topic among former volunteers and their contemporaries, though the frequency of accidents was far less than the number of such tales would indicate. Percival Mannassi told of a real life version from his days as a University of Liverpool engineering student. Mannassi wrote that he himself impersonated his tutor on the telephone in order to volunteer at the Liverpool Central power station. Mr Pryce-Jones, another student, 'was allowed to take a train from Liverpool Central to Warrington (The C.L.C. Railway) but as the signalling was not too safe they only allowed the one train to run. On reaching Warrington, it was reversed and he drove it back to Liverpool.' The rest of the students played a joke on Pryce-Jones and put a notice in the entrance hall of the engineering building, which stated, '"We the undersigned do not want to hear how you saved the C.L.C. Railway." It had about fifty signatures on it. He was annoyed but as the case was locked he could not get at it to take it down' (Mannassi, Letter, 1987).

The general media, if not always the university and society journals, focused on the glamour jobs and the glamorous or well-known participants, emphasizing exciting episodes and parodying mundane ones. Possibly because detailed and humdrum accounts would have bored those accustomed to reading society magazines, such narratives did not appear in more expensive journals, which tended instead to publish accounts regarding certain aspects of the strike or lighter, more humorous stories and parodies of strike doings, especially ones emphasizing the volunteers' upper-class identity.

Here are two perfectly true stories about volunteer workers:

> An omnibus stopped outside the Constitutional Club. The conductor, who had been scrupulously professional in his 'Yes, Madam,' ... vaulted lightly off, hurried in to the club and came out reading a telegram that had been awaiting him. The omnibus then continued.
>
> Passengers in another 'bus were amazed to find themselves being diverted from Park-lane down Mount-street, where the driver got out and rang a front door bell and swiftly drank a cup of tea handed to him with much ceremony by his butler. (London, Mr. 1926b: 2)

Even the dailies, which reached a much broader cross-section of society, published only a few first-hand narratives, surprisingly, given the number of journals and extended letters home that I came across (e.g. those of Edward Benn, Robert J. Cogswell, C. H. Drage, Lady Phyllis MacRae, and Jack Verdin).

Although similar in form to the personal narratives people wrote or told to me, published versions tended more frequently to adhere to a certain tale type: they emphasized the successful completion of a difficult task, usually associated with a near accident – as if a rag or prank had been pulled off successfully. In one typical article, 'a volunteer docker' told his tale about 'Raising the Dock Siege' in the *Daily Mail*:

> It was just getting dusk when our convoy of twelve lorries and two armoured cars, each filled with volunteers, swung smartly out of Hyde Park gates on their way to 'Somewhere in Dockland.' ...
>
> Inside the scene was reminiscent of 1914. Hundreds of men crowding together, each eager to know what they were going to do; the sharp command 'form fours!' then the numbering off and the roll call, a hot supper, and so to bed.
>
> We sat down to a substantial breakfast at seven o'clock, and marched to one of the great dock sheds, alongside which lay the S. S. 'Starling' and 'Rock' – both laden with food.
>
> In a few minutes we were at work. An Oxford undergraduate at the ship's steam crane. Oxford and Cambridge men jostled shoulder to shoulder with porters and clerks, every man doing his utmost to expedite the unloading and to excel at his new job.
>
> First came the unloading of the cargo of freshly killed meat, ... while ... hundreds of kegs of butter and boxes of cheese were being unloaded with equal rapidity ...
>
> All this time patrols of the Guards were constantly moving about, and the proceedings were watched by a huge crowd of strikers and women from the connecting bridges and other vantage points.
>
> * * *
>
> ... The vim and zest displayed by the volunteers were marvellous; hands unaccustomed to toil were torn and bleeding; clothes were dirty and stained; backs were strained; but not one man so much as thought of deserting his post. ('Raising the Dock Siege', 1926: 2)

Such detailed and lengthy accounts were rare, however, and most media reports focused on the anecdotal, contrasting tedious with amusing and holiday-like aspects of volunteer life. As the *Morning Post* explained:

> Strike duty is monotonous work, but ... systematic efforts, on the old-time lines, were made to keep them amused ... With characteristic generosity the members of the theatrical profession threw themselves into the work of providing programmes and excellent concerts have been given at all the barracks, at Deptford, at Victoria Park and even at the docks ... The military authorities are full of gratitude to these volunteers; and as for the troops themselves, the uproarious welcome given to each performer has been sufficient proof of their appreciation. Cinema shows have been given at many stations. ('How London was Made Safe', 1926: 4)

Full-blown strike narratives, whether published or privately related, usually began with an account of where the speaker or writer was when he or she first heard of the strike and his or her motives for volunteering; the latter vary somewhat. Next was the protagonist's removal to the strike's temporary and potentially chaotic world, which generally involved the exchange of usual occupation and clothing for a strike-time job and work or leisure apparel. Once the narrator joined a volunteer corps at the local Guild Hall, police station, or whatever, he was sworn in, given an assignment, and, in some cases, special markers of his new status, such as overalls, tin hat, armband, truncheon or even a chair leg when the batons ran out, depending upon the task to follow. As political journalist David Walter put it, 'final examinations were postponed as mortar boards were exchanged for peaked caps' (Walter, 1984: 60–1).

In contrast to what the mainstream print media conveyed, many of my correspondents and interviewees related that the next step was waiting and more waiting. It was often necessary to travel several miles to port towns or to London, where officials provided minimal instructions at the docks, in barracks, or in underground railway stations, bus and tram depots, and in railway sidings, print works, offices, and electrical plants. But in spite, or because, of their amateurish confidence, the volunteers plunged in and did the jobs, though not necessarily as the regular workers would have. Photographs and captions in the *Illustrated London News* explained, emphasizing the playful aspect of the strike, especially for the volunteers. 'However inconvenient and menacing the General Strike may have been, it certainly varied the monotony of life and led to many unwonted scenes ... Not least remarkable ... was the way in which the love of our national game showed itself among the volunteer workers in Hyde Park, where an improvised game of cricket took place in Rotten Row, with boxes for wickets and sticks as bats' ('Curious Effects ...', 1926: 866; see figure 2.1(c)).

Like the bus slogans, most of the shorter, published anecdotes were meant to be funny and focused on just a few topics – the social class of the volunteers, the ability of the undergraduates to beat the strikers at their own 'game' (albeit in a rather eccentric fashion), the failure of the strike to turn into a revolution, and scepticism regarding the value of what the volunteers had actually accomplished. Women volunteers were most frequently the focus of the last subject.

Humorous anecdotes about social class centred on absurdities that resulted when the leisure class took on workers' jobs (but also implied the latter's superiority) or emphasized the social status gained by doing jobs as 'lowly' as possible, for example, 'The Editor of *The Isis* wishes to contradict the rumour that he was driving a lorry of vegetables. Nothing so bourgeois! Milk, yes; and newspapers. Vegetables, No! ... The Sub-Editor, on the other hand, has sunk so low as to be a mere dockyard labourer ... Mr. Barnes has not been heard of, but it is rumoured that he has joined the looters ...' ('Our Staff', 1926: 4). The Cambridge *Gownsman and Undergraduate* commented in a section on 'strike reflections ad nauseam' that 'we went to the slums to discover the University' – again, that emphasis on a reversible world, at least for the elite. 'Nearly everyone one meets starts talking about his strike experiences, and all are unanimous in their opinion that they were with the scum of the University. Men grow heated, arguing as to whether the beer-swilling set he was with were worse than the ardently religious set someone else was with' ('Flotsam and Jetsam', 1926: 2).

Individuals' tales of this type tend to demonstrate how undergraduates shocked locals with their habits (see also Mitford, 1960: 14–15). Girton alumna Lady Smith, a retired physician, told me, 'My future husband drove his 2-decker bus very fast and dangerously and didn't know exactly where he was supposed to be going. He had to keep on stopping to ask his passengers which turn to take. After a bit they all asked him to stop and let them out as they were too alarmed by his driving to trust themselves with him any longer' (Smith, Letter, 1986). Another Girton alumna, expanded on this tale type: 'There were many jokes going round Cambridge, e.g. ... the tales of rival Oxford and Cambridge men driving the trains of the London Underground Circle [line] having races ...' (Atwood, Letter, 1987a). 'Cambridge drove the trains one way round and Oxford the other (clock and anti-clock wise), racing each to be the quicker; consequently on the one way (we of course said the Oxford way!) a driver raced his train through a station packed with people, leaving them stranded for hours' (Atwood, Letter, 1987b).

There was also a more elaborated version of a similar story about the trains that ran between cities. Brenda S——, who grew up in Rugby, told me 'a delightful story ... very much appreciated at the time' (S——, Letter, 1986a); in which student volunteer drivers 'arrived at Euston Station in record time – indeed 3 hours faster than the usual crack drivers – amazed, the station master asked the two students how they did it – to receive the answer that they had not known how to stop it until a few miles from its destination' (S——, Letter, 1986b; see S——, Interview, 1987). Joan Bedale, a Girtonian living in Paris during the strike, reported a variant (presumably told by one of her brothers, who was in the Royal Navy and Stationmaster at Glasgow Central):

> The story goes (I cannot swear that it is true) that a young volunteer was allowed to drive an express train from Glasgow to Euston Station London. He arrived, very pleased with himself, five minutes ahead of schedule. The temporary Stationmaster at Euston, no doubt my brother John's superior officer, congratulated him on his achievement. 'But there is one thing that was wrong,' he said, 'You should have made a stop at Rugby Junction on the way.'
> 'I know Sir,' said the young man. 'I known I should have stopped at Rugby, but it was not until I reached Watford (a London suburb) that I found out how to stop the damned thing.' (Bedale, Letter, 1987)

These accounts took on the features of those specific dramatic forms characteristic of upper-class leisure activities detailed in Chapter 3, that is, rags, larks, jokes, and treasure hunts, which were elaborate, pre-scripted activities often planned for some social purpose; in effect, they filled in the stories encoded by 'collapsed' slogans and quips. Such stories are essentially 'trickster' tales[3] in which a fool (the trickster) triumphs over his or her seemingly bigger, cleverer, or more powerful opponent (e.g. 'Jack the Giant-Killer'; Paredes, 1966). Alternatively, the trickster can outsmart himself and end up victim to his own pranks. Lady Lindsay (Interview, 1985) and the Reverend Adeney (Letter, 1986) related variants of the train driving undergraduate story in which someone chastised the young man involved for having almost caused an accident, instead of praising him for having managed to arrive earlier than usual. The indirect criticism contained in such accounts points to an undercurrent beneath the rag-like atmosphere that, according to the standard interpretation, prevailed among undergraduates.

In those sorts of narratives, focus is on the amusing aspects of narrow escapes (Freud, 1960; Brunvand, 1981), which tend to cluster around a few iconic experiences, such as nearly crashing a train or bus or just missing injury at the docks, and turning such an experience into a joke. The Hon. John Jones, who volunteered as a London bus driver, related,

> There was one most amusing chap there, whom I knew because I'd been quite keen on racing at Brooklands in these days ... Perry Thomas ... was an absolute mad man, wild devil ... He had a jolly good drink before he started and he came along, ...
> 'I want to drive a bus! I want to drive a bus!'
> Everyone else took his turn and the inspectors there who were looking after selecting the people to do it ... didn't know who he was. I kept quiet – I knew Perry. Anyhow, when his turn came, he was so drunk he could hardly stand, but

they hoisted him up into the cab of the bus ... You had just a seat in front and a windscreen. They had nothing at each side at all ... And he got hold of this bus – they were in those days pretty ramshackle things, the buses ... And he started off with this and he drove this bus without any trouble at all, ... got right round the skid track without hitting anything! It was amazing! Everyone else had knocked down two or three of them. Anyhow, he finished it off there. So then he wasn't satisfied with that. He went and reversed the thing and he did it! (Jones, Interview, 1987).

That structure – detailing the daring deed and then making light of it – was typical of volunteer accounts, of the British gentleman amateur in a crisis. In another instance, Clare alumnus G. Murray Burton, who volunteered to unload vessels at Hull, explained how undergraduate ingenuity generally applied to pranks was transformed into a (somewhat) more pragmatic use: 'The food was so bad we brought our own food as far as possible and made good use of broken crates of oranges. If a crate of butter was broken on one occasion we would grease the planks (on which the crates were slid down) to increase the speed of movement (more broken crates I expect)!' (Burton, Letter, 1986).

Shortened versions of the trickster type were also popular, and those I interviewed reported the excitement that came from small outbreaks of violence, evening drinking and games sessions, and occasional accidents caused by volunteer pranks or their ignorance of machinery. Many tended to recall the non-traditional work habits of the volunteers, particularly their incompetence. According to Lady (Enid) Oatley, a Girtonian, 'An undergraduate acting as a conductor ... when asked the way to a certain destination of which he hadn't the answer, would reply firmly "change at Charing Cross! Change at Charing Cross!"' (Oatley, Letter, 1987). Sylvia Baron, another Girtonian, reported that undergraduates she knew 'come back with stories of how, not being familiar with the route, they had gone the wrong way, or obliged a pretty girl-passenger by taking her to her house which was off the route, or calling on a girl friend and leaving the bus outside her door during his call. Not one of them had any political convictions and volunteered solely as a lark and a nice change from academic life' (Baron, Letter, 1986). G. Murray Burton also reported hearing that 'I don't think buses' scheduled routes were adhered to. If someone of the Female sex asked nicely I rather think they would be driven to a particular destination' (Burton, Letter, 1986).

A related type of story depicted a more rag-like scenario, in which student volunteers assumed to be real workers. Joan Bedale related one incident in which an elderly servant behaved charitably and a volunteer student porter acted the cad.

> My mother was staying in London when the Strike began. But she had to try to get home to Coventry. So she went out with her case and stood in the empty

street (Belgrave Road) hoping that she might be given a lift. Soon a car drew up beside her and an old chauffeur got out of a magnificent Rolls and asked if he could help. She told me, but I am very old and my memory fails, that he was Lord Robert's chauffeur ... He took her to Euston Station where a young student looked after her and put her in a train which he said would go to Coventry when they found a volunteer to drive it ... She offered the young man a large tip by the way, which he accepted with a broad grin and slapped in his pocket. I expect he was much richer than she was! (Bedale, Letter, 1987)

The *Isis* also printed joking anecdotes about Oxford undergraduates that emphasized the more rewarding aspects of social role-switching. 'Those who went off on Tuesday filled with a burning desire to do their bit for their country and join the Territorial Reserve Force appear to have spent a quiet two weeks in barracks, and have returned in good order, with £2 5s. in their pockets' ('Our Staff', 1926: 4).

The *British Worker*, which published longer and more anecdotal commentary about stereotypical volunteers (Everard, 1926c: 8) than did the papers and magazines aimed at the middle and upper classes, was particularly fond of alternative trickster tales, which proved just how incompetent the volunteers were. One story focused particularly on their foolishness. A group of strikers was caught in the rain on their return to London from South Wales. They stopped for shelter in an inn and met up with 'an elderly lady of severe and haughty aspect. With her was a young man, evidently her son ... [He] wore a pair of the plusiest plus fours I have ever seen.' After several minutes of listening to the woman's lamenting the strike and trying to figure out what her son could do, one of the strikers asked Lady Camelia Fotheringham, 'a Primrose dame, a member of the Women's Imperial anti-Socialist Club, and the vice chair-woman of the Anti-Vegetarian League', if she could help with 'a matter of high political importance'. She agreed, and he asked her to deliver some important papers

> to Jones of High Pringleby ... 'The utmost secrecy is needed. It is for the cause of England', I added in thrilling tones. 'After explanations – somewhat prolonged, owing to [her son's] rather attenuated [*sic*] power of understanding, a bulky package ... was transferred ... to the care of Lady Fotheringham ... They set forth ... on one of the worst roads in England. There was a look of patriotic consecration on Lady Fotheringham's face. And that's how we got our stock of revolutionary pamphlets to Comrade Jones' ('England Expects——', 1926: 4).

Individuals also reported such instances, though theirs were far less elaborated than the media versions. For instance, Jim Newmark's account had the working-class protagonist (himself) effectively 'tricking' a volunteer. Newmark, who volunteered at TUC headquarters 'tying up and parcelling stacks of newspapers and leaflets to be distributed by motor cycle dispatch riders to various centres', recalled 'one memorable day at the centre of the movement' when he 'actively took part in the stirring events of those days'.

> I set out from North London to walk the six miles or so [to Eccleston Square] as all public transport was at a standstill. Fortunately, I was able to get a lift in a car driving by a Conservative MP, Derwent Hall Caine,[4] son of the famed author [Hall Caine]. I did not mention my destination to him, but on reaching the vicinity I thanked him for his help in getting me to the strikers' Headquarters. He must have felt very uncomfortable in giving unwitting support to one of the 'other side' and his face certainly showed it. (Newmark, Letter, 1985)

Parody was the real forte of both workers' and university publications. As the Cambridge *Gownsman and Undergraduate* noted,

> There were many disquieting and conflicting rumours during the recent unpleasantness, and not the least distressing of these concerned the movements of the Oxford and Cambridge lacrosse team. Jim had been seen by William driving a tram in the great Metropolis. James had seen Bill inciting the workers of North Battersea to rise. Others maintained that the whole team had formed itself into a band of roughs and was supporting whichever faction seemed in the majority at the moment of action. ('Our Staff', 1926: 4)

For many volunteers, the strike turned out not to be at all what they expected, yet there was more to it than just a feeling of discomfiture. University reports display an overt recognition too broad to miss that the country was in the midst of one of those dramatic Great Moments of British History. One article in the *Cherwell* even complained about

> the peaceful and orderly conclusion of the strike ... Something a little more showy should have been 'staged' for the benefit of the many 'Sons of Liberty' whose dry throats were ready to shout applause on witnessing a thrilling drama enacted within the bounds of our shores – something coloured with the glory of British pageantry, and showing the 'boys of the Bull Dog Breed' with their 'backs to the wall' ... But what did they find? Not a shot fired – and strikers playing with policemen at football! ('Wanted: Flamboyance', 1926: 122)

To compensate for such disappointment, university magazines and Society journals indulged in playful satires of strike experiences. They amused their readership with rhetorical flights of fancy, which had little actual content, and spoofs of their usual gossip columns or diaries, letters to the editor, poems, and plays. While such efforts were not examples of upper-class folklore in the same ways that larks, rags, fancy dress balls, and so on are, they similarly co-opted popular imagery and traditional symbols for their social critiques. And of course they were derivative of the masquerades, charades, and ragging pranks that occurred more spontaneously during university life and country house weekends.

Punch and most of the undergraduate publications that featured these parodies were well known for this particular genre. The most popular forms for the university magazines were play scripts and poems with the plays unfolding like 'shaggy dog' stories – a lot of build-up for a groaner of a pun, or an obvious joke. An *Isis* sketch, entitled *The Strike-Breakers: A Drama in Three Driblets*, detailed the foul language, hard work, and dangerous mission of two undergraduate volunteer dockers. Mourning the ruin of their Oxford bags and tiring after just a few hours of work, they went off to the canteen. In the last 'driblet' the first two undergraduates contemplated passing through some dock pickets. This was particularly dangerous because they were dressed in plus fours and look nothing like strikers. Giving a fine example of how rumours and urban legends grow beyond themselves, the first declared,

> Don't you realise we're going into the hottest district in East London? I hear a volunteer docker was lynched outside these very gates last Wednesday.
> 2nd U.V. I never heard that. You know two Specials were stabbed on Friday?
> 1st U.V. Two! Six you mean. They don't patrol this street now. It's too costly.
> ('The Strike-Breakers', 1926: 10)

Having found an explanation for the absent patrols, the undergraduates decided they must still serve their country. But the second UV thought they should go back. The first declared, 'Never! Think what headlines it will make – "Undergraduates Heroic End". "Torn in Pieces by Infuriated Mob". "Not Wearing Oxford Trousers".' And going to the heart of the matter: 'We can't disappoint the Press'. So the two lads proceeded and met up with a fearsome picket, who politely asked them '"Well, young 'uns, 'ow d'yer like shiftin' butter?"' Before the curtain fell, they replied in unison, '"Not bad, old son"' ('The Strike-Breakers', 1926: 10).

University magazines aimed their jibes at the hypocrisy inherent in the Englishness promoted by the government, the press, and those undergraduates who took themselves too seriously. Society journals tended to parody letters and diaries that detailed social events. Like undergraduate texts, they caricatured volunteer patriotism as well as the media's attempts to turn mundane, if unusual, efforts into heroic battles.

Punch's satirical methods, though amusing, were not terribly complex or creative and relied on the structures of well-known tales. The little piece 'What did you do?' transformed the mundane details of volunteering into a fanciful tale of heroism that managed to skewer Mr Cook, the *British Worker*, and the general populace as well as the volunteers. Truthfully answering the patriotically loaded question, 'What did you do in the Great Strike?' would not do, so the narrator persuaded his brother to agree to his revised account of volunteer bus-driving. When his son asked the pre-ordained question, the father responded with a stirring tale of how the two fought off a dangerous mob by reading to them Mr Cook's statement in the *British Worker*, which claimed how peaceful and sportsmen-like the strikers were. Faced with such a challenge, the crowd rushed off singing and dancing. "'All except one, who hit Uncle Alan on the head again with another piece of coal", added John quickly. But I soon dealt with him. "Will you stop that, Harold, or must I slap you? Wasting coal at a time like this ... He burst into tears and went away ... And that's how I won my stripes", he finished, producing a blue-and-white armlet [the special constable's insignia] from his pocket' ('What did you do?', 1926: 568). Faced with a giggling boy and a stern-looking woman, the heroes walked off.

Where this satirical account differed from most, however, was in its disparagement of war-time service. The tale concluded with one volunteer's commenting to the other, 'Very disappointing ... just as sickening as the War. You do your best to make it sound interesting and then you get looked at like that. Most disappointing' ('What did you do?', 1926: 568). Instead of the Great War's hallowing the events of 1926, the paradigm was stood on its head: the volunteers' activities in 1926 were used to question British soldiers' involvement in the First World War, a literary theme that began to emerge during the war and which was becoming even more evident by the mid-1920s (Fussell, 1975).

Exaggeration for humorous effect was also a favourite technique of *Punch* essayists who, like other satirists, used this tool to make explicit the humbuggery of schoolboys eager to volunteer for a new adventure. One letter from 'Smith Major' detailed this brave lad's disappointment with 'the absolutely rotten way in which the General Strike came to an end'. Smith was unable to volunteer immediately because, as a schoolboy, he needed to have his parents' permission to do so. His letter took longer than usual to reach 'the Pater', who did send a telegram

> saying O.K. ... As I am in the Cadet Corps I did not see why I should not convoy food lorries from the docks. I have never driven anything, but I was quite willing to have a shot and to run over anyone who tried to stop me.
>
> And then on Wednesday afternoon the Government let them call the strike off ... I call it rotten that just when a fellow is ready to go out and has got permission and everything is practically fixed up, they let the strikers chuck it, and a fellow has to start prep. again instead of giving the country a leg-up.
>
> There are a number of us here who will be much obliged if you will let Baldwin have the tip that, unless he gives the next strike a decent run, we shan't bother about it, and he can save the Constitution by himself. (Evoe, 1926b: 541)

Undoubtedly there were many people who felt similarly to Smith Major, though few were willing to express themselves so bluntly.

While there were obviously plenty of tales that pointed to male volunteer incompetence, media stories that most actively denigrated volunteer efforts were frequently aimed at women, particularly at those who took on tasks ordinarily associated with men or with working-class women. The *Evening Standard* rather cattily reported that 'many ladies, royal and otherwise, who having discovered the satisfaction of doing real work during the war, have since been loath to leave their "jobs"' ('A Modern Princess', 1926: 6). More direct in its attack than middle-of-the-road media could afford to be, the Labour-oriented *Sunday Worker* published a photograph of two well-dressed women presiding over frying pans with a pointed caption, 'Lady members of the idle class "caught" doing something useful in Hyde Park' ('Lady Members', 1926: 8), which other papers also published but with different commentary, as in figure 5.15 (e).[5]

The *Queen*, *Punch*, *Sphere*, and *Tatler* featured a series of parodies, giving the distinct impression that female interest in the strike rested solely in the benefits women could derive from it (see figure 5.16). *Punch*'s 'Diary of a Mondaine' recorded, 'It was easy to see what was in the wind that blew Lady Manœuver (*sic*) in on me the other day looking so chirpy ... "To mothers of daughters one general strike is worth five hundred dances ... April and I helped with the milk in Hyde Park. Dear Lord Sideshire was one of the milkmen; and so – and so – overalls and milkcans and a crisis did what three seasons of dance-frocks and foxtrotting failed to do, and darling April's engaged"' (Mayfair Mansions, 1926: 572).

This characterisation's significance was not just the 'woman catches man thanks to the strike' theme. Typical debutante tactics had failed to secure a husband for April. Her appearance in overalls – women's work clothes – and her performance of maid's work were what won her a man – and a lord at that. Traditional motifs regarding disguised lords, challenges met, and rewards won were recycled for a modern folk tale. And the moral was clear: if young women acted like 'real' women and attended to appropriately maternal and domestic tasks (dealing with milk and helping men), rather than wasting their time at dances, they would receive their well-deserved reward. And if upper-class folks engaged in physical labour, their lives would be both more enjoyable and more satisfying. Only the temporary nature of this particular dramatic encounter and the popularly acknowledged victory of the volunteer forces enabled magazines to discuss explicitly the advantages of a society in which the leisure class did the jobs of idle workers.

The sheer amount of satirical comment directed at this topic gives some hint as to just how disturbing such a possibility actually was in the mid-1920s. It also pointed to the very real anxiety that middle and upper-class young women had about finding husbands at a time of increased competition for those men who had survived the Great War. Such narrative genres foreground both the threat and absurdity of such a topsy-turvy world.

At the universities, another level of critique emerged, along with a more profound mysogynism. The male publication staff of the *Isis*, *Cherwell*,

Cambridge Gownsman and Undergraduette, and *Oxford Magazine* often attached feminine pen names to their columns, a fairly transparent practice of gender switching also common to charity rags and the popular parties of the 1920s. The 'Letters from Ermyntrude' column in the *Isis* was 'a weekly letter about Oxford society gossip [by] a well-known society lady, [who] having rolled up *his* shirt sleeves and lit *his* pipe will now commence' ('Letters ...', 1926: 11). As in similar Society magazine columns, the thrust of this 'gossip' was that women were far more interested in the romance (adventure), the 'divinely fetching uniform[s]' ('Letters ...', 1926: 11), and the shortage of rouge occasioned by the strike. According to Aunt Ambrosia of the *Isis*, 'undergraduettes' at Oxford spent 'a large portion of the week annoying the officials at the Town Hall by vainly demanding jobs'. To keep them under control, 'the policy was initiated of sending one in every hundred applicants to take a message somewhere on her bicycle – the message was usually to her college Principle [*sic*] – to beg her to restrain the ardour of her students'. When others proposed to start a free canteen in order to draw the crowds away from Labour meetings, the authorities turned it down because 'such action might be interpreted as showing that its originators had taken up an almost definitely political view. The dangerous conditions of the Oxford streets during the past week has [*sic*] been due to the patriotic action of the undergraduettes' (Aunt Ambrosia, 1926b: 13).

Only male undergraduates, those with the most acknowledged licence in British society, had the power to make such critiques. Although Society women and Bright Young Things might have attempted to co-opt this role, they were more frequently the targets of such jibes. As Marion Massey of Girton explained to me:

> This was still a time when women were tolerated at Cambridge but not particularly welcomed, certainly not by some of the older academics. A story went round about a particular lecturer, I think in Philosophy. Each time his lecture came round during the strike, the men attending diminished in numbers, but the number of women remained the same. One day he came in to the hall – looked round and saw no men there. So he announced 'since no one is here, I will not give my lecture today'. Whether this is true or not, I don't know, but the story went round as a good joke. (Massey, Letter, 1986; see also Aunt Ambrosia, 1926b: 13)

Gender switching for public performances, which was and is part and parcel of mummers' plays, Carnival, and Mardi Gras performances, formed the basis for much of the type of humour found in *Beyond the Fringe* or *Monty Python's Flying Circus*, and is still the practice in Christmas pantomimes popular in present-day Great Britain. It is no coincidence that tricksters are often characters of ambiguous gender identity. During the French Revolution, the Rebecca Riots in early nineteenth-century Wales, the Irish Molly McGuire uprisings, and in a variety of 'blood and bread' protests throughout the eighteenth century, men disguised themselves as women to censure or attack perceived violations of tacit inter-class obligations. By masquerading as women, men could criticize without fear of personal reprisal – and, not coincidentally, relinquish responsibility for attacks on the dominant culture and its leaders, enabling all concerned to blame frivolous and emotional women if their words or deeds backfire. Characteristic of this technique of disguise, however, is the almost total lack of pretence, making clear the source of the critique but making it impossible for anyone to complain about the 'joke'. Drawing on such play traditions further emphasized the non-ordinary aspects of life during the strike, the upside-down world both volunteers and strikers had created. More to the point, such a conceit enabled male undergraduates to praise the volunteers' efforts and, at the same time, to ridicule the new women who were encroaching on their turf.

What all those humorous accounts and comments from various sources have in common is that all describe undergraduate volunteers and similar types doing what young men and women with few obligations do – commit reckless and even dangerous acts just because they can. As an article in the *Cambridge Gownsman and Undergraduette* commented, some people 'treated the crisis as a form of amusement kindly staged by the T.U.C. for the amusement of the undergraduates' ('Strike and Service', 1926: 1). Sophia Baron, at Oxford in 1926, affirmed: 'All the strike volunteers were male and regarded it as a great lark' (Baron, Letter, 1986). Some of their reckless abandon might be attributed to a 1920s' ethos of post-war anomie, or even Dadaesque bursts of creativity. But I suspect the primary source of their pleasure in such rags at the expense of others stems from the fact that these young people could afford to take life and work lightly. Girton alumna Lady Bullard noted that, 'young upper-class undergraduates at Oxford and Cambridge regarded the volunteer work in the strike as a <u>lark</u> and a change from their ordinary lives' (Bullard, Letter, 1987). They were simply of an age when they did not yet have to take much of anything seriously. And not incidentally, they had an explicit licence to pull such pranks and be subject to no penalties.

Such licence and related dramatic activities dated back to an earlier time, to the days of the Swing, Rebecca, Luddite, and other uprisings noted above. This particular kind of social protest tradition, which relies for its inspiration on models derived from folk dramas that mark calendar customs, rites of passage, and other holiday quêting[6] traditions, included fancy dress or cross-dressing and demands for money, free food and drink from middle and upper-class land and business owners (e.g. Alford, 1959; Rose, 1962; Smith, 1966; Williams, 1971; Thompson, 1971, 1974, 1991; Hobsbawm and Rudé, 1975; Burke, 1983; Pattison, 1977; Peel, 1978; Simms, 1978; Hay *et al.*, 1975;

Hebdige, 1979; Green, 1980 and 1981; Russell, 1981; Bushaway, 1982; Pearson, 1983; Pettit, 1984; Underdown, 1985). During the eighteenth and nineteenth centuries, the English upper classes were highly involved in enacting public symbolic ceremonies that marked the structural relationships between classes and the rules for appropriate behaviour for different status groups. Much of the ritualized behaviour of power and deference occurred during everyday life – in the marketplace, at home, on the streets, within the politico-legal bureaucracy, and in more formally designated public places such as churches and theatres. Calendar festivals, however, tended to be more symbolically loaded with both expressive and functional representations of communal obligations. Because the participants expected Christmas and Harvest Homes, as well as the various forms of ceremonial house visiting that occurred between Christmas and Oak Apple or Empire Day at the end of May, to demonstrate the actual existence of such relationships, the highly dramatized behaviour that characterized such occasions was intended to convince everyone that the ideal and the reality were one.

At these events there were certain ceremonial ways of marking class distinctions. Abundance, elaborate settings, dramatic costumes, and public enactments of ideal relationships usually occurred during calendar festivals as well as rites of passage celebrated by the aristocracy and gentry. As interconnected communities grew into industrial villages, the more elaborate and privately controlled dramatizations of the obligations implicit in a hierarchical small community faded and were replaced by increasingly public displays of 'good works' performed throughout the year, as well as on holidays (Laslett, 1971; Houghton, 1979; Cohen, 2002: 51). In the twentieth century, such dramatic public exchanges tended toward more pragmatic representations of hierarchical structures (Cohen, 2002: 51); there were few opportunities to express the reciprocal relationships of obligation – only those of power. In 1930, for example, when the Duke of Westminster married his third wife, Loelia Ponsonby, he remitted a week's rent to all his tenants, while others in similar situations invited 'coach loads of tenants up to London for their weddings' (Pine, 1956: 44).

These various social rituals were much more than just ceremonial survivals; the world-turned-upside-down motif provided a highly functional way to enact and preserve the social order (Gluckman, 1964). While the workers or servants were waited upon during designated times and places, the upper classes were doing the waiting. They did not merely 'allow' their workers to be on top. Acts such as serving one's tenants punch and food at an heir's coming of age party, presenting gifts to servants on Boxing Day, and distributing blankets, coal, soup, and unwanted advice to the needy became highly foregrounded occasions designed to demonstrate to those whose destiny it was to serve how to do it properly: cheerfully, politely, and enthusiastically. Similarly, youthful members of the establishment and Society women acted as happy workers during the 1926 General Strike and in innovative and symbolic ways every bit as meaningful as the holiday patronage their parents and grandparents had performed for their servants and tenants.

In May 1926, the Bright Young People and others were able to put their games and their humour to serious purpose. They applied what they knew to a social crisis and thus played out their own war-game fantasies of saving their country from the chaos of a General Strike. In a rather neat structural inversion, the volunteers, undergraduates and Society women in particular, defended their right not to do manual labour by doing it – temporarily. They countered the accusations of the socialist Labour movement that they were the idle, incompetent rich by demonstrating their ability to 'come through' in a crisis. They worked, together and as a temporary community, to 'keep the nation going'. They rallied to fight a limited, safe war against a known enemy designated as disorder and chaos, which attacked the Constitution and challenged the basis of their social hierarchy.

Of course, a great many of those who volunteered realized, albeit after the fact, that the General Strike did not pose the threat to democracy and civilization that the government and media made out to be the case. Somervillian Rosamund Tosh noted, 'things would be very different if a similar crisis occurred now-a-days. I should perhaps add that my own attitude has changed a good deal over the years, and that I now feel slightly ashamed of my then failure to appreciate the plight of the miners ... I would say that my generation was much less politically aware than are modern students' (Tosh, Letter, 1987b). But the volunteers, every bit as 'English' as the soldiers during the First World War, felt honour bound to perform their duty, to display their patriotism. Their verbal response in the form of the puns, parodies, anecdotes, and jokes permitted the activities of the volunteers to be reframed as play. Because their own identity was so tied up with role-switching and play acting, with trying to become what they were not, the volunteers could reflect and embrace the double image that British society imposed on them, which was part and parcel of their role as tricksters. Their complicity in this ambiguous identity enabled them to be at once heroes and buffoons, patriots and fools.

Notes

1 As per the title of an article in the popular press, 'The Humours of the Great Strike', 1926: 10.
2 Bruley found that striking miners, miners' wives, and family members also engaged in a fair amount of comedic, playful, and parodic behaviour during the strike and subsequent lockout (Bruley, 2010: 60–85).

3 Tricksters in other cultures include Coyote and Raven for American Indians in the southwest, Brer Rabbit for African Americans, or Monkey (Hanuman) for Southeast Asians.
4 Newmark had confused the Caine brothers and was actually referring to Gordon Ralph Hall Caine, elected as an Independent Conservative MP in East Dorset in 1922 and Conservative Whip in 1923. In 1929, his brother, Derwent Hall Caine, was elected a Labour MP in Everton.
5 The *Sketch* and the *Sphere* featured that same photo but with a different purpose and different captions. The *Sketch* caption read 'Armed with their frying pans: Lady Betty Butler (left) and Miss Collett Doughty' (1926: 13).
6 Quêtings are traditional house visits (frequently at Christmas); those of lower social status travel from house to house, perform skits or songs, and request something in return for not wreaking havoc. The children's custom of trick or treating at Halloween fulfils a similar function, as do Mardi Gras performances and subsequent demands in southern Louisiana.

7

The volunteers' farewell: closing rituals, genteel ironies

> **Plaudits for the Volunteers**
>
> The Last Night
>
> 'Positively our last appearance', the 'Plus Force' were yelling out on the Underground Friday night. 'Walk up, ladies and gentlemen. We promise you won't be disappointed'. The parting sally as we left was, 'Good-night, everybody, good-night', in best B.B.C. style. (London, 1926b: 2)
>
> Some of the volunteers who had served on the Underground had good-humoured celebrations ... to mark the end of their service. At one North London station they made the platform look like a ballroom with bright decorations of coloured streamers, and the lifts were hung with balloons. ('London Calling!', 1926: 2)
>
> [The end of the strike was] tinged with regret [for the volunteers. Many] were running valedictory trips ... A train with its strike name 'Nulli Secundus', chalked on the roof, was inscribed: 'In memoriam, RIP', and at the Highgate terminus farewell messages were scrawled everywhere. 'Goodby-ee', was written on the platforms ... together with such facetious announcements as, 'We've got the sack', and 'Volunteers are going cheap today'. A uniformed porter was among those who shook hands and congratulated the MPs and men of title who formed the volunteer staff at Westminster Tube station. ('The Tube Volunteers Farewell', 1926: 1)

Unlike the real goodby-ees and whizz bangs of the Great War, the playful frame the media drew around the 1926 General Strike transformed it into a joke, a lark – to be remembered and passed on as such for vicarious newspaper-reading participants. But of course it was not 'just play' for everyone, and there remained something tragically incomplete, naive even, about the closing rituals and ceremonies that marked the transition back to 'normality' (van Gennep, 1960; Geertz, 1973; Turner, 1973 and 1982; Smith, 1975; Babcock, 1984; Davis, 1986).

Some send-offs were spontaneous and conducted by the volunteers themselves or by those they had served, while others were more official (see figure 7.1). According to the *London Opinion*,

> There has been a regular epidemic of dinners to 'celebrate' the conclusion of General Strike. At one of them a party of members of the Royal Air Force Club, who worked on the Tubes ... entertained Lord Ashfield and some of the regular 'hands' who had stayed on to teach them their duties. And I have heard of at least two private little dinner parties between amateur bus conductors and ladies who had been their 'fares'! (Round the Town', 1926: 262)

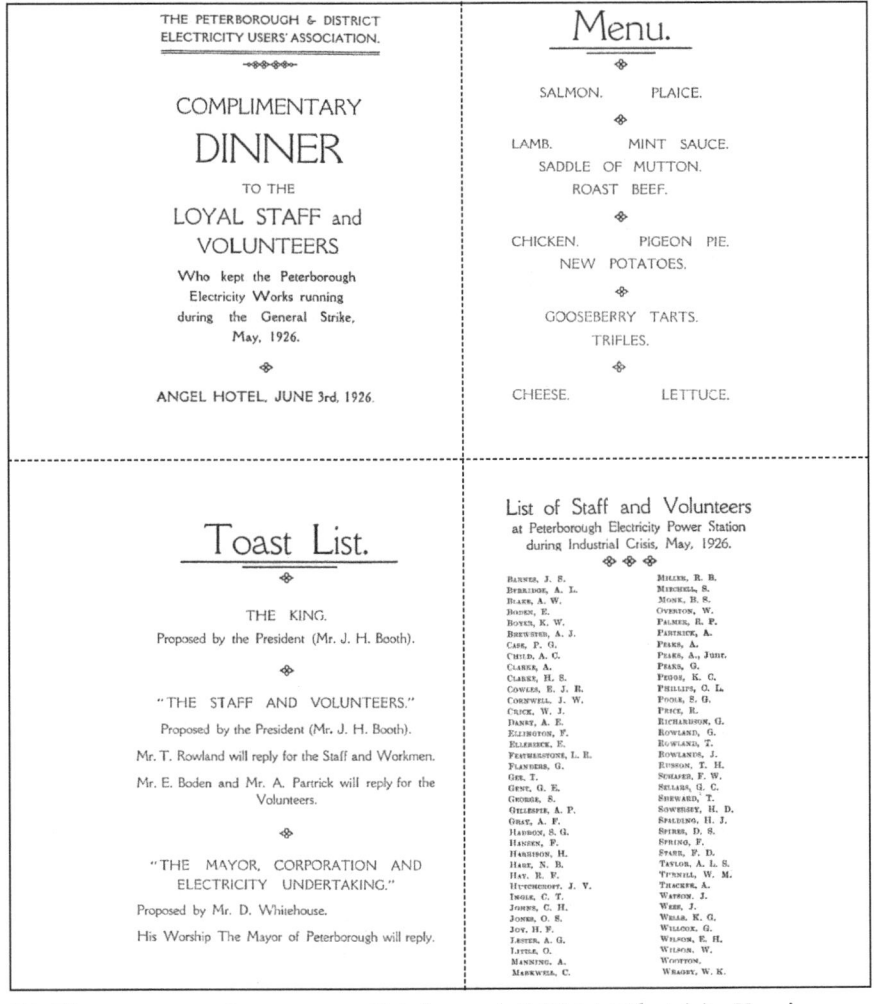

7.1 Dinner menu and programme, Peterborough & District Electricity Users' Association

The *Police Review and Parade Gossip* reported, 'The good work done by the *Wallasey* Specials is not to be allowed to pass without civic recognition. They are to be entertained at the Town Hall in two batches of about five hundred each' ('Strike Notes', 1926: 288). 'The "good-bye" dances at Earl's Court and elsewhere last Saturday night were jollier and heartier than would have been any function of a commonplace season' (A. B., 1926: 155; and see 'Good-Bye, Old Bus', 1926: 2). One of the volunteers at a bus depot even 'serenaded the neighbourhood on his ukulele [*sic*] ... for hours last night'. ('News in Brief', 1926: 2). As a personal remembrance of the occasion, special constables at Kensington autographed each other's batons ('And Then They Disbanded...', 1926: 156; Fraser, Letter, 1986b). Phineas May, who volunteered as a special constable, received a note informing him of a change in his duties (see figure 7.2). More ceremonial closures to the General Strike consisted of final assemblies, parades, and dinners at which special constables, transport

7.2 Note to Phineas May, 'May 14, 1926. The Street Patrols have been cancelled after tonight Friday so you will not have to report for that duty on Saturday morning. Please look up other duties in place of this.'

volunteers, and others were thanked formally by the Lord Mayor of London, Colonel Wilfred Ashley, MP, Ministry of Transport, and other officials in abundantly photographed occasions (e.g. 'Scenes After the Great Strike', 1926: 4; 'And Then They Disbanded . . .,' 1926: 156; 'London "Specials", "Civils", and Volunteers Disband', 1926: 889).

Besides being thanked – and paid, as were the Civilian Constabulary Reserve volunteers ('The Police and the Crisis', 1926: 279) and those who worked for privately owned firms – volunteers also received mementos of their service, usually in the form of certificates or letters (see figures 7.3–7.6).

According to *The Times* 'Financial Report' for 20 May 1926, 180 people received 'gratuities' for their help to *The Times* during the strike, 65 received £4 each, and 84 received 21s. each. The 'MET' also paid its 819 volunteer workers at the rate of the grade they worked (GLC, MET/10/564, 'Board of the Metropolitan Railway Report', 1926: 4). Some volunteers received medals for their service, such as one in the Liverpool University Archives awarded to a

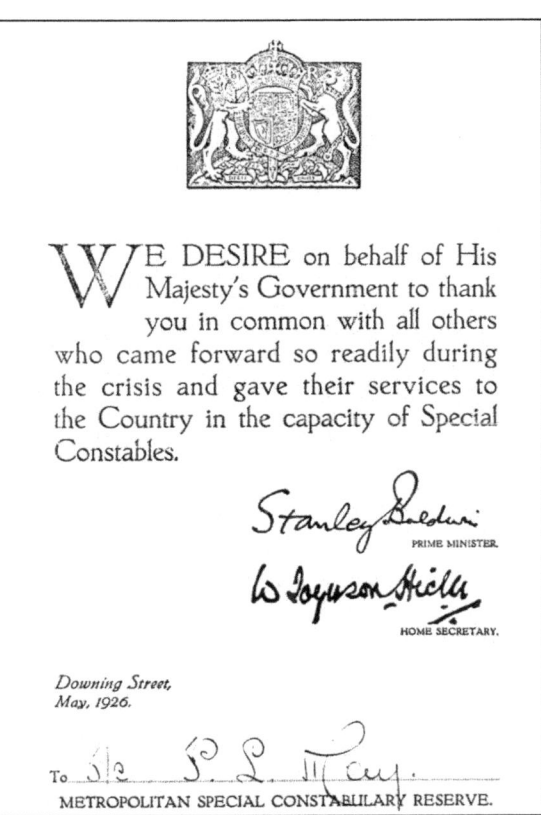

7.3 Thank you certificate issued to Phineas May, May 1926

7.4 Thank you certificate issued to Charles Cassell, May 1926

chemistry student 'for help[ing] ... the L.M.S. Railway Co ... in firing steam locomotives at Edge Hill station during the General Strike of 1926'. The legend reads '*Largitas muneris salus reimpublicae*' (Allan, Letter, 1986).

Many upper- and upper middle-class volunteers, especially those who worked with the Great Western Railway, received small silver trays. B. W. Pendred, then of Westbourne Park, who served as a 'Special Constable on the Great Western Railway based at Westbourne Park Station' explained,

> when the strike was over those of us among the volunteers who desired not to be paid were each given a solid silver ashtray 13 cm long by 9 cm wide inscribed with the Arms of the Great Western Railway and the words 'General Strike May 1926, With the Grateful Thanks of the Great Western Railway, and the name of the volunteer.' I still have mine though, apart from the name, the rest of the inscription has been almost polished out. It bears the number 714 so it is probable that over 1000 must have been presented. (Pendred, Letter, 1986a)

Prior to his memento's arrival, W. G. Massingham received a form letter (dated 21 May 1926) to from the 'Chairman and Directors of the Great Western Railway' to let him know that the 'little souvenir' was on its way

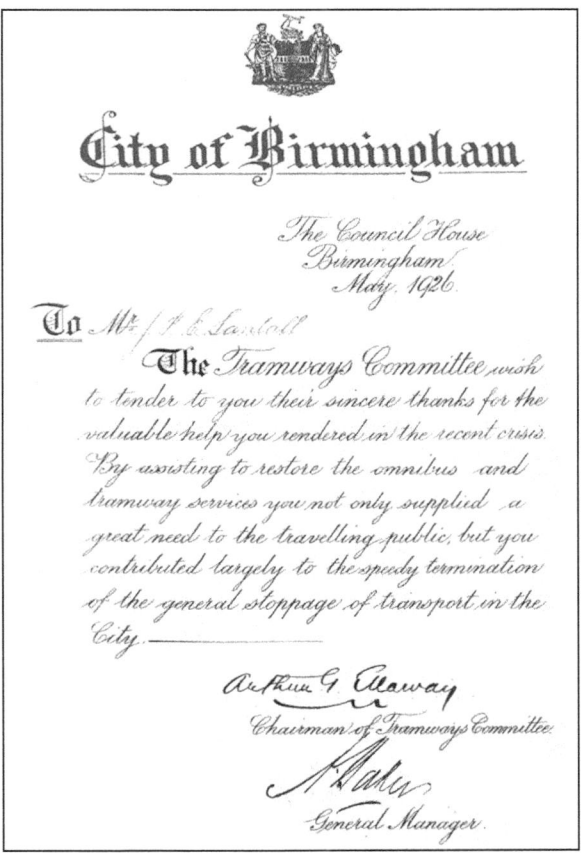

7.5 Thank you certificate issued to Jack Santall, May 1926

(Massingham, Letter, 1986). He later received a thank you certificate as well, just like the one Peter Kingsford received (see figure 7.6). Lady (Anne) Rosse, who 'served in Hyde Park in the food catering – distributing at the inhospitable hours of 4.30 am till midday' (Rosse, Letter, 1986a) also reported: 'Both my husband and I were presented with a silver emblem for our services to the General Strike Relief for food to London' (Rosse, Letter, 1986b). Diana Cooper recorded that she took 'stranded workers home in my car'. Although her husband, Duff Cooper, had forbidden to her to volunteer with those at the *Daily Express* and *The Times*, she did so anyway, and 'folded papers back to back with him all through the nights. He never knew until we both received the silver matchbox, engraved with a joke about "Strike," given by *The Times* to all helpers' (Cooper, 1959: 72).

7.6 Thank you certificate issued to Peter Kingsford, May 1926

Others had to settle for more ephemeral rewards such as postponed exams ('London University', 1926: 2; 'University News', 1926: 2). Also popular were free theatre tickets, which the BBC offered 'for volunteer workers ... at the Vaudeville Theatre' and for '"The Rescue Party" to any volunteer bus drivers, conductors, or tube workers' at the Comedy Theatre for those who showed their 'credentials' at the box office (GLC, BBC, 1926, CL/EMER/1/2: 4). In addition, volunteers received an abundance of praise in newspaper editorials, letters, and magazine articles.

Those who responded to my newspaper queries tended to structure their accounts in a particular way. First, they explained how they were the recipients of a certificate, gift, or some form of thank you for their service. Next they noted what they had done to deserve such a reward and concluded with a re-telling of the circumstances in which the reward was received. Newspaper and magazine reports had a parallel form, in which articles and letters to the editor praised and thanked volunteers for their efforts and then recounted anecdotes about their accomplishments. These stories were often didactic little tales that revealed what true gentlemen the volunteers were – especially in contrast to the strikers.

Editorials usually complimented specific individuals – government officials such as the Prime Minister and Home Secretary or certain groups, such as 'our priceless British Bobby', the 'admirable young men from Cambridge University', the BBC, and the special constables (A. A. B., 1926: 240; 'The Police and the Crisis', 1926: 279; 'Robert The Angel', 1926: 540; Seward, 1926: 10; 'Wireless Wins Through', 1926: 5). Most letters to the editor, however, maintained the widely held view that it was the average volunteers who had defeated the strikers with the 'astonishing good nature of the amateur drivers and conductors'. 'To my mind.' wrote one Lieutenant-General to the *Morning Post*, 'by their unfailing good humour they did more to keep up the spirits of the people in the last trying fortnight than anything else. Now that the bouquets are being handed out to all sorts of people I should like to add my little posy of forget-me-nots and lay it at the feet of amateur Omnibus and Train drivers and conductors' (Bethune, 1926c: 3). Bethune apparently felt so strongly about the volunteers that he sent this letter not only to the *Morning Post* but also to the *Daily Express* (Bethune, 'Public Spirit', 1926b: 2) and to *The Times* (Bethune, 'The Efficient Amateurs', 1926a: 3), which all printed it – a phenomenon that indicated either a shortage of letters or the preference such papers had for letters by high-ranking officers.

Letters in other papers provided a similar view of the volunteers' importance in defeating the strike. The *Daily Mail* published a lieutenant-colonel's letter, which insisted that the attempt to portray the strike as a government victory

> is hardly accurate. No Government with all its resources could have carried on for three days without an army of volunteers. It is to be hoped that the Prime Minister, in his natural anxiety to get things going again, will not forget those who have the first claim on him, and that he will give whole-hearted support to the Railways and other employers in their desire to find permanent employment for those of their voluntary help who need it. One may hope that when the strike is over the Government will introduce a vote of thanks to those who saved the situation. ('Work for the Volunteers', 1926: 3)

Such letters further reveal that not all volunteers were from the leisure classes, or even the middle class, or they would not have needed to make temporary jobs permanent. Several letters in the Metropolitan Railway's files also provide evidence that a great many were in as desperate a situation as some of the strikers ('General Correspondence re Volunteers Folder', 1926; 'Suggestions from Passengers', 1926; Wrigley, 1984a).

As at least one newspaper noted, the very success of the volunteers was a surprise even to them. According to the *Star*, 'the Government is to hold an inquiry into the working of the scheme for keeping essential services going during the strike ... The public was surprised at ... the scheme's ... efficiency and completeness. To the advocates of the General Strike the result must have been a shock ... It showed that the community can look after itself even when great masses of labour have been withdrawn' ('How it was Done', 1926: 4). The *Evening News* reported that 'volunteers at Hull docks are unloading ships quicker than the regular men do' ('Beaten at their Own Game', 1926: 2). University and society magazines echoed this sentiment. According to the *Isis*, 'there is no doubt that the coming of the undergraduate helpers produced a considerable moral effect'; the big towns found that the university men could do a day's work and were surprised that public school men knew about engines and had no objection to soiling their hands ('The U-C Writes', 1926: 2).

Other journals, such as the *Saturday Review*, both parodied and praised the efforts of some volunteer workers while also aiming a few barbs at the aristocrats involved. The 'overwrought' staff member wrote:

> The strike found us of the Saturday as it found the rest of Fleet Street, all dressed up and no where to print. Now our heads though bloody are unbowed ... We have done, in the simple old British way, without the least self-consciousness at the time or self-glorification afterwards, what we gather from articles in most of the daily papers was an epical thing. And we have done it alone. All through those grim days, when we rang up friends on the dailies for late news, it was necessary to begin by saying 'Would Your Grace be so good as to put the Saturday through to the News Editor?' All night long there came to our strained ears from Fleet Street the wail of infant viscounts left in the sub-editorial *crèches* while their mothers did charwomen's work for quite recently ennobled newspaper proprietors [J. J. Astor of *The Times*]. And ever and anon the tinkle of an hereditary monocle dropped in Shoe Lane, the hoot of a car in which a baronet's wife was setting off to deliver copies of some public-spirited sheet among her wide circle of acquaintances. But we, we laboured alone. Not a duchess at our switchboard [Lady Louis Mountbatten worked the switchboard at *The Times*], not even the widow of a provincial civic knight to sweep our stairs, not a single coronet displaced by mopping a weary brow in our office. (How We Did It', 1926: 612)[1]

In an editorial just before the end of the strike, the *Daily Telegraph* declared, 'All honour to them! They have saved their country from chaos and from a disgraceful surrender to revolutionary dictatorship. What they have done will never be forgotten in our time, and they have written a splendid chapter in the social history of Great Britain' ('Improving Services', 1926: 2). Even *Punch*, refraining from its usual satirical humour, printed a cartoon, entitled 'The British Worker', which depicted a cigarette-smoking volunteer at the wheel of a lorry labelled 'J. Bull' and 'Essential Services'. An upper-class Mr Punch, wearing spats and a bow-tie and carrying a cane, saluted the Volunteer with a 'Thank you, sir'; the caption below read, 'With Mr. Punch's enthusiastic compliments to the great army of amateur workers who sustained the Nation's life' (Raven-Hill, 1926: 523).

Besides letters and their own editorials, most newspapers also printed the 'Prime Minister's Message [of] Thanks to The Reserve Volunteers', which recalled that 'the salvation of the community from great peril is largely due ... to their patriotic efforts'. Even those who did not volunteer obtained membership in this praiseworthy band: over half a million 'loyal citizens', 'men and women', had offered their services, but, Baldwin explained, less than 10 per cent were actually called upon, because 'it was necessary, as in the Great War, to have and to maintain available a large service of volunteers to meet contingent demands, and to all those who so enrolled the Government desire to tender their sincere thanks' (Baldwin, Stanley, 1926b: 3; 'As In The War ...', 1926: 1).

Interestingly, those more general expressions of thanks almost always mentioned the efforts of the 'women no less than the men, ... [whose] iron endurance and good humour, has made possible the triumph we celebrate today'. Thus, at the end of the strike, as at the end of the war, women obtained full membership in 'the mass of the nation [which] has been splendid' ('Victory for Community', 1926: 2). As the *Evening Standard* put it:

> The Government deserves credit for the firmness with which it finally faced the menace ... [but] the great body of volunteers who sprang from everywhere to man essential services have placed the country under an obligation it can never sufficiently recognise. Lamentable as the business has been ... it has at least displayed before an impressed world the best qualities of the British race – its cool courage, its invincible optimism, its handiness, and its peculiar quality of humorous stoicism. ('Settle Down!', 1926: 6)

Like the Great War, even the General Strike had its justification.

In an effort to forestall continued bitterness and strife between classes, employers and employees, and individuals, the media and prominent figures tried to smooth over the rift engendered by the General Strike and responses to it ('Mr Baldwin's Thanks ...', 1926: 3). Stressing the importance of retaining that supremely British quality of order, the King urged his subjects to 'forget whatever elements of bitterness the events of the past few days may have created, only remembering how steady and how orderly the country has remained' ('The King to the Nation', 1926: 2). A lasting peace, he proclaimed, could be created only by 'forgetting the past', which would enable the nation to 'look only to the future with the hopefulness of a united people' ('Pictures of the Strike', 1926: 857; 'The King's Message', 1926: 3).

The Prime Minister, unlike George V, preferred to recall the past, to credit Britain's historic tradition with ending the strike. Welcoming the prodigal strikers back into the national fold, though not without first scolding them for 'engaging the constant attention of the Government', Stanley Baldwin stressed:

Our business is not to triumph over those who have failed in a mistaken attempt. It is rather to rally them together with the population as a whole in an attempt to restore the well-being of the nation ... It would not, however, be right that I should let to-night pass ... without expressing the heartfelt thanks of the Government to all those of our countrymen who have supported us ... We conceived it to be a matter of absolute duty to call upon the whole country to resist the menace of the general strike. The people of these islands responded ... as in our long history they have answered every claim made upon their love of freedom and sense of fair play. (Mr. Baldwin's Thanks ... ', 1926: 3)

The Liberal-leaning *New Statesman*, however, was not so fulsome in its praise, noting,

it should also be realised that the success of the various extemporised services and organisations was largely due to the fact that there was no ill-temper on either side and that the Unions had most emphatically forbidden their men to take any action which might bring them into conflict with the police. It is therefore not very wise to insist too strongly on the 'victory' of the Government. A victory it was, but for the public rather than for the Government [that] ... did everything it could, through the medium of the British Gazette, to exacerbate feelings on both sides. ('Comments', 1926: 113)

Like the *New Statesman*, the *Oxford Magazine* and other university publications printed editorials quoted Baldwin's praise for 'the commonsense of the best part of the whole United Kingdom'. Unlike the *New Statesman* article, though, this *Oxford Magazine* piece, while emphasizing that 'in no other country in the world could a national disturbance of this magnitude have been quelled so calmly, legally, and with such good humour', also took a swipe at the strike leaders, who 'tied their hands by not wishing to resort to violence, and still more because, had they wished to do so, they would obviously never have succeeded in carrying the workers with them ... The behaviour of the strikers showed that they felt their loyalty to the Unions should not entirely abrogate their loyalty to the country' ('The Non-Revolutionary Strike', 1926: 1).

While most of those on strike and those victimized by employers afterwards would not likely have agreed with this evaluation, its symbolic purpose was evident. The British character of all concerned was what really defeated the (un-British) General Strike and thus provided an implicit resolution to the 'curious, paradoxical and enlightening ... example of a general strike such as the one which has just ended' ('The Non-Revolutionary Strike', 1926: 1). Regarding this point, folklorist Moira Smith commented, 'whichever way you look at it, this is hegemony in action!' (Smith, Letter, 2010).

But besides all those editorials and articles claiming victory for the nation and the triumph of the British spirit, there were also those that explicitly blamed the strikers for the national crisis and displayed headlines of the sort that the *New Statesman* had condemned. Right-wing dailies like the *Star*, *Daily Mail*, and *Daily Express* ran banners illustrated with photographs describing 'How the Great Strike was Broken', or 'The Spirit that Broke the Strike – A Mercantile Marine Officer as a Volunteer Engine Driver' ('How the Great Strike was Broken, 1926: 4; 'The Spirit that broke the Strike ...', 1926: 4). More right-of-centre papers such as *The Times* used more subtle methods, for example, the letter of one mine owner, which noted,

> after six months of amicable conversations last year, the owners informed the miners definitely that ... they were unable to continue the old wage rates; and it was because of this situation that the Government ... granted a subsidy to tide over the period of further inquiry. Sir Herbert Samuel's Commission has reinforced the view that without such a subsidy it is impossible for the rate of wages previously in force to be paid. (Horne, 1926: 3)

In contrast, the *Scottish Worker* recommended cutting the moneys paid to royalty owners.

> The Duke of Northumberland's own admission is £75,431 last year, and admissions made by industrial royalty owners at the Sankey Commission revealed the following facts concerning their annual income from the mining industry:
>
> Marquis of Bute ... £115,772
> Duke of Hamilton ... 115,000
> Earl of Durham ... 40,522 ...
>
> So you see there appears to be a fat living in coal for everybody but the man who howks it, and gets killed in the process. ('Fat Livings in Coal, But not for the Collier' 1926: 1)

Despite similar compelling arguments,[2] an article printed the day after Horne's letter claimed that the strikers, not the employers, were 'breaking an obligation of honour ... As a matter of fact, there is no evidence anywhere that employers are trying either to reduce wages or to vary any of the conditions of employment to the detriment of their workpeople' ('Railway Work Refused', 1926: 3). This report came from the Labour Correspondent to *The Times* and contradicted the previous day's (13 May) notice by the Southdown Motor Services, which stated their refusal to recognize trade unions in the future or to employ union labour ('Non-Union Labour Only', 1926: 3). Publications such as *Punch* had no qualms about revealing their bias. One cartoon, entitled 'The Lever Breaks', pictured a working man with 'T.U.C.' on the back of his jacket. The man was struggling with a lever labelled 'General Strike' to heave a boulder labelled 'Constitutional Government' (Partridge, 1926: n.p.).

Yet not all the media were so condemnatory of strikers and their leaders, or inclined to praise so highly the feats of the volunteers or the 'calm and courage' of Baldwin and the government. Both the liberal *Oxford Magazine* and the *New Statesman* chastised Winston Churchill and his *British Gazette* for a lack of impartiality, for exacerbating the conflict with its amateurish techniques ('Parliamentary Reports', 1926: 444), and for the way it 'exaggerated, distorted or suppressed news, speeches and opinions for propagandist purposes' ('Comments', 1926: 116). Those liberal journals took a more neutral stance, for example, that of the Archbishop of Canterbury who wrote a letter advocating peace and compromise among all parties. Such a tactic provided a way to avoid mentioning vengeful motives of persons on both sides. The *Oxford Magazine* also claimed impartiality for 'that group of Oxford undergraduates who felt that ... the best way they could serve their country was to start an impartial news organ, which should freely voice the opinion of persons belonging to all parties' ('The Archbishop's Letter', 1926: 1). In the view of Michael Stew, an undergraduate at St John's College and later Foreign Secretary, 'a great many young men who had previously taken the existing distribution of wealth for granted began during the strike to think afresh and consider the conditions in which many of their fellow citizens had to live ... The members of the Labour Club ... helped the local Council of Action to organize strike meetings [and] ... bicycled round the Oxfordshire villages distributing leaflets' (Walter, 1984: 60).

Like the Archbishop, some organizations tried to distance themselves from both sides. They pointed to the existence of a different sort of community and tried to give the impression that politics need not enter into every aspect of life. An advertisement in the *New Statesman* for the life-boat service (a voluntary coastguard) claimed that it 'serves all and is supported by all without distinction of party or class, [and] was ready day and night throughout the strike to save lives. Will you help this national service? It neither asks nor receives a penny from the State' (Advertisement, 1926: 126). The *Oxford Magazine* contained a notice similar in spirit, regarding setting up a miners' distress fund. The organizers took care to note that such a fund was not intended to subsidize the strikers but to help alleviate the sufferings of the miners and their families. 'Oxford is not the enemy of the miners and trade unions', it declared somewhat defensively ('Correspondence', 1926: 507). Of course, the effect of such fundraising would not have been impartial at all, for the result would have been to free up miners' funds for less disinterested purposes.

Despite these efforts at neutrality, most of those on the Labour side were not having any parts of it. Looking beneath the guises worn for the nine-day wonder in May of 1926, *the Lock-Out Strike-Time Sentinel* pointed out that 'men in overalls were described riding in limousines along with the top-hatted – who wears top hats now? – to show the praiseworthy abolition of class distinction. We had some of this in the other war. How long will it last again? Just till the trouble is over' ('What we have Seen and Heard', 1926: 1).

The BBC itself also spoke to the notion of an ideal world, albeit in a more hopeful vein, heralding the end of the General Strike with a peculiarly symbolic gesture that pointed as well to the deeply British nature of the event. *Sphere* columnist C. Lewis Hind remained awestruck by the strangeness of the whole affair – summed up for him by the trinity of

> Mr. Baldwin's speech at the calling off of the Strike conference, and the King's address to the country, and then – I like it – a man with a caressing voice recited Blake's –
>
> > I will not cease from mental fight,
> > Nor shall my sword sleep in my hand
> > Till we have built Jerusalem
> > In England's green and pleasant land.
>
> So for me, the Strike ended – with William Blake – how strange! (Hind, 1926: 160)

It was baffling – 'strange', as Hind noted – that BBC managing director Lord Reith would invoke a poet of reform and revolution. Yet as with all symbolic tropes associated with the General Strike, multiple meanings were loaded onto yet another key metaphor. The recitation of 'Jerusalem' (Blake, 1804) was an attempt to transcend the extreme social contradictions that the strike laid bare and direct attention instead to the utopian purpose of recreating England as an exemplary society.

Notes

1. Astor had managed to get quite a number of MPs and titled acquaintances to help out at *The Times*' offices in Printing House Square.
2. According to the *British Worker*, the owners' proposals 'on the basis of a 5-day week the reductions range from 3*s* 9*d* to 17*s* 2*d* a week'. Before the strike, the highest wages were for Nottingham Hewers, who received 12*s* 1½*d* a day; that would have been reduced to 10*s* 10½*d* under the owners' proposals. The lowest daily wages were for North Wales' labourers at 6*s* 5*d* per day, which would have been reduced to 5*s*. Based on these figures, and a five and a half day week, the highest pre-strike wages would have amounted to £3 6*s* 8*d* per week and the lowest £1 15*s* 2½*d*; with the reductions, these would have amounted to £2 19*s* 9½*d and* £1 7½*s* per week, respectively ('Owners Drastic Proposals', 1926: 6).

8

From ethos to mythos: the General Strike and Britishness

Of course everyone is entitled to his or her viewpoint and recollections ... So many books dealing with history make mistakes – punctiliousness as I have inferred is essential for credulity. Hence my views on what you term 'folklore'. (Spencer, Letter, 1986b)

... in five years time, we shall be writing our novels of the Great Strike. (Herlots, 1926: 133)

Contrary to most legends the British have been every bit as vigorous as the Continentals at taking their protests to the streets. We had no *sans-culottes*, but we had Chartists and Luddites and Glasgow Weavers and Conchies and General Strikers. (James Cameron, 1986: 17) [*Radio Times* review of the BBC2 documentary *Stand Up and Be Counted*, about the history of British public protest]

Immediately after the end of the General Strike the forces of historical reproduction went into action. Reporters, playwrights, diarists, legal authorities, historians, and others did not merely repeat what others before them had said. They recorded their own versions of the strike – and their images of the volunteers – and they have continued to do so ever since.

Certain iconic images predominate in those accounts. Thus, it was no accident that so many of the people with whom I spoke and corresponded, when queried about the volunteers and the strike, recalled particular anecdotes and referenced specific activities. They remembered the undergraduate train driver's arriving early at the station, the football match between strikers and police, polite and enthusiastic undergraduate volunteer in plus fours, Society ladies serving tea, and the old gentleman in a top hat balanced on a penny-farthing bicycle. Their likening the strike and the volunteers' activities to a holiday (Webb, 1956: 92; Cootes, 1983; Wrigley, 1984b: 6), play-acting (Webb, 1956: 94; Vincent, 1974: 2; Perkins, 2006: 207), a lark or a rag (e.g. Isherwood, 1947: 177–8; Mitford, 1960: 20–3; Wrigley,

1984b: 6),[1] even among the miners (Bruley, 2004: 236–7), further came to symbolize the uniqueness of British character.

As Patrick Renshaw put it, 'The General Strike of May, 1926, like Peterloo and Tolpuddle, has passed into the folk-lore of the nation' (1975b: n.p.; see also Renshaw, 1975a: 19). His use of the older, hyphenated punctuation relegated the strike as 'folk-lore'[2] to the realm of Child ballads and mummers' plays – fragments of a long-gone past, a relic that had survived because it carried some sort of spiritual 'ur' Britishness to inspire those who hearkened to its message. The General Strike became part of a dystopic golden age – a failed revolution because strikers forgot how to strike.

Historical reproduction and the General Strike

With the exception of the Civil War and the Industrial Revolution the 1926 General Strike may well be the most written about and reimagined event in British history. Most scholarly studies detail how the strike reified the transition of government, organized labour, and big business from a paternalistic style of obligatory reciprocity to a more modern, rationalist, and reformist model (Vincent, 1974; Middlemas, 1979; Perkins, 2006). Several observe, as I have done, the apparent media dialogue in which the two sides engaged (e.g. Martin, 1926: 69–95; Mason, 1969), as well as the distortions, claims to a prerogative on peace and order, and accusations against the other for causing harm to the nation (Archard et al., 1972). A great many, notably those clearly on the left, have focused on the General Council's and others' betrayal of both the miners and the rank and file who came out solidly in support of their fellow union members (Farman, 1974; Renshaw, 1975a and 1975b; Morris, 1976; Skelley, 1976; McIlroy et al., 2006). And a few have noted that the British world was temporarily turned upside down during the General Strike, thus causing people to act with more than their notorious British sense of humour. Not incidentally, some note, this response enabled amateurs to take charge and come through (e.g. Isherwood, 1947: 176–80; Symons, 1957; Archard et al., 1972; Vincent, 1974; Cootes, 1983).

But neither those authors nor others in recent times have written extensively about the volunteers, largely because rights to the General Strike seem to have been implicitly ceded to various aspects of the left, most of whom have come to accept that 'the volunteers have been better served' by historians and that such people 'were not required to show initiative but just to carry out the tasks assigned to them' (Morris, 1976: 12). A mere survey of the literature of the time contradicts the former contention,[3] and evidence in the preceding pages dispels the latter. But this debate was less about the validity of individuals' accounts as evidence than it was about entitlement, about who had the 'right' to tell General Strike stories (Halbwachs, 1992: 63;

Shuman, 2005: 18). As Chris Wrigley has noted, 'those studying the General Strike have usually paid more attention to the strikers than to the government's volunteers. Some left wing historians have dismissed them as "blacklegs" – without really examining just who they were' (Wrigley, 1984a: 36–7). Such scholars were far more interested in explaining why the strike did not succeed and/or how unified and politically conscious were local rank and file than with investigating the conflict as a whole along with all of its players, a perspective just as crucial to understanding how strikes and revolutions fail.

In this chapter, I do refer to the strike itself from the perspective of strikers and leftist historians. Some have regarded the event as a watershed for labour, as evidence of a surprising working-class solidarity (even among women), and/or as the betrayal of the common man's cause by the TUC General Council's co-opted and reformist (not revolutionary) leaders.[4] But such issues are not my main focus; many have covered this territory extensively and exhaustively (Laybourn, 1993; McIlroy, 2006).[5] I do make mention of such interpretations, however, when they have a bearing on how and why such authors portrayed the volunteers as they did.

Those historical analyses of the strike and the volunteers are one sort of historical reproduction, akin to but somewhat different from fictional portrayals. Material from my interviews conducted in 1985–87 is included with contemporary material (vernacular representations of the strike) in previous chapters because, in most cases, such accounts were neither as self-consciously produced or motivated as those diaries, memoirs, plays, poems, and novels, which their authors sought to publish once the strike was over. Nor had most of those I contacted, or who contacted me, written or talked about the event since 1926. Contemporary published accounts and written records made for private purposes must be regarded in the same vein; there was a qualitative and functional difference between what people wrote or said to their families or to me as another individual and what they produced when they had an unknown and/or consumer audience in mind (Thompson, 1994: 9). For instance, I used Lady Lindsay's remarks to me in previous sections (Lindsay, Interview, 1985) but especially note her published accounts of her volunteer experience in this chapter. Her comments during our interview included rather more contextual discussion, which helped far more to explain the reasons she acted as a volunteer than did her memoirs (Grosvenor, 1961; Lindsay, 1983). And Jack Verdin's remarks (Verdin, Interview, 1986), made once we got to know each other, were far more revealing of his sentiments concerning his ill-treatment by officials than was the lengthy and detailed account that he wrote before we met (Verdin, MS, 1986).

The General Strike as public enactment

As it unfolded and in its retelling and reshaping over the years, the General Strike of 1926 resembled a folk drama. As a public enactment that reflected the national ethos (Paredes and Bauman, 1972; Bauman and Abrahams, 1931; Saltzman, 1995) it was not exactly like Peterloo, Tolpuddle, or the Civil War – or even those treasure hunts and fancy dress parties that continue as play traditions among certain groups of people in British society.[6] It does, however, share certain qualities with state funerals like that of Princess Diana, festivals, games, wars, rites of passage, and fancy dress parties – patterned forms of social behaviour that reaffirm community, hierarchical social relationships, tradition, and consensus. It provided opportunities to 'let go', for strangers to converse, and even for marital matches to be made. Particularly for the intellectual and political left, those features became rhetorically foregrounded and allegorized as the strike became a cultural symbol and eventually part of the national mythology (Crompton, 1988: 127; McIlroy, 2006; Perkins, 2006: 257–69; Pugh, 2006; Aughey, 2007: 49–51). As such it became available to lend new meanings to later events (Bloch, 1977), most particularly labour conflicts with government and business, which occurred on significant anniversaries of the General Strike (McIlroy, 2006), for example the coal strikes of the 1970s and especially the 1980s (Smith, 1984: 11–12; Wilsher, 1984: 18; Harris, 1985; Perkins, 2006; Bruley, 2010), the London newspaper strike of 1986–87 at Wapping, and even with modern 'Conservative' manifestations of Britishness such as the Falklands War (Jack, 1986).

For David Benedictus, who wrote the General Strike play *What a Way to Run a Revolution*,[7] the very experience of working on the production had political value in and of itself. 'It was a big thing in my life, really ... And doing that rather challenging type of a show, it gave me street cred' (Benedictus, Interview, 2009). In terms of the strike's resonance in the national imagination and the reason for writing the play, he explained:

> We then felt it did have a political message which was extremely relevant at the time, because it was when Edward Heath was having his confrontation with the miners in 1973 ... And the message of the General Strike for me then and for me today ... and this is a clear parallel between then and now, that if the Government took the view that the strike would be a useful way of breaking the power of the unions, that they would have it at the time chosen by the Government. And that in terms of Cook and Scargill [secretary of the NUM and leader of the 1984–85 strike], it was very useful to the Government, to have a figure whom they could regard as a Bolshevik influence – or whatever phrases they cared to use. (Benedictus, Interview, 1986)

In transforming the General Strike into a cultural paradigm, key symbol, and allegory, the actions and parodies of the volunteers in the General Strike became oversaturated metaphors.[8] For a metaphor to be received as its speaker intends, the audience must have the same understanding of its primary and secondary subjects (Bauman, 1983: 84–94). This was not the case for the acts of strikers or volunteers. The former tried to claim their rightful place and entitlement as integral members of the national community, while the latter were occupied with demonstrating how ideal workers might behave.

Those who reproduced the strike – the historians, cartoonists, playwrights, museum curators, novelists, poets, and educators – took volunteer parodies at face value as *play* and not as serious social commentary on the upside-down world in which they found themselves. Unless the volunteers' narratives were framed as humour, they were largely excluded from public discourse about the General Strike (Shuman, 2005: 122). Instead, amusing anecdotes took the place of reports on actual events and people – or at least as proof of a traditional, everlasting Wodehousian (Perkins, 2006: 264) or Monty Pythonesque British buffoonery. Most scholars have focused on the frame that university volunteers themselves and much of the contemporary media insisted on imposing around their acts, thus providing the rationale to marginalize and dismiss rather than to examine them as among the central actors in the strike and its resolution. Thus the contemporary meaning of the volunteers' efforts – the metonymic relationship between their ethos and actions, and their own interpretation of that meaning – collapsed into the image of their own burlesque, just as one-liners during the strike came to stand for individual narratives complete with personal details.

To admit the seriousness of their playful efforts would also mean recognizing not only the imbalances produced by the rituals of class division within British society, but also the abuse of the rights and obligations implicit in a hierarchical social contract. As Osbert Sitwell, by no means an apologist for the strike, reflected, 'to be a porter for a time, or a lorry driver, would be easy, I considered: for a *time*, but not for a *lifetime*. Only as a holiday romp did it afford the contrast that might make it seem pleasant ... (They would enjoy a battle, after the manner of the pugnacious everywhere, but they wanted still more to talk about it afterwards ...)' (Sitwell, 1948: 230–1). A similarly dismissive attitude exists toward the sort of people who produce such social critiques as *Spitting Image*, *Private Eye*,[9] or the novel *England, England* (Barnes, 1999).[10]

Interpretive models of the strike

Examination of the various scholarly and anniversary publications that reproduced and reinterpreted the volunteers' role in the General Strike reveals the predominance of only a few themes. Virtually every account noted (whether in condemnation or praise) that the Government defeated the strike because it was far better organized than the strikers. But in their attempts to explain why, some scholars assumed that both the strike and its failure were inevitable (Postgate *et al.*, 1927; Leeson, 1973; Laybourn, 1993; cf. McIlroy, 2006: 70–3; Perkins, 2006). Most deemed the TUC General Council as – at best – having resigned itself to the inevitable and thus ended the strike (Symons, 1957; Morris, 1976; Jeffery and Hennessy, 1983; Laybourn, 1993 and 1999; Perkins, 2006), or – at worst – having betrayed the cause of miners and all strikers because it feared the success of the monster it had created (Arnot, 1926; Skelley, 1976; Klugman, 1980). Even the Communist party and the Co-operative movement came in for a certain amount of criticism for not properly educating the workers – who were apparently far more conscious and capable of displaying more solidarity than anyone thought possible (Carter, 1974: 25–6; Farman, 1974 and 1976: 9; Trory, 1975: 17; Davies, 1976: 1–12; General Strike 50th Anniversary, 1976; Morris, 1976; Skelley, 1976; Porter, 1978: 352–3; Hills, 1980: 18). Such studies have characterized the volunteers as the incompetent sons and daughters of an outmoded leisure class who, in their ignorance and in the process of fulfilling childhood dreams of playing at trains (Symons, 1957; Farman, 1974; Perkins, 2006), managed to kill people and damage property (Renshaw, 1975a and 1975b; Morris, 1976: 70–3; Watson, 1976: 368–71; Klugman, 1980).

Some of the more left-leaning accounts further insisted that volunteers acted and dressed not only unconsciously but explicitly to demonstrate their class solidarity and defend their privileged interests (Farman, 1974: 240; McLean, 1976: 7–9, 13, 16). This interpretation appeared in strike chronicles published within a year or two of the event (Burns, 1926: 47–51 *et passim*; Fyfe, 1926: 60–83; Parker, 1926; Postgate *et al.*, 1927: 20–1, 52). In some of the fiftieth anniversary local studies, which were among the more leftist in sympathies, students and society women were not even mentioned. Rather, the right-wing cabinet members responsible for the OMS and local Fascist or Loyalist organizations and activities were cited as representative examples of the 'volunteers' and their oppressive tactics (e.g. Trory, 1975; Durr, 1976: 6; Farman, 1976: 9; McLean, 1976: 7–9, 13–16; Newitt, 1976: 2; Hills, 1980: 11; Klugman, 1980: 121, 222). Particularly significant about this shift, besides its production during a time when Labour was in power, was that it made the Fascists, a group whom almost everyone who survived the Second World War regarded as extremist outsiders, the villains in the General Strike drama. By virtue of their not even being named, the students regained membership in the community. Adrian Mellor, Chris Pawling, and Colin Sparks in their essay, 'Writers and the General Strike', noted that 'the proliferation of left-wing journals enabled working-class writers to begin to speak for themselves. Consequently, their perspective on 1926 is often focused through the lens of the 1930s' (Mellor *et al.*, 1976: 348), and, I would add, the 1940s, 1950s, 1960s, and 1970s. Thus, this particular model used the theme of conflict with an almost universally agreed 'other' to recreate a model of social consensus, not too far removed from that which contemporaries siding with the government attempted in 1926. If those who incited the strikers and who acted as hooligans and revolutionaries could be designated as alien, so, too, could Fascists, fifty years later (Darnton, 1984; Bodnar, 1992; Halbwachs, 1992: 46–51; Tuleja, 1997).

A more sophisticated and wide-ranging argument placed the General Strike in a larger and more far-reaching economic perspective. Scholars who took this view portrayed the General Strike as the watershed for modern labour-industrial conflicts, demonstrating the power and necessity of organization and unity, as well as the uselessness of the old violent methods of labour protests (e.g. Morris, 1976: 13; Middlemas, 1979; Perkins, 2006). Still others argued that while the strike was the most important, significant, or critical event in twentieth-century industrial relations, it was a result of the transition and not the cause of it (Laybourn, 1993: 6, 120; McIlroy, 2006). In other words, the failure of the General Strike was a necessary rite of passage from the old-style confrontations between management and labour, in which neither side attempted to understand the other, to a more rationalized 'business-like' approach (Vincent, 1974; Middlemas, 1979; Laybourn, 1993 and 1999a).

In some of its incarnations, this model credited the working classes with the volunteers' victory and thus the necessary defeat of the strikers. While upper-class undergraduates and Society women received most of the publicity, the government's plans for an emergency situation succeeded only because vast numbers of unemployed workers were eager for even a temporary job. It was *their* skilled knowledge that enabled the successful running of one-tenth of the trains and power stations in Great Britain. Because of *their* inherently reasonable British demeanour, and that of their fellows who struck peacefully and maintained good order, the General Strike was defeated (Hornsey, 1976; SEARCH Project, 1979; Wrigley, 1982: 2, 6; Crompton, 1988).

An interesting inversion of this inevitability model, and one most often iterated in volunteers' memoirs, favoured the 'loyal' ordinary citizens who supported the government. Such accounts claimed that they (often people whom others might label upper class and who describe themselves as middle or at most upper-middle class) and other ordinary citizens of Britain defeated the strike with their determination to carry on. The everyday difficulties created by the strike motivated their actions. In fact, they enjoyed the chance to prove themselves in a crisis, to talk to strangers and even to marry them, to demonstrate their refusal to be bullied into something for which they were not responsible. The majority of British people felt sympathy for the miners and little but disdain for mine owners. Yet they also felt that the method of a general strike did not justify its ends, which, even if they were not intentionally revolutionary, was their implication. Thus, those who acted as strike-breakers during the strike and who gave their monies to charities for miners' wives and children during the seven subsequent months the miners were out were also portrayed as having exemplary British qualities: they were compassionate but not willing to be victims themselves (Cartland, 1971: 274; Cogswell, n.d.).

Diaries and memoirs

Published diaries and memoirs as well as in novels written at the time and after presented a more elaborated version of this last model. Some described a uniquely British characteristic in which the holiday-like attitude of the volunteers was meant to be understood as just one more (peculiarly British) way of making the best of a bad situation. This interpretation came closest to the ways volunteers at the time described the strike and themselves, and not surprisingly, since many of the authors were former volunteers (see Bibliography: Biographies and memoirs).

Such a perspective, however, differed from the satirical and sardonic portraits painted in university and Society magazines in that they attempted to explain, rationalize, or otherwise justify why individual volunteers acted as they did. Excuses ranged from not having known what the strike was about, to pleading a youthful desire to have a good time, to outright apologies for having behaved in thoughtless and foolish ways, or to a combination of these reasons along with a continued insistence that patriotism required such action, no matter how callous it may have seemed at the time and to their heirs. Using hindsight to reframe their stories and thus the event itself, those diary and memoir accounts reaffirmed and rationalized the existing ideology (Shuman, 2005: 82–6): in sum, this was how British people behaved and that was that – a sentiment echoed by many of those with whom I was in contact, as well as by written sources (e.g. Balfour, 1933; Mellor *et al.*, 1976; Lindsay, 1983; Perkins, 2006).

Christopher Isherwood's memoir, *Lions and Shadows: An Education in the Twenties* (1947),[11] first published in 1938, contains a scathing commentary about the volunteers' role. His account, however, differs somewhat from the rest of the memoirs in that he does not quite align himself with the status quo. Instead, he created a finely crafted send-up of all the pertinent issues concerning the volunteers: larks, rags, a joke, social class, extreme civility, and even war. Describing the start of 'the tremendous upper-middle-class lark', Isherwood wrote, by lunch-time, the Poshocrats were down from Oxford and Cambridge in their hundreds – out for all the fun that was going. And the medical students ... paraded the streets in their special constables' armlets, licensed to punch at sight. Every bus and underground train was a ragtime family party ... If you fussed ... you were a spoil-sport, an obstructionist, even a trifle unpatriotic. Not that anybody talked about patriotism – this wasn't 1914. Everything was perfectly all right, really. The strikers were all right – except for a few paid agitators controlled by Moscow, and some gangs of professional roughs. The great mass of the working class entered into the 'spirit of the thing'. (Isherwood, 1947: 177)

Isherwood continued, tongue-in-cheek, retelling an anecdote about Sandy, a friend who had volunteered as a driver; this particular tale perfectly exemplifies the fool story, in which the volunteer tricks the workers and triumphs. Sandy ended up in a 'bad' area, and escaped by shouting 'with his best accent: "Are there no Scotsmen here?" And at once, a dozen voices had answered him: "Aye, laddie, we're with ye." And every day ... these compatriots had formed a bodyguard ... till he was safely through the district. Such anecdotes ... showed the Englishman's heart was in the right place' (1947: 177–8).

Further along in the passage, Isherwood cut to the quick, likening the strike to a generational rite of passage, comparable to the Great War (note his reference to war poet, Wilfred Owen), in its magnitude – and in its betrayal:

It wasn't that I seriously expected street fighting or civil war. But 'war' was in the air ... This was a dress rehearsal of 'The Test' and it found me totally unprepared ... I tried to get on with my novel; instead, I found myself opening Wilfred [Owen]. He, at least, had understood what I was feeling: 'Waving goodbye, doubtless they'd told the lad. ...' But Wilfred hadn't buried his disgust in the cushions of a Kensington drawing-room ... isolated above the battle. (Isherwood, 1947: 179–80)

Isherwood's solution to this intellectual dilemma was to do penance: he volunteered to work on a sewage farm. But the strike ended before he was required. An ironic disclaimer, typical of many volunteer narratives, concludes the passage. But Isherwood's condemnation of his class surpassed irony and laid bare the nature of its hegemony: 'The Poshocracy had won, as it always did win, in a thoroughly gentlemanly manner ... so now it was quite prepared magnanimously to pretend that nothing more serious had taken place than, so to speak, a jolly sham fight with pats of butter' (Isherwood, 1947: 180).

Historian A. J. P. Taylor, who was up at Oxford in 1926, also invoked the Great War in his recollections. 'No one even among the rowing men had any feeling that the miners were wrong or the government right. But when the general strike started ... *it was August 1914 all over again* [emphasis added]. One of the departing heroes even said to me, 'I wonder if I shall ever come back again', quite in the spirit of Rupert Brooke' (Taylor, 1983: 79).

In quite a different spirit, Christ Church (Oxford) alumnus and author Emlyn Williams recalled going off with a group of thirty undergraduates to Hay's Wharf, where after eating, they 'milled around aimlessly in the gangways, holding mugs of beer while a piano played and the hearties gathered round and swung their jorums to the inevitable Gilbert and Sullivan choruses. Everybody was excited to be playing trams in such a new way [...] The cheery come-and-go was stimulating, and at the same time I was a workman doing a foolproof job ... I was a potato at peace' (Williams, 1976: 388–9).

Besides noting their own and their friends' automatic responses, still others commented on the social function such crises served. In his memoir entry for 4 May 1926, photographer Cecil Beaton observed, 'people felt important for being a part of the general crisis. Apart from the many pedestrians, a stream of unfamiliar traffic moved slowly through the streets. Lorries were piled high with giggling typists; old carts were chock-a-block full of women dangling legs and loving it all. "Such a lark", they seemed to be saying, "so new, so amusing, so bohemian"' (Beaton, 1961: 92).

Novelist Graham Greene, then working for *The Times*, remarked on the implicit class divisions apparent during the strike and the free-for-all atmosphere it called into being:

> A few years later my sympathies would have lain with [the strikers], but the great depression was still some years away: the middle class had not yet been educated by the hunger marchers. On the side of the Establishment it was a game, a break in the monotony of earning a secure living, at its most violent the atmosphere was that of a rugger match played against a team from a rather rough council school which didn't stick to the conventional rules. 'I'm almost sorry now that it's over', I wrote home, 'as we had as much free beer as we wanted at the office while it was on ... I felt accepted now. I even received a silver matchbox from the management ... In the camaraderie of free beer and unusual duties I had become an established member of the staff.' (Greene, 1971: 178)

Beatrice Webb recorded a more critical, patronizing response in her diary for 14 May 1926, observing that the strike was

> little more than a nine days' wonder, costing Great Britain tens of millions and leaving other nations asking whether it was a baulked revolution or *play-acting on a stupendous scale* [emphasis added] ... A strike which opens with a football match between the police and the strikers and ends in unconditional surrender after nine days with densely-packed reconciliation services at all the chapels and churches of Great Britain attended by the strikers and their families, will make the continental Socialists blaspheme ... Let me add that the failure of the General Strike shows what a *sane* people the British are. If only our revolutionaries would realise the hopelessness of their attempt to turn the British workman into a Russian Red and the British business man and country gentleman into an Italian Fascist! (Webb, 1956: 92–8)

Diana Cooper's comments in the first volume of her autobiography, with their allusion to the Russian Revolution and implicit reference to the English Revolution of 1648, give some hint as to the very real fear that lay beneath all these responses and later observations about them. Wrote Cooper, when the General Strike began, 'I could hear the tumbrils [sic] rolling and heads sneezing into the baskets, and yet and yet, the English could not be like that. Then where would it end?' (Cooper, 1959: 71).

Fiction: novels, plays, and television

Unlike its appearances in memoirs and autobiographies, most fictional representations of the General Strike gave a bit more space to the main event, though even they devoted at most only one chapter or segment to the volunteers. Novels usually focused on one of two images: the devil-may-care student out for a lark, which Evelyn Waugh's hero in *Brideshead Revisited*, whose actions greatly resemble Waugh's own, epitomized; or they indicted the Fascists, also known as Loyalists, for their aggressive and destructive role as members of the OMS and/or special constabulary (see Cary, 1955; Mellor *et al.*, 1976: 356–7). R. F. Delderfield's novel, *To Serve Them All My Days*, invoked the image of the undergraduate bus driver and the general public enjoying an 'impromptu national spree' as an implicitly understood code to castigate insensitive members of the upper classes (Delderfield, 1973: 209).[12]

Ellen Wilkinson, a Labour MP as well as a popular speaker and organizer during the strike, wrote her novel, *Clash*, shortly after the event. She portrayed the volunteers as gentleman (and lady) amateurs, 'young men in plus fours' operating on the general assumption 'that the whole thing had been rather a lark' (Wilkinson, 1989: 50, 148, 126, 149). Besides making significant points about the role of women in the work place, marriage, and politics, her book, like Isherwood's, unsheathes the class consciousness of the era. Gerry Blaine, the novel's hero, wounded in the Great War and a fervent convert to the miners' cause, has devoted his work and inheritance to the labour struggle. In a conversation with Joan, the female protagonist, torn between her upper-middle-class and upper-class friends and her labour work, Gerry argues against her continued involvement with the former.

> I know they have nice manners. They don't care enough about the miners – at least, when they are not dangerous – not to be perfectly charming to anyone who cares enough to defend them. But you think what that crowd did during the General Strike ... We saw them with bared teeth all right when their class-privileges were in danger ... It's not what their class consciously does to the workers' leaders that matters, Joan. It's easy to fight against that, but it's the mass of idea which they take for granted, and which they assume ... all decent people will take for granted, the atmosphere they create that is so difficult to fight

against.... All their class privileges are bound up with not being converted, not seeing the ugly truth ... [B]etween them and the working class the gulf is fixed, and when a crisis like the General Strike comes they make no bones about which side they are on, even when the best of them admit that the workers have a case. (Wilkinson, 1989: 293–5)

In contrast, Galsworthy's *A Modern Comedy* (1950), focused on the uniquely English character the strike called forth. This book also represents one of the few novels in which women had an active role as volunteers. Although Galsworthy's characters did escape the strictures imposed on women in other novels, they also conformed to the stereotypes, the available categories, of office flappers and canteen workers. The latter, though they did a certain amount of work, did it in the service of grateful and well-mannered menfolk and in places where they got to meet those whom they would normally meet at social events (Galsworthy, 1950: 608–10).

> It would not have been natural that Fleur should rejoice in the collapse of the General Strike. A national outlook over such a matter was hardly in her character... Recruited by Norah Curfew, by herself [Fleur], Michael, and his Aunt Lady Alison Charwell, she had a first-rate crew of helpers of all ages, most of them in Society. They worked in the manner popularly attributed to negroes [*sic*] ... They got up at, or stayed up to, all hours. They were never cross and always cheery. In a word, they seemed inspired. (Galsworthy, 1950: 630)

A young cockney woman, whom Soames Forsyte's driver picked up, represented her gender and class: '"I think it's rather fun, don't you?" said the young lady. "Carrying on – you know, like we're all doing"' (Galsworthy, 1950: 601). Forsyte, whom some strikers called a 'bloated plutocrat' (1950: 599), regarded himself as a solid member of the English middle classes – 'modestly attired in a brown overcoat and soft felt hat' (Galsworthy, 1950: 599) – though all alone in his chauffeur-driven car. Despite his initial disdain for the cockney lass, he found himself enjoying their conversation, even catching a bit of her enjoyment of the strike, though he did not really understand her, her generation, or their music. For Forsyte, the strike posed a test of British character for men and women of all classes: as in the Great War, 'with a grim humour the Briton had just "carried on", unornamental and sublime, in the mud and the blood, the stink and the racket ... The Briton's defiant humour that grew better as things grew worse, would ... get its chance again now' (Galsworthy, 1950: 581–2). Yet Soames Forsyte was not a Churchillian extremist, something which his late-night thoughts on hearing the tanks rolling through London revealed. 'Those great crawling monsters! ... Playing the strong man! Something in Soames revolted slightly. Hang it! This was England, not Russia, or Italy! They might be right, but he didn't like it! Too-too military! ... No sense of proportion in things like that! And no sense of humour!' (Galsworthy, 1950: 606–7).

The television series *Upstairs, Downstairs* took a middle-of the-road stance and devoted one of its episodes, 'The Nine Days Wonder', to the General Strike (Paul, 1975). Lord Bellamy's son, a wealthy war veteran with nothing else to do, drove a bus in the strike. Although he started off to do his duty for God and country, by the end of the programme he has come to the unprecedented (for his class) notion that perhaps the conflict was not as simple as it seemed. One of the young male servants came to the same conclusion; he even wondered if perhaps they ought to come out in sympathy with the miners. Much like Galsworthy's Soames Forsyte, Lord Bellamy, a member of the government, was against the strike but also indicated that such things as tanks and armed soldiers in the streets of London were just not quite English. The butler was the only person in the cast, besides the strikers who disabled young Bellamy's bus, who was positive that his views were correct. Always the Conservative, unquestioning supporter of traditional hierarchy and authority in the show, the butler strongly sympathized with Baldwin's methods and position. Oddly, given their usually prominent roles in the programme, the women did not have much to say on the topic – or do, for that matter. Housemaid, Ruby Finch, whose uncle was a miner in Barnsley, did speak up for the miners, but (before the butler and the cook told her to keep silent) only as the female relative of miners and not as a woman in her own right.

Two plays, G. D. H. Cole's *The Striker Stricken* (1926) and David Benedictus's *What a Way to Run a Revolution* (produced in the West End in the 1970s and shown on television in May 1986), fostered the popular and stereotypical view of the volunteers, albeit the more self-aware one popularized more by contemporary Varsity publications. Benedictus explained:

> Most of the university places at the big universities would be paying places ... You had in the twenties, a university structure that applied to Lloyd's, to the Baltic Exchange, as they say in the show, and the big London money markets, just as the Civil Service, the Foreign Office, and Parliament to a large extent, was basically part of the upper-class structure of the country. And Joynson-Hicks, the Home Secretary, knew that he could call on these people, who came from basically Conservative backgrounds, to support their government, right or wrong. There were a few who refused to do so, and they were mainly intellectuals, from amongst the upper classes, people like the Webbs and so on ... If you read all the political diaries of that period, you see just how little understanding how many of them did have ...
>
> The song of the Plus Four Boys, I tried to show, that the reason they did it really [was] because ... it was wonderful to play at trains. It's what they all wanted to do. (Benedictus, Interview, 1986)

<u>The Song of the Plus-Four Boys</u>

Claude was knocking back the champers
and Hilary was sloshed on beer
When we heard that Jix was in a bit of a fix
And he wanted us to volunteer.
Well, ...

We are the Plus 4 Plus 4 Boys
A credit to our Varsity and nation
We get the Plus 4 Plus 4 joys
of working for a while beneath our station.
For Hilary is working on the buses – what a larf;
While Claude is on the footplate shovelling coal
from here to Barf;
... Charles is bashing pickets on the bottom
With his bat
And I am in the tram-supply
And wear a stunning hat.
And actually I'm driving an underground train
and it's all rather jolly actually, and I've only
had two collisions in the last two days ...
Shut up Charles.
We are the Plus 4 Plus 4 boys.
They call us blacklegs.

(Benedictus, 1985: 37–8)

Benedictus's volunteers were either frivolous, childlike, irresponsible Bright Young People or undergraduates, out for a good time and with little knowledge or interest in the political-economic conflict that called them into action. While his depiction includes ironic and explicit references to the class disparity between volunteers and the strikers, what also comes through is that the volunteers were able to combine fun with patriotic action. A more naïve and gentler image of the gentleman amateur, rather than the somewhat sinister one Benedictus puts forward, comes across in a song written and apparently performed in 1926. It appeared in *Upside Down – A 'Striking but Unofficial Commentary on the Work of London's Underground Volunteers'*, a magazine that the Metropolitan District Railway distributed to volunteers in July 1926. Certain pages of the manuscript were included in an unpublished typescript in the Clare College Archives, Cambridge University, *Cambridge University and The Great Strike, the 'Log' of three Undergraduates from Clare College Cambridge, written by one of them*.[13] These lyrics reference the First World War but differentiate the General Strike as a sort of happy-go-lucky adventure rather than a battle. At the very end, however, is a subtle jibe at their (apparent) ignorance about the strike; like Benedictus's Plus 4 Boys, they were just doing their duty.

A SONG OF THE VOLUNTEERS
Written at a few minutes notice for a Concert at Earl's Court.

With a ho! heave ho! and away we go,
The train pulls out of the station.
If you're bound for North, South, East or West,
We'll get you to your destination.
It doesn't matter if your home's in town,
Or fifty miles away,
We guarantee to get you there,
So roll along to the U.D. [underground] Fair,
And it's three pence all the way:

Refrain:
Roll up! Roll up! Roll up! Roll up!
There's room for one and all;
And if the train is full, you find,
Be sure there's another one just behind.
So don't you worry, nothing's quite as black as it appears;
Until the spot of trouble's gone
We'll stick to it and carry on
And you can bet your shirt upon
The jolly old Volunteers. Roll up!

With a 'Tickets, please', and 'Mind your knees',
We push them into the train, sir.
If it's wet outside, come and take a ride,
We never feel the rain, sir.
So, pack your troubles in the old kit-bag,
And lend a helping hand;
We're here to do the best we know,
And if we're just a trifle slow –
We crave indulgence, and:

[Refrain: ...]
If you are squeezed till you're black and blue,
Well, so are the other people too,
Just pay your money, take a trip, and put away your fears;
We've got a job; we'll see it out,
We don't know what it's all about,
But when it's over, give a shout
For the jolly old Volunteers. Roll up!

(J. A. L., 1926)

Throughout *What a Way to Run a Revolution*, Benedictus collapsed and extended the Bright Young People's fancy dress proclivities into a society bash for the socially prominent of the 1980s. Part and parcel of his conceit was to obfuscate which characters were real and which were merely costumed actors, further demonstrating the continued relevance of this form of traditional play.

> Oh, there was Leonard, Virginia
> And Lytton looking miserable
> Conan Doyle increasingly invisible ...
> And Nancy Lady Cunard
> Al Capone and Peter Pan
> Over in a corner there was charming Cecil Beaton
> Trying to take a photograph of Buster Keaton
>
> 'Clap if you believe in fairies' ...
>
> At Maisie's at Maisie's
> The world decays in many ways
> Empty phrases, vain displays
> And nothing lasts and nothing stays
> Except the memory of the days
> We spent at Maisie's for the general strike ...
>
> Agate and Beerbohm, Winnie the Pooh
> Princess Margaret and you know who
> Julius Caesar, Ben Hur in his chariot
> Enoch Powell, Judas Iscariot
> Jack the Ripper, Atilla the Hun
> Margaret Thatcher, everyone!
> Not forgetting Koo Stark! ...
>
> (Benedictus, 1985: 42–5)

Benedictus made the underlying connections between prominent social and political figures then and now explicit – a method that 'shows what lies underneath, in the same way that *Spitting Image* and *Private Eye* do' (Benedictus, Interview, 1986). He used this tactic to draw an analogy between the actions of former Secretary of State for Defence Michael Heseltine, who resigned in 1986, and those of William Joynson-Hicks, Home Secretary in 1926. In the play, each of the leading characters

> had a song in which you saw symbolically how they saw their role. And it's nothing very subtle to say that Joynson-Hicks ... did say, 'I am the ruler of England.' And that therefore was important to point up, that Home Secretaries tend to get above themselves. After all, we have a clear memory – and that's why we had [Joynson-Hicks] picking up the mace – of Heseltine doing just that in the House of Commons. He picked up the mace from the table of the House of Commons and he threatened the Labour front benches with it, like that. But for those who wished to pick it up, I had Joynson-Hicks doing exactly the same thing. (Benedictus, Interview, 1986)

Another, albeit accidental, connection between characters and political figures occurred, which Benedictus left in. The actor playing Joynson-Hicks imitated Margaret Thatcher's voice throughout, which further emphasized the similarities between Baldwin's Government in the 1920s and Thatcher's in the 1970s and 1980s (cf. Booth and Pack, 1985) as well as the paradigmatic meaning of gender-switching behaviours discussed in Chapter 3.

While Benedictus's play provides more of a satirical commentary on the use and abuse of political and social power by groups and individuals,[14] G. D. H. Cole's drama, *The Striker Stricken*, written just after the strike, focuses more on demonstrating the hypocrisy of politicians from across the political spectrum (Cole, 1977). The satirical styles and messages of those two plays, written fifty years apart, are quite similar, however. Judging by media reviews (Aubrey, 1976), other plays, most of which Labour or other left-wing groups produced for fiftieth anniversary celebrations and symposia (McIlroy, 2006: 78–83), did not portray the volunteers very differently from either Cole or Benedictus.

That references to a multitude of historical and contemporary cultural meanings occur in the plays, poetry, sermons, and other forms of verbal art concerning the strike is not surprising. Some sort of creative reframing of the General Strike, or any topic, is necessary to catch paradigmatic historical relationships and convert them into recognizable symbols and useful allegories. Yet such layering of symbolic references is not nearly so common, or particularly acceptable, for those who perceive their function to be to uncover the 'facts' about an event – rather than to discover just why those 'facts' have been so obscured (Shuman, 2005: 18, 26, 82, 87). And perhaps that is why so few have indicated the symbolic importance of the folkloric images of the General Strike and the volunteers. Historian John McIlroy's most recent essay illustrates this point. McIlroy has made a considerable contribution to our understanding of 1926 as well as to its commemoration and influence on other industrial conflicts. But when he cited my article (Saltzman, 1994a), which focused specifically on working-class critiques of the 1926 volunteers, he mentioned neither the volunteers nor their role in the event (McIlroy, 2006: 96).

Public histories: anniversary studies, exhibitions, and educational packets

There was one more version of the strike and the volunteers' role in it – that of the contained conflict – most often found in books and publications for school children and in museum exhibits, as well as implied by private memorabilia collections,[15] institutional exhibits, and anniversary publications of General Strike editions of various newspapers (e.g. '1926 Strike', 1972).[16]

The fiftieth anniversary of the strike seemed to provoke most of this need to exhibit and reassess the past. But while that was most likely due more to a cultural obsession with round numbers and half-century markers, that anniversary conveniently coincided with labour victories of the early 1970s, which, in the minds of many, were vengeance for 1926 (McIlroy, 2006: 77).

Literally scores of local histories and exhibits were produced for the fortieth and especially for the fiftieth anniversaries. A particular focus was on the 'good times' or 'lighter-side', which emphasized exemplars of real British behaviours and spirit (Renshaw, 1975b: n.p.; Cootes, 1983: 54–5). Just after the fortieth anniversary, Michael Hughes's compilation of strike cartoons and accompanying commentary came out. While in sympathy with the strikers, whom he depicted as wholeheartedly supportive of the miners, Hughes emphasized that 'the public's good humoured response to the Strike and the light-hearted seriousness of the volunteers were celebrated as a uniquely British characteristic. If anyone deserved praise for these qualities, it was surely the strikers, the majority of whom conducted themselves like the Rotarians' (Hughes, 1968: 54). Hughes observed that, for 'a large proportion of the population, it was not a revolutionary threat or a challenge to the constitution, but a lark – a holiday with entertainment provided free' (Hughes, 1968: 46). Yet he also pointed out that the 'surprisingly high proportion of the volunteers were undergraduates, who in plus fours and the newly fashionable pull-overs became the public's favourites' were also the darlings of the media, especially the cartoonists (Hughes, 1968: 48). As Hughes noted, 'if Dunkirk had not lain in the future its spirit would have undoubtedly have been invoked' as evidence of this characteristically British reaction (Hughes, 1968: 54). Felicia Stallman claimed the opposite, however; the strike was not like Dunkirk, because the latter signified defeat (Stallman, Interview, 1986). Either way, the good humour and typical British reaction under fire were credited with the strike's resolution.

One key to this model was the statement that 'no one was killed', or some variation of it – violence was denied or diminished Thus, all involved were responsible for what became construed as a victory for all British people. A slight variation on this interpretation can be found in many of the fiftieth anniversary exhibitions and educational packets, which located the General Strike in a visitable past (Karp et al., 1992). One exhibition catalogue pointed out: 'the political drama, the unity of the workers, and the loyalty of the patriots are all brought vividly to life in this splendid collection of newspapers published at the time, photographs taken at the time, and a host of other documents and personal records'. It invited the reader to 'travel with us into the past and re-live the strike that shook a nation' (Hornsey, 1976: 1). Because those involved believed they acted sincerely and in the best interests of their country, even if they might have been mistaken, everyone could be regarded as part and parcel of the same British heritage. Thus the conflict of the strike itself, in which persons on each side attempted to designate themselves as British and their opponents as 'others' and therefore not truly British, had its resolution in the bounded space of a museum exhibition or a social studies packet (e.g. Tames, 1972; SEARCH, 1979; Labour Museum, n.d.; Cootes, 1983; Harris, 1985; Spencer, 1988).

This contained-conflict model is the one most commonly used for educational purposes (see MacCannell, 1976; Curtis, 1978; Deetz, 1981; Fortin, 1981; Norberg, 1981; Nye, 1981; Nichols, 1984; Wright, 1985), though General Strike exhibitions and educational packets have included more controversial issues than one might expect (Tames, 1972; SEARCH Project, 1979; Spencer, 1988), especially for products aimed at students. Nonetheless, the overall conflict was packaged as a marketable past (MacCannell, 1976; Wright, 1985; Karp et al., 1992; Barnes, 1999).

The Jackdaw packet (Tames, 1972) took the strikers' side in its presentation of issues, documents, and images. Its explanatory essay pamphlet started out with a photo of 'Society ladies manning the tea urns at the Scotland Yard Special Constables Canteen' as well as the obligatory photograph of the 'police v. strikers football match, played at Plymouth', both pointing to the democratic all-encompassing nature of the strike. Unlike other such materials aimed at students, however, Tames hinted that not all were in consensus by including a little-known cartoon caricature of J. H. Thomas, leader of the railway men (and hardly, as Tames indicated, on the miners' side). While Tames acknowledged the volunteers' efforts in beating the strike, he also noted that most were just 'doing their bit', though some of 'the younger ones were "out for a lark"'. Tames' presentation also had a subtly misogynistic message, surprising for its time but apparent through his choice of two *Punch* cartoons: one (see figure 5.16) with a maid's asking her mistress what she'd like to wear for the strike (Reynolds, 1926a: 525) and the other (see figure 15.17), with two status-climbing female office workers' comparing who managed to ride in the higher class of vehicle to work (Mills, 1926: 541); this section was captioned, 'Social attitudes of the day are captured in these two cartoons' (Tames, 1972).

In contrast, the Factpack about the General Strike (Spencer, 1988), produced around the time of the 60th anniversary, and just after the miners' devastating defeat in 1984–85, was somewhat more sympathetic to the volunteers and supportive of the government's efforts to defeat the strike – not the usual stance taken in modern histories of the event. This educational packet also contained far more extensive materials than the Jackdaw packet and was most likely aimed more at advanced secondary or undergraduate students. Beyond the photos, cartoons, reproduced newspapers, and a striker's letter, Spencer also and surprisingly included letters from volunteers, thank you certificates to volunteers from various businesses, strike bulletins, strike and volunteer statistics, and sympathetic photos of volunteers and women workers.

Regardless of their differing stance and inclusion of primary documents pointing to the complexities of the times, the effect of such educational modules was to represent the General Strike as only one more significant event in British history, like the Civil War or the Great Reform Act, to be consumed by school children and/or tourists (Karp *et al.*, 1992; MacCannell, 1976, 1992). Volunteers and strikers became merely two sides of the same coin, and people in other countries were designated as the 'others' who looked on in amazed admiration at a Great Britain in which such a momentous event could be conducted peacefully, in an orderly manner, without revolutionary consequences, and with an even more solid constitutional and parliamentary government its unprecedented (except in England) result (Barnes, 1999).[17] Education modules portrayed this behaviour during the General Strike as inevitable, fated even, and such narratives reaffirmed belief in the national mythos that Great Britain was somehow different from other nations, not prone to revolution or contamination from alien outsiders (Shuman, 2005: 96).[18]

Nothing like the amount of material produced in 1976 appeared in 1986, which, given the then recent 1984–85 miners' strike, should have been a far more politically, if not symbolically, relevant time – a point that John McIlroy in his analysis of memory, commemoration and the strike did not make; nor did he mention the various iterations of the strike produced in the 1980s and noted below, in this paragraph (McIlroy, 2006: 84). For instance, there was an unadvertised exhibit at the Royal Festival Hall, a lecture at the Marx Memorial Library by historian Margaret Morris (Morris, 1986), as well as an article in the *Morning Star* and some requests (not mine) for strike memories by the *Sheffield Weekly Gazette* (13 February 1986). *What a Way to Run a Revolution* was shown on Channel 4 at the beginning of May 1986, and there was an exhibit at the National Portrait Gallery. *The Times* produced a magazine entitled *The Times – Past, Present, Future* on 1 January 1985, which included a page on the strike. That same year, Sarah Harris's textbook, *How and Why: The General Strike* appeared, decidedly on the side of the strikers, despite the book's intended use to teach students how to weigh and analyse historical evidence. Three works were published in 1988: Gerald Crompton's article on railway volunteers; R. H. Haigh, D. S. Morris, and A. R. Peters' *Guardian Book of the General Strike*; and Ralph Spencer's Factpack, *The General Strike – Living History*. I found little else to mark the General Strike's 60th anniversary. Yet all these pieces were filtered by the trauma of the 1984–85 miners' strike and could not help but portray the strikers as inevitable victims, even martyrs for the cause – betrayed by the TUC and the government, the latter assisted by the volunteers.

Unlike materials aimed specifically at a school-age audience, museum exhibits about the General Strike provided a more orthodox take on the past. The London Museum, which presented British history in its vast panorama, from Roman times to the present, had a one-panel strike display. A paragraph explained that the strike was called to support the coal miners and, indeed, there were photographs of miners and pickets. But the implication, given the London Museum's inevitably telescopic view of British history's triumphant trajectory into the present, was that the strike was just one more crisis averted, thanks to that unexplainable quality of British character – as displayed by strikers and volunteers. John McIlroy noted this same characteristic for those General Strike exhibits on display at Covent Garden in 1976 (McIlroy, 2006: 76).

I was privileged to have the opportunity to observe one exhibition from planning stages through to completion. From November 1986 until February 1987, the National Portrait Gallery put on a medium-sized one-room (seven panels of text, two exhibit cases, numerous photographs, paintings, and a short video) exhibition about the strike. According to the curators, who were not initially overly enthused by the topic dropped in their laps, the museum customarily put on one documentary exhibition per year, and this was it. I would not even have known about the topic had not Barbara Rusbridger, mother of my London host, Alan Rusbridger, seen a National Portrait Gallery flyer listing future exhibitions. Running concurrently with the General Strike display was a much more publicized one about Queen Elizabeth II, who was celebrating her 60th birthday (see figure 8.1). The juxtaposition of two such themes (embodied in the posters displayed on the railings outside the museum), in such a place as the National Portrait Gallery, gives some sense of how much the General Strike has become a part of the modern British mythos – at a time when the government openly approved of and encouraged union-busting.

Despite the polarised political climate at the time and their space limitations, Robin Gibson and Honor Clerk, the exhibition curators, created a reasonably fair-handed and in-depth treatment (see figure 8.2). Their written explanations for dense displays of artefacts, photographs, newspaper clippings, and paintings made it clear that the curators (and presumably the museum administration) sided with the intellectual and moderate left's consensus about the strike, that is, that the miners were victimized by both larger economic forces and mine owners, not to mention some over-zealous police constables (though the specials probably did not intimidate the strikers as much as the exhibition text claimed). Gibson and Clerk depicted Churchill as one of the villains of the drama and A. J. Cook as a brave man sincerely fighting for his men; the TUC General Council members came off as naive pawns. A largish bust of James Ramsay MacDonald with its accompanying

8.1 National Portrait Gallery railing with General Strike and Queen Elizabeth II exhibition posters

8.2 Interior of National Portrait Gallery's General Strike exhibition

text identified him as the 'strikers' chief spokesman' in the House of Commons – and not as the betrayer of union interests, as most of the rank and file thought him. J. H. Thomas, who spoke up far more in the House of Commons on the miners' behalf than did MacDonald (House of Commons, 1926), received little mention. Gibson and Clerk gave the impression overall that 'compared with later industrial conflicts, the General Strike was notably well-mannered' (Waymark, 1986).

But the volunteers themselves did not get much coverage in this exhibition. They appeared in a video of university students driving buses and in newspaper photographs with the occasional titled lady serving tea and food to them. The exhibition implied that non-strikers had a rather good time and a chance to demonstrate their patriotism. The video also conveyed that despite some violence on the strikers' side, being a volunteer was a bit of a lark, though perhaps not as much of one as the volunteers would have liked.

In one of two glass cases were displayed some of the volunteers' mementos from the strike, including Lady Lindsay's souvenir sterling silver ashtray (see figure 8.3), a selection of certificates, a special's armband and truncheon, and a letter and programme about a dinner (at 20s. per guest, not including wine) honouring special constables. The other case contained a series of mostly leftist publications about the strike, a photograph album of press pictures showing the hard conditions in a Fife mining community, and so on. Visitors were not given a sense of the vast numbers of ordinary men and women who did so much of the volunteer work or what they received for their volunteer efforts, though it was abundantly clear from newspaper clippings that prominent members of Society were quite active in support of the government. Ironically, I may have been responsible for this neglect, since I did make more of a point of stressing the dominant image of privileged volunteers in the strike when I discussed the matter with the curators during the planning stages of the exhibition.

But aside from the issue of volunteers, a more subtle subtext was present in the tertiary text,[19] the small print – and not the larger captions – explaining the newspapers and items on display. While the larger type tended to describe what was on display, the smaller and harder-to-read labels noted, for example, that 'many national and provincial newspapers managed to produce makeshift editions during the strike. These were complemented by the hundreds of propagandist bulletins and information sheets issued by unions and other organizations.'

What can we make of this? At whom were such comments aimed? They were not intended for school children, or the elderly: the print was too small. And they probably were not directed at the average, casual museum visitor who may have stumbled upon the strike exhibition, for they would take too

8.3 Lady Lindsay's Great Western Railway silver tray, Inscription: 'General Strike, May 1926, To Miss L. Ponsonby, with the grateful thanks of the Great Western Railway'

much time and effort to read (Karp and Lavine, 1991). Although I did not deliberately engage anyone in conversation, since I was busy taking pictures and looking at the exhibition myself, from the talk I overheard and from the comments directed at me, most of the visitors on that afternoon seemed to be former strikers – an unlikely audience for commentary framing their perspective as propaganda. Eventually I came to the conclusion that such comments were indeed meant to be subtexts – indicative of a dissenting, alternative point of view. In the course of sixty years, a vaguely leftist interpretation of the General Strike had become the dominant one – yet the other side was acknowledged in this National Portrait Gallery exhibition, as it was in a fiftieth anniversary exhibition at the TUC (Hornsey, 1976; cf. McIlroy, 2006).

But why should anyone really care about any of this? How many people went to such exhibitions or encountered educational strike packets? Or read books on the topic? Judging by the number of people with whom I was in correspondence who asked if I had been to the National Portrait Gallery exhibition, there were a surprising number still concerned. And not just on the Labour side, for most of those with whom I was in touch were volunteers or sympathized with them. Many of these people had saved newspapers from sixty years ago. Several offered them to me to make copies; others just sent theirs for me to keep. Lady Lindsay was quite pleased to show and allow me to photograph her souvenir sterling silver ashtray, given her by the Great Western

Railway in thanks for her volunteer service in the Paddington canteen (see figure 8.3). Lord Denning still had his truncheon (see figure 5.7). And a great many correspondents had kept their certificates of service and sent me copies (see figures 7.1–7.6 *et passim*).

This response could be attributed to older people simply wanting to share their memories and knowledge, especially of such a nationally significant event experienced during their youth, with a younger person (Thompson, 1994: 11). After all, most westerners like to think what they have done will be of more than a transitory importance and existence. What they did, tried to do, and why they did it, as well as what they thought about it, ought to be acknowledged.

The General Strike volunteer as cultural symbol

In so many histories, memoirs, plays, and novels, the General Strike tends to boil down to a highly condensed picture, a part of which almost always includes those colourful volunteers in plus fours who drove buses and trains (Renshaw, 1975a: 19; Perkins, 2006). This image itself does not mean much, for it depends on how people interpreted it – how they used it for their own purposes – to explain what they remembered and felt about the General Strike and about being British (Thompson, 1994). Osbert Sitwell commented that when he sat down to record his feelings about the strike, 'I could not but notice with what singular persistence, as I approached the subject, the clichés clustered round and clotted the nib of my pen … and even such ancient sobriety tests as "the British Constitution" rang in my head, and leapt in and out of my inkpot while I wrote' (Sitwell, 1948: 229; Passerini, 1984; Eber and Neal, 2001: 176–7; Shuman, 2005: 87–8).

The condensation of such a complex event admittedly distorts the 'real' meaning of it and its participants, for it does not begin to answer to those complexities, as John McIlroy pointed out in his analysis of the memory and commemoration of 1926 (McIlroy, 2006: 73, 104, 107). But in another sense, it does far more than that. The image of the General Strike distils rather than distorts more culturally significant meanings and preserves their complexities in the very paradoxical ways it enables people to interpret it. The parodic subtitle – '1926 and All That' – to John McIlroy, Alan Campbell, and Keith Gildart's introduction to their edited collection (McIlroy *et al.*, 2004), made this point explicit. And John Halstead's review of that collection, entitled '1926, 1984 … And All That!' (2005) took the irony still further.

As Shuman (2005) and others (Geertz, 1968; Turner, 1973; Ortner, 1979; Sahlins, 1981; Passerini, 1984; Vansina, 1985: 137–46; Portelli, 1991; Bodnar, 1992; Halbwachs, 1992; Tuleja, 1997) have observed, such key cultural symbols, such commonplaces (Renwick, 1980), become so powerful *because* they are clichés, because they can be reproduced and used in a multiplicity of ways – in jokes, in restaurants, in local histories, in museums, or even on souvenir coffee mugs.[20] And in fact, such seemingly inexplicable excess can be necessary for meanings to emerge (Shuman, 2005: 160), especially as significance has shifted over time and for different groups. The photographic display at the restaurant Strikes! is a pointed example of how the past can be co-opted for purposes that contemporaries could not begin to imagine (see figures 1.1 and 1.2).

Those who spoke and corresponded with me insisted on a particular image of themselves as volunteers: they were serving their country by keeping things moving. Several could not understand why a folklorist was interested in the volunteers; still others regarded folklore itself as having debased the volunteers' image and hindered political advance for organized labour. Correspondents and interviewees who placed themselves to the left politically required less explanation as to my interest in the volunteers. As either union members and/or former strikers, self-styled outsiders in mid-1980s' England, they had a better sense of the folkloric nature of the volunteers' image – its importance as a cultural signifier. And a few of those who had been volunteers were concerned to set me straight as to what the volunteers were really like and to dispel what they believed to be my misconceptions or 'folklore' about them (Spencer, Letter, 1986b).

Yet the persistent image of the volunteer is that of a fool, someone considered by many to be a somewhat effeminate, effete, and mannerly university lad out for a good time. Like the man-woman character in mummers' plays, adolescents in 'pre-industrial' societies, tricksters, and other liminal beings, volunteers had licence to play fools – without any consequences. They used their suddenly public and publicized position to comment on various aspects of their society, though their critiques were certainly neither as blunt as those of strikers nor taken as seriously. Women volunteers were not permitted nearly so much latitude, though some women's magazines did attempt a more covert sort of criticism of the men in charge. But even their satire was taken in the spirit of holiday tomfoolery and received nowhere near the serious attention paid to relatively minor attempts at opposition from the strikers' side.

Such dismissive treatment, combined with the fact that the volunteers were also young at a time when meaningful rites of passage were not available for young men or women of their class, added another layer to the symbolic value *they* placed on the General Strike and their memories of it. These young people did not have a Great War to usher them into a disillusioned adulthood (Fussell, 1975); thus the General Strike provided the next best thing – even better, because so few were killed.[21] According to one Cambridge undergraduate who worked at Grimsby docks, 'I thoroughly enjoyed the strike. That and the Anti-Aircraft mobilization in 1938 have been the high spots of my life – much more fun than the war' (Symons, 1957: 88). A national crisis coincided with both a social rite of passage and a traditional calendrical occasion (May Day) to add further layers of significance to such an event.

That concurrence of ritual times (Leach, 1979b) gave rise to an emergent allegory that gave the volunteers' participation a meaning qualitatively different from other experiences in their lives (Coser, 1992: 28–9; Halbwachs, 1992: 48–9). The generation before them had the First World War, the one after had the Spanish Civil War, the next, the Second World War. Without a doubt, those events reduced the strike's importance for those who had volunteered as well as for future generations who might have behaved in similar ways, had they the chance. Because of those other larger and more tragic national events, and as a result of the Left's largely undisputed entitlement to interpret the General Strike's meaning, the volunteer has been reduced to a lad in plus fours – the men, and especially the women, who served without any pay, have been almost entirely excluded.[22]

The result of this reproduction of the past has involved a marginalization of the volunteers and their role by all. Neither the British political nor academic Right have made much, if any, effort to challenge Labour and Marxist interpretations of the General Strike; there was little to be gained from celebrating the Right's heroes or reproducing their ideological interpretation because victory was so complete. Only sacrifice needs to be legitimized by cultural reproduction, such as remembrance and veterans' days, Easter, saints' days, or 9/11. Societies commemorate victories only when loss is involved, and neither the volunteers nor the government suffered any losses for which they had to compensate. Nor would they have gained anything by celebrating anniversaries of the General Strike's defeat, for that would have served to emphasize needlessly the social and economic divisiveness whose existence both the government and the TUC had an interest in denying.

Furthermore, as a result of Labour historians' casting (correctly, in my opinion) the General Strike as *the* political and economic rite of passage for organized Labour, most downplayed and trivialized the volunteers' efforts as well as their humour and that of the strikers.[23] From the Establishment side, such innovative, out-of-context use of commonplace traditions represented a challenge to the socio-political order, despite the advantageous use to which that sort of method can be, and has been, put. Bureaucracies in business, labour, and government did manage to instil these forms of popular protest with more rationalized meanings. But to admit openly that the Establishment could co-opt the verbal art, and particularly the vernacular aesthetic, of its most unjustifiably frivolous sector, would have reduced government, publicly and explicitly, to the level of schoolboy silliness. The persistence of this particular image of the General Strike volunteers attests to its relevance for modern-day British society (Santino, 2004: 370).

Notes

1. One of Jessica Mitford's sisters used the strike as an opportunity to dress up as a tramp and frighten the others, who were running a canteen for volunteers during the strike (Mitford, 1960: 14–15).
2. John Dummelow of Lincoln noted that his great-grandfather, William John Thoms, coined the word 'folk-lore' in the early 19th century (Dummelow, Letter, 1986a).
3. See discussion near the end of Chapter 1.
4. In his 1942 memoir, Brockway argued that 'the General Strike was led by people who did not believe in it. They rather than the workers, cracked. Of course a General Strike must be revolutionary; it is of necessity a conflict between the workers and the capitalist state' (Brockway, 1942: 193).
5. Both Laybourn and McIlroy have written illuminating, extensive, and nearly exhaustive historiographic analyses about the General Strike.
6. While travelling one evening on the tube in London during the Christmas holidays in 1985, I overheard some young people of university age talking about having to count the railings at Buckingham Palace. I realized they were on a treasure hunt.
7. Benedictus wrote this musical play in the early 1970s, and it was performed at the Labour and Conservative party conferences in 1973. It was also performed at the Young Vic theatre in London, and then filmed by Channel 4 and shown on television at the beginning of May in 1986 on the strike's 60th anniversary. Benedictus told me in our 2009 talk that the earlier productions were more satisfying than the 1986 one; the grittier milieu made it much more exciting than the polished televised version.
8. In *Let Your Words Be Few*, folklorist Richard Bauman discusses the concept of oversaturated metaphor. In the chapter entitled 'Going Naked as a Sign' Bauman describes William Simpson's appearing unclothed in public to make the point that we all come naked (physically and spiritually) into this world, and that we should strive to divest ourselves of corrupt, worldly religion. Simpson's appearance so overwhelmed his performance with secular meaning that observers saw only his actual physical nakedness; his metaphorical intent and meaning were missed entirely (Bauman, 1983: 84–94).
9. According to an article in the *Observer Magazine*, *Private Eye* is 'a tacky, badly printed, crudely put together and wickedly puerile paper', produced in 'dusty, untidy and somewhat stark' offices in which a 'school-like atmosphere' pervades. 'The staff and contributors are irrepressibly noisy and boisterous, shouting insults at each other, and making rude signs and even faces from time to time ... It is this blend of privilege and irresponsibility that makes the Eye so uniquely and proudly what it is ... Auberon Waugh ... says, "... it's a particular form of English humour which produces completely intemperate attacks on people"' ('Who's Who at Private Eye', 1986: 36).
10. In the novel, *England, England*, the country's historical imagery and pageantry becomes 'Disney-fied', commodified to the extent that the country consumes itself, leaving only its image.
11. I am indebted to Peter Kingsford for the relevant pages from Isherwood's 'mainly

autobiographical' account. As Peter noted, 'the passage in question is quite a little gem' (Kingsford, Letter, 1986c).

12 See also Ian Jack's (1986) review of three books, one a novel and two life histories, concerned with the mining industry, in which the Falklands, the General Strike volunteers, the Wild West, and the 1980s miners' strike were invoked to describe a certain mentality, for example Thatcher's speech to the Parliamentary 1922 Committee in the early months of the 1984–85 miners' strike: 'in the Falklands we had to fight the enemy without. Here the enemy is within, and it is more difficult to fight and more dangerous to liberty' (in reference to Ian MacGregor's *The Enemies Within*, Collins, 1986, with Rodney Tyler); 'The Wild West appeals to him. In Martin Adeney and John Lloyd's admirable analysis of the strike he [MacGregor] is, in his own words, "a hoary old bastard who only wants to win" by "pulling our wagons round in a circle"' (in reference to Adeney and Lloyd's *The Miners' Strike: Loss Without Limit*, Routledge, 1986); and also in reference to MacGregor, 'His brothers drove trams in the General Strike. He has always known what he believed and perhaps for this reason, seems never to have felt at ease in England.' As Ian Jack wrote with regard to a fired miner's wife in Tony Parker's novel, *Red Hill: A Mining Community* (Heinemann, 1986), 'She has quite failed to understand that her husband's sacking is a sacrifice for the greater good' (Jack, 1986: 28).

13 I have not been able to locate the original of the *Upside Down*.

14 Benedictus, reflecting upon the evolution of the show, told me: 'When I first did the show I think I regarded Cook as the hero of the piece. Certainly his speeches are inspiring stuff. Now, I believe that in a way he's the biggest betrayer of them all. Because he must have known if he wasn't living in a world of fantasy that he could not win. And I had a line in the ... television show where the Miner, after the song of the destruction of the House [of Commons], the call for let it all come down, and ... he said "So much for Cook and his fantasies." And I'm afraid to say that the commissioning editor here at Channel 4 insisted on that line being taken out. He would not conceive that Cook could be the villain of the piece.'

'There was also a song called "The Song of Working-Class Solidarity", which [is] to the tune ... of "Ten Green Bottles" ... and one by one the other workers, like in "Ten Green Bottles", make an excuse ... Gradually they peel off until there's only the Miner left ... In that song it seemed to me the encapsulation of the other message you should take from '26 or from '84–85, which is that, unless there is working-class solidarity you cannot win. And the mistake that Scargill made was, he wasn't able to carry the TUC with him, and he should have stopped in his tracks' (Benedictus, Interview, 1986).

15 Just after the strike, three volunteers from Clare College, Cambridge University, put together a diary of their experiences, complete with a list of the 'dramatis personae'. They presented this book to H. H. Thirkell, their senior tutor (Cambridge University and the Great Strike, 1926). While others with whom I was in contact did not keep such elaborate records of their participation in the strike, several did have collections of newspapers and other memorabilia; some had written out their experiences for their families or for limited circulation.

16 Other reprints in this series include the *Daily Express* (World War II 1939) and the *Daily Mirror* (Abdication of Edward VIII).

17 Following the strike, the *Survey*, an American magazine with vaguely liberal leanings, printed a series of articles about the event. One, entitled, 'Plus-Fours to the Rescue', by Cornelia Stratton Parker (Parker, 1926: 411–15) was specifically about the volunteers. According to the author, 'the organization of the voluntary service during the strike and the English temperament' were what kept Londoners from suffering, although the strikers as well deserved 'a large bouquet' for their 'calm and good temper' (Parker, 1926: 412). While Parker mentioned nothing about Society women running canteens (she credited the YMCA), she did note that women volunteers drove lorries (Parker, 1926: 413–14) – a fact not advertised in the British press and most likely due to the greater degree of freedom accorded women in the United States. Parker's impression was of an egalitarian, working holiday and not a class war at all.

In the same magazine, William Crook commented that the university volunteers regarded the whole experience as a lark. He also gave several examples of how the British seem to think nothing of opposing opinions and actions being permitted and expressed, frequently by the same people at the same time (Crook, 1926: 419).

18 The two most extensive and educationally-based online sources (Simkin, 2009; Trades Union Congress, 2009) also tend to follow this model, though they do tend to tilt toward the strikers' perspective. The BBC's site is considerably smaller and leans a bit more to the right of centre, declaring the 1926 General Strike a failure. Interestingly, however, and taking in that larger view, it also links to Simkin's Spartacus Educational site, which provides more extensive and more left-leaning coverage (BBC, 2009). Renaissance London's website, Exploring 20th Century London (produced by a consortium of London museums), also seems to be trying to have it both ways. The General Strike portion of the website has far more volunteer-related images than those for strikers, but the site also refers visitors to the TUC site (Renaissance London, 2009).

19 Museum exhibits traditionally use three levels of labels with correspondingly sized type: primary (headline labels), secondary (basic information), and tertiary (detailed explanations and arguments) text.

20 In 1986, Marion Bowman, a fellow folklorist and kitsch aficionado, spotted a General Strike souvenir mug in one of the tourist shops near Whitehall.

21 A song line in G. D. H. Cole's play, 'So, pack your troubles in the old kit-bag', clearly referenced the Great War (J. A. L., 1926).

22 Taking women seriously has never been a part of the British ethos. It has continued to be much easier and more acceptable to criticize women for acting in 'unfeminine' ways and for bothering men, than to praise their strengths. In the mid-1980s, 'Spitting Image', a Channel 4 political satire, portrayed Margaret Thatcher as a domineering nanny in control of an infantile all-male cabinet.

23 Sue Bruley's *The Women and Men of 1926*, which focuses on the role of working-class women in the coalfields of Wales, is a notable exception to this omission. Bruley's chapter on 'Having Fun, Getting by, and Outside Help' (60–85) examines the carnivals, jazz bands, fancy dress parties, comic cricket matches, Ladies football and other 'comedy' football matches, and the like, which did much more than just pass the time for members of coal mining communities during the nine days as

well as the ensuing seven months' lockout. Bruley especially looks at the role of women pickets and notes their continued use of 'public shaming' rituals, such as white-shirting, which has its roots in the *ceffyl pren* tradition, to censure scabs (2010: 108–9). As she notes, this behaviour was clearly not 'just a game' (2010: 111).

9

1926 and all that ...[1]: Britishness and the volunteers

According to Girton alumna, 'People used rags, larks, jokes as things that cloak/covered serious purposes or ideas.' (Atwood (pseudonym), Letter, 1987a)

At a football match at Plymouth on Saturday afternoon, which was attended by several thousands of persons, the strikers' team defeated the police team by two goals to one. The wife of the Chief Constable kicked off. (*British Worker*, 1926c: 4; *Daily Chronicle*, 1926a: 3; *Daily Telegraph*, 1926b: 3; *Sphere*, 1926b: 180; *Tatler*, 1926: 240; *The Times*, 1926c: 4) (see figure 9.1)

When essential identities depend upon narrative ... identity must be continually performed, re-enacted, and retold. (Shuman, 2005: 161)

In 1926, the Government and the TUC forced into the public domain the usually tacit connections between economic and social reproduction, allowing those implicit structural relationships to be questioned, played with, and potentially realigned. Those normally unquestioned paradigms or structures with which individuals in society think and act are reconstituted when political, economic, and social conflicts come into conjunction. Apparently immutable social structures and relationships became changeable, and it becomes obvious that people are actively involved in their ordering and reconstruction process (Sahlins, 1981 and 1985; Bourdieu, 1982; Johnson *et al.*, 1982; Popular Memory Group, 1982; Wright, 1985). As well, readily identifiable individuals and groups reify conflicting social, economic, and political relationships, a process that can obscure by its very specificity the very real battle for control and definition of the social discourse (Schwartz *et al.*, 1986; Nasson, 1987; Thompson, 1991; Shuman, 2005: 26; Ware, 2007: 171–85).

During the General Strike, the very juxtaposition of traditional forms in a non-traditional context empowered the volunteers – just as such innovative actions had empowered workers in previous times. Taking their cue from their

9.1 'Football match between police and strikers: A unique event of the General Strike was a football match between police and strikers on the Plymouth Argyle ground. The strikers won by 2–1.'

traditional leisure genres, university students, young businessmen, titled folk, and Society women enacted larks, rags, fancy dress, and leg-pulls, activities also used to raise charity funds, criticize others, or 'cloak serious purposes or ideas' (Atwood (pseudonym), Letter, 1987a). They embraced such forms of play in the midst of a political crisis to present to strikers the ideal ways in which they might resume their proper places in the community: by cheerfully accepting their duties as conductors, drivers, maids, or whatever; conducting themselves in a gracious, mannerly fashion; and willingly doing the jobs that the community designated as theirs. What they also did, however, was to unmask the conceit that eighteenth and nineteenth-century traditions of reciprocity and social obligation among classes were anything more than a form of fancy dress in the 1920s.

Accordingly, the strikers interpreted the volunteers' activities not only as a betrayal of an upper-class social contract to serve the entire community (instead of their narrow class interests) but also as an explicit act of violence against the working classes. Much as the upper classes tolerated a degree of lower-class festival licence on designated occasions (Gluckman, 1964), the working classes condoned upper-class play genres only when they were used as charity fund raisers or to bestow largesse. Such behaviour removed from its implicit context of social service was understood by the working classes as sanctioned hooliganism (Humphries, 1981; Pearson, 1983). Rose Kerrigan (see figure 9.2), a founding member of the Scottish Communist Party, recalled:

> They had what they called their rags for charity. They came dressed up and made a bit of fun in it ... They'd dance around the street. They did all sorts of things that if ordinary chaps would do they'd get jailed for it in many cases. Jumping onto trams and walking along the tram, shaking the box in the tram. We would never have been allowed to do that sort of thing ... They were doing it for a good cause, but ... They do it still in many places.
> ... [After the strike] when they used to come out in the rags for charity, we never, ever supported them. People who were politically aware had no time for them ... We had a terrible contempt of them. If I wanted to give to charity I gave it, but I didn't give it to them! ... You couldn't forgive them for what they'd done during the strike. They were your enemy – they were no longer a part of you. (Kerrigan, Interview, 1985; see Saltzman, 1995)[2]

In the aftermath of the strike, Siegfried Sassoon, better known for his devastating, poetic critique of the Great War, also penned some verses that unmasked those hegemonic processes, revealing the relentless paradigmatic relationship of such historical moments:

> *The New 'Black & Tans'*[3] *(from White's).*
> 'The members of White's club have joined en bloc, and will be used as a flying-column' – Daily Mail
>
> Before we lorry away to smash the Workers
> Let's order treble whiskeys and be solemn;
> Let's pray for Tanks in Piccadilly Circus,
> And Ciro's (captured by our flying column.)
> Let's thank that bounder Winston for this chance
> To crack the craniums of those Cup-Tie lads
> Who (though a few of them were out in France)
> Are now unpatriotic curs and cads.
>
> Then, to explain our motive for the fight
> Let's make quite certain that we never knew it
> (In times like these there's neither wrong nor right;
> There's only Trouble; and we're motoring to it.)
> Finally, for our future guidance, let's remember
> Sidney Street, Boat-Race Night, and the Fifth of November.[4]
>
> Sassoon, 1926)[5]

As Sassoon's poetics and Kerrigan's comments make clear, folkloric forms were put to what seemed a non-ordinary use, publicly displayed and

9.2 Rose Kerrigan

performed *not* for the sake of play but to assert the 'natural' right of privilege over others (Thompson, 1971 and 1991; Bloch, 1978; Brow, 1978; Samuel and Thompson, 1987; White, 1987; Bodnar, 1992). Like the wars and games to which its actors have compared it, the strike was characterized by a competition over the power to define what was or was not British behaviour. It divided the participants into us and them, self and other – though in this case those 'others' were also British. This paradoxical phenomenon – a people making war on itself – had to be transcended, and contemporaries used terms that framed the strike as an imitation of everyday life, a parody of it, in which Society did the work of the strikers. By making the buffoons of British society into soldiers and servants, even comic heroes, the general public and the media could all too easily characterize this event into one in which it was permissible, even necessary, for there to be opposing sides.

But characteristic of both war and games are the coexistent meanings available by virtue of the 'not real' frame around both event and actors. Playacting, games, and even war imply recognition of non-ordinary time, a suspension of belief that another reality exists, but also recognition that the display will end at some point and ordinary time resume its flow. The 'as if' frame implies a knowledge of both real and extraordinary contexts that give an event its meaning relative to other events in the same paradigm – in the case of the General Strike, both contemporary play genres and other key historical symbols.

To make sense of the times, contemporaries employed parody and particularly puns to contextualize the strike as real and not real, the volunteers as heroes and buffoons, the strikers as victims and traitors, and society women as glamorous kitchen maids (peeling potatoes): e.g., 'the Strike to end Strikes', 'the Plus Force', 'We are warned not to look on the whine when it is red', and 'Special Peelers' (Mr Mayfair, 1926b: 5; 'Special Peelers', 1926: 427; Tristram, 1926: 327). Shifting double meanings are at the centre of how those who experienced the General Strike comprehended it. The jibe, 'special peelers', for instance, represented a peculiar and perhaps not accidental conflation of the upper-class men and women acting like kitchen servants with the organized metropolitan police force that Sir Robert Peel formed in 1829, a decade after the Peterloo massacre and just before the Swing rebellions and Tolpuddle. With a less ominous but still pointed meaning, the description of the volunteers in the article 'Taking it Standing up, Hats off to the People who took their Coats off'[6] reads like a review of a charity ball's fashions and faces, just as song lyrics by G. D. H. Cole and David Benedictus do in their respective plays (Cole, 1977; Benedictus, 1986).

Such puns and instances of word play underscored a subversive salvation motif (made even more explicit when Lord Reith, managing director of the BBC, read William Blake's 'Jerusalem' over the radio at the close of the strike) – in which playful but polite volunteers saved England from the threat of topsy-turvydom. The volunteers and their behaviour intensified that sense of social structural inversion, thus demonstrating its absurdity – for strikers, volunteers, and foreign observers, as well as the 'general public'. As Cambridge alumna J. L. Dawson explained to me (unwittingly providing the title for this book), 'many undergraduates looked on their efforts in the general strike as a lark – for the sake of their country' (Dawson, Letter, 1986).

The volunteers tried to refute the well-publicized notion that they were impotent and frivolous by demonstrating their ability to 'come through' in a national crisis. They donned plus fours to become the 'Plus Force' to overcome the symbols of disorder and chaos: the strikers, possessed by the notion that they, too, had a stake in the polity. Like gentlefolk who acted out the roles of ideal servants at Harvest Homes and Boxing Day balls, the volunteers continued to enact an elite tradition of representing ideal workers in an ideal world.

But while the volunteers may have aimed to create a utopia in which personal relationships were privileged over market ones, the context of their recreation was a strike in which that was precisely the strikers' objective as well. University undergraduates who worked as train and bus drivers and society women who saw to their welfare knew they were acting temporarily and extra-ordinarily. 'As if' implied not only the creation of a pretend world but also contained the unspoken and clearly understood antecedent of the real world and its structural relationships for British society. The 'rightness' of the class system was the primary subject of the volunteers' actions and their self parodies, which were based on such indices of social class as clothing, accent, manners, and attitude.

The volunteers' traditional style of playing for laughs enabled them to transform a war into a game in which their rules prevailed – over the government and over the strike. Yet because that joking/play frame has such enormous power 'to encompass contradictions, and, as Gary Alan Fine says, to mean both less and more than it says' (Fine, 1984; Smith, Letter, 2010), that framing device permitted and even obligated others to regard volunteer activities as play, and not as a protest against the disintegration of traditional social relationships (Turner, 1974; Sapir and Crocker, 1977).

Thus, those who acted as volunteers had their own understanding of the purpose and form of their actions. 'These young people had a lot of fun while the more serious social problems were forgotten in the call to keep essential services running', recalled David Smithers, MD, a Clare College alumnus, whose father was a Conservative MP (Smithers, Letter, 1986a). When I asked explicitly if the volunteers' participation could be compared to a charity rag, he responded, 'Yes, that is what it became. The English have a habit of turning serious matters into lighthearted [*sic*] pranks ... The more dangerous the more off-hand the surface reaction' (Smithers, Letter, 1986b; see also Freedman, 1999; Paxman, 1999: 86–7; Ward, 2004: 59). Such a treatment, while not exactly whistling in the dark, also speaks to the volunteers' conscious and explicit denial of the government's attempts to cast the strike as a war. As Marjorie Shipley Ellis, OBE, once a magistrate as well as a Conservative party leader in Peterborough, remembered, while everyone had their stories 'just as you had in Dunkirk', the strike was in many ways quite different from the war. As she told me, 'We young things didn't realize the seriousness of the situation. We all thought it was a *huge joke*! Being allowed to do all these lovely jobs! ... You see every boy in those days wanted to drive a train or drive a bus, you see. That was the young people's idea of bliss, you see' (Ellis, Interview, 1985).

Ellis's words reference not only the prevalent playful attitude but also introduce the most commonly told tale about the volunteers – that of the reckless undergraduate train driver. Volunteers, sympathetic observers, and strikers alike told the story with little variation. As with any trickster tale type, this displayed a certain structure that shaped the listener's expectations.[7] As Lady Lindsay told me,

> There was always this story, that one of the young men was driving a train. And he clattered into Paddington station and there was a frightful crash, stopped it. And somebody said, 'Good heavens! That doesn't look very good! You driving at that speed and the buffers –'
> And he said, 'Well! I only found out how to do it when we were two hundred yards away from the platform!' ...
> That was a story; whether it was true I don't know. (Lindsay, Interview, 1985)

As in many such tales, the joke was on the audience within the story, the archetypal lower-middle-class station master, rather than the ostensible victims: the strikers. The volunteer's competence turned out to be a lucky accident, not the result of innate amateur skill. While the gentleman's sincerity merited applause, the implicit moral of this oft-told tale warned against depending upon volunteers, whose luck could just have easily gone the other way. In fact, a number of one-time volunteers told me that they could not have succeeded in their jobs without the tutelage and help of experienced regular workers who remained on the job (Laybourn, 1993 and 1999a).

Of course there was a darker side to this story, and to the sport it mimicked. Failure is part of any game, and volunteer train drivers had their share of it. But very few mentioned the lives lost as a result of volunteer-driven trains gone out of control. Leonard Amey, whose father was chief clerk in the locomotive running office of the Cambridge Railway District and treasurer of the Cambridge Trades Council during the strike, remembered trains driven by undergraduates and by volunteers with overseas experience.

> One undergraduate guard who was compelled by the absence of a crossing keeper to operate the road gates found himself abandoned in the country. A more serious affair was the mishap of a driver whose experience did not cover British stations. He was given a goods train from London and strictly instructed not to exceed 10 miles an hour. A little more than an hour later & 26 miles down the line he somehow fouled a platform awning & brought the structure down on a would be passenger, who was killed. The inquest was very discrete about the circumstances. (Amey, Letter, 1985)

Most did not speak of such incidents, and instead emphasized mishaps that caused no harm – incidents that therefore became repeatable exemplars of the volunteer experience as lark (Shuman, 2005: 143, 146–7, 153–5). Far more common were stories like the one Marjorie Shipley Ellis told me: 'Another friend of mine, a grown man this was, who was a very impatient person, and if the gates were closed, he just drove straight through them. He didn't bother [to stop]' (Ellis, Interview, 1985). Rosamund Tosh, at Somerville College in 1926, related a similar story about an undergraduate who, while driving his train from Paddington to Bristol at great speed, failed to make any stops along the way because he'd only just learned how to use the brakes five minutes before his arrival in Bristol (Tosh, Letter, 1987a).[8] That ever-present theme of escape from serious injury or death was precisely what enabled the volunteers' activities to be labelled 'jokes'.

The volunteers' obsession with game-playing, with turning battlefields into playing fields (Fussell, 1974), provides a key to the dominant ideal of Britishness in the first third of the twentieth century (Paxman, 1999: 196–9; Ward, 2004: 74–85), and to the reason why certain themes emerged in General Strike narratives. In games there are rules, boundaries, beginnings, ends, timeouts, players, and spectators (Bateson, 1972; Goffman, 1975), and whoever plays the best, wins. That such an ethos existed is not surprising, given the British Empire's expansion in such a way that gave proof to the 'fact' of social Darwinism. That this ethos continued into a period when the Empire was in a serious decline is also understandable. But faith in this aspect of Britishness also carried with it a more moralistic, even Puritanical belief that life was fair. For young people brought up to the public school ideal before, during, and after the First World War, but especially during and after, there was a real need to believe that fair play ensured, if not success, at least not abject failure. As one reporter put it,

> 'The war is o'er and I return
> To 'Ackneystadt – but not the same!'
>
> I can't swear that these are the exact words of Kipling's cockney soldier, but the sentiment is sufficiently accurate to suit my purpose. Our little war is over; we are all friends again, and if there is one thing that isn't quite the same, it is that we are even better friends than we were before. ('Bystander Comments', 1926: 419)

Thus, the General Strike was reframed as a transformative process, as a sport that renewed the nation.[9] As A. A. B. wrote in the *Tatler*: 'England, personified by the man in the street, looks, walks and talks like a different being from what he was a month ago. He bears himself like a man who has won a battle or a bet or a golf match – Pride in his port, defiance in his eye' (A. A. B., 1926b: 288).

In games, even war games, rules, fair play, and the victory of the best (in moral and physical terms) were assumed. This was particularly important to a Britain still reeling from the cruel consciousness that 'victory' in war made for a no-win situation in terms of human sacrifice.

Thus, it was no accident that sports metaphors had such appeal and appeared so frequently in articles about the 1926 General Strike, another indication of its place in the popular imagination. In particular, the media cited the Plymouth football match between strikers and police. And most contemporaries seemed to go along with the assessment of A. A. B.: 'what beat the foreigner [at home and abroad, apparently] was the football match played between the strikers and the police at Plymouth, or was it Portsmouth? *It is perhaps destined to be as famous as Drake's game of bowls, finished while the Armada was sailing up the Channel* [emphasis added]'(A. A. B., 1926b: 288).

While framing and viewing contemporary events through such key moments can create a revised understanding of the world that actually changes the world (Shuman, 2005: 26), I would propose further that it is the accumulation and repeated invocation of such powerful cultural symbols that realigns understanding.[10] Elevated to the status of one of England's 'great victories', the General Strike, and the football game epitomizing it, achieved a mythical status before either had ended – enabling the British to continue in their belief that life, or at least socio-economic conflict, was a good-natured and reasonable sporting match. And while it might seem as if those in charge had relinquished control of the outcome by turning the dispute into a competition, established authority had sanctioned this match; this was no rough game organized by street hooligans. According to the *Illustrated London News*, 'There cannot be much wrong with a country where the love of sport and the sense of comradeship could thus make itself felt at such a time. Civil strife among a people so constituted would seem to be almost unthinkable' ('Impressions of Life During the General Strike', 1926: 854).

British and foreign correspondents commented repeatedly on the meaning to be drawn from 'the now historic [football] match at Plymouth between strikers and police which has provided a seven days' wonder for the French press. "Imagine the same strike in France and draw your own conclusions", the writer exclaims' (*Daily Chronicle*, 1926c: 3). Oddly and ironically, that match occurred on 8 May, the same day as the Plymouth tram riot (strikers against blacklegs), in the same town (Laybourn, 1993: 66), though the two occurrences were never mentioned in tandem. Instead, reporters used the football match to epitomize the difference between Great Britain and all other nations and peoples (*Daily Chronicle*, 1926c: 3). To further emphasize the carefree spirit, pictures appeared of 'Hospital Volunteers – light-hearted students from King's College Hospital photographed in Downing-street' (*Daily Express*, 1926: 8) and soldiers and sailors – all kicking a football for the cameras ('Soldiers and Sailors', 1926: 1; see figure 1.3(a)). Members of the former group were laughing, waving their hats, and running toward the photographer. And despite much media commentary about hard labour, most photographs were of young men larking about and posing for the camera – not at work. Sixty years later, such images anachronistically adorned the walls of Strikes!, that barbecue restaurant near Trafalgar Square (see figures 1.1 and 1.2).

Examination of the ways individuals drew on the football match and the train stories demonstrates how certain incidents encode a variety of meanings about British society.[11] For most, recounting the football match summarized what being British meant in terms of fair play[12] – good sportsmanship towards one's opponents.[13] For others, it showed how the British differed favourably from people of any other nationality,[14] what Arthur Aughey has referred to as the 'English[/British] exemplary' (Aughey, 2007: 32–7). Joan Bedale's comments go directly to this point: 'Waiting quite light-heartedly in Paris [in 1926], I soon heard that the police had organized a grand football match, Police versus Strikers, which was a huge success. I knew then that the Strike would fail in its objective, organized, as no doubt it was, by a foreign revolutionary party – and fail it did. And everyone went back to work with no ill-feelings on either side' (Bedale, Letter, 1987). Its quintessential characteristic, good and right order, overshadowed the strike's meaning for all concerned and, ironically, became the General Strike's legacy in the national mythos (e.g. Perkins, *A Very British Strike*, 2006).

The tale of the undergraduate volunteer train engineer revealed yet another side of British identity – that of the fun-loving amateur gentleman, the ultimate trickster, capable of keeping his head in the midst of danger, and somehow or other pulling through – unless, of course, the story was told by someone not so enamoured of the undergraduates' activities during the strike. But what both stories accentuated was a potentially disorderly, even dangerous, situation made safe and controllable because it had only certain permissible outcomes; neither encoded a series of random events. Thus it was the use of those tales, which portrayed only certain aspects of the strike and the volunteers, that transformed them into symbolic narratives, allegories aimed at restructuring the meaning of the strike and the volunteers' role in it.

The most popular stories and images from 1926 further underscored the importance of just plain luck in surviving a crisis. The *Bystander* had an entire page devoted to cartoons of figures such as a tuxedoed gentleman in a top hat teetering on a penny-farthing bicycle and gay office flappers balancing precariously on some City gentleman's knee or on a hay cart (Cottrell, 1926: 421). Those images along with those of lucky volunteer train drivers all pointed to the precarious nature of the situation.

Related to that sensibility was yet one more motif, commonly cited during the strike and in later recollections: the marriages that resulted from chance encounters. Many contemporaries observed that the strike gave way to unexpected unions (though, in fact, according to one newspaper, the number of marriages went down during May 1926) as emblematic of what the strike's spirit had wrought. The *London Opinion* was not alone in noticing that 'many engagements have resulted from business girls riding to and fro from work in young men's cars during the General Strike' ('Whipped Topics', 1926: 259; 'The Humours of the Great Strike', 1926: 10). Most journalistic commentary, however, tended toward the misogynistic, pointing to the dangers of such unusual mingling between the sexes and classes, that is, male volunteers from higher classes being caught by girls of lower social standing. Many a journal noted along with reports about girls becoming 'engaged to motorists who gave them lifts ... [that] it is now being widely recognised that volunteer drivers ran considerable risks' ('Charivaria', 1926: 565).

Not by accident was this column named 'Charivaria', which references the tradition of not-so-playful community censureship and warning – shivaree or charivari – that usually occurs at weddings or times of seasonal change, times that acknowledge the threat and potential of new liaisons, of transitions. The May Day revelry that the strike seemed to countenance – the free-for-all mixing that occurred along with the ubiquity of alcohol noted by so many –

placed the event within the realm of the carnivalesque, and the dangers as well as the possibilities such Rabelaisian upheavals create. Contemporary fears about classes mingling (not just in temporary social settings but in marriages),[15] were precisely the subject of Mayfair Mansions (*Punch*), who described 'Lady Manœuver's' [*sic*] delight when the strike resulted in her daughter's engagement (Mayfair Mansions, 1926: 572). Commenting on the same topic, Evelyn of the *Tatler* mused:

> I wonder how many romances the 'lifting' business has given birth to. I saw one car the other day, driven by a real charmer in the way of young men, which bore the placard 'For Flappers Only' and he had certainly gathered an attractive collection. And one of our star racing motorists ... found that every woman occupant of the bus he was driving came to thank him personally, and his wife got so worried about it that she threatened to add her chaperonage to that of the usual policeman's to protect him from worse perils than flying stones and bottles. (Evelyn, 1926: 234)

In contrast to fears expressed in the media, individual men and women who mentioned marriages that resulted from the strike implied that such transformative events ensured Britain's continuity (Marsh, 1969). One of my correspondents told me that she had 'heard of two people staying in the country, unable to leave because of lack of transport. How ever [*sic*] it gave way to romance and a long and happy marriage' (Gage, Letter, 1986).

Oddly, the hope for such fairy-tale happy endings was also the intended meaning behind the radio broadcast of 'Jerusalem' at the end of the strike – despite its ironic effect. The plays about the General Strike by G. D. H. Cole and David Benedictus make clear that strikers regarded this symbolic gesture with stunned incredulity (Fairlie, 1959: 194–6).[16] But Blake's verses do evoke the dream of utopia *in England*, which was why his poem and not another was chosen at the General Strike's end, even though the gesture was buried during the seven long months of the miners' strike, the ensuing and vindictive Trade Disputes Act of 1927, and the years of on and off struggle among unions, management, and government in Great Britain. Post-strike and anniversary museum exhibitions as well as children's books also convey this message of British consensus, of a diverse community striving, in different ways, to achieve a cooperative society (Powell, 2002: 250–6; Ward, 2004: 170–3).[17]

Ironically, both volunteers and strikers were fighting a battle to retain an older, Liberal vision for British society – a society of social obligations and communal responsibilities. Yet the strike's very failure entitled only strikers, or those who claimed to speak for labour, to tell its stories. This class-based response cast the volunteers and their stories as inauthentic, undeserving of memory (Irwin-Zarecka, 1994: 127). Left out of serious consideration in the official historical record, the popular image of the volunteer found its way into the more creative venues of parodies, poetry, novels, plays, memoirs, and folklore.

The very condensation of the volunteers' role into an upper-class masculine image was what has enabled it to be so easily invoked as a symbol of eccentric Britishness, of good humour in a crisis, of the gentleman amateur par excellence. That image represented the continuity of a nineteenth-century paradigm that categorized life as a sporting competition not to be taken too seriously and English lads of a certain class as the ones capable of winning it – and showing others how to play the game. Thus, that image of the happy-go-lucky volunteers has persisted in British society, a humorous testament to England's ability to 'carry on'.

Notes

1 This title refers to John Halstead's (2005) review article, '1926, 1984 ... and all That!', which itself references Sellar's and Yeatman's (1930) *1066 and all That: A Memorable History of England, Comprising all the Parts you can Remember, Including 103 Good Things, 5 Bad Kings and 2 Genuine Dates.*
2 Peter Kerrigan's comments substantiate this interpretation (Leeson, 1973: 90).
3 The 'Black & Tans' were the British force used in Ireland during the 'troubles' in the early 1920s. They had a widespread reputation for violent and destructive behaviour.
4 In 1919 guns and tanks were turned on suspected communists in a private house in Sidney Street. The media lambasted Churchill for his excessive use of force against citizens and endangerment of others on the street.

Boat-Race Night is an occasion for Oxbridge undergraduates to indulge in public drunkenness and hooliganism in the streets of London.

The Fifth of November commemorates the death of Guy Fawkes, who supposedly tried to blow up the Houses of Parliament in the Gunpowder Plot in 1605. Before the holiday, children and adolescents demand 'a penny for the guy' from strangers and friends – the money to go for fireworks and a bonfire. This celebration represents not only what did not happen to Parliament, but what does happen to those who dare to protest against it. Children and adolescents were the status groups generally accorded licence during this holiday.
5 Jean Moorcroft Wilson, one of Sassoon's biographers, noted that this one was one of three poems Sassoon wrote about the strike; they were published posthumously but not until 1976, on the occasion of the 50th anniversary of the General Strike, in the *New Statesman*, 30 April 1976 (Wilson, 2003: 449–50; Wilson, 2010, email). I became aware of the *New Statesman* publication only recently, having discovered a typed copy of this poem in the TUC Library, General Strike collection in 1986.
6 See epigraphs at the beginning of Chapter 5, 'Images of the Volunteers'.
7 Paul Thompson made this comment about form and meaning in his discussion of Luisa Passerini's study (1984) of the stories told by Turinese Communist militants (Thompson, 1994: 9).
8 See Chapter 6 for accounts from Brenda S—— and Joan Bedale.

9 Lord Ruthven, the General Officer Commanding the London District, noted in his post-strike report that the army's commanding officers believed that the strike 'was the best training for war young officers had obtained since the war' (Jeffery and Hennessy, 1983: 129).
10 See Arthur Aughey's discussion about Joan Scott's analysis of the role 'fantasy echoes' play in identity formation (Aughey, 2007: 11–12) and Stefan Rohdewald's comments on those 'long living points of crystallisation of collective memory and identity' with regard to those places, images, and figures of memory on which history hangs its hat, so to speak (Rohdewald, 2008: 287).
11 See Canadine (1984) on coronation ceremonies and state funerals, Bocock (1974) on ritual in industrial society, Moore and Myerhoff (1977) on secular ritual, and Lewis (1980) on understanding ritual.
12 M. R. Pratapsinhji volunteered at the Southampton docks with others from Clare College, Cambridge in 1926. 'Another thing I remember that once there was a football match with teams of some strikers and volunteers!' (Pratapsinhji, Letter, 1986).
13 For more on British identity and the concept of fair play, see Newsome (1961), Fussell (1974), Girouard (1981), Colls and Dodd (1986), Paxman (1999: 86–7, 196–205), Ward (2004: 77, 84), and Aughey (2007: 207).
14 For more on this sense of British and especially English uniqueness, see Baldwin (1973), Paxman (1999), Powell (2002: 178–9), Ward (2004: 3, 88, 116, 124, 126, 141, 153), Kumar (2006), Perkins (2006), and Aughey (2007: 32–36, 50–52).
15 See this section in Chapter 6.
16 Benedictus attributed the irony to Baldwin and his image as a 'man of peace', rather than explicitly dealing with the broader social implications of the BBC's broadcast.
17 While it may be a bit of a stretch to fold the 1926 strike into this utopian vision of British society, it is not insignificant that such a perspective is aimed at children and the (perhaps) historically unsophisticated average museum visitor or consumer of popular history. Such an interpretation also points to the redemptive and transformative functions of the General Strike (Shuman, 2005: 154, 161).

Bibliography

Primary works

Archival sources and private manuscripts

Boodles' (London), 2735, 'Minutes of Proceedings of General committee', May 1926.
Bullivant, Otho, 1980, 'The Mostly Good Old Days', in the possession of Penelope Bullivant (England).
'Cambridge University and The Great Strike, The "Log" of three Undergraduates from Clare College Cambridge, written by one of them', 1926. Clare College Archives (Cambridge).
Cogswell, Robert, n.d., 'General Strike Engineman', Wiltshire County Record Office (Trowbridge, England), Accession #1784.
Drage, C. H., 1926–29, 'The 1914–1933 Diaries of C. H., Drage, RN, 1926–1929', Imperial War Museum Archives (London), Reel 3, PP/MCR/99, Vol: 5, pp. 15–20.
Dummelow, John, 1949, 'History of Metropolitan-Vickers Electrical Co. Ltd' (for the Company's Gold Jubilee), Manchester, in the possession of John Dummelow.
Greater London Record Office, London (hereafter GLC), ACC 1297 MET 10/564, General Strike 1926, 'Alphabetical List of all Volunteers employed by the Company during the Strike', 1926.
GLC, ACC 1297 MET 10/564, 'Volunteer Lists' Box, Folder 1926, 'General Correspondence re Volunteers'.
GLC, BBC, 1926, CL/EMER/1/2: 4.
GLC, MET 10/564, 'Volunteer Lists' Box, Folder 1926, 'Letters of Appreciation from passengers, Traders, etc.'
GLC, MET 10/564, Folder 1926, 'Volunteer Lists' Box, 'Letters of Thanks to Volunteers'.
GLC, MET 10/564, Folder, 1926, 'Volunteer Lists' Box, 'Suggestions from Passengers'.

GLC, MET/10/564, 'Volunteer Lists' Box, 'Some Copies of Circular Letters' Folder, 'Board of the Metropolitan Railway Report', 13 May 1926, p. 4.

GLC, ACC 1297 MET 1/103, Numbers 1854–2100', 'Minutes of the Metropolitan Railway Officers' Monthly Conference', January 1926–December 1927.

House of Commons, 1926, *Parliamentary Debates: Official Report*, vol. 195 H.C. Debates, Fifth Series (3–14 May), His Majesty's Stationery Office (London).

J. A. L., 1926, 'A Song of the Volunteers', in *Upside Down, A 'Striking' But Unofficial Commentary on The Work of London's Underground Volunteers* (July), n.p., Clare College Cambridge Archives (Cambridge).

Kerchway, L., Letter to Edward Benn, 5 June 1926, The Nation, New York (given to author by Glanville Edward Benn).

Liverpool University Archives (Liverpool), D181/36, Dickinson, Robert, BSc, PhD, Bronze Medal, 1926.

Millard, W.G., Letter, 1926, 'The Mining Crisis and the General Strike, 1925–26', Trades Union Congress Library (London), Reel 22 (141).

Murray, Commander J., RN, 'The Secret People', Imperial War Museum, Department of Documents (London).

Oxford and Cambridge Club Minutes, 5 May 1926.

Pirie-Gordon, Harry, 1926, 'The Story of 'The Times' During the General Strike', *The Times* Newspaper Archives (London).

PRO, HO 45/13364, Part 2, 1923–29/Special Constables/447.130/108, HO Minutes/Letters of thanks to special constables/counties and boroughs, by A. L. Dixon, Esq., CB, CBE, 26 May 1926.

PRO, HO 45/12336/2130/1926/OMS/484.910.

Public Records Office, Kew (hereafter PRO), HO 45/13364, Part 1/1923–29/Special Constables/447.130/ HO Minutes by J. H. Watson, OBE, 11 May 1926.

Sassoon, Siegfried, 1926, 'The New "Black & Tans" (from White's)', General Strike Files, Contemporary Documents, Trades Union Congress Library (London).

The Times Newspaper Archives, London (hereafter TNA), letter by J. J. Astor, 24 August 1926.

TNA, General Strike Files, 'Financial Report', 20 May 1926.

TNA, General Strike: 1926, 'General Papers', letter by A. E. S. Cheeps, 7 July 1926.

TNA, General Strike: 1926, 'General Papers', letter by A. W. Dickson, 26 June 1926.

TNA, General Strike: 1926, 'General Papers', letter by Alasdair D. Ennistoun, 11 July 1926.

TNA, General Strike: 1926, 'General Papers', Notes by J. J. Astor, 1926.

TNA, General Strike: 1926, 'General Papers', 'Receipts', 1, 29, and 31 July 1926.
TNA, General Strike: 1926, 'General Papers', 'Volunteer List – General Strike', May 1926.
TNA, General Strike: 1926, letter by Winston Churchill to Lord Northcliffe, London, England, 8 May 1926.
Trades Union Congress Library, General Purposes committee, General Council of the TUC, letter by Herbert N. Elvin, 13 May 1926.
Trades Union Congress Library, TUC General Council, 1926, *The Mining Crisis and the Nation Strike* (London: TUC), June.
Verdin, Jack, MS, 1986, untitled and unpublished General Strike manuscript, in the possession of Jack Verdin (England) and Rachelle H. Saltzman (USA).

Personal correspondence and recorded interviews with author

Adeney, Rev. A. W., Letter, 1986, 17 April, Brockenhurst, Hampshire.
Aird, Ronald, Letter, 1986, 14 April, Yapton, Sussex.
Allan, Adrian, Letter, 1986, 24 June, from the Liverpool University Archives, Liverpool.
Allan, Adrian, Letter, 1987, 24 April, from University Archivist, University of Liverpool.
Allport, Marjorie, Letter, 1985, December, Cambridge.
Amey, Leonard, Letter, 1985a, 19 November, Cambridge.
Amey, Leonard, Letter, 1985b, 3 December, Cambridge.
Anonymous, Raynes Park, Letter, 1985, 3 December, Raynes Park.
Ashley, Tom, Letter, 1986, 28 January, Peterborough.
Atherton, N., Letter, 1985, 15 November, Abingdon-on-Thames, Oxon.
Atwood (pseudonym), Letter, 1987a, 9 June, Bexhill-on-Sea, Sussex.
Atwood (pseudonym), Letter, 1987b, 22 July, Bexhill-on-Sea, Sussex.
Band, Roy, Letter, 1985, 8 January, Peterborough.
Baron, Sophia, Letter, 1986, 5 December, Stanmore, Middlesex.
Bawtree, Alec, Letter, 1986, 17 April, Murroe, County Limerick, Ireland.
Bedale, Joan, Letter, 1987, 6 January, Effingham, Surrey.
Bemrose, Clive, Letter, 1986a, 14 April, Weston Underwood, Derbyshire.
Bemrose, Clive, Letter, 1986b, 12 May, Weston Underwood, Derbyshire.
Benedictus, David, Interview, 1986, 11 June, London.
Benedictus, David, Telephone conversation, 1987, February.
Benedictus, David, Telephone interview, 2009, 3 November.
Benn, Glanvill Edward, Letter, 1986, 15 April, Aldeburgh, Suffolk.
Benson, T. G., Letter, 1986a, 16 April, Langho, Blackburn.
Benson, T. G., Letter, 1986b, 2 May, Langho, Blackburn.
Booth, Vernon, Letter, 1986a, 29 May, Girton, Cambridge.

Booth, Vernon, Letter, 1986b, 12 June, Girton, Cambridge.
Bowes Lyon, Lady Rachel, Letter, 1986a, 23 April, Hitchin, Hertfordshire.
Bowes Lyon, Lady Rachel, Letter, 1986b, May, Hitchin, Hertfordshire.
Brady, Erika, 2010, Letters, January, Bowling Green, Kentucky.
Brockway, Archibald Fenner (Lord), Letter, 1986, 21 May, Bushey, Hertfordshire.
Brockway, Archibald Fenner (Lord), Interview, 1986, 11 June.
Buckland-Evers, Cyril, 1985, Interview, 24 October, London.
Buckley, Anne, 1985, Interview, 12 November, London.
Bullard, Lady, Letter, 1987, 10 January, Melton Constable, Norfolk.
Bullivant, Penelope, Letter, 1986, 25 April, Crewkerne, Somerset.
Bullock, Irene, Letter, 1987, 4 January, Hingham, Norwich.
Bulmer-Thomas, Ivor, CBE, Letter, 1986, 26 May, London.
Burton, G. Murray, Letter, 1986, 10 April, Crowborough, Sussex.
Burton, Nancy H., Letter, 1987, 10 June, Bath, Avon.
Casselden, Sarah, Letter, 1986, 16 July, of *The Times* Newspaper Archives, London.
Cassell, Charles, Ret., RN, Letter, 1986, 18 May, Isle of Wight.
Cavendish, Pamela, Letter, 1986, 17 April, Cark-Cartmel, Cumbria.
Chandler, Mrs J. M., Letter, 1986a, 5 March, United Oxford and Cambridge Club, London.
Chandler, Mrs J. M., Letter, 1986b, 14, May, United Oxford and Cambridge Club, London.
Chitty, Mrs Mary, Letter, 1986a, 3 December, Gwynedd, North Wales.
Chitty, Mrs Mary, Letter, 1986b, 16 December, Gwynedd, North Wales.
Chitty, Mrs Mary, Letter, 1987, 30 January, Gwynedd, North Wales.
Churchill, Harold, Letter, 1986, 18 May, East Dereham, Norfolk.
Clark, A. M., Letter, 1986a, 3 May, Shirley Solihull, West Midlands.
Clark, A. M., Letter, 1986b, 23 May, Shirley Solihull, West Midlands.
Cogswell, Lt Cdr R. J., Letter, 1986, 25 October, Weymouth, Dorset.
Connolly, Ruth, Letter, 1986, 26 November, Cambridge.
Coombes, Frederick, Interview, 1985, 15 November, London.
Coulson, Dina, Letter, 1986, 24 April, Bromley, Kent.
Craske, E. J., Letter, 12 November, Peterborough.
Crawford and Balcarres, Mary, Dowager Countess of, Letter, 1986, 22 April, Colinsburgh, Fife.
Crivan, Harry, Interview, 1985, 10 November, Glasgow.
Croft, Dr Phyllis G., PhD, DVM, Letter, 1987a, 2 March, Basingstoke, Hampshire.
Croft, Dr Phyllis G., PhD, DVM, Letter, 1987b, 4 April, Basingstoke, Hampshire.
Croft, Dr Phyllis G., PhD, DVM, 1987c, 14 April, Basingstoke, Hampshire.

Davison, Margaret, Letter, 1985a, 23 November, Cambridge.
Dawson, Mrs J. L., 1986, Letter, 3 December, Hartwith, Harrogate.
Denning, Lord, Letter, 1986, 17 March, London.
Denning, Lord, Interview, 1986, 21 April, London.
Dickson, Edna R., Letter, 1986a, 1 March, Sheffield.
Dickson, Edna R., Letter, 1986b, 1 April, Sheffield.
Dickson, Edna, Letter, 1986c, 8 May, Sheffield.
Diggle, Margaret, Letter, 1986, 29 November, Ringmer, East Sussex.
Diggle, Margaret, Letter, 1987, 24 January, Ringmer, East Sussex.
Dobbs, Phyllis, MD, Letter, 1987, 28 February.
Dover, Leslie, Letter, 1986a, May, Pewsey, Wilts.
Dover, Leslie, Letter, 1986b, June, Pewsey, Wilts.
Dummelow, John, Letter, 1986a, 10 April, Lincoln.
Dummelow, John, Letter, 1986b, 17 May, Lincoln.
Dunbar, A. L., Letter, 1986, 28 April, Harrogate, Yorkshire.
Dunham, Edward, Interview, 1986, 4 February, Northwood, Middlesex.
Eccles, Viscount, Letter, 1986, 13 June, London.
Ekevall, Kay, Interview, 1986, 2 April, Bromley, Kent.
Ellis, Marjorie Shipley, Interview, 1985, 10 December, Peterborough.
Elsdon, John, Interview, 1986, 28 January, Peterborough.
Errington, Robert, Letter, 1986, 18 May, London.
Evans, Frank G, Letter, 1986, 6 June, Upton-By-Chester, Chester.
Fraser, Colin, Letter, 1986a, 25 April, Grappenhall, Warrington.
Fraser, Colin, Letter, 1986b, 13 May, Grappenhall, Warrington.
Fremantle, David, Interview, 1986, 2 May, Twickenham, Middlesex.
Gage (Diana), Viscountess, Letter, 1986, 28 April, Grange-Over-Sands, Cumbria.
Gerald, Sir (pseudonym), Letter, 1986, 4 May, Devon.
Goodby, Harry, Interview, 1985, 9 December, Peterborough.
Goodby, Betty, Interview, 1985, 9 December, Peterborough.
Greenfield, R. H., Letter, 1986a, 15 January, Foxwood, York.
Greenfield, R. H., Letter, 1986b, April, Foxwood, York.
Hambleden, Patricia (Viscountess), Letter, 16 April, 1986, Oxfordshire.
Hamilton, S. E., Letter, 1986a, 27 June, West Chiltington, West Sussex.
Hamilton, S. E., Letter, 1986b, 10 September, West Chiltington, West Sussex.
Harman, Ken, Letter, 1985a, 25 November, London.
Harman, Ken, Letter, 1985b, 16 December, London.
Harper, A. C., Retired Wing Commander, Letter, 1986a, 5 May, Lymington, Hampshire.
Harper, A. C., Retired Wing Commander, Letter, 1986b, 14 May, Lymington, Hampshire.
Harrod, Lady Wilhelmine, Letter, 1986, 21 May, Holt, Norfolk.

Havelock, Ellen, Letter, 1987, 7 January, Marblehead, Massachusetts.
Hobson, Gordon, Letter, 1985, 4 December, Wirral, Liverpool.
Hobson, Gordon, Letter, 1986a, 2 January, Wirral, Liverpool.
Hobson, Gordon, Letter, 1986b, 24 January, Wirral, Liverpool.
Hodgkiss, Winifred Haward, Letter, 1986, December, Dewsbury, Yorkshire.
Jones, John, Honourable (pseudonym), Interview, 1987, 2 February.
Jones, Bill (J. W.), Letter, 1985, 29 December, London.
Jackson, Leslie, Interview, 1985, 14 November, London.
Jeffcoate, Professor Sir Norman, 1987, 13 April, Letter, Liverpool University.
Kannreuther, J. A., Letter, 1986, 24 April, Pershore, Worcestershire.
Kay, Harry, Letter, 1985, 15 November, London.
Kerrigan, Rose, Interview, 1985, 3 December, Sydenham.
Kerrigan, Rose, Interview, 1986, 20 January, Sydenham.
Kingsford, Peter, PhD, Letter, 1986a, 11 March, Hatfield, Hertfordshire.
Kingsford, Peter, PhD, Letter, 1986b, 2 April, Hatfield, Hertfordshire.
Kingsford, Peter, PhD, Letter, 1986c, 29 August, Hatfield, Hertfordshire.
Lathbury, Marjorie, Letter, 1987a, 1 March, Mayfield, Sussex.
Lathbury, Marjorie, Letter, 1987b, 17 June, Mayfield, Sussex.
Legh, Phyllis, Letter, 1986, December, Tunbridge Wells, Kent.
Lindsay, Lady Loelia, Letter, 1985, 2 November, Send, Near Woking, Surrey.
Lindsay, Lady Loelia, Interview, 1985, 11 November, Send, Near Woking, Surrey.
Lloyd, Patricia, Letter, 1986, 2 May, Glascoed, Gwent, Wales.
Longford, Elizabeth, Countess, CBE, Letter, 1986a, 6 June, London.
Longford, Elizabeth, Countess, CBE, Letter, 1986b, 18 June, London.
McGlashan, Dr Alan, Letter, 1986, 4 May, London.
MacRae, Lady Phyllis, Letter, 1986a, 25 April, Bury St. Edmonds, Sussex.
MacRae, Lady Phyllis, Letter, 1986b, 13 May, Bury St. Edmonds, Sussex.
Maddox, Mrs A. M. S., Letter, 1987, 28 January, London.
Makower, Sylvia, Letter, 1987a, 22 March, Barnes, London.
Makower, Sylvia, Letter, 1987b, 30 April, Barnes, London.
Man, Andrew, Letter, 1985, 18 December, Dyfed, Wales.
Man, Andrew, Letter, 1986, 10 January, Dyfed, Wales.
Managing Editor, Letter, 1926, from the *Nation*, New York, to Edward Benn in Cambridge, England, 5 June.
Mander, Lady Rosalie, MA Oxon, Letter, 1986a, 16 April, Wolverhampton.
Mander, Lady Rosalie, MA Oxon, Letter, 1986b, 30 April, Wolverhampton.
Mannassi, Percival, MA, Letter, 1987, 14 April, Liverpool.
Marmorstein, Bruno, Interview, 1985, 7 November, London.
Massey, Marion E., Letter, 1986, 16 December, Petersfield, Hampshire.
Massingham, C. H., Letter, 1985, 14 December, Lee-on-Solent, Hampshire.
Massingham, C. H., Letter, 1986, 14 January, Lee-on-Solent, Hampshire.
May, Phineas, Interview, 1986, 15 January, London.

McDonald, Lady (Mary J.), Letter, 1986, 31 (*sic*) November, Lymington, Hampshire.
McGlashan, Alan, Letter, 1986, 4 May.
Mellanby, John, Letter, 1986, 5 June, Cambridge.Mellor, Norman, Letter, 1985a, 13 November, Cambridge.
Mellor, Norman, Letter, 1985b, 26 November, Cambridge.
Moore, Doris Langley, Letter, 1986, 8 May, London.
Morgan, Thomas (T. F.), Letter, 1985, 16 December, London.
Morgan, Thomas (T. F.), Letter, 1986, 22 January, London.
Mullet (pseudonym), Letter, 1986, 29 November, Solihull, W. Midlands.
Newmark, Jim, Letter, 1985, 9 November, Christchurch, Dorset.
Norman, Alf, Letter, 1985, 15 December, Gwent, Wales.
Nottage, Catherine, Interview, 1985, 8 November, London.
Oatley, Lady (Enid), Letter, 1987a, 26 January, Cambridge.
Oatley, Lady (Enid), Letter, 1987b, 8 February, Cambridge.
Oldham, L, Letter, 1986, 26 April, Dronfield, Sheffield.
Owen, William, Lt, Colonel, Ret, RN, Letter, 1986a, 18 May, Wilford, Surrey.
Owen, William, Lt, Colonel, Ret, RN, Letter, 1986b, 31 May, Wilford, Surrey.
Paten, Peggy, Interview, 1985, 10 December, Peterborough.
Paul, Victor, 1985, Letter, 14 December, Peterborough.
Paul, Victor, 1986, Interview, 27 January, Peterborough.
Paulson, G. M. E., Letter, 1986, 1 June, Hampstead Norreys, Berkshire.
Pendred, B. W., Letter, 1986a, 3 May, Newbury, Berks.
Pendred, B. W., Letter, 1986b, 14 May, Newbury, Berks.
Plate, Rev. Ria., Letter, 1986, Fife, Scotland.
Pratapsinhji, M. R., Letter, 1986, 28 July, Saurashtra, India.
Richardson, George, Interview, 1985, 10 December, Peterborough.
Richardson, George, Interview, 1986, 28 January, Peterborough.
Richmond (9th) and Gordon (4th), Duke of, Letter, 1986a, 16 April, Chichester, Sussex.
Richmond (9th) and Gordon (4th), Duke of, Letter, 1986b, 4 May, Chichester, Sussex.
Rosenberg, Sid, Interview, 1985, 26 November, London.
Rosenberg, Sid, Interview, 1986, 13 January, London.
Rosse, Lady Anne, Countess of, Letter, 1986a, 20 April, Handcross, Sussex.
Rosse, Lady Anne, Countess of, Letter, 1986b, 14 May, Birr Castle, Ireland.
Roud, Stephen, Letter, 1987, 13 June, Croydon, Surrey.
Rowntree, Jean, Letter, 1987a, 4 May, Tenterden, Kent.
Rowntree, Jean, Letter, 1987b, 27 June, Tenterden, Kent.
Santall, Jack, Letter, 1985, 5 December, Bournemouth, Dorset.
Santall, Brenda, Letter, 1985, 23 December, Bournemouth, Dorset.

Saunders, Christopher, Letter, 1986, 5 June, Hove Sussex.
Schofield, Winifred, Letter, 1986, December, Fleet, Hampshire.
S——, Brenda, Interview, 1987, 2 February, Ipswich, Suffolk.
S——, Brenda, Letter, 1986a, 16 October, Ipswich, Suffolk.
S——, Brenda, Letter, 1986b, November, Ipswich, Suffolk.
Segal, Alf, Interview, 1985, Interview, 9 November, London.
Segal, Burt, Interview, 1985, 6 November, London.
Segal, Esther Cohen, Interview, 1985, 6 November, London.
Shelton, Robert, CPO, RN, Letter, 1986, May, Pembrokeshire, Wales.
Smith, Lady, MD (pseudonym), Letter, 1986, December, Fulbourn, Cambridge.
Smith, Lady, MD, Interview, 1987, 30 January, Fulbourn, Cambridge.
Smith, Moira, Letter, 2010, 17 March, Bloomington, Indiana.
Smithers, David, MD, Letter, 1986a, 27 April, Knockholt, Kent.
Smithers, David, MD, Letter, 1986b, 8 May, Knockholt, Kent.
Speed, Sir Robert, Letter, 1986, June, Wargrave, Berkshire.
Spencer, Cyril, Letter, 1986a, 2 January, Lewes, East Sussex.
Spencer, Cyril, Letter, 1986b, 16 January, Lewes, East Sussex.
Spires, Ted, Interview, 1985, 10 December, Peterborough.
Stallman, Felicia, Interview, 1986, 23 April, London.
Stamp, Elizabeth, Letter, 1985, 18 November, Oxford.
Steel, Ralph, Interview, 1986, 28 January, Peterborough.
Studley, L. T., Letter, 1985a, 6 December, Southampton.
Studley, L. T., Letter, 1985b, 23 December, Southampton.
Talbot, Mary, Letter, 1986, 11 February, London.
Talbot, Mary, Interview, 1986a, 15 January, London.
Talbot, Mary, Interview, 1986b, 30 January, London.
Thompson, John S., Letter, 1986, 29 April, Bedford.
Toms, Allene, Interview, 1985, 18 December, Warlingham, Surrey.
Tosh, Rosamund, Letter, 1987a, 4 May, Wimbledon, London.
Tosh, Rosamund, Letter, 1987b, 29 June, Wimbledon, London.
Verdin, Jack, Interview, 1986, 19 May, London.
Vincent, Marjorie, Interview, 1986, 3 June, London.
Webb, Helen, Letter, 1986, Athenaeum Club (London), 7 March.
Whittle, Dorothy, Letter, 1985, to Mary Talbot (London), December, Callington, Cornwall.
Whittle, Dorothy, Letter, 1986, 19 April, Callington, Cornwall.
Williams, R. A. J., Letter, 1985, 13 December, Dyfed, Wales.
Williams, R. A. J., Letter, 1986, 2 January, Dyfed, Wales.
Wilmer, Professor Neville, Interview, 7 May, Cambridge.
Wilmer, Professor Neville, Letter, 1986a, 24 March, Cambridge.
Wilmer, Professor Neville, Letter, 1986b, 14 April, Cambridge.
Wooster, Dr N. A., Letter, 1986, December, Cambridge.

Zeitlyn, Alice, Letter, 1985a, 24 November, Cambridge.
Zeitlyn, Alice, Letter, 1985b, 1 December, Cambridge.

Contemporary periodicals

A. A. B., 1926a, 'All in the Game', *Tatler* (26 May), p. 240.
A. A. B., 1926b, 'All in the Game', *Tatler* (2 June), p. 240.
A. B., 1926, 'Week by Week', *Sphere* (22 May), p. 155.
A. E., 1926, 'Convictions Or What We Believe', *Isis* (May), p. 17.
Advertisement (Life Boat service), 1926, *New Statesman* (15 May), p. 126.
'After a Famous Victory', 1926, *Bystander* (26 May), p. 440.
'"All Aboard", or How Bournemouth Got its Potatoes', 1926, *Cambridge Gownsman and Undergraduette* (22 May), p. 6.
'All Strike Pay Illegal – Except to Miners', 1926, *Daily Chronicle* (12 May), p. 3.
'And Eve Said Unto Adam', 1926, *Eve* (26 May), p. 347.
'And Then They Disbanded – The Specials Dismiss', 1926, *Sphere* (22 May), p. 156.
Answers, 1926 (22 and 29 May), p. 10.
'The Archbishop's Letter', *Oxford Magazine* (20 May), p. 1.
'Armed with their Frying Pans: Lady Betty Butler (left) and Miss Collett Doughty', 1926, *Sketch* (12–19 May), p. 13.
'As in the War, Prime Minister to the Volunteers', 1926, *Daily Express* (17 May), p. 1.
'Astbury Judgement', 1926, *The Times* (14 May), p. 3.
'Asterisks', 1926, *Star* (17 May), p. 8.
Astor, Nancy, Maude Roydon, and M. Wintringham, 1926, 'Through Women's Eyes', *The Times* (12 May), p. 3.
'Attack on Omnibuses', 1926, *The Times* (10 May), p. 2.
Aunt Ambrosia, 1926a, 'Place aux Dames', *Isis* (5 May), p. 14.
Aunt Ambrosia, 1926b, 'Place aux Dames', *Isis* (19 May), p. 13.
Baldwin, Stanley, 1926a, 'The Nation's Duty', *The Times* (13 May), p. 3.
Baldwin, Stanley, 1926b, 'Editorial', *The Times* (17 May), p. 3.
Barnestein, Hugo, 1926, 'The Rumour, An Historical Drama of the Great Strike', *Isis* (12 May), pp. 7–8.
'Barricades in the London Streets', 1926, *Sphere* (15 May), p. 174.
'Beaten at their Own Game', 1926, *Evening News* (11 May), p. 2.
Benn, Edward, 1926, 'Mr. Benn Sees It Through', *Nation* (16 June), pp. 666–7.
Bethune, Edward, Lt-General, 1926a, 'The Efficient Amateurs', *Daily Mail* (17 May), p. 3.
Bethune, Edward, Lt-General, 1926b, 'Public Spirit', *Daily Express* (17 May), p. 2.
Bethune, Edward, Lt-General, 1926c, 'Splendid Amateurs', *Morning Post* (17 May), p. 3.

Beveren, 1926, 'The Clubman', *Sketch* (26 May), p. 270.
Blam, 1926, 'Our Plus Force! None But the Brave Deserved the Fare!' *Bystander* (26 May), p. 428.
Blanchette, 1926, 'Après Le Déluge', *Bystander* (26 May), p. 454.
Boale, C. H., 1926, Cartoon, *Eve* (12 and 19 May), p. 327.
Bott, Alan, 1926, 'The Volunteers Play Their Part, How all Classes of the Country came Forward to Perform National Service', *Sphere* (15 May), pp. 170–6.
British Gazette, 1926 (12 May), pp. 1–4.
British Worker, 1926a (7 May), p. 4.
British Worker, 1926b (9 May), pp. 1–2.
British Worker, 1926c (11 May), p. 4.
'British Legion's Appeal', 1926, *The Times* (10 May), p. 2.
'A British Observer', Letter, 1926, *The Times* (17 May), p. 3.
'Buns at Three a Minute', 1926, *Evening Standard* (17 May), p. 4.
'Bus Victory', 1926, *Evening News* (13 May), p. 2.
'Bystander Comments', 1926, *Bystander* (26 May), p. 419,
C. A. P., 1926, 'For Those Who Saved The Nation', *The Times* (13 May), p. 3.
'Call For Service, The', 1926, *Morning Post* (4 May), p. 11.
Candidus, 1926, 'The Sense of Things, British Sanity the admiration of Foreign Nations', *Daily Graphic* (13 May), p. 2.
'Cannibalism', 1926, *British Worker* (12 May), p. 4,
'The Canteens were Organized . . .', Caption, 1926, *Sketch* (26 May), p. 275.
'"Carrying On" During the General Strike', 1926, *Illustrated London News* (15 May), p. 859.
Cecil, Hugh, 1926, 'The Truth About the General Strike', *The Times* (11 May), p. 3.
Chadwick, Gertrude, 1926, 'The Miner's Wife', *Leeds Citizen* (8 May), p. 3.
'Chances for Cupid', *Answers* (22 May), p. 10.
'Charivaria', 1926a, *Punch* (26 May), p. 537.
'Charivaria', 1926b, *Punch* (2 June), p. 565.
'Cheery London, Business as Usual Despite the Strike', *Daily Mail* (7 May), p. 1.
Children's Newspaper, Photographs, 1926 (15 and 22 May), p. 1.
Children's Newspaper, 1926 (15 and 22 May), p. 1–2.
'The Clothes of the Volunteers show their CLASS INTEREST IN BEATING THE STRIKERS', 1926, *Westminster Worker* (May), p. 2.
'The Colleges and the Strike', 1926, *Oxford Magazine* (13 May), p. 440.
'Comments', 1926, *New Statesman* (15 May), pp. 113–16.
Corisande, 1926, 'Woman's World', *Evening Standard* (17 May), p. 11.
'Correspondence', 1926, *Oxford Magazine* (27 May), p. 507.
Cottrell, Tom, 1926, 'Wheel and Woe!', *Bystander* (26 May), p. 421.

Crave, Chas, 1926, Cartoon, *Punch* (26 May), p. 550.
Crook, William, 1926, 'Britain's Morning After', *Survey* (1 July), p. 419.
Cruikshank, R. J., 1926, 'A Diary of the General Strike', in Stuart Hodgson (ed.), *Strike Fortnight. A Diary of the Principal Events and Phases of the General Strike* (London: Fleetgate Publications), pp. 4–21.
'Curious Effects of the Strike', 1926, *Illustrated London News* (15 May), p. 866.
Daily Chronicle, 1926a (11 May), p. 3.
Daily Chronicle, 1926b, Photographs (13 May), p. 1.
Daily Chronicle, 1926c (14 May), p. 3
Daily Chronicle, 1926d (15 May), p. 3.
Daily Mail, 1926a, Photographs (12 May), p. 1.
Daily Mail, 1926b, Photographs (15 May), p. 1.
Daily Mirror, 1926 (11 May), p. 2.
Daily Telegraph, 1926a (5 May), p. 1.
Daily Telegraph, 1926b (11 May), p. 3.
Deptford Strike Bulletin, 1926 (12 May), p. 1.
'Diarie of the Weeke', 1926, *Cambridge Gownsman and Undergraduette* (15 May), p. 8.
Dixon, Roy, 1926, 'Strike Gains', *Daily Express* (17 May), p. 2.
'Dockyard Services Maintained by Volunteers', 1926, *Sphere* (15 May), p. 173.
'The Editor to his Readers' Letters', 1926, *Titbits* (8 May), p. 319.
Editorial, 1926, *Daily News* (14 May), p. 2.
Editorial, 1926a, *The Times* (12 May), p. 2.
Editorial, 1926b, *The Times* (12 May), p. 3.
Edwards, Joan Weston, 1926, 'Bolshevism in the Fashion World, The Modern Woman is Tired of Being a Robot in Matters of Dress', *Evening Standard* (17 May), p. 11.
Emergency Press, 1926 (5 May), p. 1.
Emergency Strike Bulletin, 1926 (5 May), p. 1.
'End of the Strike, An Unconditional Withdrawal', 1926, *The Times* (13 May), p. 3.
'England Expects ...', 1926, *British Worker* (16 May), p. 4.
'Enterprising Undergraduates', 1926, *Daily Telegraph* (11 May), p. 2.
'Equipped with Steel Helmets, Truncheons, and Armlets', *Bystander* (26 May), pp. 423–4.
Evelyn, 1926, 'The Letters of Evelyn', *Tatler* (12–19 May), p. 234.
Everard, C. L., 1926a, 'Would You Believe It?' *British Worker* (5 May), p. 4.
Everard, C. L., 1926b, 'Would You Believe It?' *British Worker* (7 May), p. 4.
Everard, C. L., 1926c, 'The Dope They Give Us!' *British Worker* (8 May), p. 8.
Everard, C. L., 1926d, 'Those Extra Specials', *British Worker* (10 May), p. 4.
Evoe, 1926a, 'Perfectly Lovely Times', *Punch* (19 May), p. 526.

Evoe, 1926b, 'How the Strike Struck Smith Major', *Punch* (26 May), p. 541.
Evoe, 1926c, 'Serve Britannia', *Punch* (26 May), p. 550.
Evoe, 1926d, 'The Coal Crisis', *Punch* (2 June), pp. 582–3.
'Excerpt', 1926, *Titbits* (April), p. 306.
'False News of Police Strike', 1926, *The Times* (8 May), p. 4.
'Fat Livings in Coal, But not for the Collier', 1926, *Scottish Worker* (15 May), p. 1.
'A Few Reflections', 1926, *Daily News* (14 May), p. 2.
'Fine Service', 1926, *Daily Express* (15 May), p. 3.
'Five Railway Crashes – Sequel to Blackleg and "Voluntary" Labour – Four Dead', 1926, *British Worker* (11 May), p. 1.
'Flotsam and Jetsam', 1926a, *Cambridge Gownsman and Undergraduette* (15 May), p. 2.
'Flotsam and Jetsam', 1926b, *Cambridge Gownsman and Undergraduette* (22 May), p. 2.
'Food by Convoy', 1926, *Daily Mirror* (11 May), p. 2.
'The Fortnight of Folly – Brave Volunteers – Miners Beware! – Back to Work Again', 1926, *Daily Express* (17 May), p. 2.
'Forty-one Injured', 1926, *Daily Mail* (10 May), p. 2.
Fraser, John Foster, 1926, 'Revolution Indeed! How England Carried On', *Tatler* (26 May), pp. 236–7.
Frenchman, 1926, 'Imperturbable London, the City that Laughs at Strikes', *Daily Express* (15 May), p. 3.
'French Perplexities – Commentators Nonplussed by British Calm', 1926, *Manchester Guardian* (14 May), p. 2
'From Midnight to Noonday', 1926, *Children's Newspaper* (15 and 22 May), p. 2.
'From Town and Country – A Striking Contrast', 1926, *Lady* (27 May), p. 666.
Gadfly, 1926, 'The Spatted Calves', *Daily Herald* (3 May), p. 5.
G. B., 1926, 'Alarmists', *Isis* (12 May), p. 1.
G. H., 1926, 'Revue Feminine', *Cherwell* (15 May), p. 104.
'Getting Nervous', 1926, *Sunday Express* (9 May), p. 1.
'A Glasgow Incident', 1926, *Manchester Guardian* (5 May), p. 2,
'Glasgow Rioting', 1926, *Daily Telegraph* (8 May), p. 3.
'Gloucester Solid', 1926, *British Worker* (8 May), p. 3.
'The Good side of it all', 1926, *Children's Newspaper* (15 and 22 May), p. 2.
'Good-Bye, Old Bus', 1926, *Evening News* (15 May), p. 2.
'The Great Exodus, or How it was Arranged', 1926, *Cambridge Gownsman and Undergraduette* (15 May), p. 13.
H. A. and C. U. III, 1926, 'The Gallant Six Hundred', *Cambridge Gownsman and Undergraduette* (22 May), p. 12.

Haselden, W. K., 1926, 'Some Humours of the Strike Days', *Daily Mirror* (18 May), n.p.
'Helpers at the Y.M.C.A., Canteen in Hyde Park busy Serving out "Rations"', 1926, *Bystander* (26 May), p. 427.
Herlots, Hugh G. G., 1926, 'Cambridge Letter', *Cherwell* (22 May), p. 133.
'High Hearts and High Heels', 1926, *Daily Mirror* (14 May), p. 3.
Hind, C. Lewis, 1926, 'The Great Strike: How it Came and Ended', *Sphere* (22 May), p. 160.
'Home News in Pictures', 1926, *Sphere* (15 May), p. 180.
'Hooligans Attack Food Lorries', 1926, *Daily Mail* (10 May), p. 2.
'Hooligans Busy in Glasgow', 1926, *Manchester Guardian* (10 May), p. 3.
Horne, R. S., 1926, 'Coal-Owners' Notices', *The Times* (13 May), p. 3.
Horrabin, J. F., 1929, 'A Clean Sweep', *Horrabin's 'Election Special'* (24 May), p. 1.
'Hospital Volunteers – Light-hearted Students from King's College Hospital Photographed in Downing-street', 1926, *Daily Express* (4 May), p. 8.
'How The Flag Was Kept Flying', 1926, *Tatler* (26 May), p. 251.
'How the Great Strike was Broken', 1926, *Daily Mail* (15 May), p. 4.
'How I Saved England: A Drama, In Four Acts, Of Poignant Realism', 1925, *Isis* (19 May), pp. 17–18.
'How it was Done', 1926, *Star* (17 May), p. 4.
'How London Was Made Safe', 1926, *Morning News* (14 May), p. 4,
'How the British Empire Came on in Spite of the Strike', 1926, *Tatler* (12–19 May), pp. 240–1.
'How the Press Overcame the Attack Upon Its Freedom', 1926, *Illustrated London News* (15 May), p. 868.
'How the War Won the Strike', 1926, *Manchester Guardian* (13 May) p. 2.
'How the Women Backed the General Strike', 1926, *Labour Woman* (1 June), p. 85.
'How they Helped in Hyde Park and Whitehall', 1926, *Sphere* (22 May), p. 158.
'How We Did It', 1926, *Saturday Review* (22 May), p. 612.
'How Will the Strike End', 1926, *Oxford Magazine* (3 June), p. 525.
'How Women Helped During the Great Strike', 1926, *Sphere* (22 May), p. 159.
'How Women Met a National Emergency', 1926, *Morning Post* (17 May), p. 4.
'Humour', 1926, *Children's Newspaper* (15 and 22 May), p. 2.
'The Humours of the Great Strike', 1926, *Answers* (22 and 29 May), p. 10.
'Humours of the Volunteers', 1926, *Star* (17 May), p. 5.
'Hyde Park Canteen', 1926, *Daily Express* (12 May), p. 1.
'Hyde Park as London's Food "Citadel"', 1926, *Illustrated London News* (15 May), p. 862.
'The Illegal Strike', 1926, *Daily Mirror* (12 May), p. 3.

'Impressions of Life in London during the General Strike', 1926, *Illustrated London News* (15 June), p. 854.
'An Improvement in Scotland, 1926, *The Times* (11 May), p. 3.
'Improving Services', 1926, *Daily Telegraph* (11 May), p. 2.
J. W. E., 1926, 'Wise and Otherwise', *Ladies' Companion* (12 June), p. 113.
'Keeping Smiling', 1926, *Tatler* (12–19 May), p. 246.
Kiki, 1926, 'Mainly for Women', *Sunday Pictorial* (9 May), p. 3.
'The King to the Nation', 1926, *Morning Post* (14 May), p. 2.
'The King's Message', 1926, *The Times* (13 May), p. 3.
King-Page, D., 1926, 'Strike Risks, How Insurance Firms Bore the Burden', *Daily Mail* (17 May), p. 2.
L'A., F. de, 1926, 'Outbursts of an Undergraduette of a Frivolous Nature during the Strike', *Isis* (22 May), p. 6.
'La Gazette', 1926, *Cherwell* (22 May), p. 121.
'Lady Members of the Idle Class "Caught" Doing Something Useful in Hyde Park', 1926, *Sunday Worker* (16 May), p. 8.
'Legs and the Strike', 1926, *Punch* (26 May), p. 564.
'Letters from Ermyntrude', 1926, *Isis* (12 May), p. 11.
'The Liberal Point of View', 1926, *Daily Chronicle* (11 May), p. 1.
'London University', 1926, *Morning Post* (15 May), p. 2.
London Calling!, 1926a, 'A Propaganda Error', *Daily News* (15 May), p. 2.
London Calling!, 1926b, *Daily News* (17 May), p. 2.
London, Mr., 1926a, 'Wonderful London Yesterday', *Daily Graphic* (3 May), p. 5.
London, Mr., 1926b, 'Wonderful London Yesterday', *Daily Graphic* (17 May), p. 2.
'London in Strike Time – How Citizens Kept Going – High Hearts and Good Humour', 1926, *Daily Telegraph* (14 May), p. 2.
A London Taxi Cab Driver, 1926, 'A Boxer to the Rescue – When I Lost my Cab', *Titbits* (22 May and 5 June), p. 372.
'London "Specials", "Civils", and Volunteers Disband', 1926, *Illustrated London News* (22 May), p. 889.
'London's Day of Disillusion', 1926, *Daily Chronicle* (14 May), p. 2.
'London's Quiet Sunday', 1926, *Daily Mail* (10 May), p. 2.
'Loyalty', 1926, *Oxford Magazine* (6 May), p. 420.
Lt. Colonel, 1926, 'Work for the Volunteers', *Daily Mail* (17 May), p. 3.
M. S. L., 1926, 'Back to Work', *Isis* (19 May), p. 1.
Man In The Street, 1926, 'Steady!', *Daily Sketch* (3 May), p. 7.
Martha, 1926, 'Letters from Home', *Queen* (26 May), p. 28.
Mayfair Mansions, 1926, 'The Diary of a Mondaine', *Punch* (2 June) p. 572.
Mayfair, Mr., 1926a, 'Nuts and Wine, Gossip for the After-Dinner Hour', *Sunday Pictorial* (9 May), p. 3.

Mayfair, Mr., 1926b, 'Nuts and Wine, Gossip for the After-Dinner Hour', *Sunday Pictorial* (16 May), p. 5.
Mee, Arthur, 1926, 'The Country's Nine Days Wonder', 1926, *Children's Newspaper* (15 and 22 May), p. 1.
'Meeting for Wives', 1926, *British Worker* (7 May), p. 4.
Merseyside Strike Bulletin, 1926 (10 May), p. 1.
'Miles of Smiles', 1926, *Evening News* (12 May), p. 2.
'Military Force Displayed But Not Used', 1926, *Illustrated London News* (15 May), pp. 856–7.
'Milk and Potatoes for London', 1926, *The Times* (10 May), p. 3.
Mills, Arthur Wallis, 1926, 'Riding Pillion', *Punch* (26 May), p. 541.
'Miners as Railway Workers', 1926, *The Times* (10 May), p. 2.
'Miners' Wives', 1926, *British Worker* (10 May), p. 2.
'Miss Edwina Ashley', Caption, 1926, *Sketch* (26 May), p. 275.
'Mobs Wreck Tramcars and Omnibuses in London', 1926, *Daily Mail* (6 May), p. 1.
'A Modern Princess', 1926, *Evening Standard* (17 May), p. 6.
'Mr. Baldwin's Thanks, Broadcast Message', 1926, *The Times* (13 May), p. 3.
'Mr. Baldwin's Statement', 1926, *The Times* (13 May), p. 3.
'Nation Behind the TUC', 1926, *British Worker* (10 May), p. 2.
'Nearly 100% Out', 1926, *British Worker* (8 May), p. 3.
'News in Brief', 1926, *Evening News* (15 May), p. 2.
'Noblesse Oblige', 1926, *Eve* (26 May), p. 340.
'The Non-Revolutionary Strike', 1926, *Oxford Magazine* (20 May), p. 1.
'Non-Union Labour Only', 1926, *The Times* (13 May), p. 3.
The Old Guard, 1926, 'Mob Rule', *Bystander* (26 May), p. 428.
'On Ants and Grasshoppers', 1926, *New Statesman* (8 May), pp. 103–4.
'Once More into the Breach …', 1926, *Tatler* (26 May), p. 245.
Onlooker, 1926, 'Cloth Cap as a Symbol', *Daily Graphic* (3 May), p. 6.
'Our Staff', 1926, *Isis* (19 May), p. 4.
'Our Witty Bus Drivers', 1926, *Isis* (19 May), p. 3.
'Over in Ireland, and the Strike from the Social Point of View', 1926, *Tatler* (26 May), pp. 245–6.
Owner-Driver, 1926, 'The Girl in the Mauve Hat, And Some Other Passengers', *Evening News* (15 May), p. 2.
'Owners Drastic Proposals', 1926, *British Worker* (5 May), p. 6.
'Oxford and the Strike', 1926, *Oxford Magazine* (20 May), p. 456.
Parker, Cornelia Stratton, 1926, 'Plus-Fours to the Rescue', *Survey* (1 July), pp. 411–15.
'Parliamentary Reports', 1926, *Oxford Magazine* (13 May), p. 444.
Partridge, Bernard, 1926, 'The Lever Breaks', *Punch* (19 May), n.p.
'The Passing Hour', 1926, *Isis* (5 May), pp. 3–4.

'Peer as Signalman', 1926, *Daily Graphic* (12 May), p. 3.
Phillida, 1926a, 'What the Women are Doing', *Daily Mirror* (12 May), p. 4.
Phillida, 1926b, 'The Ladies' Mirror', *Daily Mirror* (13 May), p. 4.
'Pictures of the Great Strike', 1926, *Daily Telegraph* (14 May), p. 4.
'Pictures of the Strike – The Police Cope with Disturbances', 1926, *Illustrated London News* (15 May), p. 857.
'Plus-Fours and Flannel Bags …' 1926, *Tatler* (26 May), p. 267.
'The Police and the Crisis', 1926, *The Police Review and Parade Gossip* (21 May), p. 279.
'A Pot-Pourri of Post Strike Impressions', 1926, *Sphere* (22 May), p. 154.
'The Present Emergency is not National, but Personal', 1926, *Cambridge Gownsman and Undergraduette* (15 May), p. 4.
'Prince Visits the Food Depots', 1926, *Daily Chronicle* (13 May), p. 2.
'Prison for Hooligans – Peace Breaking Roughs Sentenced', 1926, *Daily Graphic* (10 May), p. 2.
Punch, Cartoon, 1926a (16 May), p. 513.
Punch, Cartoon, 1926b (19 May), p. 534.
Punch, Cartoon, 1926c (19 May), p. 535.
Punch, Cartoon, 1926d (26 May), p. 513.
Punch, Cartoon, 1926e (2 June), p. 569.
'Railway Collision at Edinburgh', 1926, *The Times* (11 May), p. 3.
'Railway Work Refused', 1926, *The Times* (14 May), p. 3.
'Raising the Dock Siege', 1926, *Daily Mail* (15 May), p. 2.
Rambler, 1926, 'Today's Gossip by Rambler', *Daily Mirror* (14 May), p. 3.
Raven-Hill, I, 1926, 'The British Worker', *Punch* (19 May), p. 523.
'The Real Spirit', 1926, *Punch* (26 May), p. 513.
Reed, E. T., 1926, 'Some "General" Favourites', 1926, *Bystander* (26 May), p. 445.
'Re-Engagement of Strikers, Government Statement', 1926, *The Times* (13 May), p. 3.
Reynolds, Frank, 1926a, 'Repercussions of The Strike', *Punch* (19 May), p. 525.
Reynolds, Frank, 1926b, 'Your Son is Looking very Bored', *Punch* (2 June), p. 578.
'Right or Wrong?' 1926, *Halifax Courier and Guardian* (15 May), p. 4.
'Riotous Scenes in Glasgow', 1926, *The Times* (8 May), p. 2.
'Robert The Angel', 1926, *Punch* (26 May), p. 540.
'Round the Town', 1926, *London Opinion* (5 June), p. 262.
'Running a Lorry', 1926, *Daily Express* (17 May), p. 2.
S. R. L., 'Week by Week', *Sphere* (22 May), p. 155.
Sabretache, 1926a, 'Hats Off to Our 'Reserve Army', *Tatler* (26 May), pp. 268–9.
Sabretache, 1926b, 'Pictures in the Fire', *Tatler* (26 May), p. 272.
'Saklatvala Sent to Prison', 1926, *Daily Mail* (7 May), p. 1.

'Scenes After the Great Strike', 1926, *Daily Telegraph* (17 May), p. 4.
'Scrap of Conversation, A', 1926, *Oxford Magazine* (20 May), p. 460.
'Settle Down!' 1926, *Evening Standard* (17 May), p. 6.
Seward, A. C., 1926, 'Cambridge Men and the General Strike, Letter from the Vice-Chancellor', *Cambridge Gownsman and Undergraduette* (29 May), p. 10.
'Shakespeare at Stratford', 1926, *The Times* (10 May), p. 4.
Simplicissimus, 1926, 'Volunt-Hearing', *Isis* (19 May), p. 18.
'Signalmen in Fair Isle Jerseys and "Plus Fours": Two Volunteer Undergraduates in Charge of the Chief Signal Box at Bletchley Station', in 'The Spirit of England at Work', 1926, *Illustrated London News* (15 May), p. 858.
'Sir H. Samuel's Basis, No Authorization From Government', *The Times* (14 May), p. 3.
'Soldiers and Sailors on Duty at Lots Road Power Station hold a Services' Match', *Daily Graphic*, 1926 (11 May), p. 1.
'Solid and Orderly', 1926, *British Worker* (8 May), p. 3.
'Some Strike Snapshots', 1926, *Church of England Newspaper* (15 May), p. 2.
'Special Peelers', 1926, *Bystander* (16 May), p. 427.
'Specials' Fine Work', 1926, *Daily Telegraph* (14 May), p. 4.
'"Specials" of Both Sexes at Ranelagh where Polo Players Enrolled in the Mounted Section', 1926, *Daily Graphic* (17 May), p. 4.
Sphere, 1926a (15 May), Cover.
'The Spirit of England – "Carry On"', 1926, *Illustrated London News* (15 May), p. 854.
'The Spirit that Broke the Strike – A Mercantile Marine Officer as a Volunteer Engine Driver', 1926, *Daily Mail* (15 May), p. 4.
'The Spirit of England at Work', 1926, *Illustrated London News* (15 May), p. 858.
'The Strike and After', 1926, *Evening Standard* (17 May), p. 6.
'Strike Brevities', 1926a, *Evening News* (11 May), p. 2.
'Strike Brevities', 1926b, *Daily Mirror* (13 May), p. 3.
'The Strike-Breakers: A Drama in Three Driblets', 1926, *Isis* (26 May), p. 10.
'Strike Diary', 1926, *New Leader* (21 May), p. 3.
'Strike News in Brief', 1926, *Evening News* (12 May), p. 2.
'Strike Notes', 1926, *Police Review and Parade Gossip* (28 May), p. 288.
'Strike Notes', 1926, *Punch* (19 May), p. 527.
'Strike Reminiscences', 1926, *Cherwell* (22 May), p. 122,
'Strike and Post-Strike Incidents, Including Trainwrecking', 1926, *Illustrated London News* (15 May), p. 865.
'Strike and Service', 1926, *Cambridge Gownsman and Undergraduette* (8 May), p. 1.

'The Strike a Sin', 1926, *Daily Mail* (10 May), p. 3.
'Strike Sparks', 1926, *Eve* (12 and 19 May), p. 327.
'Strike Volunteers – And "A Duchess or Two" The Prince Drops in', 1926, *Evening News* (12 May), p. 2.
'Strikers' Parade', 1926, *Halifax Courier and Guardian* (8 May), p. 5,
'Striking Snapshots', 1926, *British Worker* (11 May), p. 2.
'Surrender of the Revolutionaries', 1926, *Daily Mail* (12 May), p. 1.
'Surrey Fowl Bus Driver', 1926, *Daily Mail* (8 May), p. 1,
'The Surrey Fowl', 1926, *Daily Telegraph* (8 May), p. 4.
'Taking It Standing Up, Hats Off to the People who took their Coats off', 1926, *Eve* (12 and 19 May), p. 323.
Terry, Sir Richard, 1926, 'Provincial London', *Queen* (2 June), p. 7.
Tatler, Photographs, 1926 (12–19 May), p. 240.
'Thanks to the Volunteers', 1926, *Daily Mail* (17 May), p. 2,
'These Troubled Days', 1925, *Spectator* (8 May), p. 7–8.
'Through Foreign Glasses', 1926, *Tatler* (26 May), p. 238.
The Times House Journal, 1925–6, 6, pp. 183–96.
The Times, 1926a (3 May), p. 15.
The Times, 1926b (7 May), p. 3.
The Times, 1926c (10 May), p. 4.
'Tittle-Tattle', 1926, *Bystander* (26 May), pp. 424–6.
'Today', 1926, *Sunday Express* (9 May), p. 1.
'Topsy-Turvy Ways', 1926, *British Worker* (9 May), p. 3.
'Towards Peace', 1926, *Manchester Guardian* (10 May), p. 1.
'Tram Cars Attacked', 1926, *Daily Mail* (10 May), p. 2.
Tristram, Arthur, 1926a, 'Seeing it Through', *Eve* (12 and 19 May), p. 327.
Tristram, Arthur, 1926b, 'Strike Sparks', *Eve* (12 and 19 May), p. 327.
'Truth on Rail Transport – Survey of Position at London Termini Traffic Paralysed', 1926, *British Worker* (9 May), p. 3.
'Twenty Civilians Injured, Police in Motor-Coaches with Wire Netting', 1926, *Daily Mail* (10 May), p. 2.
'The Tube Volunteers Farewell', 1926, *Star* (15 May), p. 1.
'The U-C Writes', 1926, *Isis* (1 June), p. 2.
'Undemonstrative Crowds', 1926, *The Times* (10 May), pp. 3–4.
'Undergraduate Porters at Dover', 1926, *Daily Mail* (10 May), p. 3.
'University News', 1926, *The Times* (12 May), p. 2.
'The Varsities Vindicated', 1926, *Isis* (26 May), p. 8.
'A Versatile Volunteer Worker', 1926, *Punch* (26 May), p. 540.
'Victory for Community', 1926, *Daily Graphic* (13 May), p. 2.
'The Voluntary Staff at the Horse Guards Parade', 1926, *Eve* (26 May), p. 347.
'The Volunteer's Plea', 1926, *Star* (17 May), p. 1.
'Volunteer Stablemen', 1926, *Daily Telegraph* (14 May), p. 4.

'Volunteers at Paddington deal with Food from the West Country and Western Ports', *Daily Graphic* (17 May), p. 4.
'Volunteers – And the Others', 1926, *Daily Chronicle* (12 May), p. 3.
'Waifs and Strays', 1926, *Sphinx* (3 June), p. 241.
'Wanted: Flamboyance', 1926, *Cherwell* (22 May), p. 122.
'War On Work-Girls', 1926, *Daily Telegraph* (6 May), p. 2.
'Wear and Tear, The London Shops and the Strike', 1926, *Eve* (12 and 19 May), p. 335.
'Wear Your Medals', 1926, *British Worker* (9 May), p. 4.
'Well Done – The Light (Hearted) Blues!' 1926, *Tatler* (26 May), p. 267.
'Were we Downhearted? The Answer is in the Negative', 1926, *Tatler* (12–19 May), p. 235.
Westminster Worker, 1926 (10 May), p. 2.
'What We Have Seen and Heard', 1926, *Lock-Out Strike-Time Sentinel* (13 May), p. 1.
'What Did You Do?' 1926, *Punch* (2 June), p. 568.
'Whipped Topics', 1926, *London Opinion* (5 June), p. 259.
'Who, When & Where', 1926, *Bystander* (26 May), pp. 422–7.
'Why They Had to Walk – Volunteer Driver Who Touched the Wrong Handle', 1926, *British Worker* (12 May), p. 2.
Wilson, David, 1926, 'We Take our Hats Off To—', *Bystander* (26 May), p. 429.
'Wireless Wins Through', 1926, *Answers* (22 and 29 May), p. 5.
'Without Permission of the T.U.C.', 1926, *Evening News* (11 May), p. 2.
'Women as Volunteers', 1926, *Daily Mail* (10 May), p. 3.
'Women Taxi Drivers', 1926, *Daily Mirror* (13 May), p. 3.
'Women Helping', 1926, *Daily Mail* (7 May), p. 1.
'Women with Men', *Workers' Daily* (3 May), p. 2.
'Women Work in Canteens', 1926, *Daily Mail* (10 May), p. 3.
'Women's Organisations', 1926, *The Times* (8 May), p. 4.
'Women's Work in the Crisis', 1926, *Daily Express* (12 May), p. 1.
'Wonderful London Yesterday', 1926, *Daily Graphic* (12 May), p. 2.
'Wonderful Police', 1926, *Daily Express* (14 May), p. 3.
Wood, T. R., Joseph Barcroft, Humphrey Rolleston, F. C. Bartlett, H. F. Howard, F. G. Hopkins, and Arthur Quiller-Couch, 1926, 'Cambridge Appeal', *The Times* (11 May), p. 3.
'The World of Sport', 1926, *Time and Tide* (14 May), p. 22.
X. X., 1926, 'The Lighter Side of Life', *Sphere* (15 May), p. 179.
Y. Y., 1926, 'On Tapping a Bloke On The Shoulder', *New Statesman* (15 May), pp. 118–19.
Young, Florence, 1926, Letter, 'Volunteer Omnibus Men', *The Times* (15 May), p. 3.
'Zinoviev on the Strike', 1926, *Daily Mail* (12 May), p. 1.

Plays, novels, poetry

Allen, Jim, 1975, *Days of Hope* (London: BBC).
Barnes, Julian, 1999, *England, England* (London: Picador).
Benedictus, David, 1985, *What a Way to Run a Revolution* (London: Channel 4).
Blake, William, 1804, 'Jerusalem', *Milton*.
Cary, Joyce, 1955, *Not Honour More* (New York: Harper).
Cole, G. D. H., 1977 (1926), 'The Striker Stricken', in Asa Briggs and John Saville (eds), *Essays in Labour History* (London: Croom Helm).
Delderfield, R. F., 1973, *To Serve Them all my Days* (New York: Pocket Books).
Galsworthy, John, 1950, *A Modern Comedy* (New York: Charles Scribner's Sons).
Hartley, L. P., 1953, *The Go-Between* (London: H. Hamilton).
Lee, Jennie, 1939, *Tomorrow is a New Day* (London: Cresset Press).
Marsh, Ngaio, 1969 [1957], *Off With His Head* (London: Fontana Books).
Paul, Jeremy (scriptwriter), Simon Langton (director), 1975, 'The Nine Days Wonder', *Upstairs, Downstairs* (London: BBC; first aired 2 November).
Waugh, Evelyn, 1946 [1930], *Vile Bodies* (Boston: Little, Brown and Company).
Waugh, Evelyn, 1979 [1944], *Brideshead Revisited* (Boston: Little, Brown and Company).
Williams, Raymond, 1964, *Border Country* (London: Penguin).
Wilkinson, Ellen, 1989 [1929], *Clash* (London: Virago).

Secondary works

Biographies and memoirs

Asquith (Emma Alice Margaret), Countess of Oxford and Asquith, 1943, *Off the Record* (London: Frederick Muller Ltd).
Beaton, Cecil, 1961, *The Wandering Years, Diaries 1922–1939* (London: Weidenfeld & Nicolson).
Brockway, Fenner, 1942, *Inside the Left* (London: George Allen & Unwin Ltd).
Campbell, John, 1977, *Lloyd George: The Goat in the Wilderness* (London: Jonathan Cape Ltd).
Cartland, Barbara, 1970. *We Danced All Night* (London: Hutchinson & Company).
Clephane, Irene, 1933, *Ourselves, 1900–1930* (London: John Lane, the Bodley Head Ltd).
Clynes, J. R., 1937, *Memoirs, Volume 2* (London: Hutchinson & Company).
Cooper, Diana, 1959, *The Light of Common Day* (Boston: Houghton Mifflin Company).
Cooper, Artemis (ed.), 1983, *A Durable Fire: Letters of Duff and Diana Cooper* (London: Collins).

Cooper, Diana, 1979, *Autobiography: The Rainbow Comes and Goes, Light of Common Day, Trumpets from the Steep* (London: Michael Russell).
Granville, George, Duke of Sutherland, 1957, *Looking Back: The Autobiography of the Duke of Sutherland* (London: Oldhams Press Ltd).
Graves, Robert and Alan Hodge, 1941, *The Long Week End: A Social History of Great Britain 1918–1939* (New York: The Macmillan Company).
Greene, Graham, 1971, *A Sort of Life* (New York: Simon & Schuster).
Grenfell, Joyce, 1976, *Joyce Grenfell Requests the Pleasure* (London: Macmillan).
Grieg, Daisy, 1979, *Daisy Reminisces* (London: Bachman & Turner Ltd).
Grosvenor, Loelia, Duchess of Westminster, 1961, *Grace and Favour* (London: Weidenfeld & Nicolson).
Hannington, Wal, 1977 [1936], *Unemployed Struggles 1919–1936* (London: Lawrence & Wishart Ltd).
Isherwood, Christopher, 1947 (1938), *Lions and Shadows: An Education* (Connecticut: New Directions).
Jones, Thomas, 1951, *Lloyd George* (Cambridge: Harvard University Press).
Jones, Thomas, 1969, *Whitehall Diary, Volume II, 1926–1930*, ed. Keith Middlemas (London: Oxford University Press).
Lindsay, Loelia, 1983, *Cocktails and Laughter: The Albums of Loelia Lindsay, Loelia, Duchess of Westminster*, ed. Hugo Vickers (London: Hamish Hamilton).
Margetson, Stella, 1974, *The Long Party* (Farnborough: Saxon House).
Mitford, Jessica, 1960, *Daughters and Rebels* (New York: Holt, Rinehart & Winston).
Montagu, Duke of Manchester, 1932, *My Candid Recollections* (London: Grayson and Grayson).
Moore, Doris Langley, 1929, *Pandora's Letter Box: Being a Discourse on Fashionable Life* (London: Gerald Howe).
Sitwell, Osbert, 1948, *Laughter in the Next Room* (Boston: Little, Brown and Company).
Stansky, Peter, 2003. *Sassoon: the Worlds of Philip and Sybil* (New Haven: Yale University Press).
Taylor, A. J. P., 1983, *A Personal History* (London: Hamish Hamilton).
Waugh, Evelyn, 1976, *The Diaries of Evelyn Waugh*, ed., Michael Davie (Boston: Little, Brown and Company).
Webb, Beatrice, 1956, *Beatrice Webb's Diaries 1924–1932*, ed. Margaret Cole (London: Longman's, Green and Company).
Williams, Emlyn, 1976, *George – An Autobiography* (Middlesex: Penguin).
Wilson, Jean Moorcroft, 2003, *Siegfried Sassoon: The Journey from the Trenches: A Biography (1918–1967)* (New York: Routledge).

General strike histories and anniversary publications

Archard, David, Brian Harrison, and Tony Heath, 1972, 'Corpus in the 1926 Strike', *Pelican*, 2:1, 11–21.
Arnot, Robin Page, 1926, *The General Strike, May 1926: Its Origin and History* (London: Labour Research Department).
Aubrey, Crispin, 1976, 'Fifty Years On', *Time Out* (30 April), 13–15.
Bruley, Sue, 2004, 'Women', in John McIlroy, Alan Campbell, and Keith Gildart (eds), *Industrial Politics and the 1926 Mining Lockout: The Struggle for Dignity* (Cardiff: University of Wales Press).
Bruley, Sue, 2010, *The Women and Men of 1926: A Gender and Social History of the General Strike and the Miners' Lockout in South Wales* (Cardiff: University of Wales Press).
Burns, Emile, 1926, *The General Strike May 1926: Trades Councils in Action* (London: Labour Research Department).
Carter, Paul and Carol, 1974, *Our History: The Miners of Kilsyth in the 1926 General Strike & Lockout*, Pamphlet 58, General Strike 50th Anniversary Studies (London: The Journeyman Press).
Cootes, R. J., 1983 (1964), *The General Strike 1926* (Essex: Longman Group Ltd).
Crompton, Gerald W., 1988, '"Some Good Men, Some Doubtful Men ..." The Role of Railway Volunteers in the General Strike', *The Journal of Transport History*, 9:2, 127–48.
Crook, W. H., 1931, *The General Strike: A Study of Labor's Tragic Weapon in Theory and Practice* (Chapel Hill, North Carolina: University of North Carolina Press).
Davies, Trevor, 1976[?], *Bolton May 1926: A Review of the General Strike as it Affected Bolton & District* (Bolton: Bolton Trades Council).
Durr, Arthur, 1976, *Who Were the Guilty? General Strike Brighton May 1926* (Brighton: British Labour History Press).
Farman, Christopher, 1974 (1972), *The General Strike – May 1926: Britain's Aborted Revolution?* (St Albans: Panther Books Ltd).
Farman, Christopher, 1976, 'London and the General Strike', in *Remember 1926, An Exhibition to Commemorate the 50th Anniversary of the General Strike* (London: Organising Committee and the GLC).
Florey, R. A., 1980, *The General Strike of 1926: The Economic, Political and Social Causes of that Class War* (London: John Calder).
Foster, John, 2004, 'Prologue: What Kind of Crisis? What Kind of Ruling Class?', in John McIlroy, Alan Campbell, and Keith Gildart (eds), *Industrial Politics and the 1926 Mining Lockout: The Struggle for Dignity* (Cardiff: University of Wales Press).

Francis, Hywel, 1976, 'South Wales', in Jeffrey Skelley (ed.), *The 1926 General Strike* (London: Lawrence & Wishart).

Fyfe, Hamilton, 1926, *Behind the Scenes of the Great Strike* (London: The Labour Publishing Company Ltd).

General Strike 50th Anniversary, 1976, *Socialist Worker*, Special Issue.

John Halstead, 2005, '1926, 1984 ... And All That! (review of *Industrial Politics and the 1926 Mining Lockout*)' *History Workshop Journal*, 60:1, 222–9.

Harris, Sarah, 1985, *How and Why: The General Strike*, 'Weighing Up the Evidence' series, general ed. Sarah Harris (London: Dryad Press Ltd).

Haigh, R. H., D. S. Morris, and A. R. Peters, 1988, *Guardian Book of the General Strike* (London: Wildwood House).

Hattersley, Roy, 2006, 'The Legacy of Black Friday' (review of *A Very British Strike* and *Challenge to Democracy*), *Guardian*, Books (15 July). At: www.Guardian.co.uk/books/2006/jul/15/highereducation.history.

Hills, R. I., 1980, 'The General Strike in York, 1926', in *Borthwick Papers*, 57 (York: St Anthony's Press).

Hornsey, Pat (ed.), 1976, *The General Strike 1926–1976* (Exhibition Catalogue) (London: New English Library).

Hughes, Michael (compiler and writer), 1968, *Cartoons from the General Strike* (London: Evelyn, Adams & Mackay).

Klugman, James, 1980, *History of the Communist Party of Great Britain, Volume 2: The General Strike 1925–1926* (London: Lawrence & Wishart).

Labour Museum, n.d. *General Strike 1926*, Teachers' Notes, 4 (London: Labour Museum).

Laybourn, Keith, 1993, *The General Strike of 1926* (Manchester: Manchester University Press).

Laybourn, Keith, 1999a [1996], *The General Strike: Day by Day* (Gloucestershire: Sutton Publishing Ltd).

Leeson, R. A., 1973, *Strike: A Live History, 1887–1971* (London: George Allen & Unwin Ltd).

McIlroy, John, 2006, 'Memory, Commemoration and History – 1926 in 2006', *Historical Studies in Industrial Relations*, 21, 65–108.

McIlroy, John, Alan Campbell, and Keith Gildart, 2004a, 'Introduction: 1926 and All That', in John McIlroy, Alan Campbell, and Keith Gildart (eds) *Industrial Politics and the 1926 Mining Lockout* (Cardiff: University of Wales Press).

McIlroy, John, Alan Campbell, and Keith Gildart (eds), 2004b, *Industrial Politics and the 1926 Mining Lockout* (Cardiff: University of Wales Press).

McLean, John, 1976, *Our History: The 1926 General Strike in Lanarkshire*, Pamphlet 65 (Spring), General Strike 50th Anniversary Studies (London: History Group of the Communist Party).

Martin, Kingsley, 1926, *The British Public and the General Strike* (London: Hogarth Press).

Mason, Anthony, 1969, 'The Government and the General Strike, 1926', *International Review of Social History*, 14, 1–21.
Mellor, Adrian, Chris Pawling, and Colin Sparks, 1976, 'Writers and the General Strike', in Margaret Morris (ed.), *The General Strike* (Middlesex: Penguin Books).
Morris, Margaret, 1976, *The General Strike* (Middlesex: Penguin Books).
Morris, Margaret, 1986, 'The 1926 General Strike – 60 years on', 1986 Annual Lecture (London: Marx Memorial Library).
Newitt, Ned., 1976, *The General Strike in Leicester* (Leicester: Gadfly Designs).
Noel, Gerard. 1976, *The Great Lock-out of 1926* (London: Constable).
'1926 Strike', 1972, *Great Newspapers Reprinted*, 6 (London: Peter Way Ltd).
Perkins, Anne, 2006, *A Very British Strike: 3 May – 12 May 1926* (London: Pan Books).
Phillips, Marion, 1927, *Women and the Miners' Lock-out – The Story of the Women's Committee for the Relief of the Miners' Wives and Children* (London: The Labour Publishing Company Ltd).
Porter, J. H., 1978, 'Devon and the General Strike, 1926', *International Review of Social History*, 23, 333–56.
Postgate, R. W., Ellen Wilkinson, and J. F. Horrabin, 1927, *A Worker's History of the Great Strike* (London: The Plebs League).
Pugh, Martin, 2006, 'The General Strike', *History Today*, 56:5, 40–7.
Renshaw, Patrick, 1975a, *The General Strike* (London: Methuen).
Renshaw, Patrick, 1975b, *Nine Days in May* (London: Methuen).
Saltzman, Rachelle H., 1988, 'The 1926 General Strike and the Volunteers: Upper-class British Play Genres and the Maintenance of Social Class' (PhD dissertation, University of Texas at Austin).
Saltzman, Rachelle H., 1994, 'Folklore as Politics in Great Britain: Working-class Critiques of Upper-class Strike Breakers in the 1926 General Strike', *Anthropological Quarterly: Symbols of Contention, Part II*, 67:3, 105–21.
Saltzman, Rachelle H., 1995, 'Public Displays, Play, and Power: the 1926 General Strike', *Southern Folklore: Façade Performances*, 52:2, 161–86.
Schenker, Rebecca, 1978, 'To Strike: A May-Day Tune', English Department, University of Texas at Austin.
SEARCH Project, 1979, *The General Strike on Merseyside, 1926*, Pack 15 (Liverpool: St Katharine's College).
Skelley, Jeffrey (ed.), 1976, *The General Strike 1926* (London: Lawrence & Wishart).
Skelley, Jeffrey, 1976, 'Chronology', in Jeffrey Skelley (ed.), *The 1926 General Strike* (London: Lawrence & Wishart).
Smith, Dai, 1984, 'The Longest Strike', *Listener*, 112 (15 November), 11–12.
Smith, Harold, 1976, *Remember 1926: A Book List* (Covent Garden: Remember 1926).

Spencer, Ralph (ed.), 1988, *The General Strike – Living History*, No. 11, GCSE Factpacks Series, general series ed. Michael Ryan (Huntingdon: ELM Publications).

Strike Nights at Printing House Square, 1926 (London: The Times Newspapers Ltd).

Symons, Julian, 1957, *The General Strike* (London: Cresset Press).

Tames, Richard (compiler), 1972, *The General Strike*, Jackdaw 105 (London: Jackdaw Publications Ltd).

Trory, Ernie, 1975, *Brighton and the General Strike* (Brighton: Crabtree Press Ltd).

Tucket, Angela, 1976, 'Swindon', in Jeffrey Skelley (ed.), *The General Strike* (London: Lawrence & Wishart).

Union Place Community Resource Centre, 1976, *Nine Days 1926: The General Strike in Southwark* (London: Dustbin Press).

'Unrecorded Fighters', 1976, *Socialist Worker: General Strike 50th Anniversary* (May), 4.

Usherwood, Stephen, 1972, 'The BBC and the General Strike', *History Today*, 12:22, 858–65.

Vincent, David, 1974, 'The General Strike of 1926', *Listener*, 91:2352, 1–4.

Watson, Harry, 1976, 'An Incident on the River Thames', in Jeffrey Skelley (ed.), *The General Strike 1926* (London: Lawrence & Wishart).

Waymark, Peter, 1986, 'Nine Days that Split the Nation', *The Sunday Times Magazine* (November).

Wilsher, Peter, 1984, 'How it all Ended in 1926', Week in Focus, *The Sunday Times* (25 November), pp. 18–19.

Workers Educational Association, West Midlands District, 1976, *Nine Days in Birmingham: The General Strike 4–12 May, 1926* (Birmingham: Birmingham Public Libraries, Social Sciences Department).

Wrigley, Chris, 1982, *The General Strike 1926 in Local History* (Loughborough: Department of Economics, Loughborough University).

Wrigley, Chris, 1984a, 'Local History, Part One: The Government's Volunteers', *The Local Historian*, 16:1, 36–49.

Wrigley, Chris, 1984b, '1926, Social Costs of the Mining Dispute', *History Today* (4 November), 5–10.

Wrigley, Chris, 1993a, 'Introduction', in Chris Wrigley (ed.), *Challenges of Labour, Central and Western Europe 1917–1920* (New York: Routledge).

Wrigley, Chris, 1993b, 'The State and the Challenge of Labour in Britain, 1917–20', in Chris Wrigley (ed.), *Challenges of Labour, Central and Western Europe 1917–1920* (New York: Routledge).

Historical and theoretical works

Books and articles

Abrahams, Roger, 1972, 'Christmas and Carnival on St Vincent', *Western Folklore*, 31, 275–309.

Abrahams, Roger, 1981, 'Shouting Match at the Border: The Folklore of Display Events', in Richard Bauman and Roger Abrahams (eds), *'And Other Neighborly Names': Social Process and Cultural Image in Texas Folklore* (Austin: University of Texas Press).

Abrahams, Roger D., 1987, 'An American Vocabulary of Celebrations', in Alessandro Falassi (ed.), *Time Out of Time: Essays on the Festival* (Albuquerque: University of New Mexico Press).

Alford, Violet, 1959, 'Rough Music or Charivari', *Folklore*, 70:4, 505–18.

Anderson, Benedict, 2006, *Imagined Communities: Reflections on the Origins and Spread of Nationalism* (London: Verso).

Andrews, Irene Osgood and Margaret A. Hobbs, 2010 [1918], *Economic Effects of the War upon Women and Children in Great Britain* (Memphis, Tennessee: General Books).

Aughey, Arthur, 2007, *The Politics of Englishness* (Manchester and New York: Manchester University Press).

Babcock, Barbara, 1976, *The Reversible World* (Ithaca: Cornell University Press).

Babcock, Barbara, 1984, 'Arrange me into Disorder', in John MacAloon (ed.), *Dramas, Rites, Spectacles and Festivals: Rehearsals Towards a Theory of Cultural Performance* (Philadelphia: Institute for the Study of Human Issues).

Bagwell, Philip S., 1971, 'The Triple Industrial Alliance, 1913–1922', in Asa Briggs and John Saville (eds), *Essays in Labour History, 1986–1923* (London and Basingstoke: The Macmillan Press Ltd).

Bakhtin, Mikhail, 1968, *Rabelais and His World* (Cambridge: Massachusetts Institute of Technology Press).

Baldwin, Stanley, 1971 [1926], *On England, and other Addresses* (Freeport, New York: Books for Libraries Press).

Balfour, Patrick, 1933, *Society Racket: A Critical Survey of Modern Social Life* (London: John Long Ltd).

Barth, Fredrik (ed.), 1969, *Ethnic Groups and Boundaries* (Boston: Little, Brown and Company).

Bateson, Gregory, 1972, 'A Theory of Play and Fantasy', in Gregory Bateson (ed.), *Steps to an Ecology of Mind* (San Francisco: Chandler Publishing Company).

Bauman, Richard, 1983, *Let Your Words Be Few: Symbolism of Silence Among Seventeenth-Century Quakers* (Cambridge: Cambridge University Press).

Bauman, Richard, 1986, *Story, Performance, and Event* (Cambridge: Cambridge University Press).

Bauman, Richard and Roger Abrahams (eds), 1981, *'And Other Neighborly Names': Social Process and Cultural Image in Texas Folklore* (Austin: University of Texas Press).

Berberich, Christine, 2007, *The Image of the English Gentleman in Twentieth-century Literature: Englishness and nostalgia* (Aldershot, Hampshire: Ashgate Publishing Ltd and Burlington, Vermont: Ashgate Publishing Company).

Ben Amos, Dan and Liliane Weissberg (eds), 1999, *Cultural Memory and the Construction of Identity* (Detroit: Wayne State University Press).

Benbow, William, 1936 [1832], *The Grand National Holiday and Congress of the Productive Classes*, ed. A. Ruter, *International Review of Social History*, facsimile reproductions.

Bendix, Regina, 1997, *In Search of Authenticity: The Formation of Folklore Studies* (Madison: University of Wisconsin Press).

Bennett, Diane O. (ed.), 1994, 'Symbols of Contention', *Anthropological Quarterly*, 67:1–2.

Bloch, Maurice, 1978, 'Disconnection between Power and Rank as a Process', in J. Friedman and Ruth Rowlands (eds), *The Evolution of Social Systems* (Pittsburgh: University of Pittsburgh Press).

Bloch, Maurice, 1977, 'The Past and the Present in the Present', *Man*, 12, 278–92.

Bloom, Leslie, 1997, 'Locked in Uneasy Sisterhood: Reflections on Feminist Methodology and Research Relations', *Anthropology & Education Quarterly*, 28:1, 111–22.

Bocock, Robert, 1974, *Ritual in Industrial Society: A Social Analysis of Ritualism in Modern England* (London: Allen & Unwin).

Bodnar, John, 1992, *Remaking America: Public Memory, Commemoration, and Patriotism in the Twentieth Century* (Princeton: Princeton University Press).

Booth, Alan and Melvyn Pack, 1985, 'Baldwin, Thatcher and the Aftermath of Industrial Disputes', *Political Quarterly*, 56:3, 271–8.

Bourdieu, Pierre, 1982, *Outline of a Theory of Practice* (Cambridge: Cambridge University Press).

Brandes, Stanley, 1988, *Metaphors of Masculinity: Sex and Status in Andalusian Folklore* (Philadelphia: University of Pennsylvania Press).

Branson, Nora, 1976, *Britain in the 1920s* (Minneapolis: University of Minnesota Press).

Brow, James, 1978, 'Class Formation and Ideological Practice: a Case from Sri Lanka', *Journal of Asian Studies*, 40:4, 703–18.

Brunvand, Jan, 1981, *The Vanishing Hitchhiker: American Urban Legends and*

Their Meaning (New York: Norton).

Buchan, David, 1972, *The Ballad and the Folk* (London and Boston: Routledge & Kegan Paul Ltd).

Buckle, Richard (ed.), 1978, *U & Non-U Revisited* (London: Debrett's Peerage Ltd).

Burke, Peter, 1983 [1978], *Popular Culture in Early Modern Europe* (London: Harper & Row).

Butler, Robert N., 2007, 'Forward', in John A. Kunz and Florence Gray Soltys (eds), *Transformational Reminiscence: Life Story Work* (New York: Springer Publishing Company, LLC).

Bushaway, Bob, 1982, *By Rite: Custom, Ceremony, and Community in England 1700–1888* (London: Junction Books).

Caillois, Roger, 1961, *Man, Play, and Games* (Illinois: The Free Press of Glencoe, Illinois).

Cameron, James, 1986, Review of *Stand Up and Be Counted* (BBC 2 documentary), *Radio Times* (11 May), p. 17.

Cannadine, David, 1980, *Lords and Landlords: The Aristocracy and the Towns, 1774–1967* (Leicester: Leicester University Press).

Cannadine, David, 1985, 'The Context, Performance and Meaning of Ritual: the British monarchy and "the Invention of Tradition", c.1820–1972', in Eric Hobsbawm and Terence Ranger (eds), *The Invention of Tradition* (Cambridge: Cambridge University Press).

Cohen, Debra Rae, 2002, *Remapping the Home Front: Locating Citizenship in British Women's Great War Fiction* (Boston: Northeastern University Press).

Cole, G. D. H., 1948, *History of the Labour Party from 1914* (London: Routledge & Kegan Paul).

Cornbluh, Joyce (ed.), 1998 [1964], *Rebel Voices: An IWW Anthology* (Chicago, Illinois: Charles H. Kerr Publishing Co.).

Colls, Robert, 1986, 'Englishness and the Political Culture', in Robert Colls and Philip Dodd (eds), *Englishness: Politics and Culture 1880–1920* (London: Croom Helm Ltd).

Colls, Robert and Philip Dodd (eds), 1986, *Englishness: Politics and Culture 1880–1920* (London: Croom Helm Ltd).

Coser, Lewis A., 1992, 'Introduction' in Maurice Halbwachs, *On Collective Memory*, ed. and trans., Lewis A. Coser (Chicago: University of Chicago Press).

Cunningham, Hugh, 1986, 'The Conservative Party and Patriotism', in Robert Colls and Philip Dodd (eds), *Englishness: Politics and Culture 1880–1920* (London: Croom Helm Ltd).

Curtis, James, 1978, 'Clio's Dilemma', in Ian M. G. Quimby (ed.), *Material Culture and the Study of American Life* (New York: W. W. Norton and Company Inc.).

Dangerfield, George, 1935, *The Strange Death of Liberal England 1910–1914* (New York: G. P. Putnam's Sons).
Darnton, Robert, 1984, *The Great Cat Massacre* (New York: Basic Books).
Davidoff, Lenore, 1973, *The Best Circles: Women and Society in Victorian England* (London: Rowman & Littlefield Publishers, Incorporated).
Davis, Natalie Zemon, 1975, *Society and Culture in Early Modern France* (California: Stanford University Press).
Davis, Susan, 1986, *Parades and Power* (Philadelphia: Temple University Press).
Dawes, Frank, 1974, *Not in Front of the Servants: A True Portrait of English Upstairs/Downstairs Life* (New York: Taplinger Publishing Company).
Deetz, James, 1981, 'The Link from Object to Person to Concept', in Zipporah W. Collins (ed.), *Museums, Adults and the Humanities* (Washington, D.C.: American Association of Museums).
Douglas, Mary, 1966, *Purity and Danger* (New York: Praeger).
Dundes, Alan, 1965, 'What is Folklore?' in Alan Dundes (ed.), *The Study of Folklore* (New Jersey: Prentice-Hall).
Durkheim, Emile, 1965, *The Elementary Forms of Religious Life* (New York: The Free Press).
Eber, Dena Elisabeth and Arthur G. Neal, 2001, 'The Individual and Collective Search for Identity', in Dena Elisabeth Eber and Arthur G. Neal (eds), *Memory and Representation: Constructed Truths and Competing Realities* (Madison, Wisconsin: University of Wisconsin Press).
Fairlie, Henry, 1959, 'The BBC', in Hugh Thomas (ed.), *The Establishment* (London: A. Blond).
Falassi, Alessandro, 1987, 'Festival: Definition and Morphology', in Alessandro Falassi (ed.), *Time Out of Time: Essays on the Festival* (Albuquerque: University of New Mexico Press).
Farman, Christopher, 1974 [1972], *The General Strike – May 1926: Britain's Aborted Revolution?* (St Albans: Panther Books Ltd).
Feldman, Paul, 'Nine Days that shook Britain' (Review of *A Very British Strike*), *A World to Win*. At: www.aworldtowin.net/reviews/generalstrike.html.
Fine, Gary Alan, 1984, 'Humorous Interaction and the Social Construction of Meaning: Making sense in a Jocular vein', *Studies in Symbolic Interaction*, 5, 83–101.
Fortin, Roger A, 1981, 'The Challenge of a Humanities Approach', in Zipporah W. Collins (ed.), *Museums, Adults and the Humanities* (Washington, DC: American Association of Museums).
Freedman, Jean R., 1999, *Whistling in the Dark: Memory and Culture in Wartime London* (Lexington, Kentucky: University Press of Kentucky).
Friedman, Jonathan, 1992, 'Myth, History, and Political Identity', *Cultural Anthropology*, 7:2, 194–210.

Freud, Sigmund, 1960, *Jokes and Their Relation to the Unconscious*, trans. and ed. James Strachey (New York: Norton).
Fussell, Paul, 1975, *The Great War in Modern Memory* (London: Oxford University Press).
Geary, Roger, 1985, *Political Industrial Disputes: 1893–1985* (London: Cambridge University Press).
Geertz, Clifford, 1968, *Islam Observed* (Chicago: University of Chicago Press).
Geertz, Clifford, 1973, *The Interpretation of Cultures* (New York: Basic Books).
Geertz, Clifford, 1980, 'Blurred Genres: the Refiguration of Social Thought', *American Scholar*, 49, 165–79.
Girouard, Mark, 1981, *The Return to Camelot: Chivalry and the English Gentleman* (New Haven: Yale University Press).
Gluckman, Max, 1964, 'The Frailty of Authority', in *Custom and Conflict in Africa* (New York: Barnes and Noble).
Goffman, Erving, 1975, *Frame Analysis* (New York: Harper & Row).
Goodhart, A. L., 1927, 'The legality of the General Strike in England', reprint, *Yale Law Journal* (February), n.p.
Graham, Laura R., 1995, *Performing Dreams: Discourses of Immortality among the Xavante of Central Brazil* (Austin: University of Texas Press).
Green A. E., 1980, *Performance and Politics in Popular Drama* (Cambridge: Cambridge University Press).
Green, Thomas A., 1981, 'Introduction', *Journal of American Folklore*, 94:374, 421–32.
Green, Thomas A. and W. J. Pepicello, 1984, *The Language of Riddles: New Perspectives* (Columbus: The Ohio State University Press).
Greenhill, Pauline, 1994, *Ethnicity in the Mainstream: Three Studies of English Canadian Culture in Ontario* (Montreal and Kingston: McGill-Queen's University Press).
Guss, David M., 1993, 'The Selling of San Juan: the Performance of History in an Afro-Venezuelan Community', *American Ethnologist*, 20:3, 451–73.
Halbwachs, Maurice, 1992, *On Collective Memory*, ed. and trans. Lewis A. Coser (Chicago: University of Chicago Press).
Harker, Dave, 1985, *Fakesong: The Manufacture of British 'Folksong', 1700 to the Present Day* (Milton Keynes and Philadelphia: Open University Press).
Hawarth, T. E. B., 1978, *Cambridge between Two Wars* (London: Collins).
Hay, Douglass, Peter Linebaugh, John G. Rule, E. P. Thompson, and Cal Winslow, 1975, *Albion's Fatal Tree* (New York: Pantheon Books).
Hebdige, Dick, 1979, *Subcultures: The Meaning of Style* (London: Methuen).
Hill, Christopher, 1978, *The World Turned Upside Down* (Great Britain: Penguin Books).
Hobsbawm, Eric, 1959, *Primitive Rebels* (London: W. W. Norton and Company).

Hobsbawm, Eric and Terence Ranger (eds), 1985, *The Invention of Tradition* (Cambridge: Cambridge University Press).

Hobsbawm, Eric and George Rudé, 1975, *Captain Swing* (London: W. W. Norton and Company).

Houghton, Walter, 1979, *The Victorian Frame of Mind* (New Haven: Yale University Press).

Huizinga, Johan, 1955, *Homo-Ludens: A Study in the Play-Element in Culture* (Boston: Beacon Press).

Humphries, Stephen, 1981, *Hooligans or Rebels? An Oral History of Working-Class Childhood and Youth 1889–1939* (Oxford: Basil Blackwell).

Hutchinson, John, Susan Reynolds, Anthony D. Smith, Robert Colls, and Krishan Kumar, 2007, 'Debate on Krishan Kumar's *The Making of English National Identity*'. *Nations and Nationalism*, 13:2, 179–203.

Hutt, Allen, 1937, *Post-war History of the British Working Class* (London: Gollancz).

Irwin-Zarecka, Iwona, 1994, *Frames of Remembrance: The Dynamics of Collective Memory* (New Brunswick and London: Transaction Publishers).

Jack, Ian, 1986, 'MacGregor on the Warpath', *Observer* (12 October), 28.

Jarvis, Anthea and Patricia Raine, 1984, *Fancy Dress* (Great Britain: Shire Publications Ltd).

Jeffery, Keith and Peter Hennessy, 1983, *States of Emergency: British Governments and Strikebreaking since 1919* (London, Boston, Melbourne and Henley: Routledge & Kegan Paul).

Jenkins, Mick, 1980, *The General Strike of 1842* (London: Lawrence & Wishart).

Johnson, Paul, Gregor McLennan, Bill Schwarz, and David Sutton (eds), 1982, *Making Histories: Studies in History-Writing and Politics* (London: Hutchinson & Company Ltd).

Kalčik, Susan, 1975, '"… like Ann's Gynecologist or the Time I was almost Raped": Personal Narratives in Women's Rap Groups', in Claire R. Farrer (ed.), *Women and Folklore: Images and Genres* (Austin: University of Texas Press).

Karp, Ivan and Steven D. Lavine (eds), 1991, *Exhibiting Cultures: The Poetics and Politics of Museum Display* (Washington, DC: Smithsonian Institution).

Karp, Ivan, Christine Mullen Kreamer, and Steven D. Lavine (eds), 1992, *Museums and Communities: The Politics of Public Culture* (Washington, DC: Smithsonian Institution).

Knuuttila, Seppo, 2008, 'Memory, Anachronism, and Articulation', *Trames: Mediation of Memory: Towards Transdisciplinary Perspectives in Current Memory Studies*, 12:3, 264–75.

Kumar, Krishan, 2003, *The Making of English National Identity* (Cambridge: Cambridge University Press).

Kumar, Krishan, 2006, 'English and French national identity: comparisons and contrasts', *Nations and Nationalism,* 12:3, 413–32.
Ladurie, Emanuel LeRoy, 1979, *Carnival in Romans,* trans. Mary Feeney (New York: W. W. Norton and Company).
Lambert, Angela, 1984, *Unquiet Souls: The Indian Summer of the British Aristocracy 1880–1918* (London: Macmillan).
Landsman, Gail and Sara Ciborski, 1992, 'Representation and politics: contesting histories of the Iroquois', *Cultural Anthropology* 7:4, 425–47.
Lane, Crystal, 1981, *The Rites of Rulers* (Cambridge: Cambridge University Press).
Laslett, Peter, 1971, *The World We Have Lost* (New York: Charles Scribner's Sons).
Laybourn, Keith, 1999b, *Modern Britain since 1906: A Reader* (London and New York: Tauris and Co. Ltd).
Leach, Edmund, 1979a, 'Ritualization in Man in Relation to Conceptual and Social Development', in William Lessa and Evon Vogt (eds), *Reader in Comparative Religion,* 4th edn (New York: Harper & Row).
Leach, Edmund, 1979b, 'Two Essays Concerning the Symbolic Representation of Time', in William Lessa and Evon Vogt (eds), *Reader in Comparative Religion,* 4th edn (New York: Harper & Row).
Leacock, Eleanor and Helen I. Safa (eds), 1986, *Women's Work: Development and the Division Labor by Gender* (Massachusetts: Bergin & Garvey Publishers).
Lester, Geoff, 1979, *Handsworth Traditional Sword Dancers* (Sheffield: Handsworth Traditional Sword Dancers).
Lewis, Gilbert, 1980, *Day of Shining Red: An Essay on Understanding Ritual* (Cambridge: Cambridge University Press).
MacAloon, John (ed.), 1984, *Rites, Dramas, Festival, Spectacle: Rehearsals Towards a Theory of Cultural Performance* (Philadelphia: Institute for the Study of Human Issues).
MacCannell, Dean, 1976, *The Tourist: A New Theory of the Leisure Class* (New York: Schocken Books).
MacCannell, Dean, 1992, *Empty Meeting Grounds: The Tourist Papers* (London and New York: Routledge).
Mace, Rodney, 2005 (1976), *Trafalgar Square: Emblem of Empire* (London: Lawrence & Wishart).
Mackay, Jane and Pat Thane, 1986, 'The Englishwoman', in Robert Colls and Philip Dodd (eds), *Englishness: Politics and Culture 1880–1920* (London: Croom Helm Ltd).
MacKenzie, John M., 1984, *Propaganda and Empire: The Manipulation of British Public Opinion 1880–1960* (Manchester: Manchester University Press).

McKibbin, Ross, 2000 [1998], *Classes and Cultures: England, 1918–1951* (Oxford: Oxford University Press).
Mangan, J. A., 1986, *Games Ethic and Imperialism* (London: Viking Press).
Mannin, Ethel, 1971, *Young in the Twenties* (London: Hutchinson).
Middlemas, Keith, 1979, *Politics in Industrial Society* (London: Andre Deutsch).
Mintz, Jerome, 1982, *The Anarchists of Casas Viejas* (Chicago: University of Chicago Press).
Moore, Sally and Barbara Myerhoff (eds), 1977, *Secular Ritual* (Aspen: Van Gorcum).
Mowat, Charles Loch, 1971 [1955], *Britain between the Wars, 1928–1940* (Boston: Beacon Press).
Nasson, Bill, 1987, 'Abraham Esau's War, 1899–1901: Martyrdom, Myth, and Folk Memory in Calvinia, South Africa', in Raphael Samuel and Paul Thompson (eds), *The Myths We Live By* (London and New York: Routledge).
Newby, Harold, 1980, *Green and Pleasant Land? Social Change in Rural England* (New York: Pelican Books).
Newsome, David, 1961, *Godliness and Good Learning* (London: John Murray).
Nichols, Susan K (ed.), 1984, *Museum Education Anthology: Perspectives on Informal Learning, A Decade of Roundtable Reports, 1973–1983* (Washington, DC: Museum Education Roundtable).
Nicolson, Harold, 1946, *The English Sense of Humour – An Essay* (London: The Dropmore Press).
Norberg, Arthur L., 1981, 'Humanities Themes and Process Approach to Exhibits', in Zipporah W. Collins (ed.), *Museums, Adults and the Humanities* (Washington, DC: American Association of Museums).
Noyes, Dorothy (ed.), 1995, *Façade Performances* (special issue), *Southern Folklore*, 52:2.
Nye, Russell B., 1981, 'The Humanities and the Museum: Definitions and Connections', in Zipporah W. Collins (ed.), *Museums, Adults and the Humanities* (Washington, DC: American Association of Museums).
Ortner, Sherry, 1979, 'On Key Symbols', in William Lessa and Evon Vogt (eds), *Reader in Comparative Religion*, 4th edn (New York: Harper & Row).
Paredes, Américo, 1966, 'The Anglo-American in Mexican Folklore', in Ray Browne (ed.), *New Voices in American Studies* (Indiana: Purdue University Press).
Paredes, Américo and Richard Bauman (eds), 1972, *Towards New Perspectives in Folklore* (Austin: University of Texas Press).
Passerini, Luisa, 1984, *Fascism in Popular Memory: The Cultural Experience of the Turin Working Class*, trans. Robert Lumley and Jude Bloomfield (Cambridge: Cambridge University Press).

Pattison, Susan, 1977, 'The Antrobus Soulcaking Play: an Alternative Approach to the Mummers' Play', *Folklife*, 15, 5–11.

Paxman, Jeremy, 1999, *The English: A Portrait of a People* (London: Penguin Books Ltd).

Pearson, Geoffrey, 1983, *Hooligans: A History of Respectable Fears* (London: Macmillan).

Pearson, Michael, 1984, *Traditional Knitting: Aran, Fair Isle, and Fisher Ganseys* (New York: Van Nostrand Reinhold).

Peel, Frank, 1978, *The Rising of the Luddites* (New York: Augustus M. Kelley).

Pegg, Bob, 1981, *Rites and Riots: Folk Customs of Britain and Europe* (Dorset: Blandford Press).

Pettit, Tom, 1984, '"Here Comes I, Jack Straw": English Folk Drama and Social Revolt', *Folklore*, 95, 3–20.

Pine, L. G., 1956, *Tales of the British Aristocracy* (London: Burke Publishing Company Ltd).

Popular Memory Group, 1982, 'Popular Memory: Theory, Politics, Method', in Richard Johnson, Gregor McLennan, Bill Schwartz, and David Sutton (eds), *Making Histories: Studies in History-writing and Politics* (London: Hutchinson & Company Ltd).

Portelli, Alessandro, 1991, *The Death of Luigi Trastulli and Other Stories: Form and Meaning in Oral History* (Albany, New York: State University of New York Press).

Powell, David, 2002, *Nationhood and Identity: The British State since 1800* (London and New York: I. B. Tauris & Co. Ltd).

Propp, Vladimir, 1968, *Morphology of a Folktale*, 2nd revised edn (Bloomington: Indiana University Press).

Radner, Joan Newlon (ed.), 1993, *Feminist Messages: Coding in Women's Folk Culture* (Urbana and Chicago: University of Illinois Press).

Renwick, Roger deV., 1980, *English Folk Poetry: Structure and Meaning* (Philadelphia: University of Pennsylvania Press).

Renwick, Roger deV., 1981, 'The Mummers' Play and *The Old Wives Tale*', *Journal of American Folklore*, 94:374, 433–55.

Richardson, J., 2003 [1954]. *An Introduction to the Study of Industrial Relations* (London: Routledge).

Rogers, Susan Carol, 1978, 'Woman's Place: A Critical Review of Anthropological Theory', *Comparative Studies in Society and History*, 20, 123–62.

Rohdewald, Stefan, 2008, 'Figures of (Trans-)National Religious Memory of the Orthodox Southern Slaves before 1945: An Outline on the Examples of SS. Cyril and Methodius', *Trames: 'Mediation of Memory: Towards Transdisciplinary Perspectives in Current Memory Studies'*, 12:3, 287–98.

Rose, R. B., 1962, 'Eighteenth Century Price Riots and Public Policy in

England', *The International Review of Social History*, 7:2, 277–92.

Royce, Anya Seton, 1982, *Ethnic Identity, Strategies of Diversity* (Bloomington: Indiana University Press).

Rubin, David C., 1995, *Memory in Oral Traditions: The Cognitive Psychology of Epic, Ballads, and Counting Out Rhymes* (New York & Oxford: Oxford University Press).

Rudé, George, 1979, *The Crowd in the French Revolution* (London: Oxford University Press).

Russell, Ian, 1981, 'In Comes I, Brut King: Tradition and Modernity in the Drama of the Jacksdale Bullguisers', *Journal of American Folklore*, 94:374, 456–85.

Sahlins, Marshall, 1981, *Historical Metaphors and Mythical Realities* (Ann Arbor: University of Michigan Press).

Sahlins, Marshall, 1985, *Islands of History* (Chicago: University of Chicago Press).

Saltzman, Rachelle H., 1980a, 'The Ideal Victorian Woman: An Instrument for Social Equilibrium' (History Department, University of Texas at Austin).

Saltzman, Rachelle H., 1980b, 'Matthew Arnold: A Study in Cultural Authoritarianism' (Masters thesis, University of Texas at Austin).

Saltzman, Rachelle H., 1982, 'How they Played the Game: English Ritual and the First World War', American Folklore Society Annual Meeting.

Saltzman, Rachelle H., 1987, 'Folklore, Feminism, and the Folk – Whose Lore Is It?', *Journal of American Folklore: 'Folklore and Feminism'*, 100:398, 548–62.

Saltzman, Rachelle H., 1993, 'A Feminist Folklorist Encounters the Folk: Can Praxis Make Perfect?' in Susan Hollis, Linda Pershing, M. Jane Young (eds), *Feminist Theory and the Study of Folklore* (Chicago: University of Illinois Press).

Saltzman, Rachelle H., 1994b, 'Calico Indians and Pistol Pills: Historical Symbols and Political Action', *New York Folklore*, 20:3–4, 1–18.

Saltzman, Rachelle H., 1997a, 'Folk History', in Thomas A. Green (ed.), *Folklore: An Encyclopedia of Beliefs, Customs, Music, Tales, and Art*, Volume I (Santa Barbara, CA: ABC-CLIO, Inc.).

Saltzman, Rachelle H., 1997b, 'Historical Analysis', in Thomas A. Green (ed.), *Folklore: An* Encyclopedia of Beliefs, Customs, Music, Tales, and Art, Volume I (Santa Barbara, CA: ABC-CLIO, Inc.).

Saltzman, Rachelle H., 1997c, 'Oral History', in Thomas A. Green (ed.), *Folklore: An Encyclopedia of Beliefs, Customs, Music, Tales, and Art*, Volume I (Santa Barbara, CA: ABC-CLIO, Inc.).

Samuel, Raphael, 1983a, 'The Middle Classes Between the Wars: Part One', *New Socialist* (January/February), 30–6.

Samuel, Raphael, 1983b, 'The Middle Classes Between the Wars: Part Two', *New Socialist* (March/April), 28–33.

Samuel, Raphael, 1983c, 'The Middle Classes Between the Wars: Part Three', *New Socialist* (May/June), 28–9.
Samuel, Raphael and Paul Thompson (eds), 1987, *The Myths We Live By* (London and New York: Routledge).
Sanday, Peggy Reeves, 1981, *Female Power and Male Dominance: On the Origins of Sexual Inequality* (Cambridge: Cambridge University Press).
Santino, Jack, 2004, 'Performative Commemoratives, the Personal, and the Public: Spontaneous Shrines, Emergent Ritual, and the Field of Folklore' (AFS Presidential Address, 2003), *Journal of American Folklore*, 117:466, 363–72.
Sapir, J. David and J. C. Crocker, 1977, *The Social Use of Metaphor* (Philadelphia: University of Pennsylvania Press).
Sawin, Patricia, 2004, *Listening for a Life: A Dialogic Ethnography of Bessie Eldreth through Her Songs and Stories* (Logan, Utah: Utah State University Press).
Schwartz, Barry, Yael Zerubavel, and Bernice M, Barnett, 1986, 'The Recovery of Masada: A Study in Collective Memory', *The Sociological Quarterly*, 27:2, 147–64.
Sellar, W. C. and R. J. Yeatman, 1930, *1066 and All That* (London: Methuen & Co. Ltd).
Sellwood, A.V., 1978, *Police Strike – 1919* (London: W. H. Allen).
Shils, E. and M. Young, 1953, 'The Meaning of the Coronation', *Sociological Review* 1, 63–81.
Shuman, Amy, 2005, *Other People's Stories: Entitlement Claims and the Critique of Empathy* (Urbana and Chicago: University of Illinois Press).
Simms, Norman, 1978, 'Ned Ludd's Mummer's Play', *Folklore*, 89, 166–78.
Smith, A. W., 1966, 'Some Folklore Elements in Movements of Social Protest', *Folklore*, 77, 241–52.
Smith, Moira, 1995, 'Whipping Up a Storm: The Ethics and Consequences of Joking Around', *Journal of Folklore Research: 'Arbiters of Taste: Censuring/Censoring Discourse'*, 32:2, 121–36.
Smith, Robert, 1975, *The Art of the Festival* (Lawrence: University of Kansas Library Publications in Anthropology, No. 6).
Sykes, Christopher, 1980, *Country House Camera* (London: Weidenfeld & Nicolson).
Taylor, D. J., 2007, *Bright Young People: The Rise and Fall of a Generation 1918–1940* (New York: Farrar, Straus and Giroux).
Thom, Deborah, 1998, *Nice Girls and Rude Girls: Women Workers in World War I* (London and New York: Tauris and Co. Ltd).
Thompson, Edward P., 1971, 'The Moral Economy of the English Crowd in the Eighteenth Century', *Past and Present*, 50 (February), 76–136.
Thompson, Edward P., 1972, 'Anthropology and the Discipline of Historical

Context', *Midland History*, 1, 41–55.
Thompson, Edward P., 1974, 'Patrician Society, Plebeian Culture', *Journal of Social History*, 7:4, 382–405.
Thompson, Edward P., 1991, *Customs in Common* (New York: The New Press).
Thompson, Paul, 1984 [1975], *The Edwardians* (London: Weidenfeld & Nicolson).
Thompson, Paul, 1994, 'Believe it or not: Rethinking the Historical Interpretation of Memory,' in Jaclyn Jeffrey and Glenace Edwall (eds), *Memory and History: Essays on Recalling and Interpreting Experience* (Lanham, New York, London: University Press of America).
Thompson, Paul, 2000 [1988], *The Voice of the Past: Oral History* (New York: Oxford University Press).
Tonkin, Elizabeth, 'Masks and Power', *Man*, 14:2, 237–48.
Tuleja, Tad (ed.), 1997, *Usable Pasts: Traditions and Group Expressions in North America* (Logan: Utah State University Press).
Turner, Victor, 1973, *Dramas, Fields and Metaphors* (Ithaca: Cornell University Press).
Turner, Victor, 1974, 'Liminal to Liminoid in Play, Flow, and Ritual', *Rice University Studies* 60:3, 3–92.
Turner, Victor, 1982, *The Ritual Process* (Ithaca: Cornell Paperbacks).
Underdown, David, 1985, *Revel, Riot and Rebellion: Popular Politics and Culture in England 1603–1660* (Oxford: Clarendon Press).
van Gennep, Arnold, 1960, *The Rites of Passage*, trans. Monika B. Vizedom and Gabrielle L. Caffee (Chicago: University of Chicago Press).
Vansina, Jan, 1985, *Oral Tradition as History* (Madison: University of Wisconsin Press).
Walter, David, 1984, *The Oxford Union: Playground of Power* (London Macdonald and Co. Ltd).
Walton, James K. and James Walvin (eds), 1983, *Leisure in Britain 1780–1939* (Manchester: Manchester University Press).
Walvin, James, 1978, *Leisure and Society, 1830–1850* (London and New York: Longman).
Ward, Paul, 2004, *Britishness since 1870* (Oxford and New York: Routledge).
Ware, Carolyn E., 2007, *Cajun Women and Mardi Gras: Reading the Rules Backward* (Urbana: University of Illinois Press).
Waterson, Merlin, 1985, *The Country House Remembered: Recollections of Life between the Wars* (London: Routledge & Kegan Paul).
Weinberger, Barbara, 1987, 'Keeping the Peace? Policing Strikes 1906–1926', *History Today*, 37 (December), 29–35.
White, Hayden, 1987, *The Content of the Form: Narrative Discourse and Historical Representation* (Baltimore: Johns Hopkins University Press).
'Who's Who at Private Eye', 1986, *Observer Magazine* (May), 36–7.

Wigham, Eric, 1976, *Strikes and the Government, 1893–1974* (London: Macmillan).
Williams, David, 1971, *The Rebecca Riots, A Study in Agrarian Dissent* (Cardiff: University of Wales Press).
Winder, Robert, 2004, *Bloody Foreigners: The Story of Immigration to Britain* (London: Abacus).
Woollacott, Angela, 1994, *On Her their Lives Depend: Munitions Workers in the Great War* (Berkeley and Los Angeles: University of California Press).
Workman, Mark, 1995, 'Folklore and the Literature of Exile', in *Folklore, Literature, and Cultural Theory: Collected Essays*, ed. Cathy Lynn Preston (New York: Garland).
Wright, A. R., 1928, *English Folklore* (London: Ernest Benn Ltd).
Wright, Patrick, 1985, *On Living in an Old Country* (London: Verso).
Wrigley, Christopher, 1990, *Lloyd George and the Challenge of Labour: The Post-War Coalition 1918–1922* (Hemel Hempstead: Harvester Wheatsheaf).
Zangwill, O. L., 1972, 'Psychology', in C. B. Cox and A. E. Dawson (eds), *The Twentieth-Century Mind: History, Ideas, and Literature in Great Britain 1918–1945*, Volume 2 (London: Oxford University Press).
Zipes, Jack, 1979, *Breaking the Magic Spell: Radical Theories of Folk & Fairy Tales* (Austin: University of Texas Press).

Internet sources

BBC, 2009 (14 December), 'The General Strike', GCSE Bitesize. At: www.bbc.co.uk/schools/gcsebitesize/history/mwh/britain/generalstrikerev1.shtml
de Vries, Jacqueline, 2005, Women's Voluntary Organizations in World War I, in Susan R. Grayzel, general editor, *Women, War & Society 1914–1918, Essays and Introduction, from the Women at Work Collection at the Imperial War Museum* (London). At: www.tlemea.com/devries.asp.
Grayzel, Susan R., general editor, 2005, *Women, War & Society 1914–1918, Essays and Introduction, from the Women at Work Collection at the Imperial War Museum* (London). At: www.tlemea.com/Introduction.asp.
Green, Thomas A. and W. J. Pepicello, 2000, 'The Proverb and Riddle as Folk Enthymemes', *De Proverbio*, 6:2. At: www.deproverbio.com/DPjournal/DP,6,2,00/PROVERBRIDDLE.html (17 May 2010).
Miall, Leonard, 1999, 'Obituary: Janet Adam Smith', *Independent* (13 September). At: www.independent.co.uk/arts-entertainment/obituary-janet-adam-smith-1118813.html (17 January 2011).
Ministry of Justice Opinion Poll on Identity, Belong and Values, 2008 (28 October), Fieldwork, January 2008, in 'What does it mean to be British?' *Governance of Britain*. At: www.governance.justice.gov.uk/british.

National Endowment for the Arts, 2009 (May), 'Lifetime Honors, NEA National Heritage Fellowships'. At: www.nea.gov/honors/heritage/nomination.html.

Noakes, Lucy, 2005, 'Women's Military Service in the First World War', in Susan R. Grayzel, general editor, *Women, War & Society 1914–1918, Essays and Introduction, from the Women at Work Collection at the Imperial War Museum* (London). At: www.tlemea.com/Noakes.asp.

Renaissance London (Museums for Changing Lives), 2009 (14 December), 'The General Strike 1926' *Exploring 20th Century London*. At: www.20thcenturylondon.org.uk/server.php?show=conInformationRecord.88

Simkin, John, 2009 (14 December), 'The General Strike', *Spartacus Educational*. At: www.spartacus.schoolnet.co.uk/TUgeneral.htm.

Sutton, Mike, 2008 (28 October), 'England, whose England? Class, Gender and National Identity in the 20th Century Folklore Revival', *The Magazine for Traditional Music Throughout the World*. At: www.mustrad.org.uk/articles/england.htm.

Thom, Deborah, 2005, 'Women and Work in Wartime Britain', in Susan R. Grayzel, general editor, *Women, War & Society 1914–1918, Essays and Introduction, from the Women at Work Collection at the Imperial War Museum* (London). At: www.tlemea.com/Thom.asp.

Trades Union Congress, 2009 (14 December), 'General Strike', *The Union Makes Us Strong: TUC History Online*. At: www.unionhistory.info/generalstrike/index.php.

Wills, Michael, MP, Minister of State in the Ministry of Justice, 2008, 'The Politics of Identity', speech to the Institute for Public Policy Research on the politics of national identity (Covent Garden, London: IPPR, 8 March). At: webarchive.nationalarchives.gov.uk/+/http://www.justice.gov.uk/news/sp260308b.htm (28 October 2008).

Index

Note: 'n.' after a page number indicates the number of a note on that page. Numbers in italics refer to images on that page.

60th anniversary, General Strike, 21–2, 188, 189, 197n.7

Abrahams, Roger, 25n.22, 135n.32
accent, 43, 85–6, 88, 90–1, 121, 137, 178, 205
adolescence, collective memory and, 19–20, 21
adventure, volunteering as, 36, 37, 58, 121, 131–2, 149
anniversaries, 21–2, 173, 175, 186–9 *passim*, 197n.7, 212n.5
Answers, 34
Archard, David, 13, 14
Astbury Judgement, 64
Athenaeum Club, xviii, 103
Aughey, Arthur, 21, 209

baby parties, 56–7
Baldwin, Stanley, 26n.30, 186, 213n.16
 false reporting to U. S., 41, 42n.7
 message of thanks by, 165–6, 169
 negotiation refusal by, 33
 proposals to miners sent by, 38
 speech to miners, 40
 subsidies opposed by, 29
Bauman, Richard, 174, 197n.8
Beaton, Cecil, 179, 185
Bedale, Joan, 144, 145–6, 209
Benedictus, David, 83, 173, 182–6, 197n.7, 198n.14
Benn, Edward, 111
blacklegs, 23n.4, 42n.3, 101, 139 *see also* strike-breakers
Black & Tans, 203, 212n.3
Blake, William, 169, 205
Bloom, Leslie, 18, 25n.20
Boat-Race Night, 52, 54, 212
Boodles', 34, 103

Bowes-Lyon, Rachel (Lady), 128, 135n.29
Bright Young People (BYP), 52, 57–60, 131–2, 154
 stereotypes of, 82–3, 132n.2, 183
Bright Young Things, 91, 129–30, 133n.5
British Empire, xxv, 208
British Gazette, 32, 63, 66, 80n.1, 121, 126
Britishness, xxv, 22–3, 77–8, 166–7, 194
 of all social classes, 9
 Baldwin on, 26n.30
 BYP reinvention of, 82–3, 132n.2
 collective memory and, 16
 community and, 131, 135n.32
 competition over defining, 204
 dominant ideal of, 207–8
 Englishness *vs.*, xxiv, xxvi, 22, 26n.28
 extended, 22, 26n.29
 games as, 207–8
 Great War as epitome of, 8–9
 Jewish immigrants and, 60n.2
 light-hearted attitude as, 9, 34, 187, 206, 209
 in opposition to others, 66, 78–80
 order and, xxvi, 5, 22–3, 37, 40, 66, 67, 69–70, 78–80, 79, 147, 154, 165–6, 171, 176, 205, 210
 polarized social classes and, xxvi
 post-war, 8
 press concern with, 67–71
 protest and, 170
 revolution and, 179
 strikers and, 11, 22, 67, 69, 71, 75, 136, 171, 187
 volunteers and, 201–12
 women in, 195, 199n.22
 working-class press on, 70–1
British Worker, 32, 70, 80n.1, 139, 146, 148–9
Brockway, Archibald Fenner, 32, 71, 197n.4
Bruley, Sue, 6, 14n.2, 17–19, 199n.23

bus conductors, *98*, 105, 163
  women, 115, 134n.21
bus drivers, *98*, 137–8, 144
bus slogans, 137, 142–3
BYP *see* Bright Young People
Bystander, 83, 88, 118–19, 208

calendar festivals, 153
Cambridge Gownsman and Undergraduette, 112, 119, 147, 152
  parodies on women in, 150–1
Cambridge University, xviii, 1, 16, 34, 45, 53, 87, xxin.2
canteens, 115–6, *117*, 128, 129, 197n.1
Canterbury, Archbishop of, 168
carnivalesque, 6, 13, 14, 34, 36–7, 211
Cartland, Barbara, 9, 53
cartoons, 88, *89*, 91, *92*, 119, *119–20*, 188
Cassell, Charles, *113*, 134n.20, *160*
censureship, 1, 5, 57, 152, 210
charity, 44, 46–50 *passim*, 60n.4
  rags, 54, 206
  social class behaviour category, *44*
  undergraduates', 55
charivari, 5, 210
Cherwell, 140, 147, 150–1
Children's Newspaper, 67, 68, 78, 137–8
Christ Church, 179
Churchill, Winston, 6, 47, 66, 115, 139–40
  Daily Mail print refusal viewed by, 32–3
  exhibition portrayal of, 190
  as Nero, 56
  press criticism of, 167–8, 212n.4
Civil War, symbolic use of, 65, 79
Clare College, 38–9, 72, 99, 102, 111, 198n.15
Clephane, Irene, 11, 50
clothing, 85–6, *87*, 88, 133n.4
  women in men's, 130–1
  of women volunteers, 116, 128
coal industry
  government subsidizing of, 4, 29, 31
  reform efforts, 27
coal prices, 24n.12, 28–30
Cole, G. D. H., 182, 211, 213n.16
collapsed narratives, 136–54
  humorous anecdotes, 142–52
  parody in, 136–7, 140, 147–9, 150
  slogans in, 137–8, 142–3
collective memory, 15–23, 25n.17, 25n.22, 26n.27, 26n.31, 201
Colls, Robert, xxiv

commonplaces, 20, 25n.24, 194
communism, 66–7, 68, 81n.4, 203
  Churchill incident with, 212n.4
Communist Party of Great Britain (CPGB), 29–30, 41n.2, 66
conservative press, 63, 80n.1
Constitution, 64, 65, 70–1, 80, 167
contemporary memories/resonances, 21–2, 26n.27
contested narratives, 17–20
Cook, Arthur J., 66, 67, 190
Coombes, Frederick, *106*, 106–7
Cooper, Diana (Lady), 56, 161, 180
Corpus volunteers, 13
CPGB *see* Communist Party of Great Britain
Croft, Phyllis G., 123
Crompton, Gerald, 5, 13, 80n.1
Crook, W. H., 23n.2, 199n.17
Cruikshank, R. J., 6
cultural symbols, 23, 64, 194–6, 208–12

Daily Chronicle, 63, 85, 122
  slogans in, 137
Daily Express, 45, 56, 78, 84, 161, 163, 167
Daily Graphic, 3, 67, 69, 79–80
  transportation volunteers in, 84
Daily Herald, 24n.13, 70, 139
Daily Mail, 6, 81n.3, 84, 122, 138
  article refused printing by, 31–3
  communist plot view of, 66, 81n.4
  tales about dockers in, 141
Daily Mirror, 63
Daily News, 6, 63, 79, 138
Daily Sketch, 63, 84, 155
Daily Telegraph, 65, 85, 130, 138, 164
Delderfield, R. F., 180
Denning, Lord, 95–6, *96*, 133n.9, 194
Deptford Strike Bulletin, 142
diaries, memoirs and, 177–80, 198n.15
disguises, 57–8, 152, 197n.1
dockers, 96–7, 110, 133n.10, 141
Dodd, Philip, xxiv
domestic ideal, 131
Dover, Leslie, 71, 95, *95*
dramas, 5–6, 6, 15, 23nn.3–5, 27, 44, *44*, 45–63 *passim*, 78, 91, 128, 144–5 *see also* folk drama
drivers, 109, 129, 163
  blackleg, 23n.4, 42n.3, 101, 139
  bus, *98*, 137–8, 144
  in Horse Guards Parade, 130–1

Index

women, 130–1
Duchess of Westminster *see* Lindsay, Loelia
Dummelow, John, 197n.2
Dunham, Edward, 27, 101–2, *102*

economy, 1920s, 11, 27, 30
educational packets, 188–9, 199n.18
Ellis, Margaret Shipley, *36*, 36–7, 52, 91, 115, 206
Emergency Press, 69
Emergency Strike Bulletin, 122
employment, women's, 50–1, 60nn.6–8
Englishness, xxv, 21–2
    Britishness *vs*, xxiv, xxvi, 22, 26n.28
    General Strike defining, 21, 26n.26, 62–3
    Great War and, 154
    twentieth-century, 8–9
    womanhood and, 131
Errington, Robert, 99
ethnography, 18–20
Eve, 116, 118, 119
Evening News, 63, 69, 164
Evening Standard, 150, 165
exhibitions, 187, 189, 190, 193, 199n.19
ex-soldiers, working-class, 11–12

Factpack (Spencer, R.), 188–9
Fair Isle pullover, *73*, 86, 88
fancy dress, 9, 47, 51–7 *passim*, 147, 185, 199n.23, 202
Fascists, 106, 134n.18, 175, 180
Fawkes, Guy, 212n.4
feminist methodology, 17–18
festival theory, 15, 19, 153, 173, 202
fiction, 180–6
50th anniversary, General Strike, 175, 212n.5
First World War *see* Great War
flappers, 51
folk drama, xxiv, 28, 41n.1, 132, 152, 153, 155n.6, 173, 175
    calendar festivals, 153
folk history, oral history and, 25n.21
folklore
    British understanding of, xxiv
    as folk-lore, 171, 197n.2
    scholarship, xxiii–xxvi, 16, 20–1, 25n.21, 25n.24, 135n.32, 173, 197n.8
    social class and, xxiv, 173, 174, xxvin.1
    volunteers and, 195
folklorists, xxv–xxvi, 19, 25n.22
    social historians and, xxvi

folk memory, 15
folk song theory, 20, 25n.24
football match, police-strikers, 170, 179, 183, 201, *202*, 208–9, 213n.12
foreigners
    Britishness in opposition to, 66, 78–80, 79
    General Strike as instigated by, 80
    General Strike viewed by, 77–8, 79
    strikers portrayed in opposition to, 67–8
Fremantle, David, *39*, 96–7
French Revolution, 112

Galsworthy, John, 181, 182
game-playing, 204, 206–9
gender bias, 114, 126, 127–8, 130, 135n.31, 151
gender switching, 151–2, 195
General Strike *see also* strikes; sympathetic strikes; *specific topics*
    aftermath of, 38
    anniversaries, 21–2, 173, 175, 186–9 *passim*, 197n.7, 212n.5
    beginning of, 6
    comparison of 1984-1985 strike to, 17
    duration of, 4
    end of, 38, 156–69
    foreigners' view of, 77–8, 79
    general public response to, 4–5
    Great War context for, 7–11
    holiday atmosphere of, 13, 14, 99, 105, 121, 133n.11
    as illegal, 64
    as instigated by foreigners, 80
    interpretive models and scholarship, 4, 6, 13–17, 22, 42n.7, 80n.1, 171–7, 186, 194, 196
    miners' plight after, 40–1, 42n.7
    nonviolent nature of, 5, 23n.3, 67–8, 166
    peacefulness of, 5, 23n.3, 68, 166
    railways and services during, *73*
    restaurants celebrating, 2, *2*, 4, 21–2
    Trafalgar Square location of, 4, 23n.1
    TUC on legitimacy of, 37–8, 41
    as unpatriotic, 74, 75–6
    use of term, 23n.2
    volunteer perceptions of, 36, 71–2
    as working holiday, 77
gentleman amateur, 82–3, 132n.2, 210
George V (king), 39–40
Girton, 125, 126, 143, 145, 151, 152, 201
good humour, xxvi, 13, 15, 67–70, 79, 83, *89*,

98, 110, 131, 136–55, 156, 163–6 *passim*, 171–4, 181, 187, 196, 197n.9, 212
government *see also* Parliament
  anti-strike forces of, 63
  coal industry subsidized by, 4, 29, 31
  Lloyd George's coalition, 29
  metaphors used by press and, 62
  negotiations with, 33, 38
  statement of non-obligation to union labour, 40–1
  TUC legitimacy refused by, 80
  victory for public rather than, 166
  volunteer support of, 77, 176
  women volunteers not acknowledged by, 122–3
government workers, jokes about, 140
Gownsman and Undergraduate, 143, 147
Great War, 132, 150, 156, 165, 195
  atmosphere immediately following, 7–8
  British identity epitomized by, 8–9
  Englishness and, 154
  impact on General Strike, 7–11, 178
  propaganda use of, 65
  women's employment during, 50, 60n.6
Great Western Railway, 160, *162*, *193*, 193–4
Greene, Graham, 179
Grosvenor, Loelia *see* Lindsay, Loelia

Halbwachs, Maurice, 19–20, 25n.23
Hambleden, Patricia (Lady), 108
Harrison, Brian, 13
Heath, Tony, 13
historical reproduction, xxvi, 171–2
  folk history, 19, 25n.21
  local history, 187
  oral tradition and, xxv, 17–18, 19, 25n.21
Hodgkiss, L., 127
Hodgkiss, Winifred Haward, 43, 60n.1
holiday atmosphere, 13, 14, 99, 105, 121, 133n.11
hooligans, 45–6, 55, 66–9, 106, 139, 176, 202–3, 212n.4
Horse Guards Parade, women drivers in, 130–1
house visits, 51, 54, 61n.10 *see also* quêtings
humorous anecdotes, 142–52
  on women volunteers, 139, 149–50

identity formation, xxiv–xxvi, 19–23, 25n.23, 26n.28, 26n.29, 44, 70, 131, 135n.32, 199–200, 201

Illustrated London News, 72, 98, 118, 142, 209
Isherwood, Christopher, 177–8
Isis, The, 143, 146, 148, 150–1, 164
Jackdaw packet (Tames), 188
Jackson, Leslie, *93*, 93–4
Jewish immigrants, 26n.26, 60n.2, *62*, 68
jobs, volunteer, 95, 133n.9 *see also* women volunteers; *specific jobs*
  desirable, 114, 132
  gender bias in, 114, 126, 127–8, 130, 135n.31, 151
  glamorous, 92, 96, 140
  for married women, 129–30
  physical milieu of, 97–8
  regular jobs replaced by, 103
  sexually ambiguous, 130
  tediousness of, 110–11, 112
  typical male, 36, 102–3
  for unmarried women, 114
  wages for, 92, 94, 97
jokes, 140, 201
  practical, 15, 43, 45, 52, 53–4

Kerrigan, Rose, 203, *204*
Kingsford, Peter, 103, 134n.16, 161, *162*
Knuutila, Seppo, xxiv

labour
  official spokesmen for, 211–12
  rejection of union, 40–1
Labour Party, 21, 28, 30, 76
  communism accusations of, 81n.4
  end-of-strike comments of, 168–9
  press depiction of leadership of, 66
  press of, 70–1
  rite of passage for, 196
  TUC and, 37–8
land transfer, 46
lark, 45–6, 53, 55, 132, 144, 152, 177–9, 199n.17, 201–2, 207
Lathbury, Marjorie, 24n.6, 122, 124n.25
Laybourn, Keith, 22, 29, 172, 176, 197, 207
Legh, Phyllis, 125
Liberal Party, 64, 80n.2
  press, 63–4, 139, 168
liminality, 52, 60n.7, 91, 132, 195
Lindsay, Loelia (Duchess of Westminster), 10, 24n.9, 47, 51, 57–8, *58*, 115–16, 172, 192, *193*, 193–4
  trickster tale told by, 206–7
Lloyd George, David, 7, 29, 30, 80n.1, 81n.6

local histories, 187
lockout, 12, 17, 24n.8, 31, 41, 199n.23
   date of, 30
Lock-Out Strike-Time Sentinel, 168–9
London Opinion, 137, 210
Longford, (Countess), 127, 134n.27
Lots Road Power Station, 112–13, *113*
Loyalists, 180

MacDonald, James Ramsay, 28, 30–1, 81n.4, 190, 192
MacRae, Phyllis (Lady), 10, 51, 128–9
maids, 115, 116, *119*, 131, 150, 182, 188, 202, 205
mail carriers, 36, 109, 123
male volunteers, 36
   distinguishing markers of, 84–92
   gender bias and, 126
   pattern of joining, 102–3
Mander, Rosalie (Lady), 127, 135n.28
Mannassi, Percival, 140
marriages, 210–11
married women, 48, 116, 129–30
Massey, Marion, 151
Massingham, W. G., 160–1
May, Phineas, 47, *75*, 81n.8, 158, *158*
McIlroy, John, 42n.7, 172, 176, 186–7, 189, 190, 194, 197
Mellanby, John, 109
mementos, 159–60, 192, *193*, 195, 199n.20
memoirs, diaries and, 177–80
memory, 16–23
   collective, 15–23, 25n.17, 26n.27, 26n.31, 201
   contemporary General Strike, 21–2, 26n.27
   folk, 15
   older people's, 17, 25n.17
men's clubs, 84, 103
metaphor, 62, 63, 204, 206–9
   Civil War as, 65
   oversaturated, 173–4, 197n.8
   sports, 208–9, 212
   utopian, 169, 213n.17
MFGB *see* Miners Federation of Great Britain
middle class
   charitable works by women of, 49–50
   press of, 118
   revolution feared by upper and, 29
   social behaviour, 47
   traits of upper and, *44*

upper-class women compared to, 120–1
   women volunteers, 34, 120–8
military, 70, 107, 142
miners *see also* strikers
   aftermath plight of, 40–1, 42n.7
   Baldwin and, 38, 40
   leader of, 66
   partial labour union victories for, 28
   wages of, 30, 31, 167, 169n.2
   Welsh, 72
Miners Federation of Great Britain (MFGB), 30, 31, 33, 38
Miners Union, 67
Mond-Turner negotiations, 41
Moore, Doris Langley, 83
Morning Post, 67–8, 142, 163
museums *see* exhibitions
mythos, 16, 23, 79, 189, 190, 210

narratives, 33, 36 *see also* diaries, memoirs and; *specific volunteers*
   authenticity of, 17, 19
   collapsed, 136–54
   collective memory and, 19, 25n.22
   contested, 17–20
   dramatic forms of, 144–5
   narrative theory, 17–20 *passim*, 25n.22, 25n.24, 33, 36, 136–54
Nation, 111
national identity, 22–3, 70 *see also* Britishness; Englishness
   symbolism and, 21–2
National Portrait Gallery, 189–93, *191*
National Union of Railwaymen (NUR), 12
New Statesman, 63–4, 166, 168
novels, 180–1, 197n.10, 198n.12
NUM, 173
NUR *see* National Union of Railwaymen

OMS *see* Organisation for the Maintenance of Supplies
oral history, xxv, 17–18, 19, 25n.21
orderliness, Britishness and, 69–70, 78–80
Organisation for the Maintenance of Supplies (OMS), 13–14, 139, 175, 180
oversaturated metaphor, 173–4, 197n.8
Owen, William, 109, 134n.19
Oxbridge undergraduates, 83, 92, 108
Oxford, 1, 7, 11–16 *passim*, 25n.15, 45, 52–4 *passim*, 66, *90*, 120, 124, 148 *see also* undergraduates

rivalry between Cambridge and, 143
stereotype, 86
Oxford and Cambridge Club, xviii, 103
Oxford Magazine, 31, 151, 166, 168
Oxford undergraduates, 146

paradox, 69–70, 77, 204
Parliament
  orderliness viewed by, 80
  as polarized by General Strike, 37
  propaganda and dramatic rhetoric of, 63
  Tory and Liberal members' differences, 64, 80n.2
parody, 140, 147–9, 164, 204
  gender and, 151
  true tales and, 136–7
  of women volunteers, 150–1, 155n.6
parties
  baby, 56–7
  dinner, 157, *157*, 158–9
  fancy dress balls, 47, 55–6, 185
  house visit, 51, 54, 61n.10
Paten, Peggy, 114, *114*
patriotism, 74, 75–6, 102
peacefulness, 5, 23n.3, 67–8, 68, 166
performance theory, xxvi, 20–1, 53–5, 135n.32, 151, 155, 197n.8
Perkins, Anne, 15–16
Peterborough & District Electricity Users, *157*
Peterloo, 4–5, 21, 171, 173, 205
play, 44, *44*, 46, 61n.10
  game-playing, 204, 206–9
  non-traditional context allowing, 201–2
  role reversal as, 154, 195
  social behaviour and, 174
  social class and, 34, 44, 52–3, 58, 61n.12, 91, 104, 132, 173, 174, 179, 203–9
playfulness, 110, 142
playing the game, 12, 29
plays, 148, 173, 182–6, 197n.7, 211, 213n.16
Plus Force, 86, 88, 156, 205
plus fours, *87*, 88, 91, 146
Plymouth tram riot, 209
poetry, 183, 184, 185, 203–4, 212n.5
police
  football match between strikers and, 170, 179, 188, 201, *202*, 208–9, 213n.12
police, football match between strikers and, 201, *202*, 208–9
Police Review and Parade Gossip, 158
police strike (1919), 11, 29

political unawareness, of strikers, 154
Ponsonby, Loelia *see* Lindsay, Loelia
porters, *87*
Portland, Duchess of, 48
post-war years, 7–11
  strikes during, 29
practical jokes, 15, 43, 45, 52, 53–4
praise, for volunteers, 156–66
press
  Britishness concern in, 67–71
  bus slogans in, 137
  Churchill criticized in, 167–8, 212n.4
  Conservative, 63, 80n.1
  editorials on specific volunteers, 163
  government and, 62–3
  Labour, 70–1
  leftist, 139
  Liberal, 63–4, 168
  metaphors used by, 63
  middle-class, 118
  paradoxical nature of, 69–70
  populist and elite, 66
  revolutionary threat angle of, 36, 66–7, 68, 71, 81n.4, 81n.10, 81n.11, 84n.6
  social behaviour and, 59
  social class in narratives *vs*., 93–113, 133n.7
  sympathetic, 70–1
  university, 139, 166
  volunteer praise in, 162, 163–4
  women drivers in, 130–1
  working-class, 70–1, 147
printing, 6, 31, 99, 101, 133n.13, 169n.1
Private Eye, 185, 197n.9
professional men, 46
protest *see also* social protest tradition
  Britishness and, 170
public schools, 12, 16, 28, 45, 47, 133n.14
Punch, 91, 118, 119, 147–8, 149, 167, 188
puns, 138, 148, 204–5
Pygmalion, 88

quêtings, 152, 155n.6 *see also* house visits

Raglan, Lord, 84, 132n.2
rags, 45–6, 53–4, 144, 206
railways, 42n.3, *73*, 91, 103, 133n.14, 134n.17
  Great Western, 160, *162*, *193*, 193–4
  strikes, 12, 40, 42n.3
railway telegraphs, 109
Rebecca Riots, 151–2
Reformation, 65

Renshaw, Patrick, 15, 171
Renwick, Roger de V., 20, 25n.24
research survey, 16–17
   narratives in press compared to, 142
   on rewards received, 162
   social class of respondents, 108
restaurants, General Strike celebrated by, 2, *2*, 4, 21–2, 195, 209
revolution
   Britishness and, 179
   fear of, 4, 29
   metaphor of, 63
   publicized fear of, 11, 28, 29, 36, 66, 81n.10, 81n.11, 84n.6
   volunteer lack of fear of, 36, 42n.6
rewards, for volunteers, 159, *159*, *160*, 162
Richardson, George, 99, *99*, 110
Richmond, Duke of, 107
Rosenberg, Sid, 49, *49*, 71
rough musicking, xxiii, 5
Rowntree, Jean, 125, 126
Royal Air Force Club, 157
Russian Revolution, 11, 28, 29, 65–8, 78, 81n.4, 81n.10, 81n.11, 84n.6, 180

Saklatvala, Shapurgi, 24n.11, 66, 68
Samuel Commission, 27
Samuel Memorandum, 38, 41
Sassoon, Siegfried, 203, 212n.5
satire, 147, 148, 177, 195, 199n.22
Saturday Review, 164
Scott, Joan, 21
Scottish Worker, 167
servants, 118, 120–8, 153–4
Shaw, George Bernard, 88
Shuman, Amy, 20, 23, 171–2, 186, 195, 201, 208
slogans, 137–8, 142–3
Smith, Herbert, 67
Smith, Janet Adam, 125–6, 134n.26
social behaviour, 44–7, 50, 59, 60n.4, 60n.5, 174
   categories, *44*
social class, 6
   accent marking, 43, 85–6, 88, 90–1, 121, 137, 178, 205
   Britishness across all, 9
   class war perceptions and, 32–3
   clothing as, 85–6, *87*, 88, 133n.4
   distinctions between upper and middle, 43–60, *44*

   festivals and, 13, 15, 153, 173, 202
   folklore and, xxiii–xxiv, xxvin.1, 45–6, 52–9, 147, 152–4, 155n.6, 173, 174, 195, 202,
   play and, 34, 44, 52–3, 58, 61n.12, 91, 104, 132, 173, 174, 179, 203–9, 212
   press *vs.* narratives on, 93–113, 133n.7
   of research survey respondents, 108
   social behaviour and, *44*, 44–7, 50, 59, 60n.4, 60n.5
   of volunteers, 14, 15, 34, 84, 106–7, 118, 131–2, 163
   women's work and, 50–1, 60nn.6–8, 116
   women undergraduates, 124, 126
Socialists, 127
social protest tradition, xxiii, 5, 28, 41n.1, 152–3, 155n.6, 201–5, 211–12
social rituals, 195–6
   gifts to servants as, 153–4
Society women, 128–31, 153–4
   maternal model of, 131
   in press, 113–20
   in Transportation Corps, 130–1
soldiers, ex-, 11–2
'Song of the Plus-Four Boys, The,' 182–3
"Song of the Volunteers, A" (Benedictus), 184
souvenirs *see* mementos
special constables, 84, 94–5, 104, 108, 158
Spencer, Cyril, 76, 81n.9, 104
Spencer, Ralph, 188–9
Sphere, 86, 118, 155, 169
Spitting Image, 185, 199n.22
sports, 9, 52, 59, 70, 86, 104
   cricket, 59, 112, 142, 199n.23
   football, 1, 6–7, 34, 112, 136, 147, 170, 179, 188, 199n.23, 201, *202*, 208–9, 213n.12
   golf, 16, 86, 91, 111–12, 208
   metaphors, 203–4, 208–9, 212
Stallman, Felicia, 7, 11, 120–1, 122
Steel-Maitland, Arthur, 38
strike-breakers, 5, 24, 42n.3, 42n.5, 100–1, 103, 139, 172, 177, 183, 209 *see also* blacklegs; volunteers
   playfulness of, 110
   volunteer perception as not being, 62, 77
strikers
   Britishness and, 11, 22, 67, 69, 71, 75, 136, 171, 187
   football match between police and, 170, 179, 188, 201, *202*, 208–9, 213n.12

foreigners and, 67–8
orderliness as threatened by, 67, 80, 154, 205
political unawareness of, 154
press portrayal of, 67–71, 166–7
relations between volunteers and, 77
sympathy for, 38, 76, 99, 127, 134n.27, 176–7
undergraduates' and, 168
volunteer narratives about, 62
volunteers viewed by, 202
war medals worn by, 75
working class press on Britishness of, 70–1
strikes, 9, 66, 173
aversion of railway and transport, 42n.3
comparison of 1926 to 1984, 17
1984-1985, 4, 17
policemen's (1919), 11, 29
post-war period of, 29
railway, 40, 42n.3
sympathetic, 12, 30–3, 40, 41, 42n.3, 105
transport, 105
TUC intention and image portrayal of, 5
Strikes! (restaurant), 1, *2*, 21–2, 209
Sunday Pictorial, 139
Supply and Transport Organisation, 30
Survey, 199n.17
Sutherland, Duchess of, 47
Swing rebellion, 152
symbolism, 21–2
    Civil War, 65, 79
    cultural, 194–6, 208–12
Symons, Julian, 14–15
sympathetic strikes, 12, 30, 31, 32, 40, 42n.3, 101, 105
    legality issue for, 33, 41
sympathy, for strikers, 38, 176–7
    press, 70–1
    volunteer, 76
    women undergraduate, 127, 134n.27
    working-class, 99

Talbot, Mary, 108, 121–2
tales, 141, 206–7, 209
    football match, 170, 208–9, 213n.12
    train story, 170, 206–7, 209
    true, 136–7
Tames, Richard, 188
Tatler's, 65, 67, 69, 70, 128
television series, 182
Territorial Army (Territorials), 46, 85, 101, 104, 146

Territorial Reserve Force, 146
thank you certificates, 159, *159*, 160, *160*
theatre, 69, 162
Thomas, J. H., 99, 188, 192
Time and Tide, 104
Times, The, 64, 65, 68, 79, 159, 161
    fraternity portrayed in, 111
    1986 issue, 189
Tory MPs, 64, 65
Tosh, Rosamund, 124, 125–6, 154, 207
Trade Disputes Act, 33, 41, 42n.4, 211
Trades Union Congress (TUC), 4–5, 23n.2, 152, 175
    British Worker of, 32
    communism and, 66
    General Strike viewed by, 37–8, 41
    government refusal of, 80
    MFGB offering negotiation powers to, 31
    negotiations with government, 38
    press on, 65–6, 67
    Samuel Commission and, 27, 38
    volunteer certification, 100, *100*
    war medal wearing urged by, 75
Trafalgar Square, 4, 23n.1
train driver incident, 170, 206–7, 209
transformation process, 208, 213n.17
transportation, during General Strike, 24n.6, 33–4, 74, 103, 109, 114, 121, 137
Transportation Corps, Society women in, 130–1
transportation jobs, 85, 98, *98*, 104–5, 114, 121, 126
    railway, 40, 42n.3, *73*, 91, 133n.14
transport strikes, 42n.3, 105
treasure hunts, 58, 173, 197n.6
tricksters, 144–7, 154, 155n.3, 195
    gender switching of, 151, 195
    tales, 144, 146, 206–7
Triple Alliance, 24n.10, 24n.13, 30
Tristram, Arthur, 118
true tales, parodies and, 136–7
TUC *see* Trades Union Congress

undergraduates, 13, 14, 16, 25n.15, 92, *92*, 110, 136
    charity works of, 55
    clothing of, *87*, 88
    distinction between male and female, 126
    enthusiastic volunteering of, 76–7
    humorous anecdotes about, 140–6
    images and stereotypes of, 83

jokes about, 140
lack of social purpose among, 59–60
liminal status of, 91, 132
Lots Road Power Station and, 112–13, *113*
narratives about, 106–7
parodies of, 147
poem about, 124
in press, 111
publications of, 147
rags of, 53–4
reckless train driver, 206
rewards for, 162
social behaviour of male, 45–6
sympathetic strike by, 101
women, 124–8, 134n.26, 134nn.25–7
unemployment, 24n12, 30, 51, 176
United States (U. S.), Baldwin's reports to, 41, 42n.7
University Officers Training Corps Signals, 109
university publications, 139, 147, 148, 166
university students *see* undergraduates
upper class
    accents of, 88, 90–1
    charitable works by, *44*, 46–50, 60n.4
    distinctions of, 43–60 *passim*
    jokes about, 140
    men's clubs, 84, 103
    middle-class women compared to, 120–1
    post-war women of, 7–8, 51, 60n.8
    rebels of, 57–8
    social behaviour, 47, 50, 60n.4, 60n.5
    traits of middle and, *44*
Upstairs Downstairs, 182
utopian vision, 169, 205, 211–12, 213n.17

Verdin, Jack, 172
Vincent, Marjorie, 123
violence, 5, 18, 23n.3, 67, 77, 145, 148, 166, 175, 192, 202, 207, 211
    non-, 79, 138, 187, 195, 207
volunteers, xxiii, 95 *see also* jobs, volunteer; male volunteers; women volunteers
    activities of, 5–6
    adventure perception of, 36, 37, 58, 121, 131–2, 149
    assignments of, 34
    Benedictus's characterisation of, 183
    blackleg drivers, 23n.4, 42n.3, 101, 139
    Britishness and, 201–12
    clothing of, 85–6, *87*, 88, 130–1, 133n.4

Corpus, 13
cultural symbol view of, 194–6, 208–12
dramatis personae and traits of, *44*
editorials on specific, 163
empowerment of, 201–2
folklore and, xxiii, 15–6, 45–6, 53, 55, 132, 136–54, 177–9, 195, 198n.15, 201–7, 210
General Strike viewed by, 36, 71–2
government views accepted by, 77
gratuities for, 159
Great War and, 7–11
idealism represented by, 205
inexperience of, 13
jokes about, 140
on life after General Strike, 38–9
marriages among, 210–1
mementos given, 159–60, *193*
motives of, 34, 42n.5, 72, 74, 131–2
as not strike breakers, 62, 77
persistent image of, 195–6
popular image of, 5, 14, 15, 23n.5, 34
praise for, 156–66, *157*, *159*
in press, 3, 111
railway, *73*, 133n.14
refusals, 101–2
with regular jobs, 95, 133n.9
relations between strikers and, 77
reluctant, 99
satires on, 147–9
scholarship on, 12–6, 175, 176
services performed by, 33
sleeping conditions of, 98, *98*
social class of, 14, 15, 34, 84, 106–7, 131–2, 163
social ritual, 195–6
sports team, 104
strikers' view of, 202
sympathy for strikers, 76
traits of upper and middle-class, *44*
trickster tales on incompetence of, 146
for TUC, 100, *100*
undergraduates as, 110
unofficial, 109, 122
unusual activities of, *35*
urban areas of, 33
wages of, 92, 94, 97
working-class mocking of, 90–1

wages
    miners', 30, 31, 167, 169n.2

Samuel Memorandum on reduced, 38, 41
volunteer job, 92, 94, 97
Wales, Princess of, 56
war, 123
  experiences, 130
  medals, 75
  metaphors, 62
  prevention of, 74
  service in, 149
Waugh, Evelyn, 12, 24n.13, 180
Webb, Beatrice, 179
Welsh miners, 72
Whittle, Dorothy, 121
Wilkinson, Ellen, 180–1
Wilson, Jean Moorcroft, 212n.5
women
  Britishness and, 195, 199n.22
  charitable works of upper-middle-class, 49–50
  employment and social class of, 50–1, 60nn.6–8
  General Strike role of, 17–18
  Great War employment of, 50, 60n.6
  humorous denigrations of, 139, 149–50
  married, 48, 116, 129–30
  older, 48
  play and, 52–3, 61n.12
  post-war upper-class, 7–8, 50–1, 60n.8
  power and, 130
  press about society, 113–20
  social class distinctions for, 48
  Society, 113–20, 128–31
  trivialized role of, 119
  university, 124–8
  unmarried, 51–2, 114
women undergraduates, 124–8, 134nn.25–7
  striker sympathies of, 127, 134n.27
women volunteers, 113–31, 161, 181, 199n.17
  acknowledgment of, 130–1
  as bus conductors, 115, 134n.21
  clothing of, 116, 128, 130–1
  domestic jobs of, 115–18
  end-of-strike praise for, 165
  gender bias and, 126, 127–8
  government not acknowledging, 122–3
  humorous denigrations of, 139, 149–50
  individual joining of, 115
  middle-class, 34, 120–8
  parodies about, 150–1, 155n.6
  preferred jobs of, 114
  satire of, 143, 149–51, 195
  social class and, 34, 118, 120–1
  society, 113–20, 128–31
  temporary male status of, 130–1
  in university publications, 150–1
  unofficial positions of, 122
Wooster, Bertie, 83
working class
  charity viewed by, 49
  decline of women servants of, 118
  emergency jobs taken by, 92
  ex-soldiers, 11–12
  optimism with Labour government, 28, 41n.1
  press of, 70–1, 147
  scholarship of leftists and, 21
  social class distinctions and, 47
  volunteer activities as attack on, 202–3
  volunteers mocked by, 90–1
  volunteer success credited to, 176
  wages of volunteer jobs for, 94
  women in Great War, 50, 60n.6
work pass, *95*
world-turned-upside-down motif, 153–4, 174
Wrigley, Chris, 13–14, 23n.5, 63, 80n.1, 133n.7, 172

Zinoviev Letter, 66, 81n.4, 81n.11

EU authorised representative for GPSR:
Easy Access System Europe, Mustamäe tee 50,
10621 Tallinn, Estonia
gpsr.requests@easproject.com

www.ingramcontent.com/pod-product-compliance
Ingram Content Group UK Ltd.
Pitfield, Milton Keynes, MK11 3LW, UK
UKHW042017140426
5217IPUK00015B/1225